THE CLASSICS
OF **WESTERN
SPIRITUALITY**

Alphonsus de Liguori

SELECTED WRITINGS

EDITED BY
FREDERICK M. JONES, C.SS.R.

WITH THE COLLABORATION OF
BRENDAN McCONVERY, C.SS.R., RAPHAEL GALLAGHER, C.SS.R.,
TERRENCE J. MORAN, C.SS.R., AND MARTIN McKEEVER, C.SS.R.

CONSULTANTS
SEAN O'RIORDAN, C.SS.R., AND CARL HOEGERL, C.SS.R.

PREFACE BY
SEAN O'RIORDAN, C.SS.R.

PAULIST PRESS
NEW YORK • MAHWAH

Cover art: The cover illustration of this volume is based on a detail of a painting of St. Alphonsus as Bishop by the Italian artist, *Giuseppe Capone* (1904–1971). He was a disciple of Bernard Berenson, the well-known critic of the art of the Renaissance. He belonged to the neo-realistic school, accompanying accurate reproduction of the physical characteristics of his subjects with acute analysis of their psychological and moral character. His painting of St. Alphonsus drew on the research of his brother, Fr. Domenico Capone, C.SS.R. (1907–1994) on the early portraiture and iconography of the saint, *Il Vero Volto di San Alfonso* (Rome, 1954).

Library of Congress Cataloging-in-Publication Data

Liguori, Alfonso Maria d', Saint, 1696–1787.
    [Selections. English. 1999]
    Selected writings / Alphonsus de Liguori ; edited by Frederick M. Jones, with the collaboration of Brendan McConvery ... [et al.] ; consultants, Sean O'Riordan and Carl Hoegerl] ; preface by Sean O'Riordan.
        p.   cm. – (The classics of Western spirituality)
    Includes bibliographical references (p.   ) and indexes.
    ISBN 0-8091-3771-2 (pbk.) — ISBN 0-8091-0493-8 (cloth).
    1. Spiritual life–Catholic Church. I. Jones Frederick M. II. Title. III. Series.
BX2349.L57213   1999
240–dc21   99–17472
                                                                      CIP

Published by Paulist Press
997 Macarthur Boulevard
Mahwah, New Jersey 07430

www.paulistpress.com

Printed and bound in the United States of America

CONTENTS

CONTENTS

CONTENTS

Editor of This Volume

FREDERICK M. JONES (1921-1997) was a member of the Dublin Province of the Redemptorists. He studied Literature and History at the National University of Ireland, from which he received an MA and a Traveling Studentship. He undertook postgraduate studies at the University of Louvain and the Gregorian University in Rome. He continued his researches in the Vatican Archives and in Simancas. He taught Ecclesiastical History in the Redemptorist House of Studies in Ireland, at St. Patrick's College, Maynooth, and the Milltown and Kimmage Missionary Institutes in Dublin. In addition to articles and monographs in several historical and theological journals, his published works include *Mountjoy: The Last Elizabethan Deputy* and the section "Rome and the Counter Reformation in Ireland" in the *History of Irish Catholicism*. In 1963, he was elected General Consultor to the Superior General of the Redemptorists and served in that office for six years. After years of research in the Roman and Neapolitan Archives, his *Alphonsus de Liguori: The Saint of Bourbon Naples, 1696-1787* was published in 1992. It was the first original life in English of the saint, founder of the Redemptorists and Doctor of the Church. Fr. Jones was also involved in the post-conciliar renewal of several Irish religious congregations. He died in 1997, shortly after completing the manuscript of this book.

Collaborators on This Volume

BRENDAN McCONVERY is a member of the Dublin Province of the Redemptorists. A graduate of the National University of Ireland, and of the Pontifical University, Maynooth, he specialized in Sacred Scripture at the Pontifical Biblical Institute, Rome, and at the École Biblique, Jerusalem. He was President of the Irish Biblical Association (1996-1999). He lectures in Biblical Studies at the Pontifical University, Maynooth, and at the Institute for Missionary Theology, Dublin. He is a member of the editorial board of *Scripture in Church*. He has researched the biblical background to the writings of St. Alphonsus.

RAPHAEL GALLAGHER is a member of the Dublin Province of the Redemptorists and a graduate of the National University of Ireland. He did post-graduate work in Moral Theology at the Accademia Alfonsiana, Rome, and the University of Bonn. He taught Moral Theology at the Pontifical University of Maynooth, the Milltown and Kimmage Institutes in Dublin, and at the University of St. Thomas, St. Paul, Minnesota. He spent six years as Provincial of the Irish Redemptorists. Following a sabbatical year of pastoral work in France, he was appointed Professor at the Accademia Alfonsiana. He is director of its review *Studia Moralia*.

TERRENCE J. MORAN is a member of the Baltimore Province of the Redemptorists. After ordination he spent some years in the preaching ministry, working in both English and Spanish. He continued post-graduate studies in Moral Theology at the Catholic University, Leuwen, and at the Accademia Alfonsiana, Rome. He alternates as Adjunct Professor of Theology and Religious Studies at St. John's University and Adjunct Professor of Religious Studies, College of St. Elizabeth, Convent Station, New Jersey. His publications include a number of studies in Moral Theology and Alphonsian Spirituality in both Spanish and English.

MARTIN McKEEVER is a member of the Dublin Province of the Redemptorists. He is a graduate of the National University of Ireland. Prior to ordination, he spent two years in youth ministry in Germany. He did post-graduate studies in Moral Theology at the Accademia Alfonsiana, Rome, writing his doctoral dissertation on the philosophical foundations of the ethics of St. Augustine. He has lectured in Moral Theology at the Institute for Missionary Theology, Dublin, and the Pontifical University, Maynooth. He is currently "Professor Invitatus" at the Accademia Alphonsiana, Rome.

Consultant for This Volume and
Author of the Preface
SEAN O'RIORDAN (1917–1998) was a member of the Dublin
Province of the Redemptorists. Following ordination, he graduated from the National University of Ireland with a Double First
in Classics and History. He did post-graduate studies in
Theology at the Pontifical University of Maynooth. He taught
theology at the Redemptorist House of Studies in Ireland, and
spent two sabbatical research periods in Germany and France.
He was invited to join the corps of professors at the Accademia
Alphonsiana, a specialized institute for the study of moral theology, in 1958. He taught there and guided the research of more
than ninety doctoral students until his retirement in 1987. He
directed many seminars, workshops and summer schools on
aspects of contemporary moral theology in Ireland, North
America, Europe and Asia. He was a recognized authority on
the moral theology and spirituality of St. Alphonsus.

Consultant for This Volume
CARL HOEGERL is a member of the Baltimore Province of the
Redemptorists. After ordination, he continued theological and
historical studies at the Catholic University of America and at
the University of Muenster, Germany. For many years he was a
member of the Redemptorist Historical Institute in Rome,
where he edited *The Founding Texts of the Redemptorists.*
Specializing in archival material relating to the origins of the
Redemptorists and to the life of Alphonsus Liguori, he collaborated, as Chair of the Rome-based Commission for Alphonsian
Spirituality, in editing a series of works on Redemptorist spirituality. He continues to act as editor of *Spiritus Patris*, a periodical devoted to the Alphonsian charism. Currently archivist of
the Baltimore Province, he is involved in the editing of early
Provincial texts for the ongoing publication of the general history of the Congregation of the Most Holy Redeemer, and in
preparing the *Positio super Virtutibus Heroicis* for the cause of canonization of Francis Xavier Seelos, C.SS.R.

FOREWORD

The writings of Alphonsus Maria de Liguori have had an extremely wide circulation in nearly a hundred different languages and dialects throughout the world. The mammoth task of preparing a critical edition of his 110 publications was begun in Rome in 1933 and has not yet reached completion. Eleven volumes have been published to date, not including the critical edition of his *Moral Theology*, which was edited in four volumes by Father Gaudé, C.SS.R., in 1905.

The need has been felt for some time to publish a representative selection of his writings that would demonstrate the wide scope of his work and its relevance to Christian life and spirituality in our own day. From the history of his apostolic activity and, consequently, of his writings, which he envisaged as an extension of his preaching, we become aware that his writings were not only addressed to bishops, priests, and religious but were meant more particularly for the ordinary lay faithful. Together with his great mentor, Francis de Sales, he has become the spiritual writer of the "Universal Vocation to Holiness," to use the words of Vatican II.

I wish to express our thanks to Dr. Bernard McGinn, Professor of Historical Theology and the History of Christianity at the Divinity School of the University of Chicago, for agreeing to include St. Alphonsus and his writings among the volumes of the Classics of Western Spirituality, and also to Donald F. Brophy and the staff of the Paulist Press, Mahwah, New Jersey, for their courteous cooperation.

The preparation of this volume has demanded the collaboration of specialists in different areas of Alphonsian study and

1

research. I wish to express my thanks to Fathers Carl Hoegerl and Sean O'Riordan for their expert guidance as our consultants. Without the collaboration of Fathers Terrence Moran, Raphael Gallagher, Brendan McConvery and Martin McKeever this volume would never have been prepared. Its publication is the only reward they expect.

We acknowledge the permission of the Confraternity of Christian Doctrine, Washington, D.C., to use the New American Bible translation. The abbreviations are those given in the introduction to the 1991 edition.

There are many others to whom our thanks are due for their assistance, advice and encouragement. If St. Alphonsus insisted that his writings were another way of announcing the Good News of Jesus Christ, then all those who have helped us have shared in this apostolic ministry.

Frederick M. Jones, C.SS.R.
Marianella, Dublin, Ireland

******

Shortly after consigning the manuscript of this book to Paulist Press, Frederick M. Jones passed away unexpectedly on March 8, 1997. As an historian, his area of specialization was the Counter Reformation in Ireland, to which he had made several important contributions. In 1960, he was asked by his Irish superiors to write the first independently-researched biography of Alphonsus in English. He began work the following year in the archives of Rome and Naples, but his research was cut short by his election to the Redemptorist General Council from 1963 to 1967. It was not an easy time to hold this office, as old certainties collapsed on all sides in the aftermath of Vatican II. It would be almost twenty years before freedom from other commitments would allow him to resume work on the biography of Alphonsus.

At first reluctantly, but soon with growing enthusiasm, he returned to work. *Alphonsus Liguori: The Saint of Bourbon Naples* was published in 1992. This volume in *The Classics of Western*

FOREWORD

Spirituality series is the final flowering of a project which had been maturing in Frederick Jones's mind for over thirty years. It is a volume he was uniquely equipped to write, as his introductory essay shows in its mastery of historical detail.

Father Sean O'Riordan, C.SS.R., who wrote the preface, was also destined to die before publication. He was a distinguished Irish Redemptorist professor of Moral Theology at the Alphonsian Academy, and an authority on the writings of St. Alphonsus, especially in the domain of moral theology. With the passing of these two distinguished scholars, Alphonsian studies in English are much the poorer. The younger scholars Fred enlisted as collaborators will hopefully carry on the torch. In Frederick Jones and Sean O'Riordan they have two worthy models of scholarship.

Brendan McConvery, C.SS.R.

PREFACE

Over a period of fifty years, from 1728 to 1778, Alphonsus de Liguori published no fewer than 111 works, great and small, covering a wide variety of subjects from moral theology to apologetics. He was, however, above all a spiritual writer, intent on leading people to "the practice of the love of Jesus Christ"—the title he gave to the book, published in 1768, that he considered "the most devotional, the most useful" of his works. It is in his spiritual writings, beginning with *Visits to the Blessed Sacrament* (1745), that the fundamental inspiration and significance of his whole life emerge most clearly.

It was as a spiritual writer too that he became famous in Italy during his lifetime. He appealed deeply to the minds and hearts of ordinary people who knew nothing of his scholarly work in the complex field of moral theology, though even here, as excerpts from his moral writings will show, he never lost sight of the spiritual and devotional needs of the ordinary faithful. During the nineteenth century, translations of his writings into French, German, English, and other languages spread his fame far and wide until he eventually became the most popular of all spiritual authors in the church of that time. His influence, however, extended beyond the common people. Many intellectuals, Catholic and Protestant, were impressed by the power of his single-minded concentration on God present to us in the mysteries of the redeeming Christ. One of these was the most original of all the nineteenth-century Christian thinkers, the Danish Lutheran Søren Kierkegaard (1813–1855), who read some of St. Alphonsus in a German translation and recognized him at once as a "single person." This was Kierkegaards's way of describing a true Christian—one whose entire being, mind, heart, and spirit, was focused

4

on the God of the gospel. The personality of Alphonsus, coming through in the teachings and prayers of his spiritual writings, was the most potent factor of all in making him an outstanding *maestro* of the following of Christ for Christians in the nineteenth century.

Though many new currents of spirituality developed in the twentieth century, among them the "Little Way" of spiritual childhood fostered by St. Therese of Lisieux (1873–1897), the spiritual influence of St. Alphonsus remained very strong until the middle of the present century. Then, almost suddenly, it practically disappeared from view. Few now read *The Practice of the Love of Jesus Christ* or use *Visits to the Blessed Sacrament* in their prayers. We here encounter a phenomenon that recurs regularly in the history of spirituality. Every form of spirituality is closely linked to the patterns of thought and feeling that were taken for granted when it originated and that helped to spread it. Then the patterns change, sometimes gradually, sometimes quite rapidly, and the corresponding form of spirituality recedes from prominence. This happened to the spirituality of the church of the Fathers during the Middle Ages and it happened in turn to medieval spirituality from the post-Tridentine period onward. In such times of transition new and good things emerge but many precious things from older times are forgotten. The same is true of the switch from Alphonsian spirituality during the 1950s and 1960s to new kinds of liturgical, biblical, and meditative-contemplative spirituality that reflected new thought-patterns and new ways of responding emotionally to the message of the gospel. Much was gained in that changeover but much was lost too.

It is the great merit of *The Classics of Western Spirituality* series that it presents the spiritual riches of the Western monotheistic faiths to the modern world. It retrieves the masterpieces of thought and prayer from the Christian past, which are not otherwise easily accessible, giving them new life and fresh meaning for Christians today. For a variety of reasons it is certainly fitting that an anthology of St. Alphonsus's writings should now appear in this series. It is indeed good that it does so—good for the series itself and, above all, good for the many readers who will now, perhaps for the first time, hear the voice of one who, after he was declared a Doctor of the Church by Pius IX in 1871, came to be called the Doctor of Prayer.

Sean O'Riordan, C.SS.R.
Alphonsian Academy of Moral Theology
Lateran University
Rome

GENERAL
INTRODUCTION

ALPHONSUS DE LIGUORI (1696–1787): HIS LIFE, WRITINGS, AND SPIRITUALITY

Alphonsus de Liguori is one of the most historically accessible of saints, despite the fact that 1996 marks the tercentenary of his birth. His life spanned virtually the whole of the eighteenth century from his birth in 1696 to his death at the age of ninety-one in 1787, just two years before the fall of the Bastille. The historical records for Naples, and for the regime of the Neapolitan Bourbons under whom he lived and worked for the greater part of his life, are extensive; the houses he lived in, the cathedrals and rural churches where he preached and ministered as priest and bishop, are to a large extent still in existence and not greatly altered, if at all, from his time. His extensive writings are largely available in their contemporary, if not always in their first, editions. A considerable proportion of them are still extant in manuscript form with Alphonsus's corrections and emendations. Thousands of his letters are extant, dealing, among other topics, with theological matters, spiritual direction, the affairs of his newly founded Congregation, personal family affairs, and the printing and publication of his writings.

Biographers

He was one of that minority of saints who had the dubious privilege of a contemporary biographer, in fact, two of them. Indeed, his contemporaries seem almost to have conspired to preserve for posterity every possible shred of evidence of his life and ministry. Fathers Joseph Landi and Anthony Mary Tannoia each set themselves the task of recording the details of his life. Tannoia's *Della Vita ed Istituto Del Venerabile Servo di Dio, Alfonso Maria di Liguori, Vescovo di S. Agata de'Goti e Fondatore della Congregazione de'Preti Missionarii del SS. Redentore*, in three volumes, is widely regarded as a classic of its genre. Tannoia began his recording of Alphonsus's life while still a student and while Alphonsus's mother was still alive. She provided him with intimate details of the saint's early years. Tannoia was at Alphonsus's bedside as he died in Pagani in August 1787. From then on he spent his remaining years collecting material from all the places where Alphonsus had ministered and in interviewing those who had known him personally, bishops, priests, his Redemptorist confreres, and those he had directed spiritually, both clergy and laity.

While Tannoia's *Vita* remains an indispensable basis for any study of Alphonsus, the clear though unstated purpose of the book as a prelude to Alphonsus's canonization must not be forgotten. Following Alphonsus's canonization in 1839, "official" biographies of the saint appeared in response to his popularity and considerable influence in the life of the nineteenth-century church. The reorganization and opening of the Redemptorist Archives in the General House in Rome in the middle of this century and considerable research in Neapolitan and Vatican Archives have brought to light a vast amount of new and relevant material for further study of the life and work of Alphonsus. The publications by the members of the Redemptorist Historical Institute in *Spicilegium Historicum* of important monographs have made a more accurate historical assessment of the saint possible.

Specific reference must be made, in the first place, to the work of the Spanish Redemptorist Father Raimundo Telleria, whose long years of indefatigable research came to a conclusion with the publication of his *San Alfonso Maria de Ligorio* in 1950/1951, a storehouse of new material as indispensable in its way as Tannoia. Since then important biographies of the saint have appeared in French and English: Theodule Rey-Mermet, *Le Saint du Siècle des Lumières* (1982) and Frederick M. Jones, *Alphonsus de Liguori, The Saint of Bourbon Naples* (1992).

GENERAL INTRODUCTION

Birth and Family

Alphonsus de Liguori was born on Thursday 27 September 1696 at his parents' home at Marianella on the outskirts of Naples. Two days later he was baptized in the church of Santa Maria dei Vergini in Naples itself, where he was given the names of nine heavenly patrons, Alphonsus, Maria, Anthony, John, Francis, Cosmas, Damian, Michael, Gaspar. The baptismal register of the church is still preserved with the entry of Alphonsus's baptism in the handwriting of the parish priest, Don Giuseppe del Mastro. Other hands have since completed the story of the child who was baptized on that day by adding in the margin, "Beatified, September 1816. Canonized 26 May 1839. Declared a Doctor of the Church, 23 March 1871."

Society in Naples at the time was divided into two classes, the nobility and those who could not lay claim, under any possible title, to belong to it. The Liguori family was authentically established among the ranks of the "lower nobility"; they were "patrician" in the Neapolitan sense, owing their status to royal grant for services rendered. They boasted of a coat-of-arms with the device *Sic Itur ad Astra.* In several official documents during his lifetime Alphonsus was referred to as "Patricianus Neapolitanus."

Don Joseph Felix de Liguori (Don Giuseppe), Alphonsus's father, was born in 1670 in the village of San Paolo in the diocese of Naples, making him legally a citizen of Naples; while still young he came to live in the city just outside the walls at the Porta San Gennaro. At the age of fifteen he entered the Spanish naval service. By the time of his marriage at the age of twenty-five to Donna Anna Caterina Cavalieri, he had risen to the modest position of an Ensign in the Royal Galleys. When he retired he was the commanding officer of the Flagship of the Royal Squadron. His long years in the galleys left their mark on his character, making him harsh in manner, intolerant, a martinet at home. To toughen his sons he made them, Alphonsus among them, sleep on the floor at least one night of the week when he was at home. At the same time, he was possessed of a deep faith in God, a great love for the Passion of Jesus Christ, and a piety that his rough military exterior belied. Toward the end of his life he mellowed considerably and loved nothing more than to spend some time in the quiet of Ciorani, the novitiate house of his son's missionary Congregation.

Don Giuseppe's wife belonged to the Cavalieri family, who could boast of a more authentic ancient lineage and nobility than the Liguoris. She was one of those mothers whose lives of self-sacrifice and prayer seem, in themselves, to be a sufficient explanation of the holiness of their children. Anna Caterina was the youngest of five children and was orphaned of her mother while still only a child; her eldest brother was a missionary priest and became bishop of Troia, where he died with an authentic reputation for holiness of life. Her two sisters became Franciscan nuns in Naples while her brother was a distinguished judge in the Naples courts. After her mother's death, Anna Caterina was reared in the convent where her sisters were professed nuns. She remained there for fourteen years as an *educanda* until she returned home to attend to her father, a minister of state of the Royal Council of Santa Clara.

Don Giuseppe brought his bride to live outside Naples in a country villa at Marianella. It was here that Alphonsus was born, the first of eight children. Antonio, the second child, became a Bendictine of the Cassinese Congregation and was novice master for some years before his early death. A third boy, Cajetan, ultimately became a priest of the diocese of Naples and, having obtained a lucrative benefice in the Cathedral, lived at home with his liveried staff as a cultured ecclesiastical gentleman. He caused few ripples in the pastoral care of souls in Naples. There were four girls born of the marriage, one of whom died as an infant. Two of them became nuns in the convent of St. Jerome in Naples, where the younger of the two, Anna Maria, fell into bad health both physical and mental. Her neurotic scrupulosity, which even her brother Alphonsus, despite his reputation as a spiritual director, was powerless to deal with, was widely known in religious circles in the capital. Teresa, who was Alphonsus's favorite sister, was married at the age of sixteen to the duke of Praesenzano and her unfortunate married life with a widower much older than herself certainly influenced him when he wrote of the unhappy lives of so many married couples he knew. Finally there was Hercules, the Benjamin of the family, born in 1706 and twice married. His relations with his father were never easy, with the result that Alphonsus played the role of his protector and, later in life, became virtually his guardian.

Education

With a growing family, Don Giuseppe moved into the city of Naples, the education of his children being the principal reason for the change. He opted for the private education of his sons and competent tutors for this purpose were readily available. Alphonsus's principal tutor was a Calabrian priest, Don Domenico Bonaccia, who taught Alphonsus Latin, Greek, French, Spanish, and Italian as well as history, mathematics, and the rudiments of Cartesian physics. Another priest, Don Carminiello Rocco, initiated him into the study of philosophy, mainly cosmology and psychology.

The intellectual graces were only a minor part of the cultural equipment of the Neapolitan nobleman and Don Giuseppe engaged other competent tutors to instruct his eldest son and heir in drawing, painting, and architecture, in all of which disciplines he showed considerable talent. But it was in music that Alphonsus really excelled. Surprisingly enough, his father possessed a remarkable competence in music, which his son inherited. He engaged the well-known Gaetano Greco, a pupil of Alessandro Scarlatti and teacher of Durante and Pergolesi, as music tutor for Alphonsus, who responded by devoting himself assiduously to his music studies, acquiring considerable proficiency on the harpsichord and also as a composer. His love of music never left him. He liked nothing more than to spend recreation time during his life, even up to the age of eighty, at the keyboard. As a priest and missioner he composed hymns for the people, which he taught them himself and sang with them in church; they remain favorites in Southern Italy to this day. The manuscript of a simple oratorio—*Duetto tra l'Anima e Gesù Cristo con violino*—composed by him about 1760 has found its way to the manuscript room of the British Museum.

With Don Giuseppe absent for long periods from home, the dominant formative influence on Alphonsus was his mother. She was the direct opposite of her husband in almost everything—gentle, cultured, refined, and devout with a cloistral piety that she retained from her long years in the convent. She never went to the theater or to other public amusements; she spent hours in prayer, recited the monastic breviary, fasted, and practiced corporal austerities like any contemplative nun of those days. She was inclined to be of an overanxious disposition and suffered much from scruples—which Alphonsus inherited or at least developed. Only sometime before her death did she gain complete peace of mind.

Donna Anna took her responsibility for the religious education of her children very seriously. Alphonsus was only seven when she placed him under the guidance of her own spiritual director, Father Thomas Pagano. Pagano was to remain Alphonsus's spiritual director for nearly thirty years. He was an authentic Oratorian, gentle, cultured, placid, a Christian gentleman in everything. His direction was characterized by great kindness, firmness when necessary, and emphasis on the love of God. He prepared Alphonsus for his first communion. Attached to the magnificent baroque church of the Oratorian Fathers, not far from the Liguori home, were a number of sodalities catering to the spiritual needs of the various sections of society to whom the Fathers ministered. Alphonsus, in due course, became a member of the Sodality of Young Noblemen under the patronage of St. Joseph. After graduation from university he progressed to the Sodality of Doctors. The members of these sodalities, which achieved much for the sanctification of the laity, came together regularly for conferences, spiritual reading, Mass, and the reception of the sacraments.

University

When Alphonsus had completed his humanities under the guidance of his different tutors, his father decided that he should read law at the University of Naples with a view to a legal career.

Success in the legal profession was a guaranteed entrance to success in political and royal circles in Naples. Don Giuseppe already harbored great ambitions for his eldest son. By the end of October 1708 Alphonsus, then in his thirteenth year, was registered as an *istitutista,* or first-year law student at the university. There was nothing exceptional about the age at which he matriculated; he may have been a year or so ahead of many of his contemporaries, though others may have been a month or so in advance of him. The course extended over five years, comprising the study of Roman law and of the various other legal systems that went to the making of Neapolitan jurisprudence. The law faculty had twelve chairs, seven in Civil and five in Canon or Church law. The pervading atmosphere was strongly anti-Roman in spirit. The professors by their writings and indoctrination of their students were laying the foundations for that state control of the church which characterized the Bourbons of Naples as it did many other European governments of that period. The whole system of church-state relations in Bourbon Naples, which went under the name of Regalism and which is associated with the name of Bernard Tanucci, was built on the legal foundations laid during those years.

Alphonsus's legal and philosophical formation at university level took place in a hotbed of Regalism and anti-Romanism on the one hand, and, on the other hand, in a climate of philosophical thought that, it was claimed, spawned a generation of educated intellectual atheists. He thus had an early introduction to a system and currents of thought that he was to oppose all his life. He was to become the ardent upholder of papal rights and the preacher and writer of belief in God and the love of Jesus Christ. But the picture must be carefully drawn. The general university atmosphere was not officially irreligious. Corporately the staff and students professed their religious beliefs at the opening of each academic year and at the conferring of degrees. The conferring of degrees, for example, was the occasion for expressing belief in the doctrine of the Immaculate Conception of the Blessed Virgin Mary, which had not then been defined. Despite their belief in the divine right of kings and their opposition to the power of the papacy, Charles III and his successor, Ferdinand, were intensely devout in their private lives with a simple childlike piety; their prime minister, the Regalist Tanucci, had a daughter who was a Poor Clare nun, bequeathed money for Masses for the repose of his soul, and complained bitterly when he had to accompany the king on hunting expeditions that entailed missing daily Mass.

In January 1713 Alphonsus graduated as a Doctor of Laws from the university; he was not yet seventeen. On the day of conferring, on his knees before the assembled members of the faculty, he swore to defend the doctrine of Our Lady's Immaculate Conception in a ceremony imposed by the Spanish viceroy a hundred years previously. He could hardly have foreseen that fifty years later he would strenuously defend this doctrine in his theological writings, thereby adding his support to the movement for its formal definition.

Alphonsus was now a member of a very powerful legal establishment. His degree did not mean that he immediately took his place in the courts—a further period of practical training lasting for some three years was necessary before that. Apprenticed to well-known legal practitioners, he entered fully into the activities of Neapolitan society. He was an assiduous opera goer, frequenting the San Bartolomeo opera house and the Teatro dei Fiorentini, where he would have heard the operas of Handel, Scarlatti, Mancini, and Popora. He was an avid card-player.

Alphonsus, however, continued to be faithful to his religious practices, which included making enclosed retreats with the Jesuit and Vincentian Fathers in their retreat houses in Naples. His membership of the Congregazione dei Dottori, under the guidance of his Oratorian confessors and directors, now entailed practical work of charity among the poor of the city. The Fathers of the Oratory paid for the upkeep of forty-eight beds in the hospital of Santa Maria del Popolo, a refuge for the needy and the outcast, usually referred to as the Incurabili, a name given to similar hospitals in many Italian cities in those days. On certain days each week, the young men of the Oratorian sodality attended to the needs of 310 patients assigned to them by the hospital authorities, making beds, changing linen, washing the sick, feeding the more helpless, and performing other services demanded by the care of geriatric patients. Modern hygienic methods and the advance of medical science have reduced the unpleasantness and danger of such tasks but in those days voluntary service in the Incurabili often demanded real courage and heroic charity. It was a most practical form of the lay apostolate.

Alphonsus maintained his work among the poor of the Incurabili for over eight years; it was here that he first experienced the real happiness to be found in God's service and it was here that his desire to become a priest developed and came to a positive conclusion. Don Giuseppe insisted on his son joining him as a member of another sodality, the Congregazione dei Nobili di Santa Maria della Misercordia. The Misericordiella, as the sodality was conveniently known, was an association for the lay apostolate of the Neapolitan aristocracy, whose members attended, among other charitable activities, to its own small hospital, the burying of the poor, the care of pilgrims, and the spiritual welfare of prisoners in two of the Neapolitan prisons.

Legal Career

Alphonsus's legal career progressed successfully. After some three years as an apprentice with different law firms, he began his career as a junior advocate at the Neapolitan bar where, according to contemporary sources, he enjoyed considerable success. He became the family lawyer of the important Ruffi family, while the fact that two of his uncles were judges helped to attract a clientele. Having determined his son's profession and regulated his studies, and, to a large extent, the practice of his religion, Don Giuseppe finally got round to the question of marriage. His efforts to arrange suitable partners for his son were spread over a number of years and were a constant cause of friction between father and son and a cause of pain to both. While his father had no inhibitions about suggesting possible brides for his son among the rich and the powerful on at least three occasions, Alphonsus was frustratingly uncooperative. He was confused as to his future—haunted by a desire for the priesthood, which he had confided to his many clerical confidants, and going through a period of adolescent scruples in sexual matters.

During Holy Week in 1722 Alphonsus made an enclosed retreat with the Vincentian Fathers in Naples. In later years he referred to it as his "conversion" retreat and declared that it was in the Vincentian house that he determined to abandon his legal career and become a diocesan or religious priest. His secret intention, which was concealed from his father, received confirmation in the following summer of 1723. He had been engaged as one of the lawyers in a lawsuit about lands in the area of Amatrice involving some of the most influential names among the nobility. The Grand Duchess of Tuscany was also involved, as was the Hapsburg Emperor, Charles VI. Alphonsus prepared his brief with great care, consulting the principal experts about the intricacies of land-titles in Naples, which were complicated by the existence of different legal systems. To Alphonsus his arguments seemed irrefutable. He finished his exposition confident of success. To his astonishment, the presiding judges upheld the submissions of his opponents, the Medici legal team. The whole case as presented by Alphonsus collapsed and was summarily dismissed. He had to concede defeat and retire, confused and publicly humiliated.

Historically it is now clear that there was much more to the courtroom encounter than the legal complexities of feudal tenure. Behind the scenes there was bribery and political interference at the highest level; the Medici in Florence as well as the Austrian viceroy in Naples were all involved. For days Alphonsus struggled to come to terms with his public failure; he kept to his room and to himself as he struggled to reconstruct his life. Gradually he announced to his parents and family his intention of abandoning his profession as a lawyer and the law courts. No arguments from his mother or father were able to shake his resolve; not even the parental rage of Don Giuseppe succeeded in altering his determination. Relatives and friends, both ecclesiastical and political, were enlisted in an effort to get him to see things differently. When it emerged that he was, moreover, considering becoming a priest, Don Giuseppe's frustration was unbounded; all his hopes for family advancement, which he had founded on his son's career, were shattered.

Priestly Vocation

Alphonsus spent most of the summer months of 1723 in prayer and discernment of his future. One after another, he consulted Father Pagano, his Oratorian director, the Vincentians, the Jesuits, the Benedictines where his brother was master of novices, the Theatines, and the members of the missionary society of the Pii Operai, where his relatives were influential figures. Finally, he discussed his future intentions with the members of the theological faculty at the diocesan seminary. But it was while working at the Incurabili among the sick that his final decision was made. It was there that the thought of the vanity of the world came home to him with startling clarity. The gospel words "what doth it profit a man if he gain the whole world and suffer the loss of his soul" (Mt. 16:26) seemed to resound in his ears. His hesitations were at an end. There still remained an intensely traumatic final confrontation with his father to be faced, an experience that Alphonsus never forgot for the rest of his life, as he later confided to confreres in moments of reminiscing. The upshot was that Alphonsus presented himself to the Cardinal Archbishop of Naples, who accepted him for ordination and conferred Tonsure on him on 23 October 1723. Don Guiseppe refused to be present.

The saga of Alphonsus's vocation to the priesthood has inevitably been mythologized over the years. It was too good a story not to be employed for various purposes. He became a priest because he lost a lawsuit and was humiliated in public. He dashed from the law courts exclaiming "World, I know you now!" It was while working among the outcasts of Naples that he heard a voice calling him to leave the world, whereupon he knelt before the statue of Our Lady of Mercy in the Church of Our Lady of Ransom, ungirded his sword, and placed it at Our Lady's feet as a symbol of dedication to her and of his resolve to become a priest. The truth is not so dramatic. Alphonsus had been struggling with the thoughts of the priesthood for many years. His family situation and responsibility as the eldest son, the fact that his brother was already a priest with the Benedictines, together with the condition of the clergy in the kingdom of Naples were all counterindications. His resolve matured slowly but his mind was made up over a year before the debacle in the law courts and for longer still before his experience in the hospital of the Incurabili.

Theological Studies

Alphonsus's training for the priesthood bore little resemblance to the seminary system with which we are familiar. Those who were studying for the priesthood in Naples lived at home with their families, wore ecclesiastical dress, and were assigned to a church where they assisted the incumbent priest. They studied theology privately under the guidance of appointed tutors. A decree of 1721 enjoined on candidates enrollment in one of three confraternities of priests formally recognized in the diocese. Membership in one of these sodalities was obligatory, and they provided the main source of priestly formation. Alphonsus became a member of the sodality attached to the cathedral, known as the Congregation of the Apostolic Missions or simply the Propaganda. Two of his relatives, Canon Gizzio and his tutor in moral theology, Canon Julius Torni, were influential members at the time. Alphonsus owed everything in the way of his priestly formation to the Apostolic Missions—his spirituality, his theological initiation, his practical introduction into the practice of preaching, especially popular mission preaching. If it is true that he was a Neapolitan through and through, then it is equally true that he was a genuine product of the Apostolic Missions. Every Monday the members met in the cathedral for academies in theology, spirituality, and missionary theory; attendance was carefully monitored. Meditation, assiduous study, examination of conscience, together with regular practice of corporal penance as practiced in the spirituality of the time, were inculcated as the essential basis for priestly holiness.

Twice a year a jury of twenty-four members specially chosen for the task undertook the Scrutinium, in which the lives and conduct of each member, including the superiors, were subjected to close examination, resulting in confirmation or suspension of membership as the case warranted. Eucharistic piety in the form of the Forty Hours devotion and visits to the Blessed Sacrament were a feature of their spirituality. Devotion to Our Lady under the title of Queen of Apostles as their special protectress was strongly inculcated. Their great spiritual mentor was St. Francis de Sales, whose works were read and studied. Each year in October the members made the spiritual exercises for eight days together in the cathedral complex. The annual General City Mission, held in the cathedral or in the basilica of the Holy Spirit and always conducted by the members, immediately followed. At the end of the city mission, in which all the members were expected to take part, smaller missionary bands were detailed to preach missions to the people throughout the kingdom until the following May.

Alphonsus's theological studies prior to his ordination to the priesthood lasted for not quite three and a half years. Three professors, Don Alessio Mazzocchi, Don Julius Torni, and the Oratorian Father Pagano provided the main formative intellectual influence on the future moral theologian and Doctor of the Church. Mazzocchi enjoyed a European reputation as a scripture scholar, while Torni, like Alphonsus himself, a former lawyer, was considered the great intellectual luminary of the diocese. He had studied with the Dominicans in Naples where he became, and remained all his life, a devoted adherent of Thomas Aquinas.

From his published work we can gather the theological opinions that Torni passed on to his pupils, among them, Alphonsus. He taught the doctrine of the Immaculate Conception of the Blessed Virgin and her corporal Assumption into Heaven. He encouraged the frequent reception of Holy Communion against the Jansenist teaching of Arnauld's *De la fréquente communion.* Only on the question of the efficacy of grace, the great preoccupation of rival schools of theology at the time, did he depart from the teaching of his Dominican masters. By doing so he left the way open for Alphonsus to elaborate later, in his *Prayer, the Great Means of Salvation* (1759), his own highly personal and eclectic approach to the question of the workings of God's grace. The Vincentian Louis Abelly's *Medulla Theologica* was the text used for dogmatic studies, which initiated Alphonsus into questions such as the doctrinal authority of the Pope, which he was himself to defend in his later writings.

Less felicitous was the choice of the manual used for the study of moral theology. François Genet's *Morale de Grenoble* was the bible of the Rigorist school of moral theologians. In all probability the third Venetian edition of this work, published in 1713, was the manual that provided Alphonsus with his first introduction to the study of moral theology. Every indication points to the fact that Torni was the main professor of moral theology. It is strange that he who was so liberal in other aspects of his teaching should use such a Rigorist author, even though this was the most widely used manual at the time. Alphonsus described his introduction to moral theology as follows: "I admit quite frankly that when I commenced my course of moral theology, I had a professor who followed the rigid opinion and I for my part, like so many others at the time, also defended it wholeheartedly." The development of his views over the next twenty years is a story of assiduous study, wide pastoral experience as a missioner and confessor, a deep sympathetic understanding of the lives of the simple people to whom he ministered, and long personal suffering in his own conscience as he freed himself from the agony of scruples that the various elements of his formation had induced.

Early in 1725, and still during his period of preparation for the priesthood, Alphonsus added to his commitments by becoming a member of the Confraternità dei Bianchi, an association of priests and laymen whose function was to attend to the spiritual needs of the criminals of the Naples prisons, to support their widows and orphans, and specifically to assist spiritually at the execution of condemned criminals and to bury them. The Bianchi wore a white habit with a capuche and white cincture, hence their name. Dressed in their distinctive habits, the members of the confraternity accompanied the condemned criminals on their last journey to the gallows and assisted the condemned person to the very end. The registers of the confraternity show that Alphonsus assisted at several executions after his ordination to the priesthood. The pastoral experience gathered in these circumstances was later incorporated by Alphonsus in his moral writings for priests who would have to assist at the execution of criminals. Years later he published a special pamphlet on the method of assisting those condemned to death, *Advice for Priests Who Minister to Those Condemned to Death,* which repays printing in this selection of Alphonsus's writings, not least for the gentle spirit and the sense of the mercy of God that pervade it.

The Neapolitan Clergy

Alphonsus was ordained to the priesthood on 21 December 1726 in the cathedral of Naples; he was in his thirty-first year. There was no shortage of clergy in the archdiocese of Naples when Alphonsus was added to the number. One of the great problems of the kingdom for church and government, in fact, was the excessive number of both priests and religious. For the diocese of Naples alone, with a population of less than half a million, there were at least 1,500 priests, not counting religious priests in one hundred monasteries. In an official report to the king as late as 1779 the total number of priests and religious was given as 75,000, an incredible number, seeing that the Holy See and the king had agreed in the concordat of 1742 to take steps to reduce the clerical intake. The number of churches was correspondingly excessive. It was reckoned that there were 514 churches in Naples alone requiring beeswax for their candles!

The "enormous" number of clergy—to use the word of a royal decree—was not due to any flowering of genuine vocations; it was the consequence of economic and sociological factors rooted in the position of the church in the *ancien régime.* The disedifying consequences of a too numerous, uneducated, and pastorally uncommitted clerical proletariat had occupied the Council of

Trent, whose wise decrees, if they had been courageously implemented, would have gone a long way toward remedying the situation. But little was done until the French Revolution and the Napoleonic code drastically altered the situation.

At the root of the problem in the Kingdom of Naples was the fact that church property as well as whatever property was constituted as patrimony for clerics was immune from taxation. Taxes levied at town gates on wine, corn, and fruit were not paid by clerics, who could also buy other state-taxed commodities free of impost. This immunity opened up a vast field for corruption. The kingdom swarmed with fictitious grants of property to the church with fictitiously constituted patrimonies and tonsured clerics who had no intention of proceeding to priestly ordination.

If conditions in the city of Naples were bad, the general degradation of the clergy in the rest of the kingdom was even more appalling. The numbers who became clerics for purely economic motives and were ordained without sufficient education was inordinately high. Many were not only ignorant but almost unlettered, as Alphonsus was to experience as a missioner throughout various dioceses and later as a bishop in his own. Pope Benedict XIV suggested that some southern Neapolitan clerics did not know whether the Trinity was a mystery of their faith or the name of a mountain.

The lives of the saints and their writings must always be assessed against the background of their time and milieu; this is particularly true of the long life and prolific literary output of Alphonsus de Liguori. Only against the background of the social and ecclesiastical conditions prevailing in Bourbon Naples in the *Settecento* does much of what he wrote make sense. When he urged those already ordained to lead truly priestly lives even if they had embraced the clerical state without a genuine vocation, when he urged on them zeal for souls and the necessity of making their priesthood of some spiritual value to others, he was addressing a motley crew of clerics who may never have preached a sermon, never administered a sacrament, never acquired any theological learning beyond the bare minimum.

GENERAL INTRODUCTION

Early Ministry

Alphonsus conformed initially to the pattern of priestly life in the diocese after his ordination to the extent that he lived at home with his parents for some three years until 1729. After that he left home for residence in the Chinese College, a seminary established by the great Matteo Ripa for the education of priests for the Chinese mission. From the outset of his priestly life, Alphonsus was totally committed to active pastoral ministry among the people, preaching, hearing confessions, going on missionary journeys with the members of the Apostolic Missions. When missionary activity ceased for certain months he found a further outlet for his pastoral zeal among the poor and unlettered population of Naples, the *lazzaroni,* a unique brand of urban proletariat. As a priest he consciously oriented his ministry in their direction. With a group of similarly minded priests of his own class, he established the *capelle serotine,* literally, the evening chapels, for these pastorally neglected elements of the population. The various centers that were established throughout the slums of Naples combined religious catechesis, prayer together, education, leisure activities, and charitable activities such as visiting the sick in the various hospitals for the poor. While the history of this movement has yet to be fully researched and written, it survived in one form or another right down to the end of the nineteenth century.

The ministry among the *lazzaroni* prompted the first of Alphonsus's devotional writings, a modest pocket-sized manual of twenty-four pages, containing a set of seven simple meditations, each divided into three sections, on the eternal truths, one for each day of the week. They were to be read to the men at their meetings and would then form the basis of simple, prayerful reflections. All through his missionary career Alphonsus insisted, in the face of considerable opposition from local clergy, that a simple form of meditation, with reflection and affective prayer, should be taught to the most unlettered persons whether in the cities or the rural areas of the kingdom.

Thousands of copies of this first fruit of his pen, entitled

Massime Eterne (The Eternal Truths), were printed between 1728 and 1730; they were distributed free to the men of the evening chapels and later to the people on the missions. Unfortunately, not one of these original copies has survived but the little work, reprinted tens of thousands of times since then, either alone or with other simple works of devotion, has become virtually synonymous with Alphonsus and his piety. Whatever we may think about the validity of that judgment, the publication of this first work demonstrates the motive of all Alphonsus's writings. Whether of a theological or devotional nature they were always seen by him as an instrument of the apostolate, a means of saving and sanctifying souls, an apostolic medium through which the Word of God was preached as effectively as in the pulpit.

A Missionary Group

From 1729 until the end of 1732, the story of Alphonsus's priestly activity revolves around his efforts to assemble a group of missionary priests to dedicate their lives to the preaching of the Word of God to the most abandoned souls of the Kingdom of Naples, especially those living in the countryside. It is a complicated story involving a long list of participants from the Carmelite and Visitation nun, the visionary Sister Maria Celeste Crostarosa, the bishop of Castellamare di Stabia, Monsignor Thomas Falcoia, and a long list of companions who joined Alphonsus and almost immediately abandoned him.

The founders of religious orders bear little resemblance to the romantic portrait we paint of them. Few of them cast themselves in that role either consciously or willingly. Alphonsus de Liguori was far from casting himself in the heroic role of a religious founder; the initiatives he undertook were mainly directed by others and carried out blindly in obedience to spiritual guides whom he had vowed to obey. He was still, in diocesan seniority, a "junior" priest. He was in the depths of spiritual darkness in his personal journey toward God, tortured with scruples, unsure of his future, hesitant and indecisive as he found himself playing a key role in the establishment of a new missionary society. He was the most unlikely of founders; if any man was ever led unwillingly to the task, it was he.

Leaving the details of the story to be found elsewhere, we can come to the establishment of the new missionary group of priests on 9 November 1732 in the episcopal city of Scala, high on the mountains overlooking Amalfi, on the Gulf of Salerno. The inauguration Mass celebrated in a private house belonging to a convent of nuns was on the feast of the Lateran Basilica, dedicated to the Most Holy Savior, which prompted the group to style themselves Missionaries of the Most Holy Savior. For some twelve years the small group, at times numbering fewer than five members, struggled to maintain its corporate existence. Members came and went; foundations were offered and accepted, only to fail to take root. In 1743, the seven priests of the group assembled in the one secure foundation of Ciorani to pronounce their first religious vows and to choose their first overall superior. Alphonsus was elected after some initial hesitation and remained Rector Major, at least in name, until his death, forty-four years later. From the point of view of his literary activity, the office of Rector Major provided the occasion for his *Circular Letters* to all the members, as well as for letters to individual confreres. The considerable volume of these letters gives us a unique insight into the religious, social, and political life of Bourbon Naples as well as into Alphonsus's real character and into the psychology of his Neapolitan confreres. The letter of 1754 included in this selection of Alphonsus's writings is a typical example.

The next thirty years marked the spread of the missionary group both in numbers and foundations. Approval by Rome followed in 1749, which entailed a slight change of name to that of Congregation of the Most Holy Redeemer, out of deference to the Canons of the Lateran Basilica who were known as the Canons of the Holy Savior. Requests for missions according to the method evolved by Alphonsus and his companions poured in to the four Houses. The Regalist government of the Bourbon King in Naples, Charles III, absolutely refused to permit any further foundations. Vocations multiplied, necessitating the establishment of a formal novitiate and another center for the students. Alphonsus preached throughout the length and breadth of the kingdom and was widely regarded as the foremost missioner of the day. He was in constant demand for retreats to priests and religious and became a much-sought-after spiritual director by the laity as well as by bishops priests and religious.

By 1760 his health had deteriorated considerably, though he was always inclined to exaggerate the seriousness of his condition. The government of the Congregation was making increasing demands on his time while his writings were coming more and more to occupy the major role in his apostolate. He decided that he would not be able to take part with his missionary confreres in major missionary sorties throughout the kingdom; at most he would be able to undertake some minor retreat work for priests, seminarians, and religious. For all these reasons he had settled down to a quiet tempo of life in the house at Pagani when his peace was shattered by his appointment as bishop of the diocese of Saint Agatha of the Goths in the ecclesiastical province of Beneventum. He made every effort to refuse the appointment, calling on every friendship and using every avenue of influence he could think of to get Pope Clement XIII to alter his decision. But to no avail. Somewhat irritated by the refusal, the Pope imposed a formal obedience to ensure that Alphonsus accepted the office, with the result that he was ordained bishop in the Dominican basilica of Santa Maria sopra Minerva in Rome in June 1762. He was in his sixty-seventh year. The following month he took possession of his diocese.

His appointment as bishop opened up a whole new chapter in the pastoral activity of Alphonsus; it also opened up a new and feverish chapter, as we shall see, in his literary activity. Some fifty works appeared from his pen during the years he spent in his diocese, where his health definitely deteriorated and some undiagnosed diseases that were probably arthritic in origin left him crippled and somewhat deformed.

The Moral Theology

Following on his first publication, *The Eternal Truths* in 1728, Alphonsus's commitment to the active priestly ministry as a missioner, and his involvement in the establishment of a new missionary Congregation of priests, left him little time for further literary activity. Some verses and hymns, prayers to Our Lady, a novena of prayers for the feast of Teresa of Avila culminating in 1745 in a series of reflections and prayers to assist his students in their daily visit to the Blessed Sacrament and Our Lady, were the main results of his literary efforts.

The *Visits to the Blessed Sacrament,* which had its genesis in Alphonsus's concern for his students, found a wider audience almost by accident. It was published at the expense of a friend of Alphonsus who had been deeply impressed by these devotions when he made an enclosed retreat in the monastery of Ciorani. Thus this work, the most popular and widely diffused of all Alphonsus's devotional writings, began its incredible diffusion throughout the Christian world, determining the practice of one form of Eucharistic devotion right up to modern times. The official Acts of 1870 conferring the title Doctor of the Church on Alphonsus best express the merits of this devotional booklet.

It would be false to state that

> Alphonsus de Liguori initiated the practice of visits to the Most Blessed Sacrament but his great merit is to have given this practice a definite shape and form which was easily accessible to all the faithful. Just as it is legitimate to attribute the Rosary to St. Dominic, the Way of the Cross to the sons of the seraphic St. Francis of Assisi, the Spiritual Exercises to St. Ignatius, so we can attribute the devotional practice of visits to the Blessed Sacrament to St. Alphonsus in the sense that he gave this devotion a popular form and made it easily accessible to all sections of the faithful.[1]

Alphonsus's first venture into the realm of moral theology came in 1746, when he published a short treatise (or, rather, a letter) dealing with the custom rooted in the rural society of the Kingdom of Naples of "cursing the dead." From his experience as a missioner he came to the conclusion that this did not constitute the serious sin of formal blasphemy—an opinion contrary to

29

that commonly held by Neapolitan theologians at the time. This letter was the prelude to his major work in moral theology.

For nearly fourteen years Alphonsus had been engaged in collecting material for a textbook that would provide a convenient manual of study for the young members of his missionary society. He taught moral theology for several months to his students and experienced firsthand the need for just such a suitable text. When he finally decided to prepare one he adopted the expedient of taking an established manual and reediting it with his own comments and additions. For this purpose he selected the *Medulla Theologiae* of Father Herman Busenbaum, a Westphalian Jesuit, whose work had first appeared a hundred years before in 1650.

Alphonsus began his annotations in one of the small cells in the house at Ciorani. From 1742 the tempo of his work increased as he spent eight, nine, and ten hours a day on the preparation of his text for the printers. When he left on his missionary journeys he took the manuscripts with him. By the end of 1746 he had completed the work; the *Medulla* of Busenbaum had grown from a compact volume of some five hundred pages to nearly three times its original size. It emerged from the printers in September 1746 as an octavo volume of a thousand pages with newspaper small print.

The publication of his *Adnotationes* marked the entrance of Alphonsus into the realm of moral theology where he was, without doubt, to make his greatest contribution to the life of the church. For the next forty years he devoted himself to correcting what he had written, reevaluating his opinions, defending his principles, and elaborating on his "system" of arriving at moral conclusions in order to avoid the opposing trends of laxity and rigorism. Nine editions of his work in the course of forty years bear eloquent testimony to his commitment in this field of ecclesiastical science.

A word of explanation is in order here to help understand Alphonsus's position in the history of moral theology. By the end of the eighteenth century, moral theologians were embroiled in controversies connected with the proper formation of one's conscience or, to put it simply, how to choose what course of action to follow as a Christian in doubtful circumstances. In the process of forming one's conscience there frequently occurs the necessity of weighing probabilities. Some arguments indicate one course of action as correct, other arguments seem to favor the opposite.

Toward the end of the eighteenth century, the Dominican theologian Bartholomew Medina wrote: "It seems to me that it is lawful to follow a probable opinion even though the opposite opinion is *more* probable." By the middle of the next century moral theologians were divided into opposing camps, the Probabilists and the Probabiliorists, who insisted that the more probable *(probabilior)* opinion should be followed at all times. Some theologians brought Probabilism into disrepute, pushing it to outrageous extremes by declaring that if an opinion possessed even the slightest degree of probability from whatever source, it could safely become the norm of one's Christian conduct, which led inevitably to Laxism. Then by way of reaction the pendulum swung to the opposite extreme and the Probabiliorists advocated following the obligations of law to such an extent that they became Rigorists and were identified with Jansenism.

It took Alphonsus over twenty years to work out the speculative side of this whole controversy to his own satisfaction. He was trained in the Probabiliorist or Rigorist school. From his pastoral practice as a missioner he came to realize the harm this attitude caused to souls by imposing intolerable burdens on their consciences, keeping them away in fear, if not in despair, from the frequentation of the sacraments of Penance and the Eucharist. In the years of study and writing and pastoral practice that followed he refined his attitude to the speculative aspect of the question and ended up as a Moderate Probabilist or Equiprobabilist.

But these are theological wars fought in a past age. A fresh approach based on the virtues of charity and Christian discernment make the question of Probabilism of merely historical interest.

In the same year that the *Visits* appeared, 1745, Alphonsus, greatly daring, published a series of instructions for bishops on the exercise of their pastoral duties. He was uniquely equipped for the task. Twenty years of missionary experience had given him an unequalled insight into the pastoral condition of many dioceses. Many of the bishops he knew personally before their appointment; others he was familiar with from meeting them in the course of missions or during the diocesan retreats he had preached. The *Riflessioni utili a' Vescovi* or *Reflections useful for Bishops* consisted of over one hundred pages divided into two sections. The first outlined the particular areas demanding episcopal supervision—the seminary, those preparing for ordination, the priests of the diocese, the episcopal residence, and religious. The second section listed the means the bishop should employ to achieve his goal as shepherd of his flock—prayer, good example, residence, pastoral visits throughout the diocese, missions, diocesan synods or pastoral meetings with the clergy, advice to priests, readiness to meet priests and to correct any shortcomings in their ministry.

Episcopal Ministry

With his appointment as bishop in 1762 Alphonsus was faced with the challenge of putting into practice what he had outlined in his *vade mecum* for other bishops. Had he foreseen that he would end up one himself he might have been less cavalier in his advice. At any rate, the challenge facing him was to make the transition from theory to practice. His diocese possessed all the worst features of ecclesiastical life in the Kingdom of Naples at the time, with, of course, a hard core of priests of exemplary life, well-educated and cultured, fully versed in theology and adequately equipped for their pastoral activities. For a population of less than 40,000 souls there were at least 350 diocesan priests, not counting those who lived in Naples or elsewhere, most of them employed in secular professions. This number did not include priests living in eleven monasteries. The majority of the priests in the diocese had sought ordination without the least sign of a sacerdotal vocation and with no interest in it either. Ignorant of the very fundamentals of theology, devoid, very often, of even a basic education, virtually illiterate, insufficiently instructed even in the rubrics of the Mass, many of them spent their lives gambling and drinking in the local taverns and often in other forms of licentiousness. The noblest ambition of scores of clerics was to secure one of the many benefices in the diocese where an adequate income was assured and where the obligations were, at most, a weekly Mass and attendance at the meetings of the members of the sodality attached to the benefice. Preaching, visitation, and the burdensome duty of hearing confessions were none of their concern.

Alphonsus spent thirteen years (1762–1775) in the diocese as its bishop. A full account of his episcopal activities and his efforts to root out clerical concubinage and to develop a pastorally orientated clergy belongs, like the story of the foundation of his Congregation, in another place. Suffice it to say that he followed almost to the letter the directions he had given to other bishops in his writings for them. He devoted special attention to his seminary, which he virtually rebuilt. He refused to ordain candidates for the priesthood unless he was convinced of their motivation, their religious conduct, and their theological competence. He was scrupulous in his interpretation of his obligation to reside in the diocese and to make pastoral visitation of the churches and parishes. He arranged for a series of general missions to be conducted by missioners of different religious orders from outside the diocese. And he faced up to the grave scandal of clerical concubinage, which involved some of the most powerful families of the diocese whom his predecessor had hesitated to challenge. Only with the convents of nuns did he fail to make any great headway.

Within a few years of his arrival in the episcopal city of Saint Agatha, Alphonsus's health definitely deteriorated. Advised by the doctors that the dampness and fogs that were typical of the city built on the banks of the river Isclero were injurious to his health, he moved his episcopal residence to Arienzo, where he spent the greater part of his episcopal ministry. Although his health improved initially it never again became robust, and he was forced to spend the winter months house-bound. In the summer of 1768 he fell seriously ill. The local doctors were unable to diagnose with any certainty the cause of the severe pain and fever he suffered. For six weeks he lay between life and death and prepared himself for his last moments without any signs of anxiety or scruples. After specialists had been called in and his condition was brought under control, it became clear that he would never again be able to stand erect. He could walk only with difficulty and assisted by others. His head was bent forward on his chest so that, seen from behind, he seemed to have no head at all. For the next five years he was to govern the diocese mainly from his bed.

The Enlightenment

During the thirteen years Alphonsus spent in the diocese, his literary output was phenomenal. Taking into account his pastoral activity, his general ill health, and the periods of serious illness that totally incapacitated him, what he achieved was incredible. Some fifty titles came from his pen. In the first instance he continued his defense of his *Moral Theology*, which had now gone into several editions. At least nine treatises defended his moral system.

The condition of the clergy also prompted a range of books from Alphonsus's pen directed toward assisting them in their pastoral ministry. There was a book for confessors in rural areas, *Il Confessore Diretto;* two further works were aimed at candidates who wished to engage in the ministry of the confessional. A volume on the ceremonies of the Mass was an effort to improve the celebration of the Mass by his priests and contained, at the same time, prayers to be said in preparation and in thanksgiving. *The Way of Salvation* and two works on the Passion of Jesus Christ were intended to assist his priests in their own devotion and to guide them as they led the ordinary faithful in meditation together in church.

The area of preaching next occupied his attention. He wrote two outlines of doctrinal instructions to be given to the people at Mass and finally a compendium of sermons for every Sunday of the year that concentrated on moral themes rather than on the liturgical aspects of the Eucharistic celebration.

The ideas that were beginning to circulate on a variety of topics—from the frequency of reception of Holy Communion, the position of the papacy, and the matter of General Councils to the refutation of books he considered dangerous, such as the French works *De l'Esprit* and *De la Prédication*—continued to occupy his attention. The ideas of the Enlightenment and the various theories of the French Encyclopedists, which were making their way into Italy and influencing the clergy, directed Alphonsus's literary efforts into the realm of apologetics. He cast himself in the role of a one-man counter-Encyclopedist to counteract the baneful effects the Enlightenment was having.

He published five major apologetic works in all between 1756 and 1773, three of them during his years as a bishop. The first was *Against the Errors of Modern Unbelievers Called Materialists and Deists,* which was followed by *The Truth of the Faith as Evidenced by the Motives of Credibility.* He continued his study and in 1767 as a bishop he united the arguments of these two volumes and published them under the title of *The Truth of the Faith.* This was a major work on which he claimed he had "sweated blood." The volume enjoyed considerable success as a sourcebook against the literature of the Enlightenment in Italy and represented a definite contribution to the Church's response to these particular errors within the confines of the Kingdom of Naples. Three other works during his episcopacy completed the list of his publications in this type of polemical literature: an account of the teaching of the Council of Trent aimed mainly at the teachings of Luther and Calvin, a history of all the heresies in the life of the Church published under the title *The Triumph of the Church,* and a pamphlet-sized work on the truth of Divine Revelation directed once again against Voltaire and the Deists.

Assessment of the intrinsic merit of these apologetic works is difficult. Their impact on the English-speaking world was minimal and only two of them were ever translated into that language. Their main interest nowadays is for the historian of apologetics who may seek to trace the development of this science from the *De Controversiis* of Bellarmine to modern times. Alphonsus was totally of his time in his attitude toward those he branded heretics and unbelievers. The tolerance and respect for the great religions of the world that has characterized Christianity since the Second Vatican Council was undreamed of in his day and does not find an echo in these writings.

Jansenism

The havoc wrought in religious attitudes by the writers of the Enlightenment was, to a large extent, restricted to the educated and the intellectuals; more pernicious was the threat from the Jansenists in the area of popular devotion and piety, since this affected the vast majority of the ordinary faithful. Alphonsus abhorred the cold Jansenist spirit that deprived Christian piety of its warmth, spontaneity, and tenderness. There was no place for loving contact with the person of Jesus in his sacraments, no audience of the Father in familiar prayer. Anything that enkindled tenderness in one's relationship with the forgiving Father of the parable of the Prodigal Son was frowned on. The loving-kindness of God manifested in the mysteries of the Incarnation, the Passion of Christ, and the Blessed Sacrament was neglected. Devotion to the Sacred Heart was anathema to the Jansenist spirit.

The principal battles against Jansenism were not fought in the theological lecture halls or in learned volumes of theology; rather were they fought out in the practices of popular devotion and in popular manuals of prayers and piety. The corrosive spirit of Jansenism was finally eradicated through the persistence of the ordinary faithful in their devotions to the saints, to the Mother of God, and to the love of God for us as manifested in the mysteries of the Incarnation, Passion, and death of his Son. It was in this aspect of Christian life that Alphonsus's influence was dominant. After his moral theology, this was his next greatest contribution to the life of the church. And it is against this background, as well as for their intrinsic merits, that his devotional writings must be considered.

Of the 110 works of all sizes and shapes that came from his pen, there are certainly 50 that fit into the category of devotional works. They were translated into a variety of different languages and enjoy worldwide diffusion. His themes were predictable. Devotion to the Infant Jesus in the mystery of the Incarnation, devotion to the Passion and the Way of the Cross, devotion and visits to the Blessed Sacrament, devotion to the saints and, above all, to the Mother of God.

The year 1750 saw the publication of one of the most famous and at the same time most controversial of Alphonsus's writings, *The Glories of Mary*. The work had been nearly twenty years in preparation. The idea of writing a book about the Mother of God had been with him since the early years of his priesthood. He had been encouraged in his purpose by the Neapolitan Mariologist Father Francis Pepe, S.J., with whom he discussed many aspects of Marian theology. Alphonsus set himself to study the writings of the Fathers and especially St. Bernard in their references to Our Lady. He gradually matured his theology in his mission sermons and in the novenas he preached for her feasts. By the end of 1748 he had accumulated a considerable amount of material, which he began to organize for publication.

The framework of the book was provided by the hymn *Salve Regina,* the "Hail, Holy Queen," which he took as the basic text for his commentary. Having completed the commentary on the *Salve,* he devoted the second part of the work to nine discourses for the principal feasts of Our Lady during the year, together with considerations on Our Lady's sorrows and a study of the virtues of which she gave an example during her life. The work concluded with a series of prayers and practices of devotion in her honor.

The Glories of Mary did not originate in any polemical spirit. Alphonsus saw the work as an offering from a devout child of Mary to his spiritual Mother. More significantly still, it was dedicated to Christ the Redeemer, as a "token of love for Him and his Mother"; to set it up as an effort to detract from the omnipotent salvific action of Christ in the mystery of salvation is totally unwarranted. Alphonsus saw it as an effort to nourish genuine devotion to the Mother of God among the faithful and at the same time he intended it as a theological sourcebook that would provide priests with readily available material for their meditations and sermons.

Within the space of six years, *The Glories of Mary* went into a second edition in Naples. Four years later a compact two-volume pocket edition appeared in Venice. The first German translation appeared in Augsburg a few years later and a Spanish edition followed in Valencia. Within two hundred years of its publications the work has been translated into over eighty different languages and appeared in over eight hundred known editions.

Prayer

Alphonsus realized that the question of prayer was of primary importance and not only for the educated, or for priests and religious, but also for the largely uneducated ordinary Neapolitan, whether in the cities or throughout the rural areas of the kingdom—hence the recurrence of the prayer theme to be found throughout his writings and his preaching. *A Way of Conversing Continually with God as with a Friend* is one of his earliest works on aspects of prayer and is presented in this selection in a translation by Rev. Brendan McConvery, C.SS.R. Various other, shorter publications dealing with aspects of prayer, included in devotional works on other subjects, testified to the fact that prayer was central to his whole spirituality and that he was working on a major work on the subject. This appeared in 1759, known in English as *Prayer, the Great Means of Salvation*.

The work, in two parts, was once again the fruit of years of theological study and of practical experience in the preaching of missions. Several studies of the theological basis of this work have been published, testifying to its originality, its spiritual perception, and its eclecticism. The great Dominican theologian Father Marin-Sola considered that, despite its size, it made as great a contribution to the questions of grace and predestination as many other more voluminous works of the seventeenth and eighteenth centuries.[2] Father Terrence J. Moran, C.SS.R., of the

Baltimore Province has edited the selection from the work included in this volume.

If *Prayer, the Great Means of Salvation* occupies a place apart among the ascetico-dogmatic works Alphonsus wrote, his years as bishop saw the publication of what many regard as his spiritual masterpiece, *The Practice of the Love of Jesus Christ.* Published in the summer of 1768 when Alphonsus was seventy-two years of age, it saw the light a few weeks before the illness that brought him to death's door in Arienzo. His conduct during the illness, his resignation and his patient acceptance of pain, his willingness to accept whatever the Lord permitted, translated this spiritual masterpiece into action and was proof sufficient that what he had written came from the depths of his union with God and not from any literary facility.

The Redemptorist moral theologian Father Bernard Häring wrote as follows of *The Practice of the Love of Jesus Christ:*

> This work is an outline of moral theology as it *should* be presented to the laity as well as to priests and religious—a moral theology that focuses everything in Christ and in his love for us.
>
> Modern legalists have often considered the words of St. Augustine: "Love God and do what you will" as very dangerous, if not, erroneous. But St. Alphonsus never feared that a true love of God would transgress the laws of God. Quoting this fundamental text of St. Augustine, Alphonsus explains, "A soul that loves God is taught by that very love never to do anything that might displease him."
>
> When St. Alphonsus began to write his original moral theology as a commentary on a text by the Jesuit Busenbaum, he followed an outline that was acceptable to his own contemporaries. In the final years of his life, however, he said that he wanted to write a moral theology with quite a different approach. This wonderful book, *The Practice of the Love of Jesus Christ,* reveals what his approach would have been. He returns to the fountains of Sacred Scripture and Tradition, even for the structure of his presentation. In this volume he definitely anticipated the renewal of moral theology that was

to take place in the era of Pope John XXIII and the Second Vatican council.

This is the way to teach christians morality, if we really believe with the Council that all christians are called to holiness—a holiness that will lead to an ever better fulfillment of the single commandment: "Love one another as I love you" (Jn 15:12), or "So be perfect, just as your heavenly Father is perfect" (Mt 5.48). With this love one finds in every commandment an invitation to God's love and tries to prudently find an adequate response of love in justice, temperance, fortitude and all the other virtues.[3]

Alphonsus's Spirituality

Alphonsus's religious formation was an important factor in determining the characteristics of the spirituality to be found in his writings. His early years were under the religious influence of his mother and the Oratorian Fathers. Prayer came first in importance, then the frequentation of the sacraments, confession and Holy Communion. A horror of the slightest sin that would offend God and betray considerable ingratitude for his goodness to us was a constant theme in his mother's teaching and was echoed by Pagano, his Oratorian spiritual director.

His adolescent years, which corresponded with his legal studies at the University of Naples, marked his introduction to the practice of making enclosed retreats, first under the direction of the Vincentian Fathers. Then, under the guidance of the Jesuits in their retreat houses in Naples, he made the formal spiritual exercises of St. Ignatius. There is clear evidence that in these experiences there was considerable emphasis on the Last Things, the Eternal Truths; meditations on hell with its eternity of suffering were introduced with as many dramatic effects as possible.

His admission to the clerical ranks in the Congregation of the Apostolic Missions widened still further his exposure to the prevailing spirituality. Despite the fact that Naples was politically at this time under the control of the Hapsburgs from Vienna, the dominant cultural and religious influences were Spanish. Spanish influence became even more dominant with the arrival of the first of the Bourbons in the person of Charles III in 1734. Devotion to the mysteries of the Incarnation from the infancy of the Child Jesus through his hidden life at Nazareth, his Passion, Crucifixion, and death, was widely practiced. The Blessed Sacrament was exposed for veneration in the different churches of the city and the practices of devotional visits and the Forty Hours Adoration were widespread.

Devotion to the Mother of God followed as a corollary to devotion to her Son and Spanish influence was clearly evident in the emphasis placed on her Immaculate Conception and Assumption, and on the power of her intercession. Prayers to the saints and especially the Spanish saints Teresa of Avila, John of the Cross, and Peter of Alcantara, together with devotions and novenas in their honor, were typical of popular piety. Alphonsus's first devotional publication, a slim volume *(operetta)*, was a collection of seven prayers to Our Lady, one for each day of the week, which was published in 1734. In 1742, the first of his publications that merited to be styled a "book" was a series of meditations for the feast of St. Teresa with a précis of her doctrine of perfection, *Considerazioni sopra le virtù e pregi di S. Teresa di Gesù*, etc.

Alphonsus's introduction to the practices of corporal penance, which were an accepted element of spirituality among the many religious houses and contemplative convents, probably took place with his reception as a formal member of the Apostolic Missions. Predictably, he overdid their practice in the early years of his spiritual development and had to be restrained by his spiritual director, but he maintained their practice faithfully to the end of his life and inculcated their use in his spiritual direction of priests, religious, and laity. They are a constant element in his recommendations for those who wish to grow in holiness of life.

St. Francis de Sales occupied a place apart in Alphonsus's spiritual formation. He was the principal patron of the Apostolic Missions and his writings were obligatory study for the seminarians. After Francis de Sales, Alphonsus devoted himself to the study of the writings of Teresa of Avila and, to a somewhat lesser extent, to those of John of the Cross. These three writers, whose works were readily available in Italian translations, became the source of much of his spirituality and, accordingly, of his spiritual writings. He was able to quote freely from the first two, if not always literally, then according to the sense of what they had to say. He was himself favored with mystical graces and followed the teaching of both Teresa and John of the Cross, but when he gave an outline of mystical principles for confessors in the *Praxis Confessarii,* he did not identify himself totally with their concept of perfection. For him sanctity of life was more ascetical than mystical; it did not *necessarily* entail the gift of contemplation, although it might frequently be found among those eager for growth in the spiritual life. The highest perfection, as far as Alphonsus's practical direction was concerned, was reached when, as a result of ascetical endeavors under God's grace, one achieved total conformity with the will of God. This may well explain why John of the Cross, when compared with Teresa of Avila, figures so comparatively rarely in Alphonsus's devotional writings for the ordinary faithful.

It is important to remember that Alphonsus did not devote himself consistently to writing, either theologically or spiritually, until he was well over fifty years of age and had spent over twenty years as a missioner among the ordinary people, mainly in rural areas. His publications were of a minor nature until 1748 when his writings and not the pulpit became the center of his apostolic ministry. Categorization of his vast output of 110 titles ranging in volume from pamphlets to in-quarto folios is not easy, but his works may conveniently be classified under four main headings: moral theology, dogmatic theology, apologetics, and ascetical theology. The editors of the critical edition of his works, basing their opinion on instructions given by Alphonsus himself to his publishers, argue for a distinction among ascetical, spiritual, and devotional works. These three categories, however, are included here under the single heading "ascetical."[4]

Sources

The study and reading necessary to provide a background to sustain such a variety of writings must have been considerable.

Alphonsus's dedication to study was such as to provide practical proof that he took a vow never to waste a moment of time. He also enlisted the cooperation of the members of his Congregation, priests, students, and brothers, to assist him in his researches, with the result that his spiritual writings are a tapestry of quotations from the scriptures, from the lives and writings of the saints, and from a multiplicity of different authors.

The ecclesiastical libraries of the *Settecento*–and Alphonsus insisted on building up the libraries of his Redemptorist communities from the very inception of his Congregation–were adequately provided with available editions of the works of the Fathers as well as with collections *(prontuaria)* of extracts and quotations from their writings and from theologians and spiritual writers of previous centuries. If they did not measure up to the critical standards demanded in later centuries, they were still able to provide a rich source of material for writers who, like Alphonsus, were anxious to reflect the living tradition of the Church.

Alphonsus's use of scripture makes an interesting study. He did not so much "quote scripture" to support or illustrate what he wished to say as *write* in scriptural terms. His familiarity with the Word of God was all-embracing and his power of recall so extensive that he virtually "thought" in the language of the Vulgate, which then became the appropriate vehicle to express his ideas. The same is true of his quotations from the Fathers of the Church, the medieval mystics, and the lives of the saints. He used their writings and stories from their lives to demonstrate that he was echoing the voice of Christian tradition. His approach to the texts at his disposal was not whether they were critically accurate, as the nineteenth-century critical scholar might have assessed them, but whether they expressed the *sensus fidelium* of the past. In his choice of texts he may not always have been accurate, but his theological sense was invariably perceptive.

The volumes of the critical edition of the writings of Alphonsus trace the references for each of his publications to their original sources. The number of works quoted runs into hundreds, testifying to the united efforts of the author and his cooperators. One particular aspect of his ascetical writings that demands special mention is his use of the *exempla,* the *esempi,* or, in English, the *Examples* or stories quoted in many of his devotional works from the *Glories of Mary* onward. Father Terrence T. Moran, C.SS.R., deals expertly with this matter in his introduction to his selection from *The Glories of Mary.* Suffice it to recall here that this feature of both the profane and devotional writings of medieval and later centuries has now been thoroughly studied, resulting in a more accurate assessment of this literary genre. It is now clear that the many critics who have derided this feature of the writings of earlier centuries have done so without a sufficient historical appreciation of what was involved.[5]

Spiritual Themes

Before we consider the main themes in Alphonsus's spiritual teaching, it is important to emphasize once again that his spiritual writings are really preaching under another form. He uses the preacher's techniques—a short exposé of the theme, then an incident from his own experience or from the lives of the saints to retain his reader's attention, and, finally, an outline of prayers or pious affections that should flow from what has been read and reflected on. His purpose was always to elicit personal prayers from those he addressed. His style was simple, "popular" in the best sense, conversational, reflecting the mentality of the ordinary man or woman. He himself preferred to call it "apostolic." There is no attempt at literary embellishment, no hesitation about repetition. He is not afraid to repeat in a slightly different way the same thought since this is the way we speak and interact. "It is of great help to those who are not well educated to intersperse throughout our sermons, questions and answers. It is also to be recommended to recount incidents from the lives of the saints and, at times, examples of the punishments visited by God on sinners."[6]

St. Francis de Sales, it has been said, brought the possibility of holiness from being a clerical preserve into the secular world. Alphonsus brought it one step further, that is, to the understanding and practice of the ordinary unsophisticated person without in any way diminishing the gospel's essential demands or adopting a condescending attitude toward his hearers or readers. All are called to holiness; God provides them all with the means of achieving it whatever their human, social, or intellectual condition. His teaching is in perfect harmony with Vatican II's proclamation of the universal call to holiness in Chapter 5 of *Lumen Gentium*.

Alphonus's aim in his ministry as preacher, spiritual writer, or director of souls was to lead souls from sin to union with God. The spiritual journey begins with conversion from sin and ends with the spiritual heights of union with God in perfect detachment, conformity of will, and, at times, according to the Providence of God, the graces of mystical union. For every stage of this journey Alphonsus provided meditations and reflections, advice, exhortations to personal effort, and, finally, appropriate prayers. He well knew the fickleness of the human heart and the hold that sin can have over it. Meditation on the Last Things, at times even the terrifying power of reflection on the eternity of punishment in hell, may be necessary for the soul in order to take the first step, with God's grace, on the road to holiness. To portray him as a writer inculcating nothing more than the fear of a God who can cast down to hell for all eternity is to falsify totally his teaching.

> In sermons which inspire terror the preacher must never bring his hearers to despair of their salvation or to lose hope of their conversion. At the end of every such sermon the preacher should ensure that he leaves the door open to everyone, no matter how sunk in sin, to hope for the graces necessary to alter their way of life. He should encourage them to trust in the merits of Jesus Christ and in the intercession of Our Lady. He should exhort them to have recourse in prayer to these two anchors of salvation. In every sermon he should frequently and forcefully exhort all to pray since prayer is the only means of obtaining the graces necessary for salvation.[7]

At the same time, Alphonsus does not hesitate to demand of those who set out on the road to God a simple but attainable asceticism. He does not hesitate to get them to face the challenge that holiness of life demands of human conduct. Yet he has a word of encouragement for all and for every circumstance to be met on this journey—failure, discouragement, scruples, doubts, fears, physical illness and temporal misfortunes, spiritual aridity, the dark night of the senses and of the soul, are all dealt with in a way that demonstrates his psychological perception and his mastery of the art of spiritual direction. But the most telling of all the aspects of his writings is the sense they convey that the author has been through it all himself, that he writes from lived experience.

It would be a serious misreading of his writings to imagine that Alphonsus was exclusively an *ascetical* writer in the strict theological sense of the word, that is, a writer whose main interest is in a moralizing, behavioral, and ascetical spirituality, suitable only for the early stages of one's spiritual journey. He was, in point of fact, more correctly a mystical writer whose wide study of the great mystics and whose own mystical experiences admirably equipped him to write of the highest stages of spirituality. There are mystical insights to be found everywhere in his writings and particularly in his writings about prayer and detachment. He was a spiritual writer for the generality of Christians who wished to live a sincere Christian spiritual life. Without explicit reference to mysticism or the use of mystical terminology, he led them on to union with God, simply and effectively. At the same time he was very much aware from his own experience with the contemplative convents throughout the Kingdom of Naples of the danger of pseudo-mysticism. Quietism and its attendant manifestations were still in evidence among those who professed to lead lives of deep prayer. For this reason he was cautious in allowing his penitents to read mystical writings and, in particular, the works of St. John of the Cross. They were to read the chapters he indicated and no further. Those whom the Lord favored with mystical graces were to be thoroughly tested to discern the authenticity of their experiences. Strict rules dealt with the possibility of visions and revelations, which were a feature of religious life at the time. In this context, we may find the key to Alphonsus's apparent harsh treatment of the mystic, the Venerable Maria Celeste Crostarosa, whose revelations played their part in the development of the Redemptorist Congregation and Rule.

The Love of God

There is wide agreement in regard to the main outlines of a synthesis of Alphonsus's spiritual doctrine. He began with the insistence that holiness and the highest degree of holiness are within the grasp of every human being: "God wishes that all should become saints, the priest as priest, those who are married in their married state, those engaged in commerce in the exercise of their business, soldiers as soldiers and so on for everyone else." Sanctity is not incompatible with any state of life. Alphonsus preached this doctrine along the streets of Naples, in the country villages, in the *piazze* of innumerable rural centers of population.

The holiness he inculcated is not some vague feeling or aspiration; it consists simply in the love of God. It was to be the constant effort of every confessor, even in the remotest region with the most uneducated of persons, as well as of every spiritual director, to awaken this love of God in souls. God has been infinitely good to us. We see his goodness manifested above all in the person of Jesus Christ, our Redeemer. "What more could God do for us?" is a recurring question as Alphonsus dialogues with souls to bring them to "show love for love." "So many preachers and confessors neglect to speak of love for Jesus Christ which should be the principle, if not the only devotion of a Christian," he complains in his *Novena to the Sacred Heart of Jesus.* There is nothing complicated about his exhortations to love God in Jesus Christ, as he outlines, with unashamed emphasis on the imagination and the emotions, all aspects of the mystery of the Incarnation from the birth of Jesus to his death on the Cross.

His teaching merges into the realms of mysticism as he insists on *detachment from creatures and union with God* as the practical manifestation of one's love of God. Detachment, *distacco,* is at once a feature of the purgative and illuminative ways, according to Alphonsus's interpretation of the teaching of the mystics. Union with God, the highest achievement of charity, means total indifference, the abandonment of oneself to God in every circumstance: "I have no other wish than what God wishes for me."

His doctrine of detachment is clearly stated in Chapter 17 of the *Practice of the Love of Jesus Christ:*

> God often makes use of aridity in order to draw his most cherished souls closer to himself. Attachment to our own inordinate inclinations is the greatest obstacle to true union with God. Therefore, when God intends to draw a soul to his perfect love, he tries to detach her from all affection for created things. Thus he may deprive her of temporal goods, of worldly pleasures, of property, honor, friends, relations or bodily health. By means of these losses, troubles, neglect, bereavements and infirmities he wipes out, by degrees, all earthly attachments so that the affections may be centered on him alone.
>
> When God wishes to see the soul purified even further and divested of all sensible satisfaction in order to unite her entirely to himself by means of pure love, what does he do? He places her in the crucible of desolation, more painful to bear than the most severe trials. She is left in a state of great uncertainty. Is she in God's grace or not? In the dense darkness that shrouds her there seems no prospect of her ever finding God again.

In a thousand places throughout his spiritual writings, Alphonsus insists on the means to be adopted for one's sanctification. They are simple: frequentation of the sacraments, denial of one's self, and, above all, prayer. Here we come, in his own words, to *"The Great Means of Salvation and Sanctification"*–the key that unlocks the secret of God's dealing with us and the test of our response. He exhorts to prayer in all its forms from the simplest vocal prayer through reflection, meditation, prayer of petition. He outlines simple methods of prayer, based on the mysteries of religion, the scriptures, the eternal truths, in such a way as to make them possible for the most unlettered person in his audience—even for children. From the pulpit in the village churches he leads the congregations of men, women, and children in prayer—a practice he hopes they will continue by themselves after his departure.

Prayer is a conversation with God. In your own simple words tell him your feelings, your desires, your fears and what you wish to receive from him. In return, the Lord speaks to your heart, making you aware of his infinite goodness, his love for you and what you should do to make yourselves pleasing to him.

His formulation of the theory and power of prayer as well as its place in the economy of salvation was startling in its simplicity and originality. God gives everybody the ordinary grace that is sufficient to enable them to pray. With prayer every other grace is obtainable, even graces to carry out the most difficult of the divine commandments and to fulfill all one's Christian obligations. Prayer, with due submission to the Providence of God, can obtain even those special graces that are not, as it were, on general issue. Alphonsus insisted on the obvious conclusion. We are responsible for our salvation and if we lose our souls there is no point in cursing Adam or original sin or our temptations or our environment—or, least of all, God himself. The key to salvation and to holiness is prayer to God for the assistance of his grace. He summed up his theology of prayer in an Italian jingle that was repeated over and over again until not even the most illiterate could forget it:

> Dal mundo, inferno e carne
> Al mal sei spinto.
> Prega, prega, si vuoi
> Non essere vinto.

(You are led to sin/By the world, the flesh and the devil. Pray, pray if you/Do not wish to be overcome.)

Or, to put it in one sentence, Prayer is the only way to obtain the grace necessary for salvation.

Well aware of the graces of union with God or *infused prayer,* Alphonsus limits himself to the description and practice of *active prayer* in those writings he hoped to put in the hands of everybody. But he knows that active prayer is also capable of leading souls to the higher flights of infused prayer and he advises as follows:

If during prayer one feels oneself united with God in some form of infused or supernatural recollection, one should not force oneself to continue making any other acts of affection beyond those to which one is gently led by the grace of God. One should do nothing more than give one's full attention to what the Lord is achieving in one's soul.

Teacher of the Catholic Soul

Alphonsus's resignation as bishop of St. Agatha of the Goths was accepted by Pope Pius VI in the summer of 1775. Within a few weeks he was back in his monastery at Pagani, where his health improved slightly. It was predictable that he would want to continue writing despite the strain this imposed on his helpers; the Fathers of the community had to search for the books he required and read out to him the relevant references. His failing sight made reading extremely difficult; his hearing was defective and with arthritis in his fingers he was barely able to sign his name. He informed his publishers that although he was retired "he could not remain idle." He set himself to work on a theological study of eternity and the end of creation, based on the scriptures, the Fathers of the Church, and above all St. Thomas Aquinas. The volume of just over two hundred pages entitled *A Theological-Moral Dissertation Concerning Eternal Life* was published in 1776, the last work of any length from his pen.

His last years were troubled by problems concerning the very existence of his missionary Congregation and greatly saddened by misunderstandings with the Pope and the Roman authorities. He suffered intensely both physically and mentally until on 1 August 1787 he drew his last breath quietly and without struggle. Within a few months of his death the various processes that would lead to his canonization were set in motion. Despite delays caused by the French invasions of Rome, he was beatified in 1816 and on 26 May 1839 he was canonized. Meanwhile his writings were being translated into various languages with editions following editions. His moral theology became accepted throughout the seminaries of the entire Catholic world, influencing the teaching and practice of saints such as the Cure of Ars. In March 1871 in the immediate aftermath of the First Vatican Council he was declared a Doctor of the Church. Eighty years later, in 1950, Pope Pius XII named him the patron of Confessors and Moral Theologians. The final word rests with Pope John Paul II:

> St. Alphonsus is a gigantic figure, not only in the history of the Church, but for the whole of humanity as well. Even people who would not follow his vision, still see in him "the teacher of the Catholic soul of the West." He did for modern Catholicism that which Augustine accomplished in ancient times.

ALPHONSUS DE LIGUORI'S WRITINGS

SPIRITUAL WRITINGS

Divine Love and The Means of Acquiring It

Introduction

Editor's Note: This short text was published at the end of Alphonsus's time as bishop of St. Agatha of the Goths, 1775. He was in his middle seventies when he composed it, after a period of severe illness and constant worries about whether he was obliged to remain as bishop in charge of his diocese. The themes are familiar and encapsulate the essence of his thought. An early commentator on his spiritual writings, Professor Candido Romano, correctly describes this work as the *summa* of Alphonsus's spiritual teaching, with its definite emphasis on practical application.

* * *

1. God, who is so good, loves us very much and wishes to be loved by us. Not only has he repeatedly invited us to love him, as is clear from so many examples in the scriptures, not only has he bestowed upon us individually and on the whole family so many gifts and favors, but he has also wished to oblige us, as it were, to love him, by an express command to do so. He has promised heaven to those who love him and threatened those who do not with hell. As is clear from the teaching of Saints Peter and Paul, he wishes everyone to be saved and that no one should be lost: "Who wills everyone to be saved" (1 Tm 2:4); "He is patient with you, not wishing that any should perish but that all should come to repentance" (2 Pt 3:9). But if God wishes everyone to be saved, why then has he created hell? He has created hell not to see us damned but to be loved by us! If he had not created hell, how many would have loved him? Even as it is with the existence of hell, the greater part of the human race choose to be damned rather to love God. And so I repeat, if there were no hell, how many would choose to love God? And so the Lord has threatened those who do not love him with the prospect of eternal suffering solely for the purpose of securing that those who do not love him

out of their own good will would be compelled to do so from fear of going to eternal perdition.[1]

2. My God, how greatly do those consider themselves fortunate who are invited by their king to love him: "Love me because I love you." A king would regard it as a considerable humiliation if he were to condescend to ask his subjects for their love. But God, who is infinitely good, Lord of all, all-powerful, all-wise, a God who, in a word, merits eternal love, a God who has enriched us with so many spiritual and temporal benefits, does not disdain to ask us for our love. He exhorts us and commands us to love him. And yet, in spite of everything, he does not succeed. The only thing he asks of us is that we should love him. "And now, Israel, what does the LORD, your God, ask of you but to fear the LORD, your God, and follow his ways exactly, to love and serve the LORD, your God, with all your heart and all your soul" (Dt 10:12)? For this purpose the Son of God came to be with us on earth: "I have come to set the earth on fire, and how I wish it were already blazing!" (Lk 12:49). Note the words "and how I wish it were already blazing!" It is almost as if God, who possesses in himself infinite happiness, declares that he would not be fully content unless he saw himself loved by us.[2]

3. We cannot doubt, therefore, that God loves us and loves us greatly. So much, indeed, does God love us that he wishes us to love him with all our hearts. He says to each of us: "Therefore, you shall love the LORD, your God, with all your heart" (Dt 6:5). And then he adds: "Take to heart these words which I enjoin on you today....Speak of them at home and abroad, whether you are busy or at rest. Bind them at your wrist as a sign and let them be as a pendant on your forehead. Write them on the doorposts of your houses and on your gates" (Dt 6:6–9). The important aspect of these words is the desire that the Lord has, the very hunger, as it were, that he experiences, that he should be loved by each one of us. He wishes that the words "we should love him with all our hearts" should be imprinted on our hearts. And so that we should never forget them, he wishes that we should reflect on them whether resting or engaged in activity, as we retire to rest and as we begin our day. He wishes that we should

have them always with us to remind us of our obligation no matter where we are or what we are engaged in. The Pharisees, according to St. Matthew, carried out these instructions to the letter (Mt 23:51).

4. St. Gregory of Nyssa wrote: "Blessed is the arrow which brings God, the Archer, into one's heart." This was the saint's way of saying that when God directs an arrow of love into one's heart, namely, an inspiration or a special grace of illumination, which leads us to realize the goodness of God, the love he bears us and his desire to be loved by us, at that very moment, God himself comes to us. In other words, God is both the archer and the love which the arrow brings. "For God is love," as St. John tells us (1 Jn 4:8). And just as an arrow remains fixed in the heart it has wounded, so God, who wounds a heart with love of himself, remains united with that heart. Oh, that we could all realize that only God has true and genuine love for us all. The love of parents, of friends, and of all those who say they love us (with the exception of those who love us in and on account of God himself) is not really true love since there is always some element of self-interest mixed with it. Yes, my God, I fully realize that only you genuinely love me, not from any self-interest on your part, but purely out of the love for me which comes from your infinite goodness. And I am so ungrateful that despite your love for me, I have displeased you and caused you more bitterness than I have to anyone else. Do not permit me, Jesus, to be so ungrateful to you in the future. You have genuinely loved me and now I wish to love you genuinely for the rest of my life. I wish to say to you in the words of St. Catherine of Genoa, "My love, do not allow me to offend you again. My only wish is to love you and with this I am happy."[3]

5. According to St. Bernard, a soul who genuinely loves God can only wish what God wills. Let us then pray that the Lord will wound us with the arrows of his love since souls who are wounded by these arrows are incapable of wishing for anything other than what God wills. They rid themselves of all vestiges of self-love. To this they add the total offering of themselves to the Lord and it is this to which the Lord refers when he declares in

the Song of Songs that he has been wounded by those who love him: "You have ravished my heart, my sister, my bride" (Sg 4:9).

6. St. Bernard beautifully expresses this whole idea when he says: "Let us cast our hearts up to God." When souls give themselves unreservedly to God, they in a certain sense cast their souls like javelins toward God, who in his turn expresses himself as being completely captivated by those who give themselves to him. Casting their hearts up to God then is an apt description of those who, in their prayers, give expression to their desire to give themselves wholly to him. As they pray, they make use of the following or similar short prayers: "My God and My All; My God, I want you alone and nothing more; My Lord, I give myself wholly to you and if I do not know how to give myself completely to you as I should, do you please take me to yourself."

Jesus, my love,
I want nothing but you:
To you I give myself
Do with me as you wish.[4]

7. Souls who can genuinely say in the words of the Song of Songs "My lover belongs to me and I to him" (Sg 2:16) are extremely fortunate. My God has given himself totally to me and I have given myself totally to him. Souls who are able to pray like this from their hearts are ready, in the words of St. Bernard, to accept all the pains of hell (if they could do this without losing God) rather than be separated from God for even an instant. What a wonderful treasure is the grace of divine love; happy those who possess it. Let them do everything in their power, let them take all means necessary to preserve and increase it. And those who are not yet in possession of it should make every effort to acquire it. Accordingly, let us reflect on the means that are necessary to acquire and preserve this treasure of divine love.

8. The first means of acquiring it is to detach oneself from human attachments. There is no place for the love of God in hearts that are full of earth; the more there is of earth the less there is of the reign of the love of God. This is the reason why those souls who wish to have hearts totally possessed by the love of God should devote themselves to ridding their hearts of earthly

attachments. To achieve holiness of life one must imitate St. Paul who, to gain the love of Jesus Christ, considered all the goods of this world as valueless: "I even consider everything as a loss because of the supreme good of knowing Christ Jesus my Lord. For his sake I have accepted the loss of all things and I consider them so much rubbish, that I may gain Christ" (Phil 3:8). So let us pray to the Holy Spirit that he would inflame our hearts with his holy love that we would be able to despise and regard as useless, mere vapor and dirt, all the riches, pleasures, honors, and dignities of this earth in search of which so many lose their souls.

9. When the love of God takes possession of souls, they no longer consider of any value those things the world esteems highly: "Were one to offer all he owns to purchase love,/he would be roundly mocked" (Sg 8:7). St. Francis de Sales writes that when the house goes on fire all its contents are thrown out the window, which is another way of saying that when souls burn with the love of God they cast out from their lives all earthly things such as honors and riches in order to love nothing but God. This is what the love of God in their hearts achieves; they do not need the urging of sermons nor the promptings of their spiritual directors. St. Catherine of Genoa said that she did not love God for his gifts to her but that she loved the gifts of God in order to love him more.

10. Gilberti writes that those who love God find it at the same time painful and intolerable that their love should be divided between God and the things of this world.[5] In the same strain, St. Bernard declares that the love of God is intolerant, meaning that the love of God does not tolerate other loves in the hearts of those who love him. God wants the heart wholly for himself. Some may object that God's demands are excessive when he requires us to love nothing but himself. God, who is infinitely good and deserves infinite love, can rightly demand that he should have all the love of souls whom he has created specifically for the purpose of loving him. Moreover, in order to achieve this purpose, he has sacrificed himself totally for those souls. "You have given yourself totally for me" wrote St. Bernard as he reflected on the love which Jesus Christ has shown him.

Each one of us can well say the very same thing and indeed we should do so as we reflect on the fact that Jesus Christ has given himself over to death, has shed every drop of his blood for us, consumed by sufferings on a Cross. And even after his death he has left us his body and blood, his soul and divinity, in the Sacrament of the Altar so that he could be the food and drink of our souls and so that we could be united with him.

11. St. Gregory the Great considers those souls intensely happy who find unattractive anything which is not connected with God, whom they love above everything else. We should then be on our guard that, when we give our affection to creatures, we do not, by that same fact, withdraw part of our love from God who wants it all for himself.[6] And even though our love for others may be above reproach, such as the love we have for relations and friends, at the same time, we should not forget the warning of St. Philip Neri that very often the amount of love we give to creatures is taken from the love we should have for God.

12. We should make of ourselves "a garden enclosed," to use the words of the Song of Songs: "You are an enclosed garden, my sister, my bride" (Sg 4:12). The enclosed garden signifies those souls who keep themselves free from affection for things of earth. When, then, some human affection wishes to possess our hearts we should deny it admittance and turning to Jesus Christ say: "My Jesus, you alone are sufficient for me: I do not want to love anyone but you. You are my God and my portion for ever. My God I want you to be the only Lord of my heart, my only love." For this reason we should incessantly ask from the Lord the grace of his pure love. This pure love, in the words of St. Francis de Sales, consumes in us all that is not God and, at the same time, turns all things into him.

13. The second means of acquiring the love of God is to meditate on the Passion of our Savior Jesus Christ. I recommend my readers to read the book which I have recently published entitled *Reflections on the Passion of Jesus Christ,* in which I describe at length the sufferings of our Savior.[7] I am convinced that the fact that Jesus Christ is so little loved throughout the world is due to our neglect and ingratitude in not reflecting, at least from time

to time, on the sufferings which Jesus Christ has borne for us and the love with which he suffered. St. Gregory asserts that it seems to be the height of madness that a God would wish to die to save us miserable creatures. And yet it is an article of our faith: "Christ loved us and handed himself over for us as a sacrificial offering to God" (Eph 5:2). And he willed to shed his blood to wash us clean from our sins: "To him who loves us and has freed us from our sins by his blood" (Rv 1:5).

14. St. Bonaventure exclaimed: "My God, you have loved me so much that it would appear that for love of me you were prepared to hate yourself." You even wished that you should become our food in Holy Communion. And taking up this theme, St. Thomas, the Angelic Doctor, states that God has humiliated himself for us as if he were our slave and each one of us his God.[8]

15. No wonder then that the Apostle could say: "For the love of Christ impels us" (2 Cor 5:14). St. Paul says that the love which Jesus Christ has shown toward us forces us, indeed virtually compels us, to love him. My God, what will we not do for the love of others when they show us affection? And how is it that we return so little love to a God of infinite goodness, of infinite beauty, who has died for each of us on the Cross? Should we not follow the example of St. Paul who has said: "But may I never boast except in the cross of our Lord Jesus Christ" (Gal 6:14). What greater glory can I hope to possess in this world than to have a God who for love of me has given his life's blood? Each one of us who possesses the gift of faith should repeat these same words. And if we possess this faith, how can we love anything other than our God? My God, how is it possible for souls who contemplate Jesus crucified, hanging nailed to a cross through his hands and feet, and dying of intense suffering out of love for us, not to feel drawn and even forced to love him with all their strength?

16. The third means of attaining to the perfect love of God is to unite oneself in everything to the divine will. St. Bernard used to say that one who loves God perfectly can only will what God wills.[9] There are many, of course, who profess with their lips that they are totally resigned to whatever God wills. But when they suffer some small misfortune, some unpleasant illness, they are disconsolate.

The reaction of those souls who are genuinely united with the will of God is quite different. They say in the words of St. Bonaventure: "Whatever pleases my beloved, pleases me. Everything is sweet to those who love." They realize that whatever happens in this world is either permitted or willed by God. So, no matter what happens, they accept it humbly from the hands of God and are perfectly at peace. And even though the Lord does not will that we should suffer persecution and misfortune through the actions of others, he nevertheless wishes us, for his own very good purposes, to bear our sufferings and misfortunes patiently.

17. St. Catherine of Genoa once declared that if God had placed her in the depths of hell she would have said, in the words of scripture, "It is good for me to be here" (cf. Mt 17:4). This was the equivalent of saying: "It is sufficient for me that I am where my love would have me to be. He loves me more than anyone and knows what is best for me. It is good for us to be at rest in God's hands."[10]

18. The result of one's prayers should be to conform oneself to God's will. This is the summit of perfection, according to St. Teresa of Avila. We should repeat constantly the prayer of David: "Teach me to do your will,/for you are my God" (Ps 143:9). O Lord, since you wish me to save my soul, teach me always to do your will. The most perfect act of love toward God which a soul can make is that which St. Paul made on his conversion: "Lord, what will you have me do?" ([ed.] Acts 9:6). Lord, tell me what you wish of me since I am ready to do what you want. This prayer is worth more than a thousand fasts and corporal penances. To do the divine will, then, should be our intention in all our actions, desires, and prayers. For this purpose we should pray to Our Lady, our patron saints, and our angel guardians so that they would obtain for us the grace to carry out God's will. And when certain things happen which are not to our liking, we shall be able to gain abundant treasures of merit by our acts of resignation. We shall be able to repeat the prayer which Jesus Christ has taught us by his example: "Shall I not drink the cup that the Father gave me?" (Jn 18:11). "Yes, Father, such as been your gracious will" (Mt 11:26). In other words, "Lord, I accept whatever is pleasing to you." And we should frequently repeat with Job; "The

LORD gave and the LORD has taken away;/blessed be the name of the Lord!" (Jb 1:21). The Venerable Master of Avila declared that one "Blessed be God" in trials and sufferings is worth much more than a thousand expressions of thanks when all goes well. And so to sum up, it is a wonderful grace to be able to be at peace, accepting whatever comes to us from the hands of God. The words of the Spirit of God are verified: "No harm befalls the just" (Prv 12:21).11

19. The fourth great means of acquiring the love of God is the practice of mental prayer. The great eternal truths are not perceived by the eyes of the body as are the tangible things of this earth; they are perceived only by means of reflection and meditation. So, if we do not dedicate time to reflect on the eternal truths and, above all, on our obligation to love God on account of all the gifts he has lavished on us and for the great love he has shown us, we will only with great difficulty detach ourselves from creatures and give all our love to God. It is during the time of prayer that the Lord permits us to realize the passing nature of human things and the value of heavenly realities. And it is in prayer that he inflames souls who do not resist his call with love for himself.[12]

Many souls complain that they devote time to prayer but that they do not find God in it. The reason is that they go to prayer with their hearts full of earth, as it were. Detach your hearts from creatures, says St. Teresa; seek God and you will find him. The Lord is good to all who seek him. To find God in prayer, then, we must detach ourselves from things of earth and God will speak to us accordingly: "I will lead her into the desert/ and speak to her heart" (Hos 2:16). In order to find God we need not only physical solitude but, according to St. Gregory the Great, the solitude of ours hearts as well. Our Lord made known to St. Teresa of Avila his willingness to speak to many hearts but that the world made such a din in their hearts he was unable to make his voice heard. On the other hand, when souls who are detached devote themselves to prayer, the Lord speaks to them and lets them know the love he has for them. Consequently, those souls are on fire with love for God, and in that silence which is well called the silence of love, they say more to God than all human eloquence is capable of. Their every sigh reveals their desire for God. They repeat again and again the words of the Song of Songs: "My lover belongs to me and I to him" (Sg 2:16).

20. The fifth means of acquiring the love of God is prayer. We are poor and in great need but, if we pray, we become rich and lack for nothing since God has promised to hear all those who pray to him. "Ask and it will be given to you" (Mt 7:7). What greater proof of affection can one give to another than to declare "Ask of me whatever you wish and I shall give it to you"? This is what the Lord says to each one of us. God is the Lord of all. He promises to give us whatever we ask of him. So if we find ourselves poor we have only ourselves to blame because we do not ask for the graces and favors we need. Mental prayer is morally necessary for us all because when we are involved in worldly affairs we give little thought to our souls if we neglect to pray. But when we do give ourselves to prayer, we come to realize the needs of our souls and we then ask for the graces we need.

21. The lives of the saints have been lives of meditation and prayer and all the graces which they received to enable them to sanctify themselves have come to them through prayer. If we, then, wish to save our souls and to sanctify ourselves, we too should stand as mendicants before the gates of the divine mercy praying and begging God for all the graces we need. If we need humility, let us ask for it and we shall become humble. If we need patience in suffering and tribulation, let us ask for it and we shall obtain it. If we need the love of God, let us ask for it and it shall be ours. "Ask and you shall receive" is one of God's promises in which we can never be deceived. And to increase our confidence, Jesus Christ has promised that whatever favors we ask from the Father in his name or out of love for him, or through his merits, will certainly be granted to us: "Amen, amen, I say to you, whatever you ask the Father in my name he will give you" (Jn 16:23). In another place he assures us that whatever we ask from himself in his own name he will grant: "If you ask anything of me in my name, I will do it" (Jn 14:14). This is an article of our faith since

Jesus Christ who is the Son of God can do whatever his Father can do.[13]

22. No matter how cold souls are in their love for God I cannot see how they are not able to feel themselves constrained to love Jesus Christ if they would only reflect, even in a fleeting manner, on what the scripture tells us about the love which Jesus Christ has shown us in his Passion and in the Most Holy Sacrament of the Altar. As regards the Passion, the prophet Isaiah wrote: "Yet it was our infirmities that he bore,/our sufferings that he endured....He was pierced for our offenses,/crushed for our sins" (Is 53:4-5). So our faith assures us that Jesus Christ has wished to take upon himself the pains and sufferings which we should have borne. And why did he will to do this, if not to show us the love he had for us? St. Paul says: "Christ loved us and handed himself over for us as a sacrificial offering to God" (Eph 5:2). St. John says: "[Jesus Christ] who loves us and has freed us from our sins by his blood" (Rv 1:5). As regards the Sacrament of the Eucharist, Jesus himself says to us in the words of institution: "This is my body that is for you" (1 Cor 11:24). And in another place he tells us: "Just as the living Father sent me and I have life because of the Father, so also the one who feeds on me will have life because of me" (Jn 6:57). How then is it possible for anyone with faith to read these words and not feel constrained to love our Redeemer who has sacrificed his blood and his life out of love for us and, even more than that, has left us himself in the Blessed Sacrament as the food of our souls and our constant companion?

23. I conclude with another reflection on the Passion of Jesus Christ. We see him nailed to a cross with nails that pierce his hands and feet, with blood pouring from his wounds, and agonizing in the throes of death. Why was it that Jesus wished us to see him in such a pitiable condition? Was it perhaps that we should have compassion for him? No. It was not in order that we should have compassion for him but that we should love him. And it should be more than a sufficient motive for each of us to love him to know that he has loved us from all eternity: "With age-old love I have loved you" (Jer 31:3). When the Lord realized

that this love of his was not sufficient to move us in our coldness to love him, he determined to demonstrate to us by his deeds the love he has for us. It was for this that he showed himself to us dying on a cross and covered with wounds. From this we can see the immensity of the love that he has for us. And so we have an explanation of the words of St. Paul: "Christ loved us and handed himself over for us as a sacrificial offering" (Eph 5:2).[14]

Conformity to the Will of God

Introduction

Editor's Note: This short treatise was first published sometime during 1755 as an appendix to the sixth edition of *Visits to the Most Blessed Sacrament,* etc. On 2 November of that year Alphonsus sent a copy of the new printing of his *Visits* to one of his penitents, drawing her attention to the "trattato della volunta di Dio" at the end of the work. He suggested that she use this little work as a meditation book, reading it slowly and reflecting on it. He pointed out to her at the same time that conformity to the Will of God was the secret of perfection: "mentre qui consiste tutta la perfezione" (*Lettere* Vol.1.309).

The work soon took on a life of its own and was published both separately and in conjunction with other devotional works of the saint. There were innumerable Italian editions. Within fifty years of the saint's death the work is to be found in all the main European languages. The style is simple, almost conversational. Questions and answers help to impress on the reader the clear message of the joyful acceptance of God's will in all the happenings of life. Nowhere else does Alphonsus show his mastery of the use of the *exempla* technique as convincingly as here. This was one of the devotional works that most enraged the Jansenists in the second half of the eighteenth century.

The work marks an important stage in the evolution of Alphonsus's devotional thought, which reached its full development with the publication of *The Practice of the Love of Jesus Christ* some fifteen years later.

*   *   *

Our whole perfection consists in loving God who is so deserving of our love: "And over all these put on love, that is, the bond of perfection" (Col 3:14). The perfection of the love of God consists in uniting our will with this most holy will, since the principal effect of love, as St. Denis the Areopagite says, is so to unite the wills of those who love each other that they both seem to have but one and the same will.[1] And so the more closely the will of an individual is united to the divine will, the greater will be that person's love. It is true, of course, that mortification, meditation, communions, and works of charity toward our neighbor are pleasing to God, but in what circumstances? When they are performed in accordance with his will. When they are not in accordance with his will, not only is he not pleased with them, but he considers them unacceptable and rejects them. Imagine a master with two servants, one of whom works tirelessly all day long but wants to do everything in his own way. The other works rather less but follows his master's instructions perfectly. The master will surely appreciate the second rather than the first.

In what way could our works contribute to the glory of God if they are not in accordance with his good pleasure? As the prophet said to Saul, the Lord does not want sacrifices but obedience to his wishes: "Does the LORD so delight in holocausts and sacrifices/as in obedience to the command of the LORD?...Presumption is the crime of idolatry" (1 Sm 15:22–23). Those who insist on acting according to their own will and not in accordance with the will of God are guilty of a kind of idolatry in that instead of adoring the divine will, they in some way adore their own.

The greatest glory we can give to God, then, is to do his will in everything. This is what our Redeemer taught us by his own example when he came on earth to manifest God's glory. St. Paul presents him as addressing his heavenly Father as follows: "For this reason, when he came into the world, he said:/'Sacrifice and offering you did not desire,/but a body you prepared for me..../ Behold, I come to do your will, O God'" (Heb 10:5–7). And Our Lord frequently declared that he came on earth not to do his own will but the will of his Father: "Because I came down from heaven not to do my own will but the will of the one who sent me" (Jn 6:38). It was through his obedience to his Father's will, which was that he should be sacrificed on the Cross for the salvation of all, that he wished to make known to the whole world the love he had for his Father. So it was that in the Garden, when he went forward to meet his enemies who had come to take him to his death, he said: "But the world must know that I love the

Father and that I do just as the Father has commanded me" (Jn 14:31). He also said that he recognized as his brother and sister and mother those who did the will of God—"For whoever does the will of my heavenly Father is my brother, and sister, and mother" (Mt 12:50).

All the saints knew that this is the key to the perfection of holiness and so they were constant in their efforts in doing God's will. Blessed Henry Suso said: "God does not demand that we should abound in spiritual inspirations but that we should submit ourselves in all things to his will."[2] And St. Teresa writes: "What we are to seek when we pray is the grace to conform our will to the will of God. There is no doubt that this is the highest perfection. Anyone who is exemplary in this will receive the greatest gifts from God and progress rapidly in the spiritual life."

Blessed Stefana of Soncino, a Dominican nun, in a vision of heaven which she was once granted, saw some people among the Seraphim whom she had known.[3] She was led to understand that they had been raised to this height of glory because they had united their wills perfectly with the will of God while on earth. Blessed Henry Suso, whom I have already mentioned, declared that he would rather be the vilest worm on earth doing the will of God than a seraph following his own.

We, on earth, must learn from the saints in heaven how we are to love God. The pure and perfect love of God which the saints in heaven possess consists in their complete union with his holy will. If the angels of heaven were to know that it was the will of God that they should spend their eternity building heaps of sand on the seashore or employed in the lowliest occupation on earth they would do so with the greatest enthusiasm. Even if God intimated to them that they should cast themselves into hell they would do so immediately in order to fulfil his divine will. This is what Jesus Christ instructs us when he teaches us to pray that we might do the will of God on earth as the saints do in heaven: "Your will be done,/on earth as in heaven" (Mt 6:10).

The Lord called David a man after his own heart because David fulfilled his will in all things: "I have found David, son of Jesse, a man after my own heart; he will carry out my every wish"

(Acts 13:22). David was always ready to do the will of God as he himself often declares: "My heart is steadfast, God,/my heart is steadfast" (Ps 57:8). All he asked of the Lord was that he might be taught to do God's will: "Teach me to do your will,/for you are my God" (Ps 143:10).

One act of perfect conformity to the divine will is sufficient to make a saint. Consider how Saul, while he was still persecuting the church, was shown the light and converted by Jesus Christ. What did Saul do or say? Nothing more than offer to do the will of God: "Lord, what will you have me to do?" ([ed.] Acts 9:6). And the Lord thereupon declared him to be a chosen instrument and apostle of the Gentiles: "Go, for this man is a chosen instrument of mine to carry my name before Gentiles, kings, and Israelites" (Acts 9:15). Those who give their will to God give him everything. Those who give their material goods in alms, their blood in mortification, their food in fasts, only give a part of what they have to God. But those who give him their will give him everything and can truly say: "Lord, I am poor but I give you all I have. I have given you my will and so have nothing more to offer you." And this is precisely what God expects from us: "My son, give me your heart,/and let your eyes keep to my ways" (Prv 23:26). St. Augustine says we can make no more precious offering to God than to say to him: "Lord take possession of me. I give you my whole will; tell me what you want of me and I will do it."

If we really want to please the heart of God, then we must be sure to conform to his will and not only conform but we should actually make ourselves one with whatever he ordains. Conformity means joining our will to the will of God but uniformity means making the will of God and our will into one single will, as it were, so that we do not want anything but what he wills and so his will becomes ours. This constitutes the most perfect condition to which we should constantly aspire and which should be the goal of all our actions, desires, meditations, and prayers. To obtain this grace we should invoke the assistance of the saints, our advocates before God, our guardian angels, and most of all our Mother Mary. She is the most perfect of all the saints because she most perfectly embraced the will of God at all times.

Conformity to the Will of God in All Things[4]

The most difficult thing of all is to accept the will of God, no matter what happens, that is, both in those things which are agreeable to us and in things which are not. In good times even sinners know how to unite themselves with the will of God but the saints unite themselves with God's will even in those things which are disagreeable and displeasing to them. It is here that the quality of our love of God is demonstrated. Father John of Avila said that one "Blessed be God" when things are going badly is worth more than a thousand expressions of thanks when things are going as we would wish them to.[5]

What is more, we should unite ourselves to the will of God not only in those unpleasant things which he permits, such as sickness, desolation of spirit, poverty, the death of loved ones, and so on, but also in those things which come to us through other human beings—contempt, loss of our good name, injustice, robbery, and all kinds of persecutions. On such occasions when we are offended by someone in our reputation, our sense of honor, or our material goods, it is important to realize that although God does not will the sin of the one who injures us, he does, nevertheless, will that we should learn humility, poverty, and self-denial from these experiences.

It is certain and a matter of faith that everything that happens in the world happens in accordance with the will of God. "I am the LORD, there is no other;/I form the light, and create the darkness,/I make well-being and create woe;/I, the LORD, do all these things" (Is 45:6–7). From the Lord, then, come all good things and all things that are evil—that is, those things which are not to our liking and which we falsely call evil, since, in fact, they can be blessings for us when we accept them from God's hands. "If evil befalls a city,/has not the LORD caused it?" says the prophet Amos (Am 3:6). Earlier, the wise man said, "Good and evil, life and death,/poverty and riches, are from the LORD" (Sir 11:14). It is true, as I have said, that when someone unjustly offends you, God does not will that person's sin nor share in the malice; but it is also true that God is at work through the act by which you are persecuted or robbed or injured. In this particular sense your suffering is in accordance with the will of God and comes to you from his hands.

So the Lord told David that the injuries he would receive at the hands of Absalom (2 Sm 12:11) would come from the Lord as a punishment for his sins. In the same way he told the Hebrews that, in punishment for their sins, he would send the Assyrians to ravage and ruin them: "Woe to Assyria! My rod in anger,/my staff in wrath./Against an impious nation I send him,/and against a people under my wrath I order him/To seize plunder, carry off loot" (Is 10:5–6). St. Augustine comments that the impiety of the Assyrians became the sword of God. In other words, God made use of their impiety as a sword to punish the Hebrews. And Jesus himself said that his Passion and death did not so much come to him from human beings as from his Father: "Shall I not drink the cup that the Father gave me?" (Jn 18:11).

When the messenger (who is said to have been the devil) came to tell Job that the Sabeans had carried off all his goods and had killed his sons, what did the holy man say? "The LORD gave and the LORD has taken away" (Jb 1:21). He did not say: "The Lord gave me sons and property and the Sabeans have taken them from me." This was because he well knew that this loss was willed by God and so he adds: "It has happened as it pleased the Lord, praised be the name of the Lord."

We should not, therefore, think of our troubles as happening by chance or simply through the malice of others, but rather should we be convinced that whatever happens to us is in accordance with God's will. "Know that whatever happens to you contrary to your wishes does not happen contrary to the wishes of God," said St. Augustine. The Christian martyrs Epictetus and Athio, when the tyrant had tortured them with iron hooks and burned them with flaming torches, said nothing other than: "Lord, may your will be done in us." And when they came to the place of execution they exclaimed for all to hear, "Eternal God, be praised: Your will is fully accomplished in us."[6]

Cesarius relates how a certain member of a religious community, without seeming at all different from his companions, had in fact reached such a high degree of holiness that he healed the sick simply with a touch of his garments. Amazed at this, his superior asked him one day how he could perform such miracles, seeing that his life was no more exemplary that that of the others. The religious replied that he too was amazed and could not explain it. But when the abbot asked him what were his particular devotions, he replied that he did little or nothing other than taking great care always to do only what God willed. He explained that the Lord had given him the grace of abandoning his own will to the will of God. "I do not get carried away in good times," he went on to explain, "nor do I give up when times are hard, because I accept all things as coming from the hands of God. All my prayers are for this, that his will be done in me." "So you felt no resentment at the harm that was done to us the other day," the abbot further enquired, "when our enemies took away our property and set fire to the places where we keep our corn and cattle?" "No, Father," the monk replied; "in fact, I gave thanks to God for it, as I always do on such occasions, knowing that God does everything or allows it to happen for his own glory and for our good, and so I am content with whatever happens." In the light of this the abbot, recognizing in this man such great conformity to the will of God, was not at all surprised that he was able to perform such miracles.[7]

Those who do as this man did not only become saints but they already enjoy here on earth the eternal peace which is the privilege of the blessed. Alphonsus the Great of Aragon, when once asked whom he considered the happiest people in the world, replied: "Those who abandon themselves to the will of God and accept everything that happens, good or bad, as coming from his hands." "We know that all things work for good for those who love God" (Rom 8:28).[8]

Happiness Comes from Conformity to the Will of God

Those who love God are always content, because all their pleasure lies in fulfilling God's will even in difficult circumstances, with the result that their very troubles are turned into delights at the thought that they give pleasure to their beloved Lord by accepting them. "But he who obeys me dwells in security,/in peace, without fear of harm" (Prv 1:33). In fact, what can make people more content that to see what they want to happen actually taking place? Since everything that happens in the world—with the exception of sin—happens according to God's will, it follows that for those who want only what God wills, nothing can ever happen which they do not want. In the lives of the Fathers we hear of a farmer whose land gave a greater yield than that of other neighboring farmers. When he was asked by them why this was so, he replied that it was not surprising because he always got the weather he wanted. They naturally asked how this could be. He replied: "I do not want any weather other than the weather willed by God and as I want what he wills, he gives me the crops as I want them."

Souls that are resigned to the will of God, says Salvian, when they are humbled, will their humiliation; when they suffer poverty, are willing to be poor. In a word, they will all that happens to them and on this account are always happy. If heat comes or cold or rain or wind, those who are united with the will of God say: I desire that it be as it is because it is God's will. If poverty overtakes them, persecutions, illness, or even death, they say: I desire to be poor, persecuted, sick, because such is the will of God.[9]

This is that glorious liberty which the children of God enjoy and which is worth more than all the kingdoms and riches of this world. This is that wonderful peace which the saints experience which surpasses all understanding (Phil 4:7), all the pleasures of the senses, festivals, banquets, honors, and all other worldly gratifications, which, because they are without depth and are transitory, allure our senses for a passing moment but do not satisfy the spirit in which alone real happiness can dwell. Solomon, having enjoyed all possible human delights to the full, exclaimed in affliction of spirit: "This also is vanity and a chase after wind" (Eccl 4:16).

"Ever wise are the discourses of the devout,/but the godless man, like the moon, is inconstant" (Sir 27:11). The godless persons, that is, sinners, change like the moon which today increases but tomorrow is on the wane; today they are cheerful, tomorrow

76

sorrowful, today meek, tomorrow angry. And why? Because for them happiness depends on the prosperity or adversity they meet with and hence they are changed as circumstances change around them. But the devout, those who follow the will of God, are like the sun, always radiant with serenity no matter what happens because their happiness is in their conformity to the will of God. And so they possess unalterable peace. The message of the angels to the shepherds was "And on earth peace to those on whom his favor rests" (Lk 2:14). And who are those people of good will, if not those who are always united with God's will which is supremely good and perfect?

Because they have united their wills to the will of God, the saints have enjoyed a heaven on earth. St. Dorothy says that the Fathers of the Desert were always at peace because they accepted everything as coming from the hands of God. At the very mention of *the will of God*, St. Mary Magdalene de Pazzi was so consoled that she was immediately wrapped in an ecstasy of love. At the lower level of our senses there will always be sufficient to pain us, but at the higher level of the spirit there will be peace and tranquility because our will is united to that of God. Our Savior said to the apostles: "Your hearts will rejoice, and no one will take your joy away from you" (Jn 16:22). Those who live in conformity to the will of God will have full and constant joy—full, because they have all that they want; constant, because no one can deprive them of this joy since no one can prevent what God wants.

John Tauler relates of himself that after asking the Lord for many years to send him someone to teach him about authentic spirituality, he one day heard a voice saying: "Go to such a church and you will find there the person you are looking for." He went to the church and at the door found a barefoot, ragged beggar, whom he saluted: "Good day, my friend." The poor man answered: "Sir, I never recall having a bad day." Tauler then wished the man a happy life. To this the beggar answered, "I have never been unhappy." And then he added:

> Listen, Father, it is not without reason that I say I have never had a bad day, because when I am hungry, I praise God.

When it is snowing or raining, I bless God. When someone insults me or drives me away, or if I experience any other misery, I always give glory to my God. I also said I have never been unhappy and this is true too, because I only want what God wills without any reservations. So whatever comes my way, sweet or bitter, I accept it from his hands with joy as being what is best for me and this makes me happy.

"And if God were to will your damnation," retorted Tauler, "what would you say?" The beggar replied:

If God were to will this, I would embrace my Lord with humility and love and I would cling to him so closely that if he wanted to cast me into hell, he would have to come with me too. And I would prefer to be with him in hell than to have all the delights of heaven without him.

"Where did you find God?" asked the priest. "I found him where I left all created things behind me." And when the priest asked him who he was, the beggar replied: "I am a king." "Where then is your kingdom?" countered Tauler. "It is in my own soul, where I maintain order in all things. My passions obey my reason, and my reason obeys God."

Finally Tauler asked him how he had attained to such perfection. He replied: "By means of silence. Being silent with people in order to talk with God. This and the union I have always had with Our Lord, in whom I find and have always found my deepest peace." This is what union with the will of God made of this poor man; in his poverty he was surely richer than all the kings of the world and in his sufferings he was happier than those who lose themselves in their worldly pleasures.[10]

God Desires Only Our Greater Good

It is futile to attempt to resist the will of God. Those who do so inevitably have great difficulties because no one can prevent what God wills from happening: "For who can oppose his will?" (Rom 9:19). Such people suffer in vain, calling down on themselves greater punishment in the life to come and greater unease in the present life: "Who has withstood him and remained unscathed?" (Jb 9:4). What good is it for those who are sick to complain about their pains or for those who are poor to complain to God, or curse him in anger? They only make matters twice as bad. St. Augustine says: "What more are you looking for, poor creatures, than your God; find God, unite and bind yourself to his will and you will live happily in this life and in the life to come."

After all, what else does God want more than our good? Whom could we find to love us more than God? His will is that no one should be lost but that all be saved and become holy: "Not wishing that any should perish but that all should come to repentance" (2 Pt 3:9). "This is the will of God, your holiness" (1 Thes 4:3). God has turned his glory to our good. For he is—as St. Leo says—by nature, infinitely good. Now, since goodness of its nature seeks to communicate itself, God's supreme desire is to make us partakers of his goodness and his happiness. If he sends us tribulations in this life, they are all for our good. "We know that all things work for good for those who love God" (Rom 8:28). Even chastisements, as we find in the book of Judith, do not come from God for our ruin but rather so that we might change our ways and be saved (Jdt 8:27). In order to save us from eternal woe, he surrounds us with his good will: "For you, LORD, bless the just;/you surround them with favor like a shield" (Ps 5:13). He not only desires but earnestly seeks our welfare. Confident of this, we should abandon ourselves to God's will, which is always for our good. Whatever happens, we should say: "In peace I shall both lie down and sleep,/for you alone, LORD, make me secure" (Ps 4:9). Let us then place ourselves in his hands, for he will surely take care of us: "Cast all your worries upon him because he cares for you" (1 Pt 5:7). Let us then think of God and do his will, so that he will think of us and of our well-being. "Daughter," Our Lord said to Catherine of Siena, "think of me and I will always think of you." Let us often pray with the Spouse in the Song of Songs: "My lover belongs to me and I to him" (Sg 2:16). My beloved thinks of my good and I will think of nothing but of pleasing him and of uniting myself to his will in all things.

CONFORMITY TO THE WILL OF GOD

The Abbot Nilus said that it is not for us to pray to the Lord that what *we* want should happen, but rather to pray that his will should be fulfilled in us. When unpleasant things do happen to us, let us accept them all from the hands of God, not alone with patience, but with joy, following the example of the apostles: "So they left the presence of the Sanhedrin, rejoicing that they had been found worthy to suffer dishonor for the sake of the name" (Acts 5:41).

What can be a greater source of happiness to us than to know that we are never more pleasing to God than when we endure our troubles with good will? Masters of the spiritual life tell us that while those who suffer for the love of God are pleasing to him, yet more pleasing are those who in conformity to his will desire neither to rejoice nor to suffer. They are so resigned to his will that they only want what pleases God. So, if you want to please God and live a contented life here on earth, unite yourself always and everywhere with his will. Remember that all the sins that have made your life so troubled and bitter occurred because you moved away from his will. From this day onward embrace God's will and say always and in everything that happens: "So be it, Lord, because such has been your gracious will" ([ed.] Mt 11:26).

When you feel troubled by some negative experience, remember that it comes from God. Say to yourself immediately: "This is God's will" and then be at peace. Repeat to yourself: "Lord, since you have done this, I say nothing, but accept it." "I was silent and did not open my mouth/because you were the one who did this" (Ps 39:10). All your thoughts, prayers, acts of communion, and visits to the Blessed Sacrament should be directed to the one end of asking God to help you to do his will. Offer yourself to God constantly, saying: "Lord, here I am, do with me and all that is mine whatever you will." St. Teresa did this all the time: At least fifty times a day she offered herself to the Lord, asking him to dispose of her as he pleased.

You will always be happy, my dear reader, if you do the same. You will become a holy person, you will lead a happy life and die a good death. When souls pass on to the next life, all our hope for their salvation arises from knowing that they were resigned to death when they died. So if you accept death in fulfillment of his will as you have accepted everything that came from God in life, you will surely be saved and die a holy death. Let us then abandon ourselves in all things to whatever pleases the Lord. Being most wise, he knows what is best for us and since he is most loving, even to the point of giving his life for us, he also wants what is best for us. St. Basil says that we can be quite certain that God will give us what is good for us in a way far superior to anything we could desire for ourselves.

Conformity to the Will of God in Practice

Let us consider in what practical ways we should conform our wills to the will of God.

1. The first way concerns the natural occurrences which affect us from outside ourselves, such as very hot or very cold weather, rain, famine, epidemics, and so on. We should be careful about saying: what terrible heat! what awful cold! what a pity! what evil misfortune! what terrible times! and all such expressions which express displeasure at God's will. We should want everything to be just as it is because it is God who wills it to be so. Once St. Francis Borgia arrived late at night at a house of the Society of Jesus. It was snowing. He knocked at the gate many times but because the community had retired to rest they did not hear him. Next morning they explained how sorry they were that they had made him wait outside all night, but the saint told them that he was greatly consoled during the night by the thought that it was God who was dropping the snowflakes upon him.

2. The second way in which we should unite ourselves to God's will concerns things which happen to us personally, such as hunger, thirst, poverty, desolations, dishonor. In all such circumstances we should say: Lord, do and undo as you think fit. I am content since I only want what is your will." According to Father Rodriguez this is also the way we should handle those hypothetical suggestions which the devil puts into our minds in order to lead us into some evil or at least to unsettle us. If the

devil himself were to suggest something to you or do something to you for this precise purpose, you should be ready with the answer: "No matter what happens I will say and do only what God wills." In this way we shall free ourselves from all troubles and faults.

3. Thirdly, if we have some defect of mind or body such as a poor memory, slow understanding, little ability, a physical handicap, or weak health, we should not complain about it. What claim do we have, or what obligation is God under to give us a quicker mind, or a sounder body? Could he not have made us mere animals? Or have left us in our nothingness? Does one who is receiving a gift lay down conditions? Let us rather give him thanks for what he has given us out of his sheer goodness and let us be content with the way he has made us. Perhaps if we had been endowed with greater talents, better health, or more beauty these very talents would have been our undoing. How many are there whose talents and knowledge have been the cause of their downfall in that they became puffed up with vanity or developed contempt for others, since those who are more gifted in learning and talents are prone to this danger? How many others have been led into crimes by their beauty or physical strength? And on the other hand how many have found salvation in their poverty, illness, or deformity who would have been lost had they been rich, healthy, and beautiful? So let us be content with what God has given us. "There is need of only one thing" (Lk 10:42). There is no need of beauty, of health, of quickness of mind: The only thing necessary is our salvation.

4. We should be particularly resigned in physical illness which we should willingly accept in whatever form and for whatever length of time God wills. We should, of course, make use of all ordinary means of restoring health, for this, too, is the will of God. But if these are of no avail, we should unite ourselves with the divine will for this will be of much more benefit to us than health itself. At such times we should pray: "Lord, I do not want to get better and I do not want to be ill, I only want what you want."

It is, of course, more virtuous on our part during sickness if we do not complain of our sufferings, but when these are severe it is not wrong to describe them to our friends or ask the Lord to free us from them. I mean in severe pain, for there are those who are so weak that at the slightest pain or difficulty they would wish the whole world to gather round them in pity. Even Jesus Christ, when he saw that he was approaching the bitter hour of his Passion, expressed his sufferings to his apostles: "My soul is sorrowful even to death" (Mt 26:38). He also asked his heavenly Father to deliver him from this suffering: "My Father, if it is possible, let this cup pass from me" (Mt 26:39). But Jesus himself, by adding "Yet, not as I will, but as you will" (Mt 26:39), showed us what we must do after such prayers, namely, resign ourselves immediately to God's will.

How foolish it is, then, when some declare that they want to be healthy, not in order to avoid suffering but in order to serve the Lord more fully by observing the rule, serving the community, attending church services, receiving Holy Communion, doing penance, studying, hearing confessions, preaching. But I say to you: Why do you desire to do these things? To please God? How can you desire to do these things when you know for certain that what is most pleasing to God are not your prayers, communions, penances, studies, or sermons but the fact that you suffer the illness and pains he sends you with patience. Unite your sufferings then to the sufferings of Christ. You will say: "I do not wish to be so useless and such a burden on the community." But just as you resign yourself to the will of God, so too you must believe that your superiors will also be resigned, knowing that you bring this burden on the house, not through laziness, but by God's will.

Acknowledge, then, that these desires and complaints are not born of the love of God but of self-love which seeks pretexts for avoiding God's will. Do we want to please God? Then let us say one thing to the Lord: "Your will be done." If we keep repeating this, a hundred and a thousand times, we shall please God more than any amount of mortifications or devotions. There is no better way to serve God than to embrace his will joyfully.

The Venerable Father Avila wrote to a sick priest: "Friend, do not trouble yourself with the thought of what you might be doing if you were well, but be content to remain ill as long as God so wills. If what you seek is to do the will of God, what difference does it make if you are well or sick?" This is well said because God is not so much glorified by our works as by our resignation and conformity to his holy will. This is why St. Francis de Sales said that God is better served in suffering than in good works.

It will often happen that we will find ourselves without doctors or medicine, or that the doctor will not be able to diagnose our illness. In circumstances such as these we should seek to unite our will to the will of God, who brings about our good in all things.

There is a story about a sick man who was devoted to St. Thomas of Canterbury and who went to the tomb of the saint to obtain a cure. He returned home cured but then said to himself: "What use is it being well if my illness was of greater help in bringing about my salvation?" With this thought in mind he returned to the tomb and interceded with the saint to ask God to send him whatever would be more effective in helping him toward his eternal salvation. Thereafter, he fell back into his illness and was totally at peace, confident that God was bringing about what was best for him.

Similarly, Surius tells us of a blind man who received his sight through the intercession of the saintly bishop Bedasto. Afterward he prayed that he would become blind again if sight were not good for his soul. And after his prayer he became blind as before. When we are ill, then, the best thing to do is to seek neither sickness nor health, but to abandon ourselves to the will of God that he may do with us as he wills.[11]

If we do seek health, we should at least ask for it with resignation and on condition that physical health will promote our spiritual well-being. Otherwise, it would be a defective prayer and would not be heard, because God does not listen to prayers which are not made with resignation. I call times of illness the touchstone of the spiritual life, because it is then that we can discern the caliber of a person's virtue. If a person is not troubled and anxious, does not complain, but serenely obeys the doctors and superiors in a spirit of resignation to God's will, this is a great sign of real depth of virtue.

What are we to say of sick people who complain and say that they are receiving little attention or that they cannot find a cure for their ills, or that the doctor is ignorant, or sometimes even that the hand of God presses too heavily upon them? In his life of St. Francis, St. Bonaventure writes that when the saint was suffering terribly, a well-meaning Brother said to him: "Father, ask God to treat you more gently, for his hand seems to press too heavily upon you." When St. Francis heard this he exclaimed: "Listen, if I did not know that you speak so because you do not know better, I would not want to see you again for having cast doubt on the judgment of God." Having said this, although he was very weak and in great pain, he threw himself from the bed onto the floor. Then he kissed the ground, saying: "I thank you Lord for all the pains you have sent me. I implore you to send me even more if this is what you will. It pleases me to be afflicted and I ask not to be spared in anything for to do your will is the greatest consolation I can receive in this life."

5. We should deal in the same way with the loss, which we sometimes suffer, of persons who are useful to our temporal or spiritual well-being. This is a point in which many devout people fail seriously in that they are not resigned to what God brings about. Our sanctification does not come from spiritual directors but from God. Of course, God wishes us to avail of the guidance of spiritual directors but when he takes them from us it is his will that we accept this and increase our confidence in his goodness. At such times we should say: "Lord, you have given me this help, and now you have taken it away; may your will be done always. Now, I ask you yourself to help me and guide me as to what I must do to serve you."

This is how we should accept from the hands of God all other crosses that he sends us. But you might reply that many of our troubles are punishments. I would reply by asking if the punishments of God in this life are not, in fact, blessings and graces. If we have done something wrong we must face divine justice either in this life or in the next. So, we should all say with St. Augustine: "Burn here, cut there, do not spare me as long as you save me for all eternity." Or with Job: "Let this be my consolation, that you do not spare me in afflicting me with pain" (Jb 6:10). It should surely be a consolation to one who has merited to

85

be eternally separated from God to see that God punishes here and now, and to hope that he will not punish for all eternity. When God sends us punishments let us say with Eli the priest: "He is the LORD. He will do what he judges best" (1 Sm 3:18).

6. We should also be resigned when we suffer aridity of spirit or spiritual desolation. When we give ourselves to the spiritual life it is usual for the Lord to shower us initially with consolations to wean us away from the delights of the world. But when he sees us more stable of spirit, he withdraws his hand in order to test our love of him and to see if we serve him here without the reward of sensible delights. "In this life," says St. Teresa, "our real achievement is not to be found in trying to enjoy God but in doing his will." Elsewhere she writes: "The love of God does not consist in tenderness, but in serving him with fortitude and humility," and again, "The Lord tests those who love him with aridities and temptations."

We should give thanks to the Lord when we feel the sweetness of his love but we should not become restless and impatient when we feel that we have been left in desolation. It is worth emphasizing this point because when some people experience desolation they imagine that God has abandoned them, or that the spiritual life is not for them and so they stop praying and undo the whole good their prayers have done them. There is no better time to exercise our resignation to God's will than in times of spiritual aridity. I do not say that you will not feel pain in the loss of the sense of God's presence. Of course, we feel such pain and, of course, we will lament the fact, which is not surprising when we remember that our Redeemer himself lamented it on the Cross: "My God, my God, why have you forsaken me?" (Mt 27:46). But when suffering such pain he always resigned himself totally to the will of his Lord.

All the saints have experienced similar spiritual desolation and abandonment. St. Bernard says: "What hardness of heart do I feel within me! I no longer find any joy in spiritual reading, in meditation or in prayer!" The saints have lived most of their lives in a state of desolation rather than of consolation. The Lord only rarely grants such consolation and perhaps only to those who are weaker in order that they might not give up on their spiritual journey. But he prepares all the delights of heaven for us as our prize.

Here on earth we are in a place of merit and it is through suffering that we gain merit. Heaven is the place of reward and the reward is joy. For this reason here on earth the saints have never sought for the fervor which accompanies consolation but rather that spiritual fervor which comes from suffering. The Venerable John of Avila said: "Oh, how much better it is to endure dryness and temptation in accordance with the will of God than to be lost in contemplation against God's will!" You might well say, if I knew this desolation came from God I would be content; what afflicts and disturbs me is the fear that it comes through my own fault and as a punishment for my lack of fervor. If that is the way you feel, my advice to you is to shake off your spiritual mediocrity or tepidity and be more diligent.

Perhaps you are troubled because you find yourself in inner darkness and for this reason are inclined to neglect prayer and so make the situation twice as bad. As you say, spiritual dryness may come to you as a punishment, but it is sent by God, nonetheless. You should accept it, therefore, as a deserved punishment and hold fast to the will of God. Have you not already said that you have deserved to be abandoned by God? So what are you now complaining about? Maybe you imagine that you deserve consolation from God. Come, be satisfied with the way God treats you, continue your prayers, proceed along the path you have taken, and be wary of allowing yourself to complain out of a lack of humility and little resignation to the will of God.

When we pray, we can receive no greater benefit that to unite ourselves with God's will. So resign yourself and say: "Lord, I accept this suffering from your hands, and I accept it for as long as you will. If it is your will that I remain afflicted for all eternity, I am content." Such a prayer, while painful, will be of more help to you than any consolation.

It is important to remember that spiritual dryness is not always a punishment but is sometimes permitted by God for our greater good and to keep us humble. In order that St. Paul would not boast of the gifts he received, the Lord allowed him to be tormented with impure temptations. "Therefore, that I might not become too elated, a thorn in the flesh was given to me, an angel of Satan, to beat me" (2 Cor 12:7).

To pray when prayer is a delight is not a great achievement. "Another is a friend, a boon companion,/who will not be with you when sorrow comes" (Sir 6:10). As you know, a true friend not only shares our table but is selflessly with us when we have problems. So when God sends darkness and desolation, it is a way of testing his true friends. When Palladius had suffered great dryness in prayer he went to visit St. Macarius and was told: "When you are tempted to leave your prayer say: 'For the love of Jesus Christ I am content to stay here and simply guard the walls of this cell.'" This is how you should respond when you are tempted to discontinue your prayer because it seems a waste of time to you. On such occasions say: "I am here to please God." St. Francis de Sales says that if we do nothing else during prayer than drive away temptations and distractions, we have prayed well. Tauler also claims that God will grant greater favors to the person who simply perseveres in arid prayer than to the one who prays a lot with a great deal of spiritual consolation.

Father Rodriguez tells of a man who said that he had been praying for forty years and had never experienced any consolation. But the man explained that on the days he prayed he felt strong in virtue whereas when he did not pray he felt such terrible weakness within himself that he was incapable of doing any good. St. Bonaventure and Gerson say that many people actually serve God better when they are not as recollected at prayer as they would wish, because this causes them to be more diligent and humble. Otherwise, they might perhaps become vain and luke-warm, thinking that they have already found what they are looking for.

7. What is true of spiritual dryness is also true of temptations. We must try to avoid temptations, but if God wills or allows that we be tempted to sin against faith, against purity, or against any other virtue, then we must not complain but again resign ourselves to his will. When St. Paul prayed to be delivered

from his temptations, the Lord replied: "My grace is sufficient for you" (2 Cor 12:9).

8. Finally we should unite ourselves with the will of God both as regards the time of our death and the way in which we are to die. Once when St. Gertrude was climbing a hill she lost her footing and feel into a ravine. Afterward, her companions asked her if she had not been afraid of dying without receiving the Last Sacraments. She answered: "I would very much like to die with the Sacraments but I am even more concerned that the will of God should be done, because I believe that the best disposition which one can have at the point of death is to submit oneself to God's will. For this reason I desire whatever form of death God gives me."

In his *Dialogues,* St. Gregory tells of a priest named Santolo who was condemned to death by the Vandals. When they allowed him to choose the form of death he should suffer the saint refused to choose, saying: "I am in the hands of my God and I will accept whatever death he allows you to inflict on me. I have no other wish than this." The Lord was so pleased with this act of submission to his will that when the barbarians decided to behead the priest, he held back the arm of the executioner as he was about to strike. The Vandals were so impressed with this miracle that they spared the priest's life. So the best kind of death for us is the form of death that God has determined. When we think of our death we should always say: "Save us, Lord, and let us die according to your will."

In the same way we have to accept the time at which we are to die. What is this world but a prison in which we suffer and are in constant danger of losing God? This is why David cried out: "Lead me out of my prison,/that I may give thanks to your name" (Ps 142:8). This also made St. Teresa sigh for death. When she heard the clock strike she was full of consolation at the thought that she had passed another hour of her life evading the danger of losing God.

Father John of Avila said that those who know themselves to be only half-hearted in loving God should desire death on account of the danger of losing grace in this life. What could be more precious and desirable to us than to be assured through a good death that we can no longer lose the grace of our God? You might say: "So far I have done nothing. I have gained nothing for my soul." But if it is God's will that you should die at this point, what good would it do to go on living against his will? Who knows if you would then die the manner which you can now hope to die? Who knows if you might not change your conduct, fall into other sins and be lost? In any case, you would not be able to live without committing some sins, even if not very serious. St. Bernard exclaimed: "Why do we want life, when the longer we live the more we sin?" It is certain, indeed, that God is more greatly displeased over one venial sin than he is pleased with any amount of good works we can do.

It seems to me that whoever has little desire for paradise shows little desire for God. Whoever loves, desires the presence of the beloved, but we cannot see God unless we leave this earth. That is why all the saints have sighed for death that they might go to see their beloved Lord. St. Augustine sighed: "Oh, if only I could die, that I might see you." St. Paul sighed: "I long to depart this life and be with Christ" (Phil 1:23). Similarly David: "When can I go and see the face of God?" (Ps 42:3). This is how it is with all souls who love God.

A certain author writes that when he was hunting in woods on horseback he heard a man singing sweetly. He stopped, only to find a poor leper covered in sores. He asked him if he had been singing. "Yes, sir," he replied, "it was I who was singing." "How come you can sing and be content, when you are in such pain and facing death?" The leper replied: "There is nothing between God and me other than this wall of clay which is my body; when it is gone I will go to enjoy my God. I am content and sing because I see that this wall is falling apart a little more each day."

9. We should also unite ourselves with God's will as regards the degree of grace and glory we attain. We should, of course, value things which give glory to God, but we should value his will even more. We should desire to love him more than the Seraphim, but we should not aspire to any degree of love higher than that which God has destined for us.

CONFORMITY TO THE WILL OF GOD

Father Avila says: "I do not believe the saints wanted to be better than they were. And yet, they were at peace because they did not desire to be saints out of self-love but for the sake of God. They would have been content with what they had received even if it had been less. They considered it to be a truer expression of love to be content with what God gave them than to be desirous of having more." Father Rodriguez explains what this means. On the one hand we should be as diligent as we can about attaining perfection. So we should not make excuses about being spiritually tepid and negligent as those who say "God must give me what I need. I can only do so much." On the other hand, when we do fail, we should not lose courage or peace of mind, nor should we lose our conformity to the will of God who permits our failures. Instead, we should be sorry and humbly ask God for greater help. Then we should get up immediately and continue on our course. In the same way, we may desire to be with the choirs of angels in heaven. But we must desire this not in order to have greater glory for ourselves but in order to give greater glory to God and to love him more dearly. At the same time, we should be resigned to his will and be content with whatever grace he, in his mercy, pleases to grant us.

It would be a serious fault to desire gifts of supernatural prayer such as ecstasies, visions, or revelations. Masters of the spiritual life teach us that souls who are favored by God with such graces should pray that they be taken away so that they may love God by pure faith, which is the safest way. Many have arrived at perfection without these supernatural graces. It is by virtue alone, and most of all by uniformity with God's will, that we are raised to sanctity. If God does not will that we be raised to sublime heights of perfection and glory then we should conform ourselves completely to his holy will and pray that we might at least be saved through his mercy. If we do this we shall receive no small reward from the goodness of our Lord for he loves, more than all else, souls who are resigned.

Conclusion

In conclusion, we should look upon everything that happens or will happen to us as coming from the hands of God. We should direct all our actions to the single end of doing God's will, and doing it simply because it is his will. In order to be confident that we have understood what is God's will for us, we should depend upon the guidance of our superiors in external matters and on our spiritual directors in internal matters. We should have great faith in what Jesus Christ has said to us: "Whoever listens to you listens to me" (Lk 10:16).

Above all, we should be eager to serve God in the way he would have us serve him. I say this so that we might avoid the delusion of those who waste their time on idle fancies by saying: "If I were in a desert, if I were in a monastery, if I were anywhere but in this house and far away from these relations and companions, I would become a saint. I would do such penances, I would pray so much." They keep repeating "I would," "I would," but in the meantime they bear the cross which God has sent them with reluctance and are not following the path he wills them to follow. In this way they not only fail to become holy but in fact they get worse and worse. These desires are sometimes temptations of the devil because they are not according to God's will. So we should reject them and try to serve God only in whatever way he has chosen for us. By doing his will we will become saints in whatever state of life he places us.

Let us, then, always will only what God wills. If we do so he will hold us close to his heart. To help us remember this let us recall some passages of scripture which invite us to unite ourselves with the will of God. "Lord, what will you have me to do?" ([ed.] Acts 9:6). My God, tell me what you want of me and I will do it. "I am yours; save me,/for I cherish your precepts" (Ps 119:94). I am no longer my own but yours, Lord; do with me whatever you will. Particularly when some serious hardship comes our way such as the death of a relative, material loss, and so on, we should always say: "Yes, my God and good Father, let it be so, for such is your will" ([ed.] Mt 11:26). Above all, let us treasure the prayer which Jesus Christ taught us: "Your will be done on earth as it is in heaven." The Lord said to St. Catherine of Genoa that whenever she prayed the Our Father she should dwell particularly on these words, praying that his will might be done in her as it is done in the saints in heaven. Let us do the same and we will surely become saints.

May the Divine Will be Loved and Praised Forever
Praised be the Immaculate Virgin Mary.

Motives for Confidence in the Divine Mercy

Introduction

Editor's Note: In the list of Alphonsus's publications drawn up for the Congregation of Rites in Rome in preparation for his being declared a Doctor of the Church, this work appears under the title *Motivi di Confidenza nella Divina Misericordia per i meriti di Gesù Cristo* (Concessionis Tituli Doctoris, etc., Rome, 1870, p. 90). It first appeared as an appendix to the *Condotta ammirabile della Divina Providenza in salvar l'Uomo per mezzo di Gesù Cristo*, published in Naples in 1775, and three years later was published by Remondini in Venice.

De Meulemeester (B.G.E.R., p. 167) is not convinced that this is a separate treatise in its own right but thinks that it was originally part of or complementary to *Encouragement for a Troubled Soul*. Whatever its origins, it is a devotional work of great spiritual gentleness.

*   *   *

According to what you have told me there are two principal problems which, more than any others, cause you anxiety. The first is whether you are destined to be saved and the second is whether God has forgiven you your sins. As regards the first, whether your name is written in the Book of Life or not, that is a secret which God does not wish to reveal to us for the very good reason that he wishes us to dedicate ourselves by our good works to securing our salvation and at the same time to fear the loss of God. That is what St. Peter tells us: "Therefore, brothers, be all the more eager to make your call and election firm, for, in doing so, you will never stumble" (2 Pt 1:10). It is true that the Lord is the one who has to convert and save us but it is also necessary for us to ensure that we turn to God since he, for his part, will not fail to save us. "Turn to me and be safe,/all you ends of the earth,/for I am God; there is no other" (Is 45:22).

It was blasphemous on the part of Calvin to assert that God created certain people for the sole purpose of sending them to

94

damnation. And to make things worse, he added that God himself forces them to commit sin so that they should suffer damnation, whereas it is certain that God wills all to be saved: "This is good and pleasing to God our savior, who wills everyone to be saved and to come to knowledge of the truth" (1 Tm 2:3–4). And the Lord declares that he wishes even the wicked who might justly deserve eternal death to be converted from their sinful ways and to attain salvation. "As I live, says the Lord GOD, I swear I take no pleasure in the death of the wicked man, but rather in the wicked man's conversion, that he may live" (Ez 33:11). Tertullian points out that those first words, "As I live," amount to an oath on the part of God so that there can be no possible doubt on our part as to his sincerity. "He even swears an oath in order to convince us."[1]

Petavius finds it almost incredible that anyone could doubt the fact that God wishes all to be saved. If it is possible so to twist this truth which God has confirmed by oath in the scriptures as to make it mean something quite the opposite, what truth of faith is there that can escape similar misinterpretation? And why is it that God has such an intense desire to save us all except that he has created us out of love from all eternity? The Lord speaks to us all in these words: "With age-old love I have loved you;/so I have kept my mercy toward you" (Jer 31:3).[2]

Since the Lord is fully aware of our human frailty he has, in the words of St. Peter, great patience with sinners since he does not wish that they should be lost but that they should do penance for their sins and save their souls. "He is patient with you, not wishing that any should perish but that all should come to repentance" (2 Pt 3:9). St. Augustine says that our Redeemer who has saved us from eternal death at the price of his most Precious Blood does not wish to lose souls which have cost him so dearly. In a word, God wishes to save everybody and when he sees that some, by the malice of their deliberate sins, condemn themselves to perdition, he, as it were, weeps with compassion for them: "Why should you die, O house of Israel? For I have no pleasure in the death of anyone who dies, says the Lord GOD. Return and live!" (Ez 18:31–32). It is almost as if he were to say: "My children, why do you wish to lose your souls for all eternity since I have died on the Cross to save you all? If you have wandered far from me, return to me now with sorrow and I shall restore to you the eternal life that you have lost."

From all this can you now have any doubt that God wishes to save you? From this moment onward never dare to utter again: "I wonder does God wish to save me. Maybe he wishes to see me damned on account of the sins I have committed against him." Get rid of all such thoughts, once and for all, since you must now realize that God is helping you with his graces and calls you insistently to love him.

As regards your second anxiety, namely that the Lord has not yet pardoned you the offenses of your past life, I have already told you that, in obedience to your spiritual director and confessor, you should cast aside all your anxiety in this matter and you should never again confess what you have already confessed before. Remember, as I now repeat, that, in the words of St. Teresa, whoever obeys one's confessor, whether with difficulty or not, is certain of doing the will of God. And I tell you further that, in the words of St. John of the Cross, whoever does not accept without reserve what the confessor says is lacking in faith. The simple truth is that Jesus Christ has said that whoever obeys his minister obeys him and whoever refuses to obey, refuses to obey him: "Whoever listens to you listens to me. Whoever rejects you rejects me" (Lk 10:16).

And so from this moment onward leave any anxiety you may have about your eternal salvation in the hands of the Lord since he has taken you into his care, as St. Peter assures us: "Cast all your worries upon him for he cares for you" (1 Pt 5:7).

In order to keep ourselves in the friendship of God we must totally distrust our own strength, since, without the assistance of God's grace, we can do nothing for our salvation; indeed, we could, instead, fall into every type of evil. For that reason it is essential that if we wish to obtain salvation we should continually recommend ourselves to God in prayer. Because we are in constant danger of falling we must continually seek the assistance of God's help. This assistance is available to all, according to St.

Bernard; only those who refuse to ask for it are deprived of it. Even though God offers his assistance to all, he still wishes us to ask him for it. "Ask and you will receive" (Jn 16:24). Whoever neglects to ask for it does not receive it and so is lost.

When the devil succeeds in frightening us with thoughts of our weakness and frailty, we should not lose confidence; rather should we increase our hope of receiving all the strength we need from God who is all-powerful and encourages us to have confidence. We should say with the Apostle: "I have the strength for everything through him who empowers me" (Phil 4:13). And if we place our trust in God, is it possible that he will fail us? Certainly not! "Has anyone hoped in the LORD and been disappointed?" (Sir 2:10). The very name of Jesus is sufficient to drive away the forces of evil. St. Paul declares that the Lord has given Jesus Christ a name which surpasses all names and at the sound of it all bow down: "God...bestowed on him the name/that is above every name,/that at the name of Jesus/every knee should bend,/of those in heaven and on earth and under the earth" (Phil 2:9–10). In our struggle with the enemies of our salvation very often the invocation of the sole name of Jesus is more effective than the recitation of long prayers.

As well as what I have said so far, I now wish to leave you a few other considerations which, I believe, will be of further assurance to you.

1. I repeat once more the necessity of obedience to your confessor since, from what I have been able to discern, you have not had that total faith in this obedience in the past and this is the reason why you have not achieved peace of mind. However, what I have already said on this point is sufficient. Whoever walks the path of obedience walks securely on the road to heaven.

2. When you suffer misfortune of any kind endeavor to accept whatever comes as coming to you from the hand of God. In times of illness cooperate obediently with your medical advisers in whatever remedies they prescribe; make known your sufferings without exaggeration and then do not be worried any

further. Do not seek inordinately to evoke sympathy from those who come to visit you. And when anyone happens to express their sympathies in an exaggerated fashion, reply graciously in the words of Our Lord himself: "Shall I not drink the cup that the Father gave me?" (Jn 18:11). Say simply, the Lord has permitted me to bear these sufferings not because he dislikes me but because he loves me. And shall I not therefore accept them with resignation? It is in time of suffering that one is able to discern whether a person is genuinely Christian or not. There are some so-called devout persons who are all sweetness and humble when they are well. But when the slightest illness afflicts them they immediately become impatient and intolerable and they are loud in their complaints if they do not receive attention or some remedy without delay. When you are ill bear your suffering without complaint. In all your trials remember the words of Job: "The LORD gave and the LORD has taken away;/blessed be the name of the LORD!" (Jb 1:21). Let your effort then be to bear your sufferings and disappointments without complaining. This is the true test of whether one has genuine humility.

3. The Lord is full of goodness to those who seek him. No one has ever trusted in the Lord and been rejected: "Has anyone hoped in the LORD and been disappointed?" (Sir 2:10). And the Lord is at hand even for those who do not seek for him, as St. Paul asserts, quoting the prophet Isaiah: "I was found [by] those who were not seeking me" (Rom 10:20). How much more easily, then, is the Lord to be found by those who are seeking for him? From now onward never say that the Lord has abandoned you: The Lord abandons only those who are obstinate and do not wish to change their sinful lives. And he does not in fact abandon even them. He stays at their side right up to the time of their death and assists them with every grace to secure that they do not lose their souls.

4. When souls seek to love the Lord he finds it impossible not to love them in return, according to the book of Proverbs: "Those who love me I also love" (Prv 8:17). And when he hides himself from those souls who love him he does so only for their greater good, to entice them to seek his graces more earnestly

and thus bind themselves more closely to himself. When St. Catherine of Genoa experienced great aridity of spirit, almost to the extent of believing that God had abandoned her and that she had no further ground for hope, she would then say: "How happy I am to be in this most unfortunate state. What does it matter if my heart is crushed provided the One I love is glorified. O my Love, if you receive even one more degree of glory from my suffering I pray you to allow me to remain in this terrible aridity for all eternity." And with these words she broke out in tears in the midst of her sufferings.

5. Souls who love their Crucified Lord in the midst of their own desolation grow closer to him in their hearts. Nothing makes a soul seek for God as much as desolation of spirit and nothing else draws the Lord into one's heart more effectively because in the midst of desolation, one's acts of acceptance of the will of God are purer and more perfect. The greater the desolation, the great one's humility; one's resignation is more unselfish, one's trust in God more authentic, and one's prayers more eager. God's graces, as a result, are more abundant.

6. To advance in the way of holiness it is necessary above all else to concentrate one's efforts on loving God. When the love of God takes possession of our hearts, it drives out all sinful affections. Make sure then that you repeat frequently acts of the love of God, saying, "My God, I love you," over and over again and "I hope to die repeating, My God, I love you." The saints have said that each breath that we take should be, in fact, an act of the love of God.

7. In your prayers do not neglect to offer yourself to God unreservedly. From your heart say: "My Jesus I give myself to you without reserve. I wish to be wholly yours. And if I am unable to give myself to you as I should, do you yourself receive me and make me wholly your own." St. Teresa of Avila offered herself to God time and time again each day. And you should be able to do the same. Offer the Lord your will, repeating the words of St. Paul: "Lord, what do you wish me to do?" ([ed.] Acts 9:6).[3] This prayer of St. Paul was sufficient to change him from being a persecutor of the church into a chosen instrument of God's designs. So in

your prayers repeat frequently the words of David in the psalms: "Teach me to do your will,/for you are my God" (Ps 143:10). Let this be your main prayer to God, to Our Lady, to your angel guardian, and to all the saints you pray to, so that you will have the grace to do, in everything, the will of God. In a word, let the short prayer "Thy will be done" serve you in all your sufferings and obtain for you all the graces you need.

8. When you experience great aridity of spirit be sure then to rejoice unselfishly in the bliss your God enjoys in heaven. This is an anticipation on earth of that perfect act of love of the blessed in heaven since they do not so much rejoice in their own happiness as in the infinite happiness of God himself. They love God much more than they love themselves.

9. As regards your prayers and reflections, never neglect to meditate on the Passion of Jesus Christ. There is no other subject more calculated to elicit our love than the thought of the sufferings of Jesus Christ. If, in the course of your meditations on the mysteries of our Lord's Passion, you experience a sense of tender love for Jesus, be grateful to God for this grace. But if, on the other hand, you do not experience this tenderness, be assured that you will always experience a great sense of encouragement. Go in spirit to the Garden of Gethsemane, as St. Teresa was wont to do, and there you will find the Lord alone. As you reflect on him in his agony, sweating blood and sorrowful even unto death, you will find consolation in your own distress as you realize that he suffered all this for you. And when you see the Lord ready to die for you, offer yourself to die for him. In the midst of the sufferings you experience, have the courage to say what St. Thomas said to his fellow apostles, "Let us also go to die with him" (Jn 11:16).

10. Place yourself also on the Hill of Calvary where you will find your Lord dying on the Cross consumed with sufferings. Seeing him in this terrible condition, is there any way you could refuse to undergo willingly all types of suffering for a God who dies out of love for you? St. Paul declared that he knew nothing, and wished to know nothing more in this life, than Jesus Crucified: "For I resolved to know nothing while I was with you except Jesus Christ, and him crucified" (1 Cor 2:2). St. Bonaventure

insists that those who want to have a steadfast love for Jesus Christ should always keep before their minds the thought of Jesus dying on the Cross. So, in the midst of all your anxieties, cast a glance at the Crucifix and renew your courage and determination to suffer out of love for him.

11. I recommend prayer to you above all else. When you can say nothing else, simply say, "Lord, help me and help me without delay." "Lord come to my assistance; make haste, O Lord, to help me." You are aware already that the church repeats this invocation several times a day in the liturgical prayer of priests and religious.[4] St. Philip Neri taught others to repeat this prayer many times over in the form of a rosary. Our Lord, as you know, has promised to give us whatever we ask for: "Ask and it shall be given to you." St. Bernard was filled with encouragement as he meditated on the words Our Lord addressed to the sons of Zebedee when they said: "'Teacher, we want you to do for us whatever we ask of you.' [Jesus] replied: 'What do you wish [me] to do for you?'" (Mk 10:35).

12. When you ask for graces from God make sure that you ask them in the name of Jesus Christ. Whatever comes to us from God comes to us through the merits of Jesus Christ. And Jesus our Redeemer has promised us that the Father will grant us whatever we ask of him in the name of Jesus: "Amen, amen, I say to you, whatever you ask the Father in my name he will give you" (Jn 16:23). So when you fear that God will send you to hell, think for a moment how could it be possible that the one who has said to you that whatever you ask him will be granted, would send you to hell!

13. How is it that you think you are not pleasing to God when you suffer desolation of spirit? Rather than being worried you should feel reassured, since God is dealing with you in the very same way that he treats his most intimate friends. He treated his own Divine Son in the very same way: ["But the LORD was pleased/to crush him in infirmity"] (Is 53:10). It was his will to see him crushed under the weight of sufferings and sorrow.

14. When you get anxious at the thought that the Lord will abandon you on account of your ingratitude, you should follow the example of the two disciples on the road to Emmaus. Jesus joined them under the guise of a fellow pilgrim and when they

neared their destination Jesus gave the impression that he was going on farther. But they, in the words of the gospel of St. Luke, "urged him, 'Stay with us, for it is nearly evening'" (Lk 24:29). He then went into the inn with them and remained with them. So when it seems to you that the Lord is going to depart from you, compel him to remain with you by saying: "Jesus, stay with me. I do not want you to leave me." Say with St. Peter, "Lord, if you leave me to whom shall I go for consolation and salvation?" ([ed.] Jn 6:68). Keep on praying to him with love and tenderness and have no anxiety that he will abandon you. Say in the words of the Apostle: "Neither death, nor life,...nor any other creature will be able to separate us from the love of God in Christ Jesus our Lord" (Rom 8:38–39). Say, "Jesus, no matter how displeased with me you may be, know that neither the fear of death nor the hope of life, nor anything on this earth can ever separate me from your love." When St. Francis de Sales, as a young man, experienced great aridity of spirit the devil suggested to him that he was destined for hell. The saint replied, "Well, if I cannot love my God for all eternity I will at least love him to the best of my ability while I am here on earth." In this way, he recovered his joy and serenity of spirit.

15. When you are oppressed by fears for your salvation or by desolation of spirit, do not neglect to have recourse to Our Lady who has been given to us by God as the Consolatrix of those who are afflicted. Even though Jesus Christ is the foundation of all our hope, the church still wishes us to call on Our Lady in the words of the hymn *Salve Regina,* "Hail, our Hope." All the graces that we receive come to us from God as from their source, but St. Bernard asserts that they all pass through the hands of the Mother of God, with the result that whoever omits to recommend themselves to her, closes off, as it were, the channel of graces. Our Lady never refuses to help those who call on her and so all the saints were assiduous in recommending themselves to her who enjoys such power over the heart of God.

16. Once you have the firm intention of loving God, open your heart to him. "Open wide your mouth that I may fill it" (Ps 81:11) are the words of the psalm which tell us that the more

trust we have in the Lord the more we receive from him. He himself has declared that he rewards those who trust in him: "The LORD's promise is tried and true;/he is a shield for all who trust in him" (Ps 18:31). Remember that when you doubt that the Lord is listening to your prayers, he reproves you in the very same words he addressed to St. Peter: "O you of little faith, why did you doubt?" (Mt 14:31). Why did you doubt that I would hear you since I have promised to hear all those who pray to me? And since he wishes us to know that he will hear us when we pray he also wishes us to have no doubts whatsoever when we ask him for favors: "Therefore I tell you, all that you ask for in prayer, believe that you will receive it and it shall be yours" (Mk 11:24). Note the words "believe that you will receive it." You must therefore ask God for his favors with confidence and without any hesitation, as St. James warns us: "But he should ask in faith, not doubting" (Jas 1:6). So in your relations with the Lord, be full of confidence, and cast aside all your fears and hesitations. Whoever serves God in a sorrowful manner instead of honoring him, rather dishonors him. St. Bernard tells us that whoever imagines that God is cross and severe does him an injury since God is goodness and kindness itself. How could you doubt, says the saint, that Jesus would forgive you your sins since he has already nailed them to his Cross with the very same nails which pierced his hands?

17. The Lord has declared that his great joy is to be with us: "And I found delight in the sons of men" (Prv 8:31). Since God finds his delight in being with us, it is only right that all our delight should be in dealing with him. This thought alone should encourage us to pray to God with all confidence, and to endeavor to spend what remains to us of life with God who loves us so much and in whose company in heaven we hope to spend our eternity.

18. Let us then accustom ourselves to deal with God as with our most affectionate and dear friend who loves us more than anybody else. My God! why is it that scrupulous and anxious souls treat you as if you were a tyrant who demands nothing more from your subjects than fear and trepidation? The result is they think that God gets angry at every thought that passes through their

minds and at every word that slips involuntarily from their lips and wishes to cast them into hell. No! God does not deprive us of his grace, unless, with our eyes open and fully deliberately, we turn our backs on him and reject him. When we offend him slightly by some venial sin we certainly displease him but he does not deprive us of the friendship he bears us and an act of penance on our part or an act of love restores us to his friendship once more.

19. God's infinite majesty certainly deserves all our reverence and submission but he himself prefers to receive from souls desirous of loving him their love and confidence rather than fear and servility. So do not ever again consider the Lord a tyrant. Remember all the graces and favors he has heaped upon you despite all the offenses and ingratitude you have shown him. Remember too all the loving efforts he has made to entice you away from the paths of sin, all the inspirations he has sent you to bring you to love him. From this day onward show the Lord that loving confidence which is fitting for the dearest friend you have.

20. I know there is no further need for me to recommend to you the frequent reception of the sacraments, since such is already your practice. Confess your sins twice each week, certainly at least once. As regards the reception of Holy Communion, obey your spiritual director and even if you do not experience sensible devotion do not omit to ask permission to receive Holy Communion. Spiritual directors are accustomed to grant permission for reception of Holy Communion according to the eagerness which their penitents manifest. When your director sees that you do not request permission to receive and that you show little eagerness in the matter, he will not ordinarily instruct you to receive Holy Communion. Even when you do not receive Communion sacramentally do so spiritually many times during the day.[5]

21. Your love should be centered above all else on the two great mysteries of Our Lord's love, the Holy Sacrament of the Altar and the Passion of Jesus Christ. If the love of all human hearts could be concentrated in one heart it would not approach in the slightest degree to the greatness of the love which Jesus Christ has shown us in these two mysteries. And so, in short, concentrate all your efforts for the future on love for God and confi-

dence in his great mercy. And do not lose courage when you find yourself suffering and experiencing difficulties—these are a sign of God's love for you and not a sign that he has rejected you.[6]

25. St. Liduvina suffered great desolation of spirit for over four years. In all her sufferings she displayed total resignation to the will of God and she even blessed God for the sufferings he permitted her to undergo. She united her sufferings with the Passion of Jesus Christ and was thus able to bear her heavy burden. God gave her the grace of serenity in her sufferings even though she still continued to experience great pain. She said: "When I see Jesus Christ hanging on the Cross, I do not feel any further pain. Even though my sufferings at times make me cry out in pain, my heart says "Jesus my Love, increase my sufferings but, at the same time, increase my love." To those who wished to sympathize with her she replied, "All my sufferings are as nothing since I am in the hands of Infinite Goodness. God loves me more than father and mother together."

26. In conclusion, since you love Jesus Christ do not omit to recommend sinners to him in your prayers each day. Both St. Teresa of Avila and St. Mary Magdalene de' Pazzi prayed unceasingly for sinners. We show little love for God if we omit to pray for the conversion of all those who so grievously offend him.[7]

The Practice of the Love of Jesus Christ

Introduction

Editor's Note: At the end of the Introduction to the first edition of *The Glories of Mary,* Alphonsus announced his intention of publishing a companion volume on Jesus Christ.[1] The outline for this work has survived in a notebook, the second of a series of three, probably compiled between 1741 and 1761.[2] The outline envisaged three chapters: (1) "The Love of the Eternal Father in Giving Us His Son," (2) "The Hope We Should Have in Jesus Christ," (3) "The Love Jesus Christ Has Shown Us (i) in the Incarnation, (ii) in the Passion, and (iii) in the Blessed Sacrament." This work was not destined to appear for more than a quarter of a century, by which time Alphonsus was Bishop of St. Agatha, but poor health had forced him to take up residence in Arienzo, the second city of his diocese. On 14 September 1767, he wrote to his Venetian publisher, Giambattista Remondini: "Should God give me time and strength, I hope to publish this winter another very useful work, entitled *The Practice of the Love of Jesus Christ.*" By November, he was able to report that a good portion of the work had been completed.[3] Printing began in Naples the following May, and Alphonsus was expressing confidence that the completed work would be favorably received by the public, especially by nuns and other devout persons, for "all the virtues are there discussed and I have collected therein, not without great labor, the choicest sayings and the most shining actions of the saints."[4] The first Neapolitan edition appeared in June 1768, and was promptly corrected and dispatched to Venice with the comment, "This will be my last ascetical work." While this prediction proved to be untrue, Alphonsus's assessment of its value proved to be accurate, for it has been one of the most frequently published of his works.[5]

The work belongs to a genre that had become popular among the spiritual writers of seventeenth-century France. Alphonsus was familiar with at least two examples. The first was *De la Connaissance et de l'Amour du Fils de Dieu* by the Jesuit Jean

Baptiste de St. Jure, published in French in 1638 (Italian translation, 1677) and from which he had extensively borrowed in the past.[6] The second, whose title resembles closely that of his own work, was *De l'Amour de Notre Seigneur Jésus Christ et les Moyens de l'Acquerir* by François Nepveu (1638–1708), published in French 1684 and in an Italian edition in 1716. There are, however, several distinctive features of Alphonsus's approach. He shows little interest, for instance, in following St. Jure's mathematical analysis of love into its different aspects such as "amour de bienveillance, amour aspiratif, amour appreciatif, amour douloureux de contrition," or his exhaustive enumeration of the motives of love.[7] Nor is he interested in delimiting the stages of the spiritual journey. For him, love is the starting point rather than a summit reached after years of effort on the lower slopes. According to Domenico Capone, Alphonsus's presentation of love is totally Christocentric, rooted as it is in the gospel of salvation.[8]

The long incubation of the *Practice* from draft notes to final publication entailed an important development of the original project. The final work contains seventeen chapters in two unequal parts, representing the dialogical structure of love and response. The first three chapters remained substantially as in the original draft and are an invitation to the reader to embark on the project of learning the love of Jesus Christ as shown in the Passion (Chap. 1), in his abiding presence in the Eucharist (Chap. 2), and in the present offer of salvation (Chap. 3: "The great confidence we should have in the love which Jesus Christ has shown in everything he has done for us"). The second section (Chaps. 4–17) is an addition to the original draft, and it treats the human response of love in action through a running commentary on Paul's hymn to love in 1 Corinthians 13. It is scarcely accidental that one other work of Alphonsus contains the Italian word *practicà* in its title, namely, *Pratica del Confessore* (1755). Both place the emphasis on the practical art or skill, and share a common vision of the moral life and its foundation in the redeeming love of Jesus Christ for human beings. Bernard Häring has described *The Practice of the Love of Jesus Christ* as "a kind of moral theology, for lay-people as well as for priests."[9] It is an essential work for understanding the underlying vision that informs Alphonsus's moral theology. Häring has observed that in the case of both Alphonsus and Luther, anguish regarding personal salvation led to a profound statement of a theology of a gracious God.[10] Luther's "sola gratia" has its counterpart in the motto Alphonsus gave his Redemptorist Congregation at its foundation: "with him there is plentiful redemption," taken from Psalm 130:16. As Häring elsewhere suggests, his stress on creative liberty and fidelity can be understood only in the light of his understanding of moral action as a response to divine love, which is given its fullest expression here.[11]

The argument of the work is set out clearly in the opening sentence: "A person will become perfectly holy by loving Jesus Christ, our God, our chief good and our Savior." Holiness is a matter of returning love for love, and since it is addressed to all Christians, it can never become the preserve of any single category, but each must find the way to holiness in accordance with the state of life in which providence has placed him: "the religious as a religious, the person in the world as a person in the world, priest as priest, married person as married person, soldier as soldier" (8:10). Alphonsus invites them to set their sights high. His sketch of what holiness involves is nothing short of heroic, but, anticipating the argument that it was too costly, Alphonsus depicts the even more costly foolishness of Christ's love as shown in the Passion. Brian Johnstone has remarked that when Alphonsus set out to answer the question of why Jesus suffered so much, he found the traditional Anselmian schema of the Passion as satisfaction inadequate, and attempted to give it fresh expression in terms of intense personal passion: "Alphonsus' God is an intensely passionate God, a God of the great dramatic deed, a God of burning desires. Thus, he speaks of the folly of the cross, in terms of excessive love."[12]

The *Practice* speaks the language of love, and its intention is to elicit a response of love. Alphonsus marshals his arguments in vigorously rhetorical fashion, not always easy to reproduce in contemporary English translation without running the risk of parody. Rhetoric had been an important element in Alphonsus's early legal education, and all through his life he remained conscious that words communicate to the heart and to the imagination as well as to the head, yet his rhetoric, particularly that of the spiritual writings, has received little attention to date, though one suspects that a closer study of it might yield rich results.[13] The propositions are set out simply and clearly, usually in a single sentence at the beginning of a chapter or subsection, and a variety of rhetorical devices is enlisted to hammer the point home. Sometimes, the reader is addressed directly in a series of rhetorical questions; at other times Jesus Christ becomes a partner in the dialogue, being either addressed in prayer or speaking in the author's expansionist paraphrase of the words of scripture. There are frequent changes of tone, probably an indication that material originally composed for a different setting is being put to new use. Chapter 6, for instance, has all the appearance of having been originally a conference on fraternal charity: it contains no citations from the Fathers, but includes many telling examples of charity applicable to religious communities and superiors. The mode of expression is concrete and at times humorous, with reference to street angels and house devils; the advice to leave a person who just been given a dressing-down with some self-respect still intact *(colla bocca dolce),* or to imitate the Good Samaritan by pouring on soothing oil of praise to temper the vinegar of correction, or the word-picture of an angry person "smoldering like Vesuvius," plucked straight from the landscape of Naples. The selection below contains the original first section (Chaps. 1–3) and, from the second section, Chapters 5 through 8 and Chapter 11.

Chapter 8 is the longest in the book, and comes closest to being a summary of Alphonsus's teaching on the spiritual life. He regards spirituality as essentially the formation of conscience and its fine-tuning to the point where the person instinctively makes generous moral decisions. He helps his readers to distinguish a scrupulous conscience from a delicate one, and reassures them that everyday faults, or past sins, are not a barrier to advancing in the love of God; indeed, the knowledge that one is a forgiven sinner is for him essential if one is to grasp the grace of redemption in all its fullness. For Alphonsus, the quest for holiness begins when the imagination is fired by the example of Jesus Christ, and by sayings and incidents drawn from the lives of the saints. Desire is essentially giving free rein to the spiritual imagination (1–12); he quotes with approval St. Teresa of Avila's saying "our desires must be great, and great will come from them." He recognized that a refined taste for spiritual experience was fashionable among certain sections of eighteenth-century Neapolitan society, but also that it could become simply another form of elegant entertainment with little substance. He does not flinch from an honest diagnosis and strips away the mask: "Many people feed on desires alone, but never take a step on the way that leads to God," and so desire must be transformed by the will into authentic and effective moral decisions or "good resolutions" (12–17). He sketches a brief but devastating portrait of the spiritual sluggard whose life is a series of ineffective longings (12), while pointing out the danger of scrupulosity on the other hand. Desire, and the spiritual imagination, reaches its highest point in the ambition to choose the best, and not merely opting to please God by avoiding what is sinful. The spiritual imagination is nourished by meditation on the Word, particularly the Passion (18–25), and by the celebration of the Eucharist (26–32). Holiness for Alphonsus is, however, not simply a naturalistic search for perfection that the human subject of good will can undertake with its own natural strength. It is, from beginning to end, God's work through grace, and grace can be found only through persistent and humble prayer (33–38). Since God has not created the desire for love capriciously, and even though a person may have spent much of his life struggling with temptation and the painful reality of human weakness, the genuine prayer, which no matter how inadequately expresses the desire for God, will be crowned with the grace of perseverance.

Chapter 11 is difficult because it treats a number of different subjects under the heading of detachment, and here more than anywhere else Alphonsus is reflecting critically on a social world very different from that of today. Its core idea, the importance of detachment *(distacco),* might be expressed as the ideal of spiritual freedom. From John of the Cross, he borrows the metaphor of a bird that has escaped from the cage but is still tethered by a fine but very strong thread. It can flap its wings and thus give itself the illusion of flying, but soaring flight is impossible. Alphonsus argues that people who have begun the journey toward God sooner or later have to confront the possessive power of attachment to wealth, power, and reputation, which raise for them in a way that is usually painful the question of whether they are spiritually free. He is not interested in an abstract notion of spiritual freedom, but rather in whether a person is free enough to respond to the concrete, and sometimes radical, possibilities that love lays open in the present. He analyzes some of the cultural and social forces that made the attainment of that sort of spiritual freedom difficult for his Neapolitan contemporaries, particularly the cult of the *bella figura,* of the carefully cultivated public image, and the social pressure that can arise in a society built on a highly developed system of honor and shame. The section on vocation (11–20) may seem like a digression, but Alphonsus is using it as a test case and fights the battle for spiritual freedom on two fronts. On the one hand, he is vindicating the rights of generous young people to follow a state in life in the teeth of parental opposition. To the modern reader, his strictures on family may seem excessively severe, and the examples given in Chapter 11: 14 are certainly crude and in poor taste, but his personal experience as well as several incidents in the lives of the young men of his own Congregation had made him painfully conscious of the degree to which the stifling atmosphere of the patriarchal family sought to impose its will on young people on the verge of adulthood in a way that compromised not only their own deepest aspirations but also any hope of the church being able to make effective pastoral responses. The second front on which he fights is that of calculating parental ambition. The ecclesiastical state in Bourbon Naples was in some instances a path out of penury for younger sons, or even a means to improve the lot of genteel families whose fortunes had declined. Seen in this context, Alphonsus's paragraphs on vocation may serve as a reminder that spiritual freedom can never be judged purely on the basis of personal preference, but always has important implications for the life of the whole church community.

The translation that follows is based on the text of the Italian critical edition of the *Opere Ascetiche*.[14] Brief omissions in the text are indicated by [...]; omissions of lengthier sections are noted in the text when they occur.

*   *   *

Chapter 1: Jesus Christ Deserves Our Love in Return for the Love He Has Shown Us in His Passion.

1. A person will become perfectly holy by loving Jesus Christ, our God, our chief good, and our Savior. He himself says that anyone who loves him will be loved by the eternal Father: "For the Father himself loves you, because you have loved me" (Jn 16:27). "Some people," says St. Francis de Sales, "think that perfection can be found by an austere life; others make it a matter of much prayer, or of frequenting the sacraments, or of acts of charity. They are all mistaken. Perfection consists in loving God with our whole heart. The Apostle writes: 'And over all these put on love, that is, the bond of perfection' (Col 3:14). It is love that preserves and holds together all the virtues that make a person perfect."[15] St. Augustine says: "Love and do what you wish," because love itself will teach a person who loves God never to do anything that might displease him, and to do everything that pleases him.

2. Could it be that God does not deserve our love? He has loved us from the very beginning of eternity: "With age-old love I have loved you" (Jer 31:3). God was the first to love you. Before you existed, indeed, even before the world itself existed, God was already loving you. For as long as he has been God, he has been loving you. [...]

3. When God saw how human beings were attracted by good things, he set out to win them over by his gifts: "I drew them with human cords,/with bands of love" (Hos 11:4). Every gift of his was created for human beings. First, he endowed the soul made in his image with its powers of memory, intellect, and will, and gave it a body with all its senses, created heaven and

earth and all that is in them—the sky, the stars, plants, seas, rivers, springs, mountains, plains, metals, fruits, and all the species of wild animals—everything was an act of his love. All these created things were for the use of human beings, so that they love him in return for so many gifts.[16] "The heavens and the earth and everything in them," says St. Augustine, "cry out to me that I must love you." [...]

4. St. Mary Magdalene de' Pazzi felt herself aglow with the love of God if she as much as held a beautiful flower in her hand and she would say, "My Lord has thought of creating this flower for me from all eternity." The flower seemed like an arrow of divine love, piercing her and uniting to God. The sight of trees, springs, streams, sea-coasts, or meadows caused St. Teresa to say that their beauty reminded her of her ingratitude in loving their Creator so little who had made them to gain her love. There was once a holy hermit. On his walks through the countryside, it seemed to him as if the wild flowers and plants along the way reminded him of his ingratitude to God, and he would strike them with his staff, saying, "Be silent, be silent! You call me ungrateful. You tell me that God has created you out of love for me, yet I do not love him. I understand you now. Be silent! Be silent! Do not reproach me anymore."

5. God was not content simply to give us a beautiful creation. In order to win us totally, the Eternal Father has gone so far as to give us his one and only Son: "For God so loved the world that he gave his only Son" (Jn 3:16). Seeing us dead and deprived of grace through sin, in his overwhelming love for us, he sent his Son to make satisfaction for us, and to restore to us the life which sin had destroyed. According to St. Paul, this is too costly a love: "Out of the exceeding love which he has for us, when we were dead on account of our sins, he brought us back to life in Christ" ([ed.] Eph 2:4–5).[17] With the Son, whom he did not spare in order that he might spare us, he has given us every thing that is good—his grace, his love, and paradise. Yet all these things are of much less account than his Son: "He who did not spare his own Son but handed him over for us all, how will he not also give us everything else along with him?" (Rom 8:32).

6. So, too, out of love for us, has given us himself: "He loved me, and gave himself for me" ([ed.] Gal 2:20). To redeem us from eternal death and restore to us divine grace and the paradise which we had lost, he became a human being clothed with flesh like ours: "And the Word became flesh" (Jn 1:14). This is how God has despoiled himself: "He emptied himself,/taking the form of a slave,/coming in human likeness" (Phil 2:7), the Lord of the world taking the form of a servant and submitting himself to all the miseries that other human beings suffer!

7. What is even more astonishing is that he could have saved us without dying and without suffering. Yet he chose a life of affliction and contempt, and a bitter and ignominious death. He went so far as to die on the shameful scaffold of the Cross: "He humbled himself,/becoming obedient to death,/even death on a cross" (Phil 2:8). If he could have redeemed us without suffering, why then did he choose to die, and to die on a cross? It was for no other reason than to show his love for us: He "loved us and handed himself over for us" (Eph 5:2). Because he loved us, he surrendered himself to sorrow, ignominy, and to the most painful death that anyone on earth has ever suffered.

8. That is why St. Paul, the great lover of Jesus Christ, could say "the love of Christ impels us" (2 Cor 5:14). He meant that it was not so much what Jesus Christ has suffered for us as the love he has shown in suffering for us which obliges us, and indeed forces us, to love him. Commenting on this text, St. Francis de Sales asks, "Is knowing that Jesus, true God, has loved us to the extent of suffering death on a cross for us, not like having our heart put into a wine-press, and feeling it wrenched, until love is pressed from it by a force as strong as it is loving?" He continues:

> Why, then, do we not throw ourselves on Jesus crucified to die on the cross along with him who was willed to die there for love of us? I will cling to him, and will never more abandon him. I will die with him, and be consumed by the fire of his love. Let the same fire consume the creature as consumes the creator. My Jesus gives himself totally to me, and I give myself totally to him. I will live and die on his breast. Neither death nor life will ever separate me from him. Eternal love,

114

my soul seeks you and wants to possess you forever. Come then, Holy Spirit, and inflame our hearts with your love. To love and to die. To die to every other love to live for the love of Jesus. Savior of our souls, grant that we might sing for ever "May Jesus live whom I love, I love Jesus who lives for ever and ever."

9. The love of Jesus Christ for human beings was so great that it made him long for the hour of his death so that he might show the tenderness of his love for them. During his life, he said, "There is a baptism with which I must be baptized, and how great is my anguish until it is accomplished!" (Lk 12:50). That is why in describing the night on which Jesus began his Passion, St. John writes: "Jesus knew that his hour had come to pass from this world to the Father. He loved his own in the world and he loved them to the end" (Jn 13:1). The Redeemer called that hour "his hour" because the hour of his death was the time for which he had longed.

10. Who could have forced a God to die tortured on a gallows between two criminals, suffering so much shame to his divine majesty? St. Bernard: "It was love, forgetting its dignity." When love wishes to be recognized, it does not stand on its dignity, but does what is best calculated to reveal its true self. [...]

11. Without the assurance of faith, could anyone ever have believed that an omnipotent God, Lord of all and supremely happy in himself, was capable of loving human beings to the extent of appearing to be out of his mind with love for them? As St. Lawrence Justinian puts it, "We see Wisdom become a fool through excess of love."[18] St. Mary Magdalene de' Pazzi said much the same. In ecstasy one day, she took a wooden crucifix in her hands and exclaimed, "Yes, Jesus, you are insane with love. I will say it, and will go on repeating it forever, 'you are insane with love.'" According to Denis the Aeropagite, this is not insanity, but that the ordinary effect of divine love is to make lovers go beyond themselves and give themselves totally to the object of their love: "This divine yearning brings ecstasy so that the lover belongs no longer to self but to the beloved."

12. If only people would stop to think as they look at Jesus crucified of the love he has for each one of them! St. Francis de Sales asks how we can remain untouched by love when we see the flame which burned in the breast of the Redeemer. What a fate it would be to be consumed with the same fire which consumed our God! And what a joy it would be to be bound to God with bonds of love. According to St. Bonaventure, the wounds of Jesus Christ can pierce the hardest hearts and inflame the coldest souls. [...]

13. Venerable John of Avila loved Jesus Christ so much that, in his preaching, he never ceased to speak of his love for us. In a treatise on the love of the Redeemer, he writes the following burning words which are so beautiful that I include them here.[19]

> 14. Your love for humanity is so great, our Redeemer, that no one who reflects on it can do anything less than love you in return. Your love does violence to our hearts, as the Apostle says, "the love of Christ compels us." The source of Jesus Christ's love for human beings is in the love he has for the Father. As he said on Holy Thursday, "but the world must know the love I have for the Father and that I do just as the Father has commanded me. Get up, let us go" ([ed.] Jn 14:31). Where does he go? To die for human beings on the Cross.

15. No mind can grasp the ardor of love which burned in the heart of Jesus Christ. Although he was commanded to undergo death once, he would have submitted to a thousand deaths from love, had he been so ordered. Had he been ordered to undergo on behalf of a single individual what was required for all, he would have undergone for each one what he suffered for all. He spent three hours on the Cross. Had he been required to stay there until the day of judgment, he had love enough to carry out the command. The love of Jesus was greater than his sufferings. Divine love! How much greater you are than you appear! Outwardly, you appear great, for so many wounds and bruises proclaim a great love to us. But the inner reality is even greater than what appears visible. It is only a drop from the immense ocean of your love. [...]

19. If we wish to attain perfect love for Jesus Christ, we should take the means recommended by St. Thomas Aquinas:

1. to keep ever in mind the goodness of God in general and to ourselves in particular;
2. to consider how God's infinite goodness is always engaged in doing good for us, always loves us, and seeks our love in return;
3. to avoid diligently even the least thing which might cause him displeasure;
4. to renounce all the sensible goods of this earth, namely, riches, honors, and the pleasures of the senses.[20]

Father Tauler adds that another great means of acquiring perfect love for Jesus Christ is to meditate on his Passion.[21]

20. Who could deny that devotion to the Passion of Jesus Christ is the most useful and the most tender of all devotions, that it is the one dearest to God, the one which brings the greatest consolation to sinners and inflames ardent souls? From where do all our benefits come, if not from the Passion of Jesus Christ? From where else can we have hope of forgiveness, strength against temptations, hope of heaven? From where else come so many lights of truth, so many invitations to love, so much encouragement to change our life, so many desires to give ourselves to God, if not from the Passion of Jesus Christ? The Apostle was right when he declared that anyone who did not love Jesus Christ was excommunicated—"If anyone does not love the Lord, let him be accursed" (1 Cor 16:22).

21. St. Bonaventure says that there is no devotion better calculated to sanctify people than meditation on the Passion of Jesus Christ, and he advises us to meditate every day on the Passion if we wish to make progress in the love of God. De Bustis cites St. Augustine that a single tear shed in memory of the Passion has greater value than a fasting once a week on bread and water.[22] That is why the saints have always devoted themselves to meditation on the sufferings of Jesus Christ. By this means, St. Francis of Assisi became a seraph. One day, a gentleman came

upon him weeping and crying aloud, Francis told him: "I weep because of the suffering and ignominy of my Lord, but what makes me sadder still is that the people for whom he suffered so much can live unmindful of it." With that, he began to weep again, and so did the gentleman. At another time when he was ill, someone asked him if he would like to have something read from a spiritual book. He answered: "My book is Jesus crucified," and that is why he exhorted his friars always to think on the Passion of Jesus Christ. Tiepolo writes: "No one who does not fall in love with God when they contemplate Jesus dead on a cross, will ever fall in love."[23]

Chapter 2: How Much Jesus Christ Deserves Our Love in Return for the Love He Has Shown Us in Instituting the Sacrament of the Altar.

1. "Jesus knew that his hour had come to pass from this world to the Father. He loved his own in the world and he loved them to the end" (Jn 13:1). Knowing that the time had come for him to leave this earth and that he was soon to die for us, our loving Savior wished to leave us the greatest gift his love could give, the gift of the most holy sacrament. St. Bernardino of Siena says that those tokens of love which are given at death remain firmly engraved on the memory and are the most treasured. People on their death-bed often make a last bequest of an article of clothing or a ring to their friends as a token of their affection. But you, Jesus, as you were on the point of leaving this world, what was the token of love that you left us? It was not an article of clothing or a ring, but your body and your blood, your soul and divinity, your whole self. As St. John Chrysostom expresses it: "He gave you everything, he left himself nothing."

2. The Council of Trent says that in this sacrament, Jesus Christ "poured out, as it were, the riches of his divine love on humanity."[24] The Apostle points out that it was on the very night on which his enemies were preparing to put him to death that Jesus gave us this gift: "the Lord Jesus, on the night he was handed over, took bread, and after he had given thanks, broke it and said,

'This is my body that is for you'" (1 Cor 11:23–24). According to St. Bernardino of Siena, he was not simply ready to die for us, but before dying was constrained by the excess of his love to give us his own body as food.

3. This sacrament was rightly called by St. Thomas Aquinas "the sacrament and the pledge of love." It is a "sacrament of love" because it was love alone which led Jesus to give us himself completely in it; it is a "pledge of love," so that if we were ever to doubt his love, we might have its proof of it in this sacrament.[25] [...] St. Bernard called it "the love of loves." It contains every other gift the Lord has given us—creation, redemption, the call to glory. The Eucharist is not alone the pledge of Christ's love; it is also a pledge that he wishes to give us paradise, or, as the church says, "the pledge of future glory is given to us." St. Philip Neri could call Jesus in the Blessed Sacrament by no other name than love. When viaticum was brought to him, he was heard to exclaim, "Here is my love, give me my love."

4. Could anyone ever have been able to imagine that the Word become flesh would take on the appearance of bread to become our food unless he himself had already done so? St. Augustine asks whether the saying "eat my flesh and drink my blood" is not madness. When Jesus revealed to his disciples his intention of leaving us this sacrament, they were unable to believe it and abandoned him, saying, "How can this man give us his flesh to eat?" and "This saying is hard. Who can accept it?" (Jn 6:53, 61). The great love of Jesus Christ has conceived and brought about what human beings could not imagine or even believe. What is the food, Savior of the world, which you desired to give us before you died? "This is my body" (1 Cor 11:24): This is no earthly food, it is I giving myself to you.

5. Jesus desires very much to come to us in Holy Communion: "I have eagerly desired to eat this Passover with you" (Lk 22:15). According to St. Lawrence Justinian, "This is the voice of the most outspoken love." He left himself to us under the appearance of bread so that everyone might be able to receive him. If he had left himself under the appearance of some rare or costly food, the poor would not have been able to receive him. But he

left himself under the appearance of bread, which is cheap and is available to everyone, so that people in every land could find him and receive him.

6. In order to draw us to receive him in Holy Communion, he invites us to "Come, eat of my food,/and drink the wine I have mixed!" (Prv 9:5), and "eat, friends; drink!" meaning the heavenly bread and wine (Sg 5:1). He even imposes a commandment on us: "Take it; this is my body" (Mk 14:22). He encourages us by promising us paradise: "Whoever eats my flesh and drinks my blood has eternal life" (Jn 6:54); "Whoever eats this bread will live forever" (Jn 6:58). He goes as far as threatening us with exclusion from paradise should we refuse: "Unless you eat the flesh of the Son of Man and drink his blood, you do not have life within you" (Jn 6:53). All of these invitations, promises, and threats are born of his great desire to come to us in this sacrament.

7. Here is the reason why Jesus desires so much to come in Holy Communion. According to St. Denis, love always aspires and tends toward union, or as St. Thomas puts it, "Lovers desire that the two become one." He means that people who are truly in love want to be as close to one another as though they were a single person. God's great love has so arranged things that he gives himself to us not just in the eternal kingdom, but even here below he allows us to possess him in the greatest intimacy possible, by giving himself to us under the appearance of bread in this sacrament. He is like the lover in the Canticle: "Here he stands behind our wall,/gazing through the windows,/peering through the lattices" (Sg 2:9). Even though we cannot see him in the Eucharist, he sees us and is really present there. He is present so that we can possess him, but hidden in order that we might desire him. Until such time as we come to our homeland, Jesus wishes to give himself completely to us and to remain completely united with us.

8. He was not able to satisfy his love by giving himself to the human race through his Incarnation and Passion, although he died for every human being. He wished to find a way to give himself to each one of us. He instituted the Sacrament of the Altar in order to be united with us. "Whoever eats my flesh and

drinks my blood remains in me and I in him" (Jn 6:56). In Holy Communion, Jesus unites himself to the soul and the soul is united to Jesus. It does not simply depend on feelings, for it is a true and real union. That is why St. Francis de Sales said: "Here the Savior is seen at his most tender and loving. Here, he seems to annihilate himself, and to reduce himself to food in order to enter into our souls, and be united with the hearts of his faithful." St. John Chrysostom says that it was out of his great love for us that Jesus Christ wished to unite himself to us so much in order that we might become the same thing as he is.

9. "How wonderful is your love, Lord Jesus," adds St. Lawrence Justinian, "that you wished to incorporate us into your body in such a way that we might have one heart and soul with you." St. Bernardino of Siena remarks that Jesus Christ's giving himself to us as food was the ultimate degree of love, for he gives himself to us to become totally one with us just as food becomes one with the person who eats it. [...]

10. We should be convinced that no one can do, nor even conceive of doing, anything more pleasing to Jesus Christ than of communicating with the dispositions appropriate to the great guest they are to receive. I say "with the dispositions appropriate," not "in a worthy state," for if it were a matter of being worthy, who would ever be able to communicate? Only another God would be worthy to receive God. I mean "appropriate" insofar as that is possible for a poor creature clothed with the frail flesh of Adam. It is enough that a person, ordinarily speaking, receive in the state of grace and with a lively desire to grow in the love of Jesus Christ. "You should only receive Jesus Christ in holy communion out of love, since he gives himself to us only out of love" says St. Francis de Sales. [...]

Chapter 3: The Great Trust We Should Place in the Love Which Jesus Christ Has Shown Us in Everything He Has Done for Us.

1. David placed all his hope for salvation in the coming Redeemer and said "Into your hands I commend my spirit;/you

will redeem me, LORD, faithful God" (Ps 31:6). We are even more justified in placing our confidence in Jesus Christ, since he has already come and accomplished the work of redemption. We should repeat frequently and with great confidence, "Into your hands I commend my spirit, you have redeemed me, Lord, faithful God."

2. Although we have good cause to dread eternal death on account of how we have offended God, we have still greater motives for hoping for eternal life through Jesus Christ, whose merits are of infinitely greater value for our salvation than are our own merits for bringing us to perdition. We have sinned and deserved to be lost, but the Redeemer came to take on the burden of our offenses and to make satisfaction for them by what he suffered: "Yet it was our infirmities that he bore,/our sufferings that he endured" (Is 53:4).

3. At the very moment we sinned, God had already written out our sentence of eternal death. But what did our merciful Redeemer do? "Obliterating the bond against us, with its legal claims...he also removed it from our midst, nailing it to the cross" (Col 2:14). He canceled with his blood the decree of our condemnation. Then he fixed it to the Cross so that when we looked for our sentence of judgment, we would see the Cross where the dying Jesus canceled it out with his blood and thereby take hope of pardon and eternal salvation [...]

5. It is true that we shall have to render a strict account of every sin to the eternal judge. But who is our judge to be? "The Father...has given all judgment to his Son" (Jn 5:22). Our consolation lies in the knowledge that the eternal Father has entrusted the task of judging us to the one who is also our Redeemer. St. Paul gives us heart when he says, "Who will condemn? It is Christ [Jesus] who died, rather, was raised, who also is at the right hand of God, who indeed intercedes for us" (Rom 8:34). [...]

6. If, knowing our own weakness, we fear that we will succumb to the assaults of the enemy against whom we must still do combat, we should follow the Apostle's advice: "Let us...persevere in running the race that lies before us while keeping our eyes fixed on Jesus, the leader and perfecter of our faith. For the sake

of the joy that lay before him he has endured the cross, despising its shame, and has taken his seat at the right of the throne of God" (Heb 12:1-2). We must go forward courageously to the fight, our eyes fixed on Jesus crucified who, from the Cross, offers us his help, and assures us of the victor's crown. We have fallen in the past because we left off contemplating the wounds and the disgrace suffered by our Redeemer and forgot to turn to him for help. If, for the future, we keep before our eyes how much he has suffered for us and how ready he is to help us if we turn to him, we can be certain that the enemy will not triumph. With her usual generous spirit, St. Teresa remarked, "I don't understand these timid cries of 'The devil! The devil!' when we can say 'God! God!' and make the devil tremble!" On the other hand, she also said that unless we place all our confidence in God, all our diligence will be of little or no use to us: "All is of little benefit if we do not place the trust we have in ourselves in God."

7. The two great mysteries of hope and love are the Passion of Jesus Christ and the Sacrament of the Altar. Without the assurance of faith, who could ever believe them? An omnipotent God willed to become man, to shed his blood to the last drop and to die in anguish on a gallows—why? To pay for our sins and to save us rebels! Then he wished to give us his body, once sacrificed for us on the Cross, as our food so that through it, he could become united to each one of us. Could sinners, however dissolute, ever despair of pardon if, moved by the sight of a God who loves them so much, they repent of the wrong they have done? St. Bonaventure says, "I act in faith, hoping immovably that nothing necessary for salvation will be denied me by him who did so much and bore so much for my salvation."

8. The Apostle exhorts us, "So let us confidently approach the throne of grace to receive mercy and to find grace for timely help" (Heb. 4:16). The Cross is the throne from which Jesus dispenses grace to anyone who has recourse to him. We must come to him speedily, so that we can find the help we need for our salvation, for a time will come when we will not be able to find him any more. Our wretchedness should not dishearten us: In Jesus Christ we find all the richness and all the grace we need: "In him

you were enriched in every way...so that you are not lacking in any spiritual gift" (1 Cor 1:5, 7). The merits of Jesus Christ have enriched us with wealth of God, and made it possible for us to receive every grace we desire.

9. St. Leo says that the good Jesus brought us with his death far outweighed the harm the devil wrought through sin. He is simply repeating the words of St. Paul: "The gift is not like the transgression...where sin increased, grace overflowed all the more" (Rom 5:15, 20). The Savior inspires us to hope for every favor and for every grace through his merits: "Amen, amen, I say to you, whatever you ask the Father in my name he will give you" (Jn 16:23). Could the Father deny us any grace if he has given us his only Son whom he loves as he loves himself? "He...handed him over for us all, how will he not give us everything else along with him?" (Rom 8:32). The Apostle says "everything." That means that no grace is excluded—neither pardon, nor perseverance, nor love, nor perfection, nor paradise—he has given us everything, everything. But we must ask for it. God is generous to those who pray to him, "enriching all who call upon him" (Rom 10:12). [...]

15. If you believe that the eternal Father has given you his Son, trust then that he will give you everything else, for nothing is greater than his Son. You cannot think that Jesus Christ has forgotten you when he has left you the greatest pledge of his love, his very self in the Sacrament of the Altar.

Chapter 5: Love Is Patient.
Whoever loves Jesus Christ will welcome suffering.

1. If this earth is a place for gaining merit, it follows that it will be a place of suffering. Paradise is our true homeland, and in its joy, God has prepared our eternal rest. The time we spend in this world is comparatively short, but we will have many hardships to endure. "Man born of woman/is short-lived and full of trouble" (Jb 14:1). Everyone, saint or sinner, has to suffer, has some cross to carry. Those who carry it patiently will be saved, those who carry it impatiently will be lost. St. Augustine remarks

that the same trial dispatches some to paradise, and others to perdition, and that suffering is the test which separates the grain from the chaff in the church of God. Those who are humble and resigned to the will of God are grain fit for paradise; the chaff is those who grow impatient and forsake him.

2. If we are to receive the judgment of the elect, we must live in conformity with the life of Jesus Christ: "For those he foreknew he also predestined to be conformed to the image of his Son, so that he might be the firstborn among many brothers" (Rom 8:29). The Eternal Word came among us to teach us by his example how to carry the crosses God sends us. "For to this you have been called," writes St. Peter, "because Christ also suffered for you, leaving you an example that you should follow in his footsteps" (1 Pt 2:21).

3. God treats those he loves and considers his children in the same way he treated Jesus, his beloved Son: "For whom the Lord loves, he disciplines;/he scourges every son he acknowledges" (Heb 12:6). Jesus told St. Teresa, "You ought to realize that the people dearest to my Father are those who have to endure the greatest sufferings." During one time of suffering, she said that she would not exchange her lot for all the treasures in the world. She appeared to someone after her death and told the person that the great reward she enjoyed in heaven was the result, not of her good works, but of her generosity in suffering during her life for love of God, and that if she had any cause to return to this earth, it would be so that she might suffer something more for God's sake.

4. Those who continue to love God in midst of suffering gain a double reward. According to St. Vincent de Paul, it is a misfortune not to have something to suffer in this life. He held that religious congregations and individuals who met with everyone's approval, and never experienced suffering were heading for disaster. St. Francis of Assisi believed that if a day passed in which he had no cross to bear, it was a sign that God had forgotten him. According to St. John Chrysostom, the grace of suffering is a greater gift than the power of raising the dead. When someone performs miracles, they are in God's debt, but if they have to suffer,

God places himself in their debt. He adds that anyone who suffers for God will receive a great reward, and that Paul's grace of being in chains for Jesus Christ's sake was superior to the grace he was given of being caught up to the third heaven.

5. "Patience must complete its work" ([ed.] Jas 1:4), that is to say, nothing is more pleasing to God than a person who bears patiently and in peace all the crosses he sends. Love makes the lover like the beloved. According to St. Francis de Sales, our Redeemer's wounds teach us how far we ought to go in bearing suffering for his sake. The science of the saints is readiness to suffer constantly for Jesus, for that is how we become saints. Anyone who loves Jesus Christ will be eager to be treated like Jesus, who was poor, tortured, and despised. St. John saw all the saints clothed in white garments and with palms in their hands (cf. Rv 8:9). Why were they carrying the palm, the emblem of martyrdom, if they were not all martyrs? St. Gregory replies that every saint is a martyr, either by the sword or by his or her patience.

6. Those who loves Jesus Christ gain their real reward through love and suffering. The Lord said to St. Teresa: "Do you think, daughter, that you can earn your reward through a life of pleasure? No, you will earn it through loving and suffering. Remember how full of suffering my life was. You should measure my Father's love for someone by the amount of suffering the person receives from him, for that is how love is reckoned. Consider my wounds, for your pains will never go so far. It is foolish to think that my Father will admit people to his friendship without effort on their part." Then, for our encouragement, she adds that God never sends a trial without paying it back with a favor.

Jesus Christ appeared once to Blessed Baptista Varani and told her he gives his chosen ones three great favors: first, he keeps them from sin; second, he enables them to do good works; but the third, and the greatest of all, is that he allows them to suffer something for love of him.[26] St. Teresa says he repays those who work for him by sending them a test. The saints were always grateful for the trials they had to face. In describing his time of slavery among the Turks, St. Louis of France said, "I am more grateful to God for giving me patience during my imprisonment than if I had gained the whole world." After the death of her husband, St. Elizabeth of Hungary was banished along with her son. Homeless and abandoned, she made her way to a Franciscan convent where she had a *Te Deum* sung in thanksgiving for the favor of suffering for love of God.

7. In saying "No toil is too great to gain heaven," St. Joseph Calasanctius was only repeating the words of St. Paul, "I consider that the sufferings of this present time are as nothing compared with the glory to be revealed for us" (Rom 8:18). If you were to spend your whole life enduring the sufferings of all the martyrs, it would be worth it for a single moment of paradise. You should welcome your crosses, then, knowing that the sufferings of this short life will win you eternal happiness. "For this momentary light affliction is producing for us an eternal weight of glory beyond all comparison" (2 Cor 4:17). To gain the crown of paradise, it is necessary to struggle and suffer: "If we persevere/we shall also reign with him" (2 Tm 2:12). As for the prize: "An athlete cannot receive the winner's crown except by competing according to the rules" (2 Tm 2:5), and the greater the endurance, the greater the crown. Isn't it extraordinary the effort some people put into gaining a worldly advantage, but when it comes to eternal life, they'll say "A little corner in heaven will be good enough for me." That was never the attitude of the saints. They were satisfied with the things of this life, and were even ready to renounce them, but when it came to eternal life, they tried to gain as much as they could. Which do you think is the wiser course?

8. Even considering the matter in purely worldly terms, you can rest assured that a person who suffers patiently will enjoy peace of heart. St. Philip Neri held that there is no purgatory in this life, only paradise or hell, and anyone who endures trials with patience will enjoy paradise, otherwise, they will have to endure a hell. The truth is, as St. Teresa points out, anyone who welcomes the crosses that God sends will not really feel them. At one particularly critical time in his life, St. Francis de Sales wrote: "For some time now, the opposition and criticism which have come my way have brought me a peace so calm that nothing

can compare with it. It foretells that my soul will soon be at rest in its God. In all truth, that is my ambition and my one and only heart's desire." Anyone who lives a disordered life will never have peace; it can be found only by those who live united to God and his holy will. A missionary in the Indies was once called to minister to a man on the scaffold. He told him: "Father, I once belonged to your order. As long as I kept the rule, I was content. Once I became careless, everything was a burden. Finally, I left the order and abandoned myself to every vice, and so have come to the wretched state in which you now see me. I am telling you all this so that my example can serve as a lesson to others." Venerable Father Louis da Ponte said, "Treat the pleasant things in this life as though they were bitter, and the bitter as though they were pleasant: in that way you will always find peace."[27] No matter how pleasing to the senses sweet things may be, they leave a bitter aftertaste, for they cannot bring us true satisfaction. On the other hand, once bitter things are accepted lovingly as coming from the hand of God, they become sweet and precious.

9. Since we are all wounded by sin, only those who accept and lovingly welcome suffering as coming from God's hand will find peace in this life. Saints here below suffer in love; saints in paradise enjoy in love. In a letter of encouragement to one of his penitents, Father Paul Segneri the Younger suggested that she fix to the foot of the crucifix the words "This is how you should love."[28] Readiness to suffer for love of Jesus Christ, and not the mere fact of suffering alone, is the surest measure of a person's love. "Can there be any greater possession," asks St. Teresa, "than the sign that we are doing what pleases God?" Unfortunately, many people take fright at the merest mention of words such as *cross, humiliation,* or *suffering.* On the other hand, there are many generous people who find their entire happiness in suffering and who would be almost inconsolable if they had to live without it. "Seeing Jesus crucified," said one holy person, "makes the cross so precious that it seems to be impossible to be happy without suffering. The love Jesus's Christ is enough for me." "Take up [your] cross daily and follow me" (Lk 9:23) is Jesus' invitation to

all who wish to follow him, but we must carry it humbly, patiently, and lovingly, not unwillingly or with ill grace.

10. God is pleased when someone takes up the cross he sends with humility and patience. [...] According to John of Avila, "A single 'Blessed be God' when things are not going our way is worth a thousand words of thanks when they are in our favor." Blessed Angela of Foligno said that if people understood the value of suffering for God's sake, they would almost be in competition with one another in looking for fresh opportunities. St. Mary Magdalene de' Pazzi understood the value of suffering, and wished to live rather than to go to heaven straight away, saying "in heaven, there is no more suffering."

11. Anyone who loves God will have no other aim in this life than that of reaching complete union with him. We should learn from what St. Catherine of Genoa says: "Adversity is necessary if we are to arrive at perfect union with God, for this is the means God uses to burn away all our interior and exterior sinful inclinations. That is why anything that goes against the grain is very necessary, because it throws us into battle, and with every victory, our evil desires are overcome and they no longer trouble us. We shall never arrive at union with God until adversity appears sweet rather than bitter."

12. Anyone who desires to belong completely to God will seek suffering rather than enjoyment here below, and, as St. John of the Cross teaches, will seek opportunities for voluntary mortification, or better still, for involuntary ones, as these are more pleasing to God. "A patient man is better than a warrior," says Solomon (Prv 16:32). Those who mortify themselves with fasts, chains, or the discipline please God by their strength of character, but he will be even more pleased by their strength in bearing patiently and joyfully the crosses he sends them. St. Francis de Sales says: "Mortifications coming to us either directly from God or from others with his consent are always more precious than those which are the offspring of our own will. It is a good general rule that, wherever there is less of our own choice involved, we will give more glory to God and find more profit for ourselves." St. Teresa's advice is similar: "We gain more from the trials which

129

come to us from God or from our neighbor in a single day than we would in ten years of sufferings chosen by ourselves." [...]

13. Let us ask the Lord to make us worthy of his love. If we love him perfectly, worldly things will seem like a wisp of smoke or a speck of dust, and we will value instead humiliation and suffering. "Those who have attained perfect love," says Chrysostom, "seem to be alone on earth. They care for neither fame nor insults, they discount temptations and sufferings, they lose the taste and appetite for everything. Finding no other support or rest, they go tirelessly in search of the beloved. Whether they are working, eating, watching, sleeping, their only thought and ambition is to find the beloved, because where their treasure is, there their heart is also."

Chapter 6: Love Is Kind.
Whoever loves Jesus Christ, loves kindness.

1. God is kindness itself, and so anyone who loves God will love all those that God loves and be ready to help everyone, to console everyone, and to make them happy insofar as they are able. St. Francis de Sales, a very model of kindness, says "Unassuming kindness is the greatest virtue God recommends, so it should be practiced always and by everyone." He gives the following rule: "If you see anything you can do with love, do it, and omit whatever you cannot do without strife." That is, of course, anything that can be omitted without offending God, because an offense against God should always be prevented at once, by anyone whose duty it is to prevent it.

2. Kindness should be shown to the poor especially, since they are often treated harshly simply because they are poor. It should also be shown in a particular way to the sick, who often meet with little understanding from others. Most of all, it should be shown to our enemies: "Conquer evil with good" (Rom 12:21). Hatred is overcome by love, persecution by meekness. Acting in this way, the saints won the affection of even their most stubborn opponents.

3. "Nothing," St. Francis de Sales says, "has such an influence on our neighbors as treating them kindly." He was identified by his gracious smile and by his kindly words and actions. St. Vincent de Paul said he never knew a more kind person and that he seemed the very image of the kindness of Jesus Christ. Even when he had to refuse a favor he could not in conscience grant, he did so with such kindness that people went away well-disposed toward him and at peace with themselves. He was kind toward everyone, unlike those whom he termed "house angels and street devils." He seldom rebuked his servants for their failures, or at least when he was obliged to do so, it was always with a few kindly words. It would be a blessing if all superiors could imitate him, for superiors should always be as kind as possible to those who are under them. If something needs to be done, they should request rather than command. St. Vincent de Paul says that there is no better way for a superior to be obeyed than gentleness, while St. Jane Frances de Chantal says, "I have tried several ways of exercising authority, but there is none better than gentleness and patience."

4. A superior should be kind even when pointing out faults. Firmness may occasionally be necessary, especially in a serious matter, or if a fault is repeated after it has been brought to the person's notice. Still, we should be careful about correcting someone harshly or in anger, for that does more harm than good. There are people who pride themselves in making their families toe the line, and who would claim that is the best way to keep them in order, but it is not what St. James recommends: "But if you have bitter jealousy and selfish ambition in your hearts, do not boast and be false to the truth" (Jas 3:14).[29] In the occasional rare case where a few sharp words are necessary to bring people to their senses, we should always part with a smile and a final word of kindness. Like the Samaritan in the gospel story, we should bind up the wounds, pouring on oil and wine, for just as oil rises to the surface, kindness should come out on top in everything. If the one to be corrected is worked up, it is better to leave the correction until the person has cooled down,

otherwise you will only provoke the individual further. When the house is on fire, there is no need to throw on more timber.

5. Jesus rebuked his disciples James and John for wanting to have the Samaritans who had driven them from their town repaid with fire from heaven (cf. Lk 8:55). They did not have the same attitude he did. The Son of Man came to seek out and to save what was lost. Think of the kindness with which he treated the adulterous woman: "Woman,...Has no one condemned you?...Neither do I condemn you. Go, [and] from now on, do not sin any more" (Jn 8:10–11). It was enough for him simply to admonish her not to sin any more and to send her away in peace. He won over the Samaritan woman with similar kindness. First, he asked for something to drink; then he said, "If you knew who it was asking you for a drink." Finally, he revealed that he was the expected messiah. With gentleness he tried to win back the unfortunate Judas, even allowing him to eat from the same dish, washing his feet, and in the very act of betrayal, saying to him, "Judas, are you betraying the Son of Man with a kiss?" (Lk 22:48). How did he win Peter after he had denied him? "The Lord turned and looked at Peter" (Lk 22:61). That gentle look changed him so deeply, that, for the rest of his life, Peter never ceased to regret the wrong he had done his master.

6. There is more to be gained from gentleness than from bitterness. St. Francis de Sales says there are few things more bitter than an almond, but once it is preserved, it becomes sweet and delicious. Correction can be unpleasant, but done with love and kindness, it is acceptable and produces good results. St. Vincent de Paul relates that, in the direction of his congregation, he corrected people sharply three times when he believed he had reason to do so, but none of the three occasions produced as successful results as the many times he had corrected with kindness.

7. By his kindness, St. Francis de Sales was able to get other people to do what he wanted, and was successful in attracting even obstinate sinners to God. St. Vincent de Paul gave his followers this maxim: "Courtesy, love and humility work wonderfully in winning people's hearts, and leading them to do things which nature finds distasteful." Once he sent a great sinner to

one his fathers to be prepared for confession. The priest tried everything without success, so he finally begged the saint to have a few words with him. Vincent spoke with him, and the sinner said it was Vincent's outstanding kindness which won him over. He would never permit his missionaries to treat their penitents harshly, and warned them that the devil uses the harshness of a few to bring about the ruin of many.

8. We should practice kindness toward every one, in all occasions and at all times. St. Bernard notes how some people are all sweetness and light as long as things are going their way, but, at the slightest contradiction, the begin to smolder like Mount Vesuvius. They are like burning embers hidden under the ashes. Anyone who wishes to become a saint should rather be like a lily among thorns: No matter what angle the thorns come from, they never cease being lilies of gentleness and kindness. People who love God know how to preserve their inner peace, and it even shows on their faces, for they always appear even-tempered no matter what comes their way, as Cardinal Petrucci wrote:

> Of outward things, they view the varying styles,
> While in their hearts' inmost depths,
> Undimmed, God's image lies.[30]

9. A person's real character comes through when the going gets rough. St. Francis de Sales loved the Visitation Order whose foundation had cost him so much trouble. Several times, he saw it in danger of collapse, yet he never lost his peace, and would have been content to see it destroyed if that was God's will. "For some time now, the opposition and criticism which have come my way have brought me a peace so calm that nothing can compare with it. It foretells that my soul will soon be at rest in its God which is my ambition and my one and only heart's desire."

10. If there is need to reply to someone who is treating us badly, we should be careful to do it gently: "A mild answer calms wrath" (Prv 15:1). If we are upset, we might feel justified in saying the first word which comes to our lips, but when we have calmed down, we will realize that those words would not have been appropriate, so the best rule is to say nothing for the moment.

133

11. Finally, we should be gentle with ourselves after we have committed a fault. Getting angry with ourselves is not humility; it is, rather, a subtle form of pride, which makes us forget the weak people we really are. St. Teresa says, "If humility upsets us, it is not from God but from the demon." Getting angry with ourselves after a fault is greater defect than the fault itself, for it can lead to a whole chain of other faults. It can make us give up our prayers, meditation, or holy communion, or even if we do perform them, it will be only with half a heart. St. Aloysius Gonzaga once said that the devil fishes in muddy waters. When people are upset, they forget what God expects of them. When we slip, it is best to turn to God with humility and confidence, asking his forgiveness in the words of St. Catherine of Genoa, "Lord, this is the only thing my garden can grow at the moment!" I love you with all my heart, and I repent of having offended you. With your help, I will not do so again.

Chapter 7: "Love Is Not Jealous." A person who loves Jesus Christ does not envy worldly greatness, but competes only with those who love Jesus Christ more.

1. St. Gregory explains this next sign of love: "It is not envious because, desiring nothing in this life, it is incapable of envying worldly success." There are two kinds of rivalry, one evil and the other holy. The evil kind is jealous, begrudging others the worldly goods they have. Holy rivalry is not envious; instead it pities the great ones of this world who must live in the midst of honors and worldly pleasures. Since people like this seek God alone, their only aim in life is to love him as much as possible, and they envy in a holy way those who love him more than they do, because they want to outdo even the seraphim in love.

2. This desire so charms the heart of God that he says: "You have ravished my heart, my sister, my bride;/you have ravished my heart with one glance of your eyes" (Sg 4:9). The "one glance" is a reference to the single-mindedness of their desire to please God in every thought or action. Unlike worldly people who often act with an eye to their own advantage, saints are single-minded, for in

everything they do, their one objective is how best to please God. Like David, they can say "Whom else have I in the heavens?/None beside you delights me on earth./Though my flesh and my heart fail,/God is the rock of my heart, my portion forever" (Ps 73:25–26). St. Paulinus says, "Let the rich enjoy their treasures, kings their realms, you Christ, are my glory and my kingdom."

3. We ought to realize that it is not enough merely to perform good works; it is also necessary to perform them well. If we wish our actions to be perfect, we should perform them with the single aim of pleasing God. Jesus was praised for having done all things well (cf Mk 7:37). Many things can be praiseworthy in themselves, but if they are done for some other purpose than God's glory, they are worth little or even nothing in his sight. St. Mary Magadalene de' Pazzi used to say, "God repays our actions according to the weight of their purity." She meant that if the intention is pure, God will accept them and reward us for them. It can be very difficult to find an action which is done solely for God. I remember a holy old religious, who had worn himself out in God's service and died with a reputation for sanctity, saying sadly one day, "When I look back over my life, I cannot find a single thing done solely for God." Through self-love we can lose a large part, or even all, of the fruit of our good actions. There are people, even including preachers, confessors, or missionaries, who toil and strain but gain little because they are not acting for God alone, but from motives of self-interest, or because they love the limelight, or even simply because they are following their own inclinations.

4. The Lord says, "Take care not to perform righteous deeds in order that people may see them; otherwise, you will have no recompense from your heavenly Father" (Mt 6:1). Those putting all their effort simply into suiting themselves have already received their reward. The passing satisfaction is, in any case, like a puff of smoke disappearing quickly and leaving little profit behind. The prophet Haggai says that those who exhaust themselves for any other purpose than pleasing God are like people putting their wages into a torn bag, and when they go to look for them, they find nothing: "He who earned wages/earned them for

a bag with holes in it" (Hg 1:6). If they become discouraged when their efforts fail to achieve results, it can be a sign that they are not working solely for the glory of God. When people undertake something for God's glory, they are in no way upset if it turns out to be a failure; acting with the right intention, they have achieved already what they set out to do, namely, to give glory to God.

5. Here are a few signs which may help those working in the apostolate to discern whether or not they are working solely for God. First, they do not get upset if they do not obtain the results they set out to achieve, because they are at peace in the realization that, if it is not what God wants, they should not want it either. Second, they are as pleased with the good achieved by others as they are with their own successes. Third, they express no preferences about the kind of work they do, but are content with whatever is decided by obedience. Fourth, when the work is done, they seek neither approval nor thanks from others. In fact, they do not even mind if others criticize or express disapproval, because they are satisfied that they have sought to please God. On the other hand, if they do receive a word of praise, it does not turn their heads, but, like John of Avila, they reply to any feelings of pride which might be stirred up with "Too late for vanity, everything has been done for God."

6. This is the meaning of God's promise that his faithful servants would "enter into the master's joy." If we happen to do something pleasing to God, have we a right to expect any other reward? The greatest reward or happiness a creature can have is to please the Creator.

7. Jesus asks those who love him to "set me as a seal on your heart,/as a seal on your arm" (Sg 8:6). "A seal on the heart" means that in planning, one makes the intention of acting solely for the love of God; "on the arm" means having God's good pleasure as the only goal of our thoughts and actions. St. Teresa says that a person who wants to become a saint should live with no other desire than that of pleasing God. One of her first nuns, Beatrice of the Incarnation, said, "Even the slightest action done for God is priceless." She was right, for everything done for God's sake unites us with him and wins us an eternal reward.

8. Purity of intention is the heavenly alchemy which turns iron into gold, so that even the most trivial acts, such as our daily chores, eating a meal, taking recreation or rest, become the gold of love, by being done for God's sake. St. Mary Magdalene de' Pazzi believed that anyone who had tried to act with a pure intention went directly to paradise without passing through purgatory. One of the Desert Fathers used to stop for a moment and raise his eyes to heaven before undertaking any action. He explained that he did so in order to make his aim more accurate. Like an archer looking carefully at the target before releasing the arrow, he looked toward God so that he could be sure of his aim. We might act likewise by renewing our intention of pleasing God in everything from time to time.

9. People who seek nothing but God's will enjoy the freedom of the children of God, and welcome whatever pleases him, no matter how deeply it may go against the grain of self-love or human respect. If we love Jesus Christ, we will be indifferent to everything, whether it is bitter or pleasant, and we will want nothing for ourselves, but only what pleases God. We will undertake important things and trivial, pleasant and unpleasant, with the same peace.

10. Some people want to serve God, but they set conditions about the employment, the place, the companions. If their expectations are not met, they work with an ill-will or give up altogether. People like that lack inner freedom, and, since they are slaves of self-love, they will gain little from what they do. They live without inner peace and the yoke of Jesus Christ weighs heavily on them. Those who truly love God delight in doing what pleases him and in the way he has chosen, whether it be in the public eye or in obscurity. That is what loving Jesus Christ means, and we should bend our energies toward it, fighting against any feeling of self-love which would prefer to see us in important and prestigious occupations in keeping with our own tastes.

11. We should cultivate a similar freedom even with regard to spiritual exercises, should the Lord wish to make use of us in some other way. Father Alvarez was once very busy and, feeling distant from God, wanted to take a short break for prayer. The

Lord said to him, "Even if I do not always keep you alongside me, it should be enough for you that I make use of you."[31] The same holds true for people who become uneasy when they have to omit their usual devotions through service of others or obedience. Their unease is not from God, but from either the demon or their self-love. "Please God and die," that is the maxim of the saints.

Chapter 8: Love Is Not Pompous. Anyone who loves Jesus Christ flees from tepidity and loves perfection. The means of perfection are: (1) desire; (2) resolution; (3) mental prayer; (4) holy communion; and (5) prayer of petition.

1. In his explanation of the verse "love is not pompous," St. Gregory the Great says that since it leads the way to an ever-deepening commitment to God, love makes room only for what is just and holy. St. Paul describes this precisely when he told us: "Over all these put on love, that is, the bond of perfection" (Col 3:14). Since divine love aims for perfection, it will have no time for the kind of tepidity with which some people serve God, and thereby run the risk of losing everything—love, divine grace, themselves.

2. You should understand that there are two kinds of tepidity. The first is unavoidable, but the other can be avoided. Not even the saints were free of the first kind. Some faults are committed without our ever fully willing them, for they are simply the result of our human weakness. They include, for instance, distractions at prayer, useless chatter, idle curiosity, a desire to shine, choosiness in eating or drinking, the first stirrings of sexual pleasure, and so forth. We should avoid them insofar as we are able, but since our nature is weakened by sin, it is not possible to avoid them totally. If we do yield to them, we should regret offending God in this way, but not allow them to disturb us unduly. St. Francis de Sales writes that "no thought which causes us disquiet can come from God who is the prince of peace, and so they must come from the demon, our self-love or from the exaggerated opinion we make of ourselves."

3. We should put away thoughts like that at once and make nothing of them. The same saint says that faults committed with

138

little thought are wiped out speedily by an act of sorrow or an act of love. Holy Communion does the same, as the Council of Trent teaches when it calls the Eucharist the "antidote that frees us from daily sins." Although they are certainly faults, they do not hinder us from perfection, or rather, from walking the road that leads to perfection, for no one is ever perfect until the person reaches the Kingdom of Heaven.

4. The tepidity which does slow us down on the way to perfection is the avoidable kind, that is to say, venial sin deliberately committed. Even in our present state, God's grace makes it possible for us to avoid committing faults with our eyes open. Examples of this kind of fault might be deliberate lies, grumbling, swearing, mocking another, engaging in resentful or quarrelsome talk, bragging about our own importance, nursing grievances, or sentimental attachments to the opposite sex. That is why St. Teresa said, "From deliberate sin, no matter how small, may the good Lord deliver you!" She described faults like these as mites which we only notice once they have begun to ruin our virtue, and warns us that the devil can make use of carelessness in small matters to makes holes through which greater sins can eventually make their way.

5. You should be careful about deliberate faults, if only because on their account God withholds light and help, and withdraws spiritual consolation from us. That is why some people find their spiritual duties wearisome and painful, and grow slack about prayer, communion, visits to the Blessed Sacrament, novenas, and sometimes, unfortunately, even give up everything.

6. The Lord warns such lukewarm people: "I know that you are neither cold nor hot. I wish you were either cold or hot. So, because you are lukewarm, neither hot nor cold, I will spit you out of my mouth" (Rv 3:15–16). Isn't it astonishing that he says "I wish you were cold"? How could it possibly be better to be cold, that is, deprived of grace, than lukewarm? The reason is that if you are cold, at least your conscience can still be stirred to make some improvement, whereas lukewarm people who slumber soundly despite their faults and never give a moment's thought to change make one despair that they will ever improve. Once

139

fervor begins to turn to tepidity, the outlook is bleak. Venerable Louis da Ponte admitted to numerous faults during his life, but said that he had never made peace with them. Some people destroy themselves by making peace with their faults, especially when the fault is one which has to do with their sense of their own importance, or a grudge against a neighbor, or a soft attachment to a person of the opposite sex. The danger for people like that is that fine hairs can become chains dragging them to destruction. At the very least, they will fail to become saints and will lose the great crown God had prepared for them had they remained faithful to his grace. Just as a bird soars freely when released from its cage, a person who is free from earthly attachments will fly toward God, but even the finest thread will be enough to hinder his progress. Many people could become saints if only they could summon up the strength to rid themselves of such small attachments.

7. All the damage comes from having too little love for Jesus Christ. Some people are full of their own importance or else become discouraged when things do not turn out exactly as they planned; others develop self-indulgent worries about their health or lavish their affection on anything that comes their way. They live in a state of constant distraction, craving to satisfy their curiosity about everything, including things which are not of the slightest relevance to the service of God. Others resent it if everyone is not dancing to attention for them. One day they are in a high state of devotional excitement; the next, they have become discouraged and sad, depending on whether or not things are going according to their mood. People like that either do not love Jesus Christ at all or else they love him only a little, but they bring true devotion into disrepute.

8. What remedy is there for people who finds themselves in the unfortunate state of tepidity? Although it can be difficult to recover our former fervor once we lose it in this way, the Lord does tell us that he can do what human strength finds impossible. Those who pray and take the right measures will arrive securely at their goal. There are five remedies for tepidity, which enable us to resume the journey to perfection once more: (1) the

desire to for perfection; (2) the resolution to attain it; (3) mental prayer; (4) frequent communion; (5) prayer.

9. First, the desire for perfection. Desires are the wings by which we rise above the earth. According to St. Lawrence Justinian, holy desire "helps our natural strength and makes difficulties appear light." Desire gives us strength for the journey toward perfection and sweetens its difficulties. Those who really want to be perfect will never stop making progress, and, unless they wander from the path, they will arrive safely at their goal. On the other hand, those who lack a genuine desire for perfection and who allow themselves to be carried along simply by natural weakness will find themselves going backward, for, according to St. Augustine, "not to go forward is to go backwards."

10. It would be a serious error to say "God does not want everyone to become a saint." St. Paul says, "This is the will of God, your holiness" (1 Thes 4:3). God wishes everyone to be a saint, but in accordance with their own state in life—the religious as a religious, the person in the world as a person in the world, the priest as a priest, a married person as a married person, a soldier as a soldier, and so on for every other way of life. My great patron St. Teresa has written much about this. She says, for example, "If our desires are great, great good will flow from them." Somewhere else she writes: "There is no need to lower the sights of our desire, but we should trust in God, and keep marching steadily onwards, for we will make steady progress as many saints have done before us," and she went on to give examples of people who, in her experience, had made great progress in a short time through love. She assures us, "The Lord is as satisfied with our desires as if we had already put them into practice," and again, "The Lord only gives special grace to those who desire his love very much." She writes, "God does not allow good desires to pass unrewarded in this life, for he is a friend to generous spirits, provided they do not rely on their own strength too much." Teresa herself had this kind of generous spirit. She told the Lord once that it would not bother her to see people in paradise happier than she was, but that she could not tolerate seeing anyone who had loved more than she did.

11. We should be of good courage: "Good is the LORD to one who waits for him, to the soul that seeks him" (Lam 3:25). God is more than generous to those who seek him wholeheartedly. Even our past sins are no obstacle to our becoming saints, if that is what we really want. St. Teresa warns: "The devil makes great desires or wanting to imitate the saints appear like pride, but determination to do great things is a wonderful help. Even if we find that cannot do them straight away, desire will help us to strike off boldly and arrive sooner at our goal." The Apostle writes that "all things work for good for those who love God" (Rom 8:28). The gloss adds "even sin."[32] Past sins can contribute to our sanctification, since recalling them makes us more humble and more grateful for the great favors God bestows on us despite our having offended him so much. A sinner should say, "I can do nothing, I have deserved to be lost, but I am dealing with a God of infinite goodness who has promised to listen to anyone who prays. Now that he has saved me and is offering me his help to become a saint, I know that I can do it, not through any strength of my own, but through his grace which strengthens me: "I have the strength for everything through him who empowers me" (Phil 4:13). If we begin with good desires, we will make good resolutions, and trusting in God, put them into practice. If we meet an obstacle to our spiritual progress, we should be at peace with what God wills, preferring his will to our own good desires.

12. The second means of perfection is the determination to give oneself totally to God. Many are called to perfection, are drawn toward it by grace, or even acquire the desire for it, but if they lack determination, they will live and die tepid and imperfect. Desire for perfection is not enough unless it is accompanied by a determination to attain it. Many people feed on desires alone, but never take a step on the way that leads to God! This is the kind of desire the sage spoke about: "The sluggard's propensity slays him" (Prv 21:25). A lazy person is full of desires, but never brings them to the point of resolution. He'll say: "If only I were a hermit and not living here at home. If only I could go and live in another monastery, I would serve God devotedly." Meanwhile, unable to stand his companions or bear a single word of criticism, he wears

himself out with needless worries, commits a thousand faults of greed, curiosity, and pride, and then sighs like the wind, "If only I had..., if only I could...." Desire like that does more harm than good. St. Francis de Sales said, "I would never approve of anyone who is already committed to some vocation longing for a different one, nor wanting to perform practices of piety incompatible with it. Behavior like that fritters away their heart and makes them listless in the exercises they should be performing."

13. We must desire perfection, then, and resolutely undertake the means toward acquiring it. St. Teresa writes that "God does not want us simply to make good resolutions and then leave it all to him. The devil has no fear of irresolute souls." One of the purposes of mental prayer is to enable us to lay hold of the helps which will bring us to the perfection of love. Although some people spend a lot of time at prayer, they never come to any resolution as a result of it. St. Teresa says again, "Brief prayer which produces great results is better than years of prayer where the person never reaches the resolution of doing something worthwhile for God." Elsewhere she says, "In my experience, it is more helpful to resolve at the beginning to do something, no matter how difficult. If one does it to please God, there is nothing to fear."

14. The first resolution must be to do everything in our power (even to die first), rather than to commit a deliberate sin, no matter how small. Although it is true that any effort of ours to overcome temptation will be insufficient without grace, God wishes us nevertheless to exert ourselves up to the point where he provides his grace and helps us to obtain the victory in spite of our own weakness. Resolution like this removes every obstacle to progress, but it also gives us great courage, by assuring us that we are in God's grace. St. Francis de Sales writes: "The greatest assurance of being in God's grace lies not in any feeling of love we might have, but in the pure and steadfast abandonment of ourselves into his hands, together with the firm resolve never to consent to any sin, be it great or small." That is what it meant by a delicate conscience. It is quite a different thing from a scrupulous conscience. A delicate conscience is necessary if you are to

become a saint. A scrupulous conscience is a defective conscience and will do damage. You should obey your spiritual director, and overcome your scruples, for they are nothing more than empty and irrational fears.

15. Next, it is necessary to be resolved to prefer what is best; that is, not simply to do something that is acceptable to God, but what will give him the greatest pleasure without any reservation on our part. St. Francis de Sales tells us to begin with a strong and unshakable resolution to give ourselves totally to God, insisting that from now on, we wish to be unreservedly his, and that we should keep renewing the same resolution afterward. St. Andrew Avellino made a vow to make progress toward perfection every day. It is not necessary to make vows, but we do need to take determined steps toward perfection. St. Lawrence Justinian writes, "When a person is making headway, they will want to keep going forward, and the further they advance, the more the desire keeps growing. As the light grows brighter, they will think that they are less virtuous and are doing little good. If by chance they do notice the good they have done, they think it imperfect and of little account. As a result, they keep striving toward perfection without growing tired."

16. We must act quickly, without waiting until tomorrow. Who knows if there will be time then? Listen to what the Preacher says: "Anything you can turn your hand to, do with what power you have" (Eccl 9:10), and he continues, "For there will be no work, nor reason, nor knowledge, nor wisdom in the nether world where you are going." [...]

17. David said, "Now I will begin" ([ed.] Ps 77:11). St. Charles Borromeo used to say, "Today, I must begin to serve God." We should do the same, as though we had done no good in the past. In fact, anything we can do for God is really very little, and so we should resolve each day to belong totally to him once more and without giving a thought to what others are doing or what progress they are making. Very few people succeed in becoming saints. According to St. Bernard, it is not possible to be perfect without being different. If we wish to imitate the common run of people, we will be as imperfect as they are. It is necessary to conquer in every-

thing, to give up everything in order to gain everything. St. Teresa says we never receive God's love completely because we never succeed in giving all our love to him. Everything we do for Jesus Christ is insignificant, for he has given his life's blood for us. "Everything we can possibly do," she writes, "is dross in comparison with a single drop of the blood the Lord shed for us." The saints were unsparing in seeking to please a God who gave himself totally to us simply to put us under an obligation of loving him and they denied him nothing. Chrysostom writes: "He gave himself completely to you, and left nothing for himself." If God has given himself to you so totally, there is no excuse why you should be niggardly with God. He went so far as to die for us "so that those who live might no longer live for themselves but for him who for their sake died and was raised" (2 Cor 5:15).

18. The third way to become a saint is mental prayer.[33] According to John Gerson, it is almost miraculous how anyone who does not meditate on the eternal truths can live as a Christian. The truths of faith cannot be seen with the eyes of the body, but only with the eyes of the soul when it meditates. Those who do not meditate will fail to see them, and being as it were in darkness, they will be more easily attracted by outward things and lose a taste for the things of eternity. St. Teresa wrote to the Bishop of Osma, "We may think we have no imperfections, but they will appear clearly as soon as God opens our eyes in prayer." St. Bernard wrote that those who do not meditate lack self and have no awareness of their own limitations. Prayer, he says, "orders our affection and directs our action." Without prayer, the affection can quickly become attached to earthly things, action will follow suit, and the result will be chaos. [...]

20. If people abandon prayer, they will soon cease loving Jesus Christ. Prayer is like a hearth in which the fire of divine love is kindled and kept blazing. St. Catherine of Bologna said, "Anyone who does not devote time to prayer slips the leash that binds them to God, and when the devil finds someone like that cool in God's love, he has no difficulty in enticing them to eat the poisoned fruit."[34] St. Teresa held it as certain "that anyone who perseveres in prayer will eventually reach the harbor of salvation, no

matter what obstacles the devil tries to put in its path." Elsewhere she writes, "Anyone who does not wander from the path of prayer will arrive, sooner or later, at their goal." She remarks that the devil puts so much effort into enticing people away from prayer because he knows that he has already lost anyone who perseveres in giving time to it. Prayer brings us a rich harvest. In prayer, we think good thoughts, stir up devout feelings and greater desires, make determined resolutions to give ourselves completely to God, and so are enabled to sacrifice earthly pleasures and disordered appetites. St. Aloysius Gonzaga said, "There cannot be much perfection unless there is much prayer," and anyone desiring perfection will take note of this saying of the saint.

21. We ought not go into prayer simply in order to taste the sweetness of divine love. It would be a waste of time to go for such a reason and it will bring us scant profit. We should give time to prayer simply to please God, or in other words, to discover what God wants from us and to ask his help in carrying it out. Father Anthony Torres used to say, "Carrying the cross without consolation helps a person to fly toward perfection."[35] Prayer in which we fail to experience a great deal of satisfaction for the feelings can be the most spiritually profitable, and it would be a misfortunate to give up prayer simply because we do not find it very pleasant. St. Teresa warns that a person who gives up prayer is like someone putting themselves into hell without any help from the devil.

22. Mental prayer helps a person to think constantly about God. "The true lover," says St. Teresa, "is always thinking of the beloved." Prayerful people speak constantly about God, because they know how pleased he is when his friends speak about him and about his love for them. The same saint says again, "Jesus Christ is always present when God's servants are in conversation, and he is very pleased when they delight in him."

23. One of the fruits of prayer is a growing desire for solitude to be alone with God or to help us maintain recollection of mind while we are dealing with necessary business. "Necessary" business is that which arises from family obligations or from offices imposed by obedience. Otherwise, prayerful people

ought to love solitude, and will try to prevent themselves becoming drained by unnecessary or useless business, by which the spirit of recollection is lost. "You are an enclosed garden, my sister, my bride" (Sg 4:12). A person devoted to Jesus Christ should be like a garden closed to created things and will bar the way to thoughts or business which are not of God or for God. Open hearts do not make for saints. The saints who worked at winning souls for God never lost their spirit of recollection even in the midst of absorbing activities like preaching, hearing confessions, mediating in disputes, or helping the sick. The same applies to those who are engaged in study. Despite all their study and pretensions to learning, some people never succeed in becoming either holy or learned. Genuine learning is the science of the saint, that is, knowing how to love Jesus Christ. Divine love brings wisdom in her company: "Yet all good things together came to me in her company" (Wis 7:11). Although St. John Berchmans was extraordinarily dedicated to his studies, he was a man of virtue, and never allowed them to compete with his progress in the spiritual life. Paul advises us "to think, but to think soberly, each according to the measure of faith that God has apportioned" (Rom 12:3). Priests in particular should appreciate the need to be thoughtful people, if they are to fulfill their pastoral duties properly. But they should "think soberly." Giving up prayer in order to have more time for study can be a sign of looking for personal satisfaction rather than for God's glory in study. Those who are genuinely seeking God will be prepared to leave their study aside for prayer, except when it is really necessary, but they will never give up prayer for study.

24. Above all, without mental prayer, one fails to make prayer of petition. I have already spoken frequently in my spiritual writings about the necessity of prayer, and especially in a little book called *The Great Means of Prayer,* so I will not say much about it in this chapter. It is enough to recall what Bishop Palafox of Osma said, "How can love survive unless God grants us perseverance? And how can we ask for it without prayer? Without prayer, there is not that communication with God which is the very life of virtue."[36] People who do not make mental prayer are

aware of their spiritual needs only in a very limited way. They have little sense of the dangers to their salvation, or of the ways to overcome temptation, and not grasping the importance of prayer of petition, they can easily omit it and run the risk of being lost.

25. As to subjects for meditation, the most useful are the last things—death, judgment, heaven, hell, and paradise. It can be particularly useful to imagine ourselves on our death-bed, kissing the cross and on the point of entering eternity. Anyone who loves Jesus Christ and who wishes to grow in love will know that there is nothing more useful that meditating on the Passion of the Redeemer. St. Francis de Sales calls Calvary "the hill of lovers." All those who love Jesus Christ often resort to this mountain where they breathe the very air of divine love. When we see a God who died for love of us, it is impossible not to love him passionately. From the wounds of the crucified, there come darts of fire which would wound even hearts of stone. [...]

26. The fourth means of attaining perfection and of persevering in the grace of God is frequent communication, which we have already discussed in Chapter 2 where we said that a person can give no greater pleasure to Jesus Christ that receiving him frequently in the Sacrament of the Altar.[37] [...]

33. The fifth and most necessary means for living a spiritual life and acquiring the love of Jesus Christ is prayer of petition. Let me say first of all that prayer is the expression of God's love for us. Could a person give any greater proof of love than to tell their friends, "Ask me for anything you want and I will give it to you"? That is exactly what the Lord has told us: "Ask and you will receive; seek and you will find; knock and the door will be opened" (Lk 11:9). Prayer can win any favor from God, and those who pray will obtain from God whatever they ask. David expresses it beautifully: "Blessed be God,/who did not refuse me the kindness I sought in prayer" (Ps 66:20). St. Augustine comments on these words saying: "When you see that prayer does not fail you, rest assured that the divine mercy will not fail you either." St. John Chrysostom adds, "We always obtain grace even while we are still asking for it." When we pray, the Lord gives us

the grace before our prayer is finished. If we are poor in grace, we have only ourselves to thank. We are poor because we have chosen to be poor, and we do not deserve any sympathy. Would a beggar deserve any sympathy if, in spite of having a wealthy patron willing to provide him with everything he needed as soon as he asked, he chose to stay poor rather than make his needs known? The Apostle says that our God is always "enriching all who call upon him" (Rom 10:12).

34. Humble prayer obtains everything from God. Prayer is not simply useful, but is vitally necessary to salvation. If we are to overcome the temptations of the enemy, we stand in absolute need of divine help. Sometimes, the sufficient grace which God gives to everyone is enough to enable us to resist even his most violent assaults. But in view of our evil inclinations, this is not always enough and we have need of special grace. Whoever prays will obtain it; whoever does not pray will not obtain it, and will be lost.[38] Discussing the grace of final perseverance, that is of dying in the grace of God, St. Augustine says that God only gives this grace to those who ask for it. The reason why many are lost is because they forget to ask God for this grace of final perseverance.

35. In brief, the Fathers of the Church remind us of the necessity of prayer. If not just necessary simply because there is a commandment to pray or because theologians teach that anyone who would allow a month to slip by without recommending their eternal salvation to God cannot be excused from mortal sin. Prayer is necessary as a means to salvation. To put it simply, it is impossible for anyone who refuses to pray to be saved, because we cannot obtain salvation without the help of divine grace, and God grants his grace only to those who ask for it. Since we are constantly exposed to the danger of temptation and of falling away from the grace of God, our prayer must be just as constant. That is why St. Thomas writes that constant prayer is necessary for a human being's salvation: "Constant prayer is necessary for a person to enter heaven."[39] Jesus Christ himself spoke of the "necessity...to pray always without becoming weary" (Lk 18:1) and the Apostle of "praying without ceasing" (1 Thes 5:17). Once we leave off recommending ourselves to God, the devil conquers. As

the Council of Trent teaches, we do not earn the grace of final perseverance, but there is, nevertheless, a sense in which it can be said that we can merit it through prayer, or, in St. Augustine's words, "God's gift of perseverance can be merited by supplication, that is, by asking and beseeching." The Lord desires to give us his grace, but he wishes us to pray for it, and in the words of St. Gregory, "God wishes us to pray, he wishes to be forced, he wishes somehow to be overcome by our imploring." St. Mary Magdalene de' Pazzi says that when we ask God for grace, not only does he hear us, but he is almost even grateful to us. The truth is that, since God is infinite goodness, he longs to pour himself out on behalf of others, and he has, as it were, such an infinite desire to dispense his grace that when he sees a person praying to him, he is so pleased that he seems to be grateful to them for their prayer.

36. If we wish to remain in the grace of God until death, we must become beggars, always waiting for an opportunity to ask for help, saying "Jesus, mercy; do not allow me to be separated from you. Lord help me. My God help me." This was the prayer of the ancient Desert Fathers: "Graciously rescue me, God!/ Come quickly to help me, LORD!" (Ps 70:2), and it should be ours especially in time of temptation, otherwise we run the risk of being lost.

37. We should have great confidence in prayer. God promised to hear anyone who prays to him: "Ask and you will receive" (Jn 16:24). Why should we doubt, asks St. Augustine, if the Lord has bound himself with a promise, and by this promise, he has placed himself under an obligation to us? When we recommend ourselves to God, we should trust confidently that God hears us and that we will obtain what we need: "All that you ask for in prayer, believe that you will receive it and it shall be yours" (Mk 11:24).

38. Someone might be tempted to argue, "But I am a sinner and I do not deserve to be heard." But Jesus Christ says: "Everyone who asks, receives" (Lk 11:10). According to St. Thomas, the power of prayer in obtaining grace for us does not lie in our merits, but in the mercy of God who has promised to

hear anyone who prays: "Prayer of petition does not rest on our merits but solely on divine mercy." In order to take away any anxiety we might feel when we pray, he assures us: "Amen, amen, I say to you, whatever you ask the Father in my name he will give you" (Jn 16:23). Note that the words "in my name" mean, as St. Thomas says, in the name of the Savior. The graces we ask for should be those which have to do with eternal salvation, for this promise does not apply to temporal favors, for the Lord gives or withholds from us in the measure that they are a help toward our eternal salvation. Whenever we ask for temporal graces, then, we should ask for them on the condition that they will be of spiritual benefit to us. There is no need to set such conditions in regard to spiritual graces, but we should simply ask boldly: "Eternal Father, in the name of Jesus Christ, free me from this temptation, give me holy perseverance, give me your love, give me paradise." We can ask for these graces directly from Jesus Christ himself and in his own name, that is, by his merits, on account of the promise he made: "If you ask anything of me in my name, I will do it" (Jn 14:14). When we pray to God, we should remember to recommend ourselves to Mary, who is the dispenser of graces. St. Bernard says that God is the one who gives grace, but that he gives it through the hand of Mary: "Let us seek grace, and let us seek it through Mary, because the one who seeks finds and cannot seek in vain." If Mary prays for us, we can rest secure, for her prayers are always heard, and are never refused.

Chapter 11: "Love Does Not Seek Its Own Interests." Whoever loves Jesus Christ will seek to be detached from all created things.

1. Anyone who wishes to love Jesus Christ will need to drive from their heart everything which is dictated by self-love, rather than by love of God. "Not seeking one's own interests" means not seeking ourselves but only what pleases God. This is what the Lord asks of us when he says, "You shall love the Lord your God with all your heart" (Mt 22:37). Two things are necessary if you are to love God with all your heart. The first is to raise

your heart above worldly things, and second is to fill it with love of God. A heart in which worldly affection reigns cannot belong totally to God. St. Philip Neri says that the more love we give to creatures, the more we take from God. Purity of heart is attained by mortification and by the practice of detachment from created things. People who complain that they cannot find God when they seek him should heed St. Teresa's advice: "Detach the heart from created things, then seek God and you will find him."

2. Some people make the mistake of wishing to become saints in their own fashion. They wish to love Jesus Christ, but in a way that accords with their own taste, and without leaving behind frivolous entertainments, vanity in dress, or fondness for the choicest foods. People like that love God, but they become bitterly disappointed if they fail to obtain some office or other. They are prickly about points of honor. In times of sickness, if they are not cured at once, they lose all patience. They do love God, but are unable to lay aside their preoccupation with money, status, or the prestige which goes with being considered nobler, wiser, or better than others. They can practice mental prayer, go to communion, but their hearts are so full of worldly things that none of it brings them any real spiritual profit. The Lord does not even speak to them, for it would be a waste of words. He once told St. Teresa, "I would speak to many people but the world makes so much of a din in their ears that my voice cannot be heard. If only they would withdraw from the world a little!" People full to the brim with worldly love are unable to hear God's voice speaking to them. Their attachment to their worldly goods has so blinded them that they are prepared to run the risk of losing God, the infinite good, rather than lose them. St. Teresa says, "It is clear that anyone who goes chasing perishable things will perish themselves."

3. St. Augustine describes how Tiberius Caesar wished to make Jesus Christ a member of the Roman Senate, but the senators refused to admit him on the grounds that he was a proud God who wished to be adored alone and without anyone to share his honor.[40] It is absolutely true: God wishes to be the only one we love and adore, not because he is conceited, but because it is his

due in return for having loved us so much. He wants all our love in return and is a jealous God if he sees others sharing hearts he wishes to have for himself. St. Jerome says that Jesus is jealous, and that he does not want us to place our affection in anything except in him. That is what the apostle James means in asking, "Do you suppose that the scripture speaks without meaning when it says, 'The spirit that he has made to dwell in us tends toward jealousy'?" (Jas 4:5). The Lord praises his spouse in the Song of Songs: "You are an enclosed garden, my sister, my bride" (Sg 4:12). He calls her an "enclosed garden" because she has closed her heart to every earthly love in order to keep it for the love of Jesus alone. Jesus deserves all our love on account of his goodness and the love he has for us. The saints understood that perfectly clearly, and it is why St. Francis de Sales could say, "If I knew that there was a single fiber in my heart that did not belong to God, I would be ready to pluck it out straight away."

4. David wanted to be free from any entanglement in worldly things so that he could fly away and rest in God (Ps 55:7). Many people desire to be free of all earthly ties in order to fly toward God, and they would surely make great progress in holiness if they were genuinely free, but because they harbor some small disordered affection and make no real effort to shake themselves free from it, they never succeed in getting even one foot off the ground. St. John of the Cross says, "Those who remain attached to any thing, even a very small thing, will never attain divine union despite their many virtues. It matters little whether a bird is restrained by a stout cord or a fine unbreakable thread. It is still prevented from flying. It is tragic that some people, who are otherwise rich in spiritual experiences, virtues, and divine favors, never succeed in reaching union with God because they lack the courage to put an end to some trifling affection. All they need to break the thread is one great effort to fly! God can only give himself fully to a person who is free from all attachment to created things."

5. Those who wish God to be first in their lives must give themselves totally to him. "My lover belongs to me and I to him," says the spouse (Sg 2:16). Because he loves us very much,

Jesus Christ wishes to have all our love, and will never be content until he has it all. That is why St. Teresa wrote to a prioress of one of her monasteries: "See to it that the sisters are detached from every created thing, so that they can train themselves to be the spouses of a very jealous king who wants them to forget even themselves." St. Mary Magdalene de' Pazzi once took a little spiritual book from a novice lest she become attached to it. There are people who make mental prayer, visit the Blessed Sacrament, go to Holy Communion frequently, but make little or no progress on the way of perfection because they carry some little earthly attachment in their hearts. If they continue like that, not only will they be unhappy but they will be in danger of losing everything.

6. Like David, we should pray that God will purify our hearts from every worldly attachment: "A clean heart create for me, God" (Ps 51:12), otherwise we can never belong totally to him: "Everyone of you who does not renounce all his possessions cannot be my disciple" (Lk 14:33). That is why the Desert Fathers would ask a novice seeking to join them: "Do you bring a heart empty enough for the Holy Spirit to fill?" [...]

7. As soon as the heart is free from fondness for created things, God's love enters and fills it. St. Teresa says, "Once we have turned our eyes away from things which are less attractive, our soul can concentrate on loving God." People cannot live without love. They must love either the Creator or what he has created, and if they do not love the creature, then they must love the Creator. As Thomas à Kempis puts it briefly, "totum pro toto"—we must leave everything if we are to acquire everything. St. Teresa discovered that an attachment she had for one of her relatives (and it was a chaste one) prevented her from giving herself totally to God. When finally she summoned up the courage to let go of it, she heard Jesus Christ say to her, "Now, Teresa, you are all mine, and I am all yours." If one heart is too small to love our loving God who is worthy of infinite love, how can we divide it between God and creatures? [...]

8. The prophet Jeremiah says, "Good is the LORD to one who waits for him,/to the soul that seeks him" (Lam 3:25). He means, of course, a person who seeks God alone. It is a happy

loss, and a happy gain to lose passing things which fail to satisfy the heart in order to acquire God who is the highest everlasting good. A story is told about a hermit who one day met a prince in the forest. The prince asked him what he was doing there. He replied by asking him, "Sir, what are you doing in this lonely place?" When the prince answered that he was hunting wild animals, the hermit rejoined, "And I am hunting for God," and went on his way. Our one thought and purpose in this life should be to go in search of God in order to love him, and his will in order do it, while at the same time freeing our heart from desire for created things. When any earthly good threatens to draw our love away, we should be ready to say, "I despise the kingdom of the earth and all worldly adornment for the love of Jesus Christ my Lord."[41] Worldly dignity and status are only a cloud of mist which disappears at death. Fortunate indeed is anyone who can say, "My Jesus Christ, for the sake of your love, I have left behind everything. You are my sole love. You alone are enough for me."

9. When divine love takes possession of persons, it enables them with the help of divine grace to strip themselves of any thing which hinders them from belonging completely to God. St. Francis de Sales remarked that when a house is on fire, the contents are thrown out the window. He means that when people give themselves completely to God, they instinctively free themselves from every other tie without needing to be exhorted by preachers or confessors. Father Segneri the Younger said that divine love is a thief who robs us of everything, and leaves us only God. A person who had given up everything for the sake of Jesus Christ was asked by a friend why he had reduced himself to such poverty. He drew a bible from his pocket and said, "This is what has stripped me of everything: The Holy Spirit says, 'Were one to offer all he owns to purchase love,/he would be roundly mocked'" (Sg 8:7). People who love God totally consider things like wealth, pleasure, dignity, estates, even kingdoms as unimportant, for they want only God. St. Francis de Sales writes, "Pure love of God consumes everything which is not God in order to convert everything to itself, because everything done for God's sake is love."

10. The spouse says, "He brings me into the banquet hall/and his emblem over me is love" (Sg 2:4). According to St. Teresa, the banqueting hall is divine love, which takes possession of a soul in such a way that it seems to make it so drunk that it forgets everything else. When a people are drunk, they appear to be dead to the world. The effect of divine love is somewhat similar. People seem to loose all consciousness of the things of the world to the extent that they want to think of nothing but God, to speak of nothing but God, to hear about nothing but loving and pleasing God. In the Song, the Lord forbids his sleeping beloved to be wakened: "Do not arouse, do not stir up love/before its own time" (Sg 2:7). According to St. Basil, the sleep which the soul betrothed to Jesus Christ is nothing less than total forgetfulness of everything. It is a virtuous and voluntary forgetfulness of everything created, so as to be able to attend solely to God and to be able to say with St. Francis, "My God and my all." My God, what are wealth, dignity, and the goods of this world? You are everything to me, and my every good. Thomas à Kempis writes, "My God and my all!" For someone who understands, enough is said, and for one who loves, it is a delightful thing to say "My God and my all! My God and my all!"

11. To reach perfect union with God, we need to be altogether free from created things. In concrete terms, this means first of all to be free from disordered affection for relatives.

Jesus Christ says, "If anyone comes to me without hating his father and mother, wife and children, brothers and sisters, and even his own life, he cannot be my disciple" (Lk 14:26). In what concerns our spiritual profit, we have no greater enemies than our close relatives: "And one's enemies will be those of his household" (Mt 10:36). St. Charles Borromeo said that whenever he went home to his relatives, he always returned less fervent in spirit. [...]

12. When it comes to making a choice about vocation, St. Thomas Aquinas's opinion that there is no obligation to obey our parents is sound.[42] If a young person feels called to the religious life and his parents are opposed, he is obliged to obey God rather than his parents, whose opposition may spring from their own selfish interests. St. Thomas reminds us that "frequently,

those who are our friends according to the flesh are the opponents of our spiritual progress." St. Bernard writes that some
parents would be happier to see their children lost rather than to
see them leave the family home.

13.   It is astonishing to see how even some god-fearing parents can be so blinded by passion that they will not leave a stone
unturned to prevent one of their children from following a vocation to the religious life. Except in the rarest cases, they cannot
be excused from serious sin. Some people might ask, "Well, supposing that young man does not become a religious, does it
mean that he will not be saved? Are you saying that everyone who
stays in the world is damned?" My answer is: "Those who are not
called by God to the religious life will save themselves by fulfilling the duties of their state of life in the world. Those who are
called, but do not answer the call, may well be saved, but they will
find it difficult, since they will lack those spiritual helps the Lord
had prepared for them in the religious life." The theologian
Habert writes that a person who does not follow a divine vocation is like a displaced person in the church and will encounter
great difficulty in carrying out his duties and obtaining salvation.[43] He continues, "Absolutely speaking, such a person can be
saved, but will find it difficult to enter the way and to find life."

14.   Father Granata calls the choice of a state in life "the mainspring."[44] Just as a clock won't work if the mainspring is broken, so
if the choice of a state in life goes wrong, the rest of that person's
life will be in trouble. Many young people who have lost their vocation due to their parents' interference have come to a bad end.
Some have even been the ruin of the family. One young man lost
his vocation due to his father's interference, and in his resentment,
he killed his father with his own hands and died on the scaffold.
Another young man on the point of entering the seminary was
called by God to join a religious order. He ignored the call, gave up
the practice of the spiritual life which he had been leading up until
then, and was finally murdered by a rival one night as he was leaving a house of prostitution. I could give you many other examples.

15.   To return to the main point: St. Thomas teaches that
those who are called to a more perfect life ought not to consult

their parents about it first, since in such matters, parents can sometimes be their worst enemies. If children are not obliged to consult their parents in following their vocation to a more perfect state, it follows that they are even less obliged to wait for their permission, or indeed even to ask it, if they fear that it may be withheld unjustly in order to prevent them following their vocation. Saints Thomas Aquinas, Peter of Alcantara, Francis Xavier, Luis Beltrand, and many others went off to join religious communities without even letting their parents know of their intentions.

16. Just as those who ignore a vocation in order to please their parents are in great danger of being lost, the same holds for those who would enter the clerical state without a vocation and simply in order to avoid displeasing their parents. [...]

19. The ecclesiastical state was not instituted by Jesus Christ to further the ambition of worldly families but to promote the glory of God and the salvation of souls. Some people make the mistake of supposing that the ecclesiastical state is simply another career by which a person advances in honor and wealth. If relatives put pressure on a bishop to ordain someone without the education or who is living a dissolute life by alleging that the family is poor and cannot otherwise manage, he should reply: "No my friend, the ecclesiastical state was not made to help a few families in their poverty, but for the good of the Church." He should send them away without giving them another hearing. In the ordinary run of events, unsuitable candidates destroy not only themselves but also their family and the whole locality.[45]

20. Priests living at home and who are under pressure from relatives who want them to apply their energies to advancing the family rather than to their priestly duties should give them the answer Jesus gave to his divine mother, "Did you not know that I must be in my Father's house?" (Lk 2:49). "I am a priest, my duty is not to make money or procure honors, nor to undertake the administration of the house, but to live quietly, praying, studying, and helping people." If there is some special reason for helping the family, let him do what he can but without giving up his main occupation, which is to attend to his own sanctification and that of others.

21. Whoever wishes to belong totally to God ought to be *free from attachment to worldly reputation*. Many people remain distant from God and even lose him altogether on account of their wretched preoccupation with their reputation. If their faults are criticized, for instance, they justify themselves vigorously and try to prove that it is all lies and slander. On the other hand, if they do something virtuous, they broadcast it to the whole world. Saints never behaved like that. They did not mind the whole world knowing about their faults and regarding them as the people of no account they believed themselves to be, but they wanted their virtuous acts known only to God for they were performed for his glory alone. They never forgot the saying of Jesus, "When you give alms, do not let your left hand know what your right is doing...when you pray, go to your inner room, close the door, and pray to your Father in secret" (Mt 6:3, 6).

22. Above all, it is necessary to be *free from attachment to ourselves, that is, to our own will*. Those who master themselves will easily overcome everything else that goes against the grain. "Overcome yourself" was St. Francis Xavier's advice to everyone. Jesus Christ says, "Whoever wishes to come after me must deny himself" (Mt 16:24). If we are to become saints, we must deny ourselves and not follow our own will all the time. "Go not after your lusts,/but keep your desires in check" (Sir 18:30). According to St. Francis of Assisi, the greatest gift persons can receive from God is that of conquering themselves by denying their own will. St. Bernard writes that "if self-will ceased, there would be no hell." He said that self-will often goes a long way toward making even good works defective. It would be a fault, for instance, to undertake an act of penance against the will of a confessor, simply in order to gratify one's own will. People who live as slaves to self-will are unhappy. They are always hankering after the unattainable, for they will discover many things not to their taste, but they will have to put up with them. "Where do the wars and where do the conflicts among you come from? Is it not from your passions that make war within your members? You covet but do not possess" (Jas 4:1, 2).

The first front on which the battle is fought is our appetite for sensual pleasure. If we avoid the circumstances in which temptation is liable to arise, mortify the sight, and recommend ourselves to God, the war will cease. The second front is our desire for wealth. If we cultivate a love for poverty, the war will cease. The third front is ambition for honor. If we cultivate humility and a hidden life, the war will cease. The fourth front is the most dangerous and comes from our self-will: If we can accept everything that happens to us as God's will, the war will cease. [...]

23. We must love God then, in the way that pleases him, and just not in a way that suits ourselves. God wishes people to empty themselves of everything in order to be united to him and to be filled with his divine love. St. Teresa says, "I believe that the prayer of union is nothing else than dying to everything in the world to enjoy God alone. The more we empty ourselves to make space for the love of God, the more he fills us with himself and the more united to him we will be." Many people would like to attain union with God but they cannot bear the contradictions he sends them. They hate the sickness which strikes them, or the poverty they suffer, or the insults they receive. Since they cannot be resigned, they never succeed in reaching total union with God.

24. Let me add here a practice taught by St. John of the Cross. Holding that total mortification of the senses and appetites is necessary to reach perfect union, he says: "As regards the senses, if anything pleasant comes your way which is not purely for the glory of God, put it away immediately for the love of Jesus Christ. For instance, if you feel the urge to see or hear something which will not of itself lead you closer to God, do less of it. As for the appetites, prefer always what is worse, more unpleasant, or poorer, without desiring anything other than to suffer and to be despised."

To conclude: If people are sincerely trying to love Jesus Christ, they will gradually lose their attachment to earthly goods, and will become poor in spirit in order to be more united to him. Their every desire will be directed toward Jesus; they will think of him often; they will long for him and they will seek to please him alone, always and everywhere. To arrive at such a point, we must take care that our hearts are free from any affection which is not for God.

What does it mean for persons to give themselves completely to God? It means in the first place to avoid anything which would displease God and to do everything which would please him. Second, it means welcoming everything that comes our way, no matter how hard or unpleasant, as coming from his hand. Finally, it means preferring in everything the will of God to our own will. That is what it means to belong entirely to God.

SPIRITUAL DIRECTION

Direction of Souls Who Wish to Lead a Deeply Spiritual Life

Introduction

Editor's Note: Alphonsus de Liguori's *Moral Theology* made its first appearance as *Annotations to the Medulla Theologiae Moralis* of H. Busenbaum, S.J., in 1748. Alphonsus's intention was to produce not a speculative manual but a pastoral one. He looked constantly to *practice,* or as he wrote in Italian, *pratica,* that is, to theology as it affected the daily life and conduct of every category of Christian—pope, bishop, priest, religious, judge, doctor, teacher, hairdresser, peasant, the educated and the unlettered. The *Pratica del Confessore per ben esercitare il suo Ministero,* freely translated as the *Confessor's Guide to the Correct Pastoral Exercise of His Ministry,* was first printed in Italian in 1755 as an appendix to the second Neapolitan edition of the *Moral Theology.* Here, in a popular manual of some two hundred pages, easily accessible in the vernacular, Alphonsus was able to outline his ideal of the confessor—one who was well versed in the principles of moral theology but possessing, at the same time, the holiness of life required to sustain him in the discharge of this ministry, a holiness of life centered on prayer and daily meditation on the scriptures.

Alphonsus insisted that the confessor should be able to guide souls to God, to help them to lead Christian lives to the full by the frequentation of the sacraments, by instructing them in the way of union with God in prayer, which, at times, could even lead them on to the graces of contemplation. With this in mind Alphonsus appended for the confessor a guide for directing spiritual souls in the way of holiness of life, including sections on contemplation, mortification, the frequentation of the sacraments and especially of Holy Communion. It is this section of the work that is given here.

The Italian version of the *Pratica,* revised and translated into Latin by Alphonsus himself, assisted by two of his colleagues (Fathers Gaspar Caione and Geronimo Ferrara), was published separately in Venice two years later in 1757. Edition followed edition both in Italian and Latin, and, within a few years, into other

European languages, though I am not aware of any complete English translation. The text printed here is Chapter 9 of the *Praxis Confessarii* and is translated from the Latin version.

*　　　*　　　*

1. The Lord said to Jeremiah: "This day I set you/over nations and over kingdoms,/To root up and to tear down,/to destroy and to demolish,/to build and to plant" (Jer 1:10). He says the same to confessors, whose duty it is not only to uproot vice from their penitents but also to sow the seeds of virtue in their souls. Accordingly, I have considered it useful to add this special section to what I have already written on the duties of confessors in order to be of assistance to young confessors as they undertake the direction of spiritual souls on the way to perfection.

To convert sinners from their sinful ways is certainly a ministry pleasing to the Lord, but it is still more acceptable to him to help spiritual souls practice virtue so that they will give themselves entirely to him. The Lord is more pleased with one soul who strives for holiness than for a thousand who lead imperfect lives. Therefore, when a confessor becomes aware that his penitent lives a life free from all mortal faults, he should make every effort to introduce that soul into the way of perfection and of divine love. He should point out to his penitent how much God deserves our love, the gratitude we owe to Jesus Christ who loved us to the point of dying for us. And at the same time he should point out the risk we run if we resist God's call to lead a deeply spiritual life.

Spiritual direction of those who wish to lead a more perfect life should emphasize four areas, namely, *meditation* and *contemplation, mortification* and the *frequentation of the Sacraments*. I shall deal with each of these points.

1. Concerning Meditation

2. A prudent confessor who discerns in his penitent a deep horror of serious sin and at the same time a desire to grow in the love of God should, before all else, encourage his penitent to devote time to meditating on the eternal truths and on the great

goodness of God. Although meditation, unlike the prayer of petition, is not necessary for one's eternal salvation, it is nonetheless very important for souls who wish to persevere in the grace of God. Unlike some other acts of piety which can exist side-by-side with sin in one's life, prayer and sin cannot. One will either give up sin or abandon prayer. St. Teresa of Avila said: "I am convinced that the Lord will lead to salvation the soul that perseveres in prayer, no matter how many sins the devil will urge against her." And so the devil wishes above all else to prevent souls from devoting themselves to prayer. St. Teresa declares that the devil knows he has lost the soul who perseveres in prayer. It is love which unites a soul with God but it is prayer or meditation which enkindles that love of God in souls. "In my thoughts a fire blazed up" (Ps 39:4).

3. Accordingly, a confessor should be advised to introduce his penitents to prayer. At the outset he should recommend about a half an hour; this can be gradually increased. The confessor should not yield on this point even though his penitents protest that time or a suitable place cannot be found. He should insist that, at least, every morning and evening when the house is quiet and even if his penitents are occupied in some business (provided, of course, no one is watching) that they should turn their thoughts to God, meditate on the truths of faith such as the Last Things, particularly death (which is very useful for beginners in the spiritual life). Next should come meditation on the Passion of Jesus Christ, which is universally helpful.

To facilitate progress in prayer, the confessor should recommend to his penitent the use of a suitable book of meditations. St. Teresa of Avila herself used a book. The confessor should advise his penitent to choose the subject which is most conducive to devotion and to spend more time on those subjects which prove most deeply moving. The soul should then move from reflections and engage in acts of will or prayer of petition or make appropriate resolutions. To be more explicit, encourage the soul to make acts of humility, thanksgiving, acts of faith and hope, and to repeat acts of sorrow and of love for God, at the same time offering oneself totally to God and abandoning oneself totally to his holy will. Let the soul repeat as often as possible those sentiments toward God which arise most spontaneously.

As regards prayer of petition or asking God for the graces we need, St. Augustine tells us that in the ordinary course of events God does not grant us his graces and in particular the grace of perseverance unless we ask. Our Lord said, "Ask and you shall receive." St. Teresa makes the point from this that if we do *not* ask we shall not receive. So, if we wish to save our soul, it is necessary always to pray and above all to ask in our prayers for the grace of perseverance and for the love of God. There is no time more suitable for this than the time of mental prayer. If one does not pray one is not inclined to petition God since one is not aware of one's need for grace and of the necessity of asking God for it. In a word, one who does not pray will have difficulty in persevering in God's grace.

In order that one's prayer should be effective it is important to put into practice the inspirations one receives. So, following the advice of St. Francis de Sales, we should never end our prayer without making some definite resolution, such as to avoid our habitual faults or to practice some virtue in the area in which we are weakest.

4. Confessors should demand from their penitents an account of their mental prayer and specifically if they were faithful to it. They should recommend that they accuse themselves in confession if they have omitted their prayer. One who abandons prayer cannot be saved. To quote St. Teresa of Avila, "One who, by deliberate choice, abandons prayer is heading for hell without any need for the intervention of the Devil." What great benefit confessors confer on their penitents by urging them to the practice of prayer and, on the other hand, what a serious account will those who neglect to do so have to give to God since it is their duty to procure the spiritual progress of their penitents. How many souls could not confessors lead along the way of perfection, how many grave sins could be avoided, if only confessors were to exercise even a little diligence in the matter of encouraging their penitents to pray. And then inquiring from them—at least in the beginning of their spiritual journey—if they have

been faithful to their practice of prayer. A soul who is rooted in prayer will only with great difficulty be unfaithful to God. So, not only those of delicate conscience but even those who lead sinful lives should be encouraged to pray since very often it is only through their lack of reflection on the eternal truths that they continue in their sinful ways.

5. Confessors should be particularly attentive to their penitents when they experience aridity or spiritual desolation. The Lord initially favors with special graces, insights, and even sensible consolations souls who commit themselves to lead a spiritual life. After some time, however, he deprives them of these consolations in order to test their fidelity and to lead them to greater perfection. For souls can very easily become attached selfishly to these consolations out of a certain degree of self-love. Sensible consolations, just like supernatural attractions, are indeed a gift of God but they are not God himself. And so God, in order to detach his chosen souls even from his gifts and to ensure that they love him, the Giver of all good gifts, with an unselfish love, deprives them of sensible consolation in their prayers and allows them instead to suffer disgust, aridity, upset, and at times even temptations. The confessor should be very diligent in these circumstances to encourage his penitents to persevere in prayer and above all not to omit to receive Holy Communion. The words of Francis de Sales are relevant here. "One prayer in the midst of desolation is more pleasing to God than a hundred in the midst of sensible consolations."[1] The one who loves God on account of the consolations he lavishes on us loves God's consolations more than God himself. But the one who loves God without receiving any consolation manifests authentic love.

This is sufficient about meditation or mental prayer. I think it is opportune for me now to give young confessors some general ideas about infused contemplation and its different stages of development as well as a description of some of the supernatural gifts which can accompany it. I shall outline some of the norms laid down by masters of the spiritual life for those confessors who direct those souls to whom God gives these special graces.

2. The Prayer of Contemplation and Its Different Degrees

6. It is very important that a confessor should know how to direct souls to whom God grants the grace of contemplation and at the same time how to preserve them from all danger of illusions. In this whole area the unskilled confessor can do great harm and, as St. John of the Cross warns us, will have to account to God for it. Contemplation is quite different from meditation. In meditation we find God as a result of our mental efforts; in contemplation, on the other hand, God is present to us without these mental efforts. In meditation we employ acts of our own faculties, in contemplation it is God who is active and we are the recipients of the graces which he pours into our souls without effort on our part. The divine love and light which fills our souls disposes them to contemplate the goodness of God, who fills us with his gifts.

Prayer of Recollection

7. Before the Lord grants us the gift of contemplation he leads us into the prayer of recollection, that is *active recollection* or as it is sometimes called in the language of the mystics, *contemplative repose,* or loving attention to God. This is not yet infused contemplation since the soul still remains active. The state of recollection (I am speaking here of natural recollection and not of supernatural or infused recollection which I shall deal with in number 13 below) occurs when one's intellect is able to ponder deeply some mystery or eternal truth, outside the soul, as it were. Without conscious effort, untroubled by external distractions, and totally absorbed within itself, experiencing at the same time a deep sense of serenity, the soul is able to concentrate on the mystery or the eternal truth in question.[2]

Contemplative repose or loving attention to God is virtually the same except that now the soul is focused on some spiritual thought and, absorbed in itself, feels itself gently attracted to God. In this state of recollection or contemplative repose certain mystics state that the soul should leave aside meditation, and should not make acts of love or offering of oneself or resignation to the will of God, and so forth. The soul should merely remain in its sense of awareness and love of God without any act on its part. However, I disagree totally with these ideas. Certainly, when a person achieves this sense of recollection, the soul has no need of meditation because the fruit of meditation has already been secured, as Father Segneri points out in his valuable work, *Harmony between Activity and Rest*. Meditation, he declares, leads in the ordinary course of events to what is called *acquired* contemplation—one intuitively penetrates to the heart of truths which previously required considerable mental activity or discourse.[3]

Nevertheless, I cannot see why the soul should cease to make acts of the will. What better time to do so than when the soul is deep in recollection? It is true that St. Francis de Sales advised Blessed Jane Chantal not to repeat new acts in prayer when she perceived herself united with God. And why? Because she had already arrived at the state of passive contemplation. But when the soul is still in a state of activity there is no reason why virtuous acts should be an obstacle to the flow of grace. St. Francis de Sales instructed those souls he directed to make a certain number of acts of love within a determined space of time. Even though souls which reach the state of *passive* contemplation do not acquire merit for the simple reason that they are not active but passive, nonetheless they acquire a great reserve of spiritual energy to act meritoriously afterward. But when souls are still in the active state they have to make acts if they wish to merit. These are the means by which they merit God's grace. And so Father Segneri is quite correct when he insists that when God takes the initiative in speaking and working in us we should be silent and leave aside our own efforts, doing nothing beyond turning ourselves willingly and lovingly toward him. But when God does not speak with us we must take whatever steps we can to unite ourselves with him, namely, by meditations, affections, prayers, and resolutions. But we should only make those acts which flow from us gently and without doing violence to ourselves.

171

Aridity

8. Before he leads a soul into the prayer of contemplation, the Lord usually permits a soul to be purified by undergoing a period of aridity or desolation which is called *spiritual purification*. This purifies the soul from any imperfections which would hinder the gift of contemplation. There are two types of aridity, one *sensible*, which affects our senses, and the other *substantial*, which affects the soul or spirit. There are also two types of sensible aridity, one *natural* the other *supernatural*. Natural aridity brings with it a certain disgust for spiritual matters, and a certain darkness or sense of obscurity which, however, is more or less of a transient nature. Supernatural aridity, on the other hand, leaves the soul in a deeper sense of obscurity, which is of longer duration and seems to deepen with each passing day. Souls which find themselves in this state, despite the fact that they have no desire for creatures and have their thoughts firmly fixed on God with a determination and a great desire to love Him above all, nevertheless feel themselves incapable of doing so on account of their imperfections which seem to them to be the reason why they have become unpleasing to God. They still endeavor to lead a virtuous life.

This troublesome aridity is, nonetheless, a movement of God's grace, a divine illumination which brings with it both suffering and darkness. These souls desire to unite themselves with God spiritually, but are unable to do so because their senses and their souls are not yet free from sensible attractions. Natural imaginings, ideas, and representations fill their minds. This aridity, moreover, causes the soul painful obscurity which, at the same time, can be positively beneficial since it helps to detach the soul from all sensible pleasures both natural and spiritual. In this state souls consequently acquire a deep awareness of their own misery and their inability to perform any good act by their own power. They acquire, at once, a reverential fear of God and a great veneration for him.

At this stage the confessor should encourage his penitents to understand that God's action in their lives is to be regarded as a preparation for great graces. He should suggest to them that they omit any form of discursive meditation and instead humble themselves in God's presence, offer themselves totally to him, and resign themselves to accepting his will, which always works for our good.

9. After the purification of the *senses* the Lord usually grants the grace of contemplation, sometimes styled "joyous contemplation" or the grace of supernatural recollection, quiet, and union. However, after the grace of recollection and quiet and before the gift of union the Lord purifies the soul further by *aridity of spirit* or desolation (sometimes called *substantial aridity*) by which he leads the soul to the death of all self. Aridity of the senses entails the lack of all sensible devotion. Aridity of spirit is a divine illumination which leads souls to recognize their own nothingness, with the result that they experience excruciating sufferings in themselves. Even though they are more determined than ever to overcome themselves in everything and to be ever attentive to please God they become more and more conscious of their own imperfections. They feel rejected by God, even abandoned by him on account of their ingratitude for all the graces they have received. Their acts of devotion, their prayers, communions, acts of penance, bring no sense of satisfaction. Only with great difficulty and at the cost of overcoming themselves can they continue to perform these acts of virtue. Instead of being meritorious, these acts seem to be worthy of condemnation and only render the soul more hateful in God's sight. It happens frequently that souls in this state feel that they hate God, who accordingly rejects them as his enemies. They experience the very pains of the damned since they feel rejected by God.

In addition the Lord sometimes permits a thousand other temptations to accompany this desolation of spirit, temptations to impurity, anger, blasphemy, disbelief, and above all despair. In the midst of all this, these tortured souls are unable to realize that they have, in fact, rejected these temptations; they fear they have consented and so their sense of rejection by God increases. The spiritual darkness in which they find themselves deprives these souls of all sense of being determined to resist temptations or leaves them, at best, in a state of doubt.

10. A confessor who meets these souls who have progressed in the way of perfection and assert that they have been abandoned by God should not be put off by all this confusion of soul and so many expressions of fear and despair on the part of his penitents. He should show no signs of hesitancy or timidity but should at once counsel his penitent not to fear. Above all else, he should encourage the soul to trust ever more and more in God, quoting the saying of St. Teresa that no one loses God without being aware of it. Assure the penitent that all those temptations to blasphemy, unbelief, impurity, and despair are not sins but sufferings, which, if patiently borne, bring the soul nearer and nearer to God. God never hates a soul who loves him and wishes to please him. This is the way the Lord deals with those souls who are particularly dear to him. "It is in aridity and temptations," says St. Teresa, "that the Lord tests his genuine lovers. Even if aridity lasts the whole of their lives, these souls should not abandon prayer since the time will certainly come when they will be fully rewarded." What a consoling thought this is for troubled souls! The confessor should encourage them to remain steadfast and to look forward to special graces from God, who is leading them securely in the way of the Cross. His advice to these souls should be to humble themselves before God by admitting that they deserve these sufferings on account of their past infidelities. Secondly, they should resign themselves entirely to the will of God and express their willingness to accept all these trials and even greater ones for as long as God wishes. Thirdly, they should abandon themselves, as if dead to self, into the arms of the divine mercy and commit themselves at the same time to the protection of Our Lady, rightly called Mother of Mercy and Consolation of the Afflicted.

11. The aridity of the senses will remain until the soul, purified in its senses, is ready to receive the grace of contemplation. Spiritual aridity, on the other hand, will remain until the soul is capable of the grace of divine union. Sometimes, even after union, the Lord permits souls to experience this spiritual

aridity once more, so that they should not be elated and carried away but should remember their own nothingness before God.

Contemplation

12. When the Lord has purified the soul in its senses and when the trial of aridity has come to an end, the Lord grants the soul the grace of contemplation. This is of two types, the one *affirmative* the other *negative*. In the state of affirmative contemplation, the soul without any effort on its part and solely as a result of divine illumination perceives immediately some created truth such as the torment of hell or the happiness of heaven or some uncreated truth such as the divine attributes of mercy, love, power, or goodness. In the state of negative contemplation, the soul is aware of the divine perfections in a somewhat confused and general way and not individually, although this knowledge does convey knowledge of the divine greatness with much greater clarity. In the same way the soul becomes aware in a confused sort of way of certain created truths such as the awfulness of hell.

Let us now treat of the first two grades of contemplation, *interior recollection of spirit* and, secondly, *quiet*. We shall treat of the grace of *union* later.

Supernatural Recollection

13. The first degree of contemplation is called *supernatural recollection*. We have already dealt with *natural recollection* in number 7 above. This last occurs when the faculties of the soul are gathered together interiorly to reflect on God. It is a *natural* state because the soul remains active and operates as a result of God's ordinary graces. To say that this state is *natural* does not imply that the soul is able to act, as it were, by its own strength since every act of virtue which enables us to merit an eternal reward needs the assistance of grace. Supernatural recollection comes from God by way of an extraordinary grace which leaves the soul in a passive state. Supernatural recollection, more correctly

called *infused*, is not due to the personal efforts of the soul but is brought about by means of an illumination which the Lord pours into the soul and which arouses in the soul a wonderful sense of love for God. In this state the soul must not be forced to abandon that peaceful discursive communication which God's inspiration may suggest. Nor should the soul strive to reflect on anything in particular or to make any resolutions. Neither should the soul curiously pry into the nature of the recollection being experienced. Rather should the soul allow itself to be directed by God to reflect on whatever he inspires, and to repeat those acts which the soul knows are due to divine inspiration.

Prayer of Quiet

14. The second degree of contemplation is that of *quiet*. In the state of recollection God's love is communicated to the soul directly through the external senses, which are all gathered together into one, as it were, within the soul. But, in the prayer of quiet, God's love is communicated directly to the spirit in the very center of the soul. And this love is often so ardent that it communicates itself even to the external senses, though this is not always the case. Very often the soul possesses the prayer of quiet without any external sense of sweetness. St. Teresa of Avila declares that in this state of prayer not all the powers of the soul are suspended.[4] Certainly, the will is bound, in the sense that it is unable to love any other object except God who draws the soul to himself. The intellect and memory or imagination often remain free and can roam around. But Teresa advises the soul not to be upset by this: "Let the soul make fun of these thoughts and reject them as foolishness and remain undisturbed in the state of quiet. Since one's will is dominant it will bring one's imagination under control without any further effort on the part of the soul."[5] But if these souls wish to give themselves over to reflection they will lose the prayer of quiet without any further effort. In this state of contemplative quiet, even more so than in the prayer of recollection, souls should refrain from making resolutions or any other

acts involving their own choices. They should only elicit those acts toward which God is gently attracting them.

Darkness

15. A word now about contemplative prayer, pure and simple, or *negative* contemplation mentioned in number 12, which is a much more perfect state of contemplation than the positive. It is styled *Chiaro-Oscuro* or Bright-Dark since the flood of divine light darkens the intellect just as one who looks directly into the sun is blinded and sees nothing but realizes that the sun is a great light. Into this darkness God pours his divine light with the result that the soul does not come to the knowledge of any one truth in particular but acquires a general and somewhat confused knowledge of the incomprehensible goodness of God and forms a profound, even if obscure, idea of him. When souls become aware, however imperfectly, of any of the divine perfections they are able to conceive some idea of God's goodness. But when they realize that God's perfection is incomprehensible, then they are able to come to an even better realization of God's goodness. Cardinal Petrucci in his letters described this prayer as the prayer of darkness since souls in this life are not capable of clearly understanding the Divinity. So, in this prayer of contemplation souls come to the knowledge of God not by means of their intellect but by an altogether higher mode of knowledge. They do not know intellectually since God cannot be known under any form or image subject to our senses. Souls know nothing more than that they cannot know God intellectually. The Areopagite, accordingly, calls this the *sublime knowledge of God achieved through the absence of knowledge of him.*[6] In this prayer of darkness all the interior faculties of the soul are suspended and at times even the exterior senses. Sometimes the soul seems to be intoxicated since it breaks forth in a delirium of love, cries, uncontrolled weeping, dancing, and such similar reactions as happened to St. Mary Magdalene de' Pazzi.

Active and Passive Union

16. From these states of prayer, the Lord leads souls to the state of *union*. The sole purpose of this is simply union with God and it is not necessary for a soul to possess *passive union* in order to achieve perfection. *Active union* is sufficient. St. Teresa declared that God leads very few souls by these supernatural ways and, in heaven, we shall see many souls who had never been granted these supernatural graces higher in glory than those who had received them. "Perfection," insists St. Teresa, "does not consist in ecstasy. True union with God consists in the union of our will with his." This is the union that is necessary and not passive union. "Those souls who have achieved just active union," says the saint, "have very often acquired much greater merit since they have had to overcome great difficulties. And the Lord directs them in such a way that the consolations which they have not experienced in this life will be preserved for them in the next." Cardinal Petrucci states that even without the grace of infused contemplation, souls can achieve the death of their own wills through the ordinary graces that God grants and can transform their own wills into God's will by wishing nothing more than what God wills. And even though the soul may still experience the movements of various passions, these do not form an obstacle to that transformation. Consequently, he adds, since all holiness consists in transforming our will into that of God, we should desire and ask God for nothing more than to be directed by him to make our wills one with his.

St. Teresa, dealing with the state of passive union, states that in it "the soul neither sees nor feels any sensation nor even realizes that she is in that state." The abundance of God's light and love brings about that state of darkness in which all the powers of the soul are suspended. The memory thinks only of God; the will is so joined to God that it can love nothing else; the mind is so full of God's light that it is aware of no other thought, not even of the grace that it is experiencing. The intellect knows many things but is not conscious of what it knows. In short, souls in that state of contemplative union have a clear and experimental knowledge of God, who is united with them in the very center of their being. St. Teresa points out that this state of union does not last long, at most half-an-hour. In the other states of contemplation which we have described, God manifests himself merely as being *near* to the soul; in this state, however, he manifests himself as being *present* to the soul. And souls experience that God is united with them by a sense of gentle contact. As St. Teresa points out, in other states of contemplation souls might doubt whether God was really present to them or not, but in this case they have no doubt. Despite this, the confessor should warn his penitents that they have not become incapable of sinning with the result that the more they become aware of the grace that God has given them so much the more should they be humble, totally detached, loving the Cross, and remaining in everything completely submissive to the Lord's dispositions. And they should realize that any infidelities on their part would be the more severely punished on account of the great ingratitude involved in them. St. Teresa wrote that she knew of several souls who had reached this state of union but afterward plunged headlong into mortal sin.[7]

Spiritual Espousals

17. There are three types of *union*, namely, *simple, espousal,* and *consummated union or spiritual marriage.* What we have described up to the present is simple union. Union of espousal is ordinarily preceded by substantial aridity, or purification of the spirit, which we have described above in number 8. In this espousal union there are three further grades or experiences, namely, *ecstasy, rapture,* and *flight of the spirit.* In the state of simple union the faculties are suspended, though not the bodily senses, but these last are so weak that they are barely able to function. In ecstasy, however, souls lose the use of their senses with the result that they neither see nor hear and do not feel even cuts or burns. *Rapture* is a sensation of a very powerful influx of grace by which God not only unites the soul with himself in union but

179

does so suddenly and violently. At times, the body is raised as a result and feels as light as a feather. *Flight of the spirit* occurs when souls feel, as it were, swept out of themselves and borne away with great violence. Initially, they are terrified. Flight of the spirit involves both ecstasy, which brings with it suspension of the senses, and rapture, which involves violent movement. A person who has received graces such as these told me that in these elevations of the spirit it seemed to him that his soul was torn from the body and violently lifted up as though he traversed in an instant a thousand miles. And this terrified him since he did not know where he was going. But when this experience came to an end, he knew he was enlightened by some divine secret.[8]

A problem arises here. How is it possible for the soul to know what has taken place and to speak of the hidden things of God if, during the state of union, one's faculties are suspended and one's intellect, blinded by the divine light, is unable to give its attention to what is happening? Mystics answer that when God wishes souls to know some secret or to convey to them some intellectual vision, he diminishes the divine illumination so that the soul remains capable of perceiving and understanding what God wants.

Spiritual Nuptials

18. *Consummated union,* which is a still more perfect degree of union and which is the highest form which God can grant to a soul while on earth, is called *spiritual marriage or nuptials.* In this state the soul is transformed into God and becomes one with him just as a vessel of water when poured into the sea becomes one with the water of the sea.[9] It is important to note that, as the mystics assert, while one's faculties are suspended in other states of union, this is not the case in spiritual marriage. One's faculties are purified of their sensibilities and their materiality so that they are capable of divine union. The will loves God serenely, the intellect is aware and conscious of the divine union which has already taken place in the center of the

soul. It is as if one were to gaze into the heart of the blazing sun and without any injury to one's eyes were to behold its dazzling glory. Moreover, this union is not of a transitory nature like the other two, but permanent. The soul is aware of the divine presence and is able to enjoy it in tranquillity. Passions no longer disturb the soul, which recognizes them for what they are when they manifest themselves but the soul is not upset just as one who dwells above the clouds perceives the storms raging below but is not affected by them.

Visions

19. It will not be irrelevant at this juncture to say something about *visions, locutions,* and *revelations,* if only to be able to distinguish the false from the authentic. Visions are either *external, imaginative,* or *intellectual.*[10] External visions are seen by the bodily eyes; imaginative visions are seen by the imaginative senses—the fantasy or the imagination; intellectual visions are seen, not by the eyes or imagination, but by the intellect or mind alone, helped by divine illumination, which is capable of producing an intellectual image. These last types of visions, according to St. Teresa, are totally spiritual. Neither the senses, whether external or internal, such as the imagination and fantasy, play any part in them. Souls can only perceive in corporeal form what has been represented to them through their eyes and imagination, even if these are of spiritual substances. Intellectual visions, even if they are of material substances, are always seen as spiritual. Or rather, I should say, they are *perceived* as spiritual, not *seen.* But this is a more satisfactory form of knowledge than if they were actually seen by the eyes.

20. It is important to point out that these visions, even intellectual visions, can owe their origin to the devil as well as to God. At least that is what St. John of the Cross insinuates, contrary to the opinion of Cardinal Petrucci.[11] But this is more likely to occur in the case of exterior corporeal visions which have their origin in the fantasy or imagination and with women.

There are certain indications which help to distinguish true from false visions: (a) if they occur unexpectedly without any previous reflection on the part of the soul; (b) if, initially, they cause the souls to be confused and even terrified but afterward leave them in peace; (c) if they only occur rarely, since frequent visions arouse suspicions; (d) if their duration is short. St. Teresa states that when the soul gazes on some representation for a considerable period of time the presumption is that this is an act of the imagination or fantasy. A divine vision is as transitory as a flash of lightning but remains afterward indelibly imprinted on the mind. (e) A genuine vision fills the soul with a deep peace, a sense of its own unworthiness, and at the same time with a great desire of striving for perfection. Diabolical visions on the contrary make little impression, leave souls in dryness, subject them to movements of self-esteem, and with a desire for further favors of a similar nature. However, even when all these signs are present, according to St. Teresa, the soul can have no guarantee of the nature of their experience since very often the devil knows how to simulate peace of soul, thoughts of humility, and even a desire for perfection. With the origin of these sentiments, then, uncertain, the devil is accustomed to arouse them in the soul so that he may gain credence and be able to reap the fruits of his deception.

The director of conscience, generally speaking, should permit his penitents to describe their visions and even oblige them to do so, whether they are true or false. This is according to St. Teresa.[12] But he should pretend no great interest in knowing about them and should not question his penitent on the details. And he should not ask his penitents if this is what the vision was, or did you see this or this, as it were, putting these ideas into their mouths. The soul could then very easily reply in the affirmative either from malice on the one hand or from simplicity on the other. If he is convinced that these visions are fantasy or the work of the devil which withdraws a soul from the practice of obedience, humility, or some other virtue, the confessor should make this known to his penitent immediately. But if he is unable to discern the nature of the visions, he should be advised not to persist in declaring them to be either from the devil or from the fantasy as some do who are inordinately skeptical—just as some, who are inordinately credulous, believe them all to be genuine. Instead, he should advise his penitents to ask the Lord not to guide them in these paths which are so dangerous and to assure the Lord, at the same time, that as long as they remain on earth their only desire is to know him by faith. He should so direct his penitents that they should gather from the visions, whether they be genuine or false, the only result that is necessary, namely to continue walking uprightly before God. In this way the devil will be deprived of whatever benefits he had sought to gain from these visions if they were from him.

Locutions

21. As regards *locutions,* they can be *successive, formal,* and *substantial. Successive* locutions occur when souls in the course of meditating on some truth of faith feel that they are being answered by their own spirit but, as if it were, by somebody outside themselves. When this gives rise to a beneficial effect such as an increase of love or of a remarkable act of humility it may well be a special illumination of God's grace.

When, however, there is no indication of an increase of love then it can be taken that it comes from one's own intellect. *Formal* locutions occur when souls distinctly hear definite, formed words but from outside themselves. And they can hear them with their ears, or their imagination or with their intellect. The test of whether these are from God or from the devil is to be found in what the locutions themselves say, what actions they recommend, and what effects they produce in the soul. If they come from God they will inculcate acts of patience, humility, or some other spiritual act and they will leave the soul ready to accept whatever comes from the hand of God, to do whatever he demands, and to deepen humility.

Substantial locutions are similar to formal locutions and differ from them only in their effects. A formal locution gives instruction or imposes a direction. A substantial locution achieves its effect instantly. For example, if the soul hears "be consoled," "do not fear," "love me," in that very instant the soul is filled with consolation, is encouraged, or burns with the fire of love. This final type of locution is far more reliable than the other two. Successive locutions are very doubtful; the second, that is the formal locution, is suspect especially when it orders something to be performed. The director in this case will absolutely forbid his penitent to carry out what was ordered if he judges it contrary to Christian prudence. If what was ordered is not contrary to Christian prudence, the director would be well advised to delay the performance of what was ordered until he is more convinced about it. And this particularly if what was ordered is something out of the ordinary.

Revelations

22. *Revelations* concerning secret or future things such as mysteries of faith, the reading of consciences, the predestination of certain persons, foretelling their death, elevation to higher dignities, and all such things may occur in three ways, namely, through *visions, locutions,* and by *intellectual perception* of such truths. In all cases of revelations, the director of conscience should manifest extreme caution. He should not be too ready to give credence to the revelations and he should be extremely cautious in communicating with anyone as a result of information received in the revelation. He should above all insist that his penitent should not reveal the revelation to others. He should consult with other prudent persons since very often these revelations are of doubtful origin and quite suspect. But less suspect are revelations or illuminations of basic truths concerning the mysteries of faith, the Divine Attributes, the malice of sin, the unhappiness of the damned, and such like. St. John of the Cross writes that the soul should not seek to receive these revelations but when they are in conformity with the faith, then, if they are granted, they should be received with humility and there is no need to attempt to reject them.[13]

Supernatural Gifts

23. Should all these types of graces and supernatural communications be accepted or rejected? A learned author, agreeing with St. John of the Cross, makes this distinction. All graces which come in an unusual form such as visions, locutions, and revelations are to be strenuously rejected by the soul if they distance one from the faith. Graces, on the other hand, which are in conformity with the teaching of the faith, such as general and somewhat confused communications and contact with God which unite the soul with him, are not to be rejected. They may even be desired and sought for so that the soul becomes more and more united with God and confirmed in his love. But this applies only to those souls who have already received similar graces. For others, by far the safest way is to desire and ask only for active union, which, as I have outlined above, unites our will with the divine will. In a word, then, when a director meet souls who receive these communications of contemplation, darkness, or union, he should not instruct them to reject them but rather encourage them to receive them with humility and a spirit of gratitude.

He should so communicate with his penitents that all their hesitations are not removed but that some little insecurity remains which should not, however, make them anxious but should rather confirm them in humility and total detachment. As regards extraordinary graces which are received in visions and such like, the director should instruct his penitents to reject them in a spirit of humility (but not contemptuously by spitting in the face and mocking, which many suggest). These souls should continue to protest to God that all they wish is to serve him in pure faith. For the rest, St. Teresa insists that every time souls realize that they are being gently led to a greater love for God, they have received a divine communication, not indeed to make them believe they are better than others but to help them advance more perfectly toward God. By acting in this way the Lord will see to it that if the devil has had any part in the communication he has been defeated by his very own weapons.

24. And now to sum up. The director should (a) oblige his

penitents to reveal all the communications they have received in prayer without at the same time showing any curiosity to know of them. He should never inform others of the supernatural graces his penitents have received, since they would then recommend themselves to their prayers and expose them to the danger of pride. And if afterward they noticed some defects, however slight, in the recipients of these favors they would be scandalized and hold them up to scorn. (b) The director should not show any unwonted sign of favor to souls graced with these favors and much less should he recommend other penitents to seek advice from them, or to go to them for consolation or direction. He should rather make less of them than of other souls who follow the ordinary way of faith. Souls favored with extraordinary graces should be humiliated in every way possible. (c) If the director perceives that his penitents who have received these divine communications preserve their humility and their anxiety not to offend God, he should help them and reassure them whenever he thinks it opportune. St. Teresa declares that souls will never be moved to do great things for God unless they realize that they have received great favors from him. And when she herself had been reassured by both St. Francis Borgia and St. Peter of Alcantara that the graces she had received were from God, she not only ran in the way of perfection, she virtually flew toward God.

The director should not deduce from the fact that his penitents fall into some defect (provided always that the defect is not fully deliberate or committed with stubbornness or contempt) that all the communications they have received are lies and illusions. The Lord is accustomed to grant such graces not only to those who are perfect but even to those who are as yet imperfect in order to free them from their imperfections and to urge them on to greater perfection. It is an infallible sign that these extraordinary favors are authentic if the recipients, as a result, struggle more and more to overcome their passions, grow in divine love and in their eagerness for perfection. In short, when the director encounters external graces such as visions, locutions, and revelations, it is more prudent for him, generally speaking, as we have said, not to make much of them. He can quote what St. Teresa from heaven said to a religious: "Souls should not rely on visions and personal revelations nor should they think that perfection consists in them. While many of these external graces are genuine, many are also false and deceptive. Among so many lies it is difficult to find something that is true. There are more false visions than genuine ones. The more eagerly one seeks these visions and prizes them, the more does that person stray from the simple way of faith and humility which is the surest way to heaven."[14]

The director should then advise his penitents to pray that God would grant them true ecstasy, namely, total renunciation of self and of all things earthly. Without this there is no way to perfection. If the director perceives that his penitents are not well grounded in acknowledging their own unworthiness and persist in maintaining that the communications they have received are genuine and are disturbed that their director is not inclined to accept them as such, it is not a good sign. Indeed, it can be a sign either that these communications are from the devil since they are a cause of pride in the recipient, or they are an indication that all is not well with the penitents since, if the director has doubts about these graces, they should also share them. In these circumstances the director should exercise his penitents in humility in every way possible and cultivate in their souls the fear of God. If they do not even then come round to accepting the director's assessment, he should forbid them to receive communion and penance them severely since they are in danger of being deceived by the devil.

Finally, if the director judges that he should ultimately reassure his penitents that their communications are from the Lord, he should at the same time suggest to them that in their prayers they should always recall some incident from the life or Passion of Jesus. St. Teresa says that souls which neglect to orientate themselves toward Jesus will never achieve perfect union with God. Souls at the beginning of their spiritual journey should meditate in a discursive way on the Passion of the Lord. Those favored with the grace of contemplation have no need of discursive prayer but they should recall some divine mystery and dwell on the goodness, mercy, and love of God. God will then give them the grace when he so wills, to move on to the contemplation of his divinity.

3. Concerning Mortification[15]

25. As regards the virtue of mortification, it is important to consider the following points. The Lord usually grants to those who resolve to lead a deeply spiritual life the grace of sensible consolations with the result that, in their initial fervor, these souls wish to burden themselves with many corporal penances such as the use of disciplines, hair shirts, and fasting. The director should be very slow in granting permission for such acts of mortification since, after some time, the penitent begins to suffer from spiritual aridity, loses the initial sensible fervor, and consequently abandons all these practices. With an increasing sense of disgust, the penitent then leaves prayer aside and even considers the very practice of the spiritual life as only meant for others and then abandons everything. Furthermore, it can sometimes happen that some souls, as a result of their initial fervor, abandon all restraint in their practices of mortification with consequent loss of health. In order to recuperate their strength they then leave aside totally the practice of their spiritual devotions and incur the danger of not resuming them again.

The spiritual director should ensure that this penitents are, first of all, well grounded in the spiritual life and only then, having taken into account the question of health, their normal occupations, and their spirit of fervor, should he permit them those external mortifications which he considers appropriate in the light of Christian prudence. I say *in the light of Christian prudence.* There are some spiritual directors so devoid of this that they seem to place the essence of spiritual progress in permitting their penitents to multiply practices of fasting, hair shirts, disciplines to blood, and self-inflicted burns. There are other spiritual directors, however, who totally condemn the practice of *external* mortification and place the essence of perfection in *internal* mortification. This is as much an error as the other point of view.

External mortification helps internal mortification and it is in a certain sense necessary (when it can prudently be practiced) in order to control one's senses. And so we read that it was practiced by all the saints. It is quite true that one's penitent should be directed particularly to the practice of internal mortification: not to respond to offenses, not to complain, not to reveal to others what redounds to one's personal credit, to yield in arguments, to give in to other's wishes provided there is no spiritual damage involved. At times, it is also advisable to forbid one's penitent to practice any external act of mortification until the soul's predominant passions such, for example, as vanity, anger, desire for temporal possessions, self-esteem, and one's self-will have been brought under control. But to state categorically and absolutely that external mortifications are of little or no value is a serious error. St. John of the Cross was of the opinion that no credence should be given to those who rejected external mortification even though they worked miracles.

26. The spiritual director should insist from the very outset that his penitents should be obedient, that they should not perform anything in the matter of corporal penances against his directions or without his permission. A soul who insists on performing corporal penances against the instructions of the director "makes more progress in defects than in virtues," according to St. John of the Cross. So, as I have said, the spiritual director should be quite restrained in permitting penances of this nature even though his penitent insistently requests them. He should, in the beginning, give permission for some slight and infrequent acts of corporal mortification such as the use of the hair shirt or the discipline or fasting, more with the idea of instilling in the soul a desire for mortification than with the purpose of permitting its practice. In due course, taking into account the progress in virtue that the soul has made, the director may be more liberal in granting permission. Then, when the soul is definitely established in the practice of virtue, the director should scruple to

deny permission to his penitent for the practice of appropriate practices of mortification.

The director, in the ordinary course of events, should make it a rule not to grant permission for external penances unless his penitent requests them; their value depends to some degree on the willingness of the penitent. He should always give permission for less than what is requested and, as Cassian laid down, he should more often refuse than concede. He should recommend in the first place the mortification of one's appetite, which, very often, even spiritual souls do not find attractive. This mortification can be the most difficult of all but is very beneficial for the soul and even for the body. St. Philip Neri said that the soul that does not mortify the appetite will never attain to perfection. On the other hand, the director should be very loath to give permission for mortification in the area of sleep since this can often be harmful both to soul and body. If one's penitents do not have sufficient sleep they are confused and unable to meditate and are in no form for other acts of devotion. No matter what mortifications the director permits to his penitents, he should stress that they are nothing compared to what the saints practiced and to what Jesus Christ suffered for us. In this way there is no danger to the soul of pride. St. Teresa affirmed that no matter what we do it is a mere speck of dust in comparison with a single drop of the blood that Christ shed for us.

By far the best acts of mortifications and the most useful and, at the same time, the least dangerous are negative mortifications, for which, as a general rule, one does not require the permission of one's director. Such are, for example, not looking or listening out of curiosity, restraining oneself in talking, being satisfied with the least appetizing or badly prepared type of food, not to approach the heat in winter, choosing for oneself the least desirable of things, to be happy and rejoice when one lacks something, since St. Bernard says that this is the essential element in the virtue of poverty: "The virtue of poverty is not poverty itself but the love of it." One can add to these examples others such as not complaining if the weather is inclement, having a low opinion of oneself, accepting persecutions and the infirmities of ill-health. The stones of the edifice of the heavenly Jerusalem are carved by sufferings and sorrows. St. Teresa affirms that "it is the height of foolishness to imagine that the Lord admits to his intimate friendship those who seek their own comfort. Souls who love God never seek their own ease."

27. In the gospel we read: "Just so, your light must shine before others, that they may see your good deeds and glorify your heavenly Father" (Mt 5:16). And in another place: "But when you give alms, do not let your left hand know what your right is doing" (Mt 6:3). The question then arises as to whether our acts of virtue should be seen by others or should be concealed. A distinction is necessary here. All works common to the exercise of Christian virtue should be done quite openly. Such, for example, would be the frequentation of the sacraments, mental prayer, visits to the Most Blessed Sacrament, kneeling and showing recollection during Mass, keeping custody of the eyes and preserving reverence in church, declaring: "I wish to attain holiness of life," avoiding excessive talking, dangerous conversations, and excessive curiosity. But acts which are out of the ordinary, beyond what is required, and smack of the singular, such as the practice of the above-mentioned external penances, such as the hair shirt, the discipline, praying with one's arms extended in the form of a cross, eating bitter herbs, loud sighs and tears during prayer, all these should be performed in private as far as possible. If, however, it is impossible to perform them in private, then they should not be omitted provided they are performed with the sole intention of pleasing God.

4. Concerning Frequentation of the Sacraments

28. Finally, I must say something about the advice spiritual directors should give to their penitents in the matter of the frequentation of the sacraments, that is, confession and the reception of Holy Communion.

As regards confession, it is advisable to suggest to them that they make a general confession of all their sins, if they have not already done so. If they have already made such a confession, or, if the souls are troubled by scruples of conscience, the director should forbid them to make or repeat this type of confession. Some souls with a more than ordinary delicacy of conscience are accustomed to confess each day, but, generally speaking, it is sufficient for spiritual persons, and especially if they are in any way scrupulous, to confess their sins once a week, or at most, twice. But when a soul commits some light fault and has not the opportunity of confessing, that person should on no account omit to receive Holy Communion. This is the opinion of Father Barisoni in his work on Holy Communion and he relies on the authority of St. Ambrose and of many other authors, among them St. Francis de Sales in one of his letters. The Council of Trent teaches that there are other ways besides confession to secure the remission of venial sins such as acts of contrition and love. So it is more advisable for souls, in order to be purified of their faults, to employ one of these means rather than to omit Holy Communion if a confessor is not available. A wise spiritual director has said that occasionally it is much more beneficial for certain spiritual souls to dispose themselves to receive Holy Communion by making acts in this way rather than by use of confession. Often the soul is disposed to receive Holy Communion by very fervent acts of sorrow, confidence, and humility.

29. As regards Holy Communion, I am not dealing here with the obligation that pastors of souls are under not to deny persons who are not public sinners reception of Holy Communion when they reasonably request it. I have already dealt with this matter in my work in which we saw that Pope Innocent XI decreed that the question of frequent reception of Holy Communion was a matter for the prudence of confessors. I cannot see how any pastor could, without compelling reasons, conscientiously deny the reception of Holy Communion to those who request it. Moreover, that very same decree forbids bishops to lay down certain days on which souls can communicate.[16]

I am dealing here with the question of how directors of souls should deal with their penitents in the matter of permitting them the reception of Holy Communion. In this matter, some err on account of being overindulgent, others on account of excessive rigorism. Benedict XIV is certainly correct when he declares in his admirable work *De Synodo* that it is an error to grant Holy Communion to those who frequently fall into serious sin and show no inclination to repent and to amend their ways, or to those who receive Holy Communion despite their attachment to deliberate venial sins without any effort on their part to avoid them.[17] It is certainly advisable, occasionally, to admit to Holy Communion those who are in danger of falling into mortal sins so that they might gain strength to avoid them. As regards those souls who are not in danger of falling into serious sin and who, on the other hand, commit deliberate venial sins and show no indication or desire of giving them up, the best advice is not to permit them to communicate more frequently than once a week. Indeed, on occasion, it might be a good thing to forbid them to communicate for a whole week in the hope that they will develop a horror for their sins and a greater reverence for the sacrament. It is the more commonly held opinion that to receive Holy Communion in actual venial sin or with attachment to it is itself a fault on account of irreverence toward the Blessed Sacrament. There are some authorities who allege the following Decree of Pope Anacletus: "After the consecration all who wish to remain part of the Church shall communicate. This was laid down by the Apostles and is affirmed by the Holy Roman Church." But the existence of such an apostolic precept is denied by Suarez and others. That decree, as an explanatory note attached to it declares, applied only to the ministers who were assisting at the altar. Even if such a decree ever laid down such an obligation, it is certain that it has today fallen into desuetude.

30. Many spiritual directors are in error and are lacking in the true spirit of the church when, without any consideration of the needs or spiritual progress of souls, they indiscriminately refuse to permit frequent communion for the sole reason that it is *frequent.* The *Roman Catechism,* explaining the wish of the Council of Trent that all who assist at the Sacrifice of the Mass should communicate, instructs all pastors of souls that it is their duty to encourage the faithful to receive Holy Communion not merely frequently but even daily.[18] Pastors are to instruct their

people that the soul, just like the human body, needs daily nourishment. There is no need for me to adduce here the authority of so many Fathers and saints of the church as well as masters of the spiritual life. These are readily available in the many treatises which deal with the question of frequent Communion. Suffice it to cite the *Roman Catechism* and the Decree of Pope Innocent XI to which I refer in my *Moral Theology,* which demonstrate that frequent and indeed daily communion was always approved by the church and the church Fathers. One authority points out that when the practice of daily communion began to lapse the church exerted every effort to restore it. And in the Third Synod held in the diocese of Milan under St. Charles Borromeo, pastors were instructed to exhort, in their sermons, their flock to the practice of frequent communion. The bishops of that province were obliged to forbid under pain of censure those who held differently to preach the opposing doctrine which was a source of scandal to the faithful and contrary to the whole tradition of the church. Furthermore, in the above-mentioned Decree of Pope Innocent XI, bishops were not only forbidden to deny the daily reception of communion to those who wished it but were obliged to encourage this practice among their faithful.

The more rigid theologians readily admit the lawfulness of the practice of daily communion but they declare that proper dispositions are required before this should be permitted. But what are these *proper dispositions?* If they understand by this that we should be *worthy,* who would ever be allowed to approach Holy Communion? Only Jesus Christ could worthily receive the Eucharist since only God could worthily receive God. If they understand by *proper dispositions* that those who are in actual venial sin or are attached to it without any intention of abandoning it should be denied frequent communion, I would agree that this is fair enough. But we are talking about those souls who have freed themselves from their deliberate attachment to venial sins, who have striven to overcome their sinful inclinations and have a great desire of approaching Holy Communion. St. Francis de Sales says that these souls, with the advice of their spiritual director, are to be admitted to the daily reception of communion. St.

Thomas clearly states that when a soul becomes aware of growth in the love of God as a result of daily communion and that reverence for the sacrament is in no way diminished as a result, this soul should not abstain from receiving communion daily. Here are the holy Doctor's own words: "If souls experience growth in the fervor of their love for God as a result of daily reception of communion and their reverence is not in any way diminished they should communicate daily."[19]

31. Even though it can be an act of virtue to abstain from communion on one or other day, Father Granata in his work on Holy Communion declares that it is the common opinion of theologians that it is better to receive Holy Communion daily out of love than to abstain from it out of reverence. St. Thomas endorses this opinion when he writes: "To approach Holy Communion daily and to abstain from communion now and again are both acts of reverence towards the sacrament. But love and hope towards which the Scriptures constantly exhort us are to be preferred to reverential fear." And Father Barisoni correctly remarks that the soul who communicates with the desire of growing in the love of God thereby shows reverence to Jesus Christ. The soul who receives Holy Communion makes a positive act of reverence toward the Blessed Sacrament while the action of the soul that abstains is merely negative. Many saints such as St. Gertrude, St. Catherine of Siena, St. Teresa of Avila, St. Jane Francis de Chantal, all of whom had great reverence for the Blessed Sacrament, did not abstain from daily communion. And if some authors counter this by saying that such saints do not exist today, let them not suppose that the hand of the Lord is shortened. The Venerable John of Avila did not hesitate to state that those who condemn souls who receive communion frequently are doing the devil's work for him.

32. So having considered the various opinions in this matter it seems that a spiritual director could not without scruple deny frequent and even daily communion to his penitents who wish to receive communion daily in order to grow in the love of God. When I say "daily communion," I am not excluding the possibility of excluding one day a week as is the practice of some prudent directors, or even the possibility that a director might

deny a soul Holy Communion to test obedience or humility or for some other good reason. I am supposing that the soul in question has removed all attachment to deliberate venial sin, devotes time to mental prayer, and is earnest in making efforts to strive for perfection and does not fall into sin, particularly deliberate venial sin. According to the opinion of St. Prosper of Aquitaine, this is the degree of perfection to which we can attain in this world taking into account human frailty. And when a confessor decides that it is spiritually profitable for a soul to be allowed to approach communion daily, there is no difficulty in permitting this, according to the decree of Innocent XI, both to those who are married and those engaged in business affairs. Here are his words: "Judgment in the matter of permitting frequent reception of Holy Communion is a matter for confessors. They should prescribe frequent reception for lay people, both married and those engaged in business affairs, and who are of blameless consciences, when they foresee that this will be beneficial and will assist them in making spiritual progress."

33. Of course, a soul may from time to time fall into deliberate venial sin on account of human weakness but then be sorry right away and determine not to offend again. Why should communion be denied to such a person who wishes to communicate in order to gain strength not to fall again and to continue to make progress in the spiritual life? Alexander VIII condemned Proposition No. 22 of Baius which declared: "Those who claim admission to Holy Communion before they have done penance for the sins they have committed are guilty of sacrilege." And Proposition No. 23: "Those who do not yet possess the purest and undiluted love of God are to be forbidden to receive Holy Communion."[20]

The Council of Trent stated that this sacrament "is the antidote by which we are freed from our daily faults and preserved from mortal sin." And it was for the purpose of preserving souls from relapsing into sin that the apostles permitted the early Christians to receive Holy Communion daily. Amongst them were certainly to be found many who were not yet perfect and some who were very imperfect, as can be deduced from the letters of St. Paul and St. James. In the postcommunion prayer of the Mass for the Twenty-second Sunday after Pentecost the church prays that "whatever is imperfect in our soul may be cured by the medicine of this Sacrament." Clearly then, communion was instituted also for the imperfect who are restored to health by means of this heavenly food. St. Francis de Sales in his *Philotea* states on this point:

> If you are asked why you communicate so frequently reply that there are two types of souls who should communicate frequently, the perfect and the imperfect: the perfect in order that they should remain perfect and the imperfect in order that they should become perfect. The strong lest they grow weak, the weak that they may become strong; the sick in order that they may be restored to health and the healthy lest they become infirm. And as regards yourself since you are imperfect, ill and weak, you have need of frequent communion. Say to them, moreover, that those who are not involved in worldly affairs should communicate frequently because they have the opportunity to do so and those who are caught up in worldly affairs should also do so because they have need of it.

St. Francis concludes: "Communicate frequently Philotea, even very frequently with the advice of your director. Believe me that the hares on our mountains are white for no other reason than that they feed on snow.[21] In the same way you will become totally pure by feeding on the purity of this Sacrament."

Father Granata in his treatise on communion writes: "No one should abstain from communicating on account of unworthiness. This treasure has been bequeathed precisely to enrich the poor, this medicine is destined for the sick. No one, no matter how imperfect, should be deprived of this medicine if they really wish to be cured. Indeed, the more one recognizes oneself to be weak all the more should one seek out this food." This is in agreement with the opinion of St. Ambrose: "Because I am always sinning I am always in need of medicine." And in another place: "If you sin daily, then communicate daily."[22]

34. There is a further argument from St. Thomas, who

states that, as regards the effect of the sacrament of the Eucharist, venial sins are not an obstacle to an increase of grace, provided that they are not committed in the act of communion itself. While they partially obstruct the effect of this sacrament, they are not a total block. This opinion is also held by Sotus, Suarez, Valentia, Vasquez, Coninck, and many others, as the *Salmanticenses* declare.[23] Many reliable authors hold that this sacrament remits venial sins *ex opere operato* (that is, by the very fact of receiving it) provided that the soul does not remain attached to them. This is confirmed by the *Roman Catechism,* which states: "There is no questioning the fact that the Eucharist remits and removes those lesser sins which are usually styled venial. Whatever the soul loses through the force of its passions is restored by the Eucharist which wipes out these lesser faults." It is commonly held with St. Thomas that reception of this sacrament prompts us to acts of love of God and these in turn remit our sins.

35. If it becomes evident, after some time, that those who frequently receive Holy Communion make no progress in the way of holiness, that they do not renounce deliberate sins, even venial sins, that they still give in to sensible desires in seeing, hearing, eating, and to vanity in outward comportment, then certainly serious thought should be given to the question of restricting their frequent reception of communion. Indeed, there must be serious doubt as to the authenticity of their intention of amending their lives and of their desire for perfection. At the same time it is important to note that even though St. Thomas insists that one should approach Holy Communion with great devotion, it is not necessary that this devotion should be either of the highest degree or experienced in the external senses. It is sufficient if the director discerns in his penitent a readiness to carry out what the Lord wants. Souls who stay away from Holy Communion because they do not experience in themselves a great degree of sensible devotion resemble, according to the saying of Gerson, those who feel the cold yet refuse to approach the heat because they do not experience in themselves any sense of warmth!

Those pusillanimous souls who on account of an exaggerated sense of their own unworthiness neglect to receive Holy

Communion are thereby inflicting considerable harm to their own spiritual progress. Nor is it necessary in order to continue one's practice of frequent communion that the soul should be aware of or be able to feel spiritual progress since the spiritual effects of this sacrament are not always easily discernible. St. Bonaventure wrote: "If your devotion is not of the highest order still approach this sacrament with great trust in the mercy of God. If you are conscious of your own unworthiness remember that the person who realizes the seriousness of his illness has the greatest need of the physician. You are not approaching Holy Communion because you are endeavoring to sanctify the Lord; he it is who is to sanctify you." And then he concludes: "You should not omit Holy Communion if you do not feel any depth of sensible devotion but you should make a special effort to prepare yourself either beforehand or in the act of receiving communion if you feel less devotion than you would wish to have." And the saint goes a step further when he says that even if one experiences less devotion after receiving Holy Communion than before it, one should still not omit to communicate.[24] So, if the confessor may sometimes find it advisable to test his penitent by refusing permission to communicate even when the soul most eagerly desires to do so, it is equally advisable for him to encourage the soul to frequent communion in the midst of aridity and even distaste, so that his penitent may gain strength from the sacrament. If the director perceives that his penitent is unduly disturbed when denied permission to communicate he should consider this as evidence of pride on his penitent's part which in itself could render the soul unworthy of communion.

36. In conclusion, it is my sincere wish that there should be many souls, who detesting even the slightest sin, seek permission, not only to communicate frequently, but even daily with a firm determination at the same time to improve and to grow in the love of God. (Imagine that there are some confessors so strict that they categorize these souls as irreverent and presumptuous!) If only this were so there would be greater love for Jesus Christ in this world of ours. It is the experience of all those who exercise the ministry of spiritual direction, myself included, that those

who approach Holy Communion with correct dispositions make considerable progress in their spiritual lives. The Lord, moreover, draws them wonderfully to himself, even though he may not allow them, for their own good, to be aware of this. He may even allow them to suffer spiritual darkness and desolation, without the slightest sensible satisfaction. The surest remedy for these souls, as St. Teresa of Avila and Blessed Henry Suso teach, is frequent reception of communion.

The spiritual director should urge his penitents to the reception of communion as often as they show a genuine longing for it and when he perceives that as a result of communion they make progress in the spiritual life. He should be careful to recommend that they spend whatever time they can in thanksgiving after communion. There are very few directors who encourage their penitents to spend some time in thanksgiving after the reception of Holy Communion for the simple reason that very few priests themselves spend time with the Lord in thanksgiving after having celebrated the Holy Sacrifice of the Mass. Accordingly, they are ashamed to recommend a course of action which they neglect themselves. Ordinarily, a whole hour should be spent in thanksgiving but certainly it should be at least half an hour in which the soul spends time in making acts of love of God and prayers of petition. St. Teresa commented that after communion the Lord is with us as on a throne of mercy dispensing his favors. "What do you wish me to do for you?" And in another place she urges us not to lose such a wonderful opportunity of treating with the Lord about important spiritual matters. The Divine Guest will not be lacking in generosity to those who grant him generous hospitality in their souls. She also urges us to communicate spiritually very frequently as well, a practice which is greatly encouraged by the Council of Trent. "The practice of spiritual Communions is very advantageous," says St. Teresa. "Be advised not to neglect this practice since it is in this way that the Lord becomes aware of how much you love Him."

Encouragement for a Troubled Soul

Introduction

Editor's Note: This works purports to be a spiritual conversation between Alphonsus and a soul who is troubled in spirit. Published in Naples in 1775, the year Alphonsus resigned his bishopric, it appeared as a dialogue between a soul and a bishop. In this translation I have substituted "spiritual director" for "bishop." Students of Alphonsus's writings suggest that the penitent in question may have been Sister Brianna Caraffa, a contemplative sister of the Convent of St. Marcellino in Naples whom Alphonsus directed for many years. Many of his letters to her have been preserved and published.

The work, however, deals with spiritual problems experienced by many who are neither priests or religious. It has proved a source of consolation and reassurance to many of the laity who are sincerely committed to progress in the spiritual life and would find a place in any compendium of lay spirituality.

*   *   *

Spiritual Director: Please tell me the worries of conscience which, you say, are troubling you greatly.

Soul: Father, for three years I have suffered great dryness of spirit, such desolation that I am unable to find the Lord in prayer, or before the Blessed Sacrament or even when I receive Holy Communion. It seems to me that I am devoid of all love of God, without hope and without faith. In a word, I feel God has abandoned me. Neither the Passion of Our Lord nor his presence in the Eucharist moves me to any tenderness of spirit. I am totally devoid of all devotion. At the same time, I admit that I have deserved all this on account of my sins, which have merited the pains of hell.

Spiritual Director: In a word, then, you are telling me that you have experienced great aridity of spirit for a considerable time. To give you an adequate answer I shall have to know whether your aridity is voluntary, that is, due to yourself, or whether it is involuntary. Let me explain. Voluntary aridity occurs when souls freely commit deliberate faults and have no intention of amending their ways. This state is not really aridity; it is more properly called tepidity. And if souls do not make a determined effort to overcome it, their spiritual state deteriorates. Tepidity could lead to serious consequences. This type of aridity is more or less a wasting spiritual disease which could even prove fatal. On the other hand, involuntary aridity occurs when souls strive to advance in the way of perfection, when they avoid deliberate defects, when they are faithful to prayer, the sacraments, and yet, with all that, they experience this dryness of spirit. And so we come to yourself. You have mentioned sins of your past life. Have you confessed these sins?

Soul: Yes, indeed, Father, I have. I made a general confession. To be exact, I have confessed them many times.

Spiritual Director: And what instructions has your spiritual director given you?

Soul: He has forbidden me even to mention sins of my past life but I have always been anxious, thinking that, perhaps, I did not explain myself sufficiently clearly. Moreover, I am tormented by a thousand temptations, against faith, in the matter of chastity, to pride. I endeavor to reject these temptations but I am troubled that I may have given some form of tacit consent.

Spiritual Director: And what advice does your spiritual director give you in these matters?

Soul: He forbids me to confess these matters unless I could swear beyond all doubt that I gave consent. Will you please give me some advice that will relieve my anxiety?

Spiritual Director: I can only tell you to have greater faith in obedience to your director. Haven't you read what St. Philip Neri wrote? Souls who obey their confessors will not have to give an account to God of their actions. Have faith in your confessor then since God will not allow him to err. There is no more secure way of countering the temptations of the devil than by obeying the directions of your spiritual director in all that concerns God. And, on the other hand, there is no more dangerous way than following your own inclinations.

St. Francis de Sales speaking of the obedience due to one's confessor: "This is the essential advice. No matter how much you search you will not find a safer way of discerning the Will of God than by walking in the way of humble obedience. This is the path which all the saints have followed." St. Teresa wrote in a similar vein: Choose your spiritual director with the firm intention of not being any longer preoccupied with yourself. Think only of the words of the Lord: "Who listens to you, listens to me." This acceptance of one's spiritual director is of such value in the eyes of the Lord that we have a guarantee that despite all difficulties, despite the fact that we may think the advice we receive to be inappropriate, no matter what pain we endure, we are still carrying out God's will in our regard.

Speaking, as it were, in the person of Jesus Christ, St. John of the Cross says: "If you are unfaithful to your confessor, you are unfaithful to me; 'whoever rejects you rejects me'" (Lk 10:16). And he adds, "It is an act of pride and a lack of faith not to accept what one's confessor decides and his reason for saying this is because Our Lord has said, 'whoever listens to you, listens to me.'" St. Francis de Sales proposes three very important maxims for our instruction. (1) A truly obedient soul has never been lost. (2) It is sufficient for you to know that your confessor assures you that all is well without your further probing to know the reason why. This is a very telling argument against those scrupulous souls who wish to know the reasons for the decisions of their spiritual directors. (3) And, finally, he asserts that the more perfect way for us is to walk blindly under the guidance of divine Providence through the darkness and perplexities of this life.

This principal of obeying one's spiritual director in all doubts of conscience is confirmed unanimously by all the Doctors of the Church. St. Bernard's words will suffice for all the others. "Whatever one's spiritual director decides when he speaks in the name of God, should be accepted as if it came from God himself, provided what he decides is not certainly sinful." So, in a word, obedience to God's ministers is the surest remedy given to us by Jesus Christ to secure peace for troubled consciences. And we should be grateful to him for it since otherwise how would scrupulous souls ever be able to regain peace of mind? Scrupulosity is one of the bitterest trials souls who love God can undergo, worse than ill-health, persecutions, and similar sufferings. Nearly all the saints have been afflicted by scruples at some time, St. Teresa of Avila, St. Mary Magdalene de' Pazzi, St. Jane Frances de Chantal, and many others. How did they overcome their scruples if not by obedience to their spiritual directors? Now, as regards yourself, are you convinced that by being obedient to your confessor you are following the right path?

Soul: Yes, I am convinced of that but why is it that despite the fact that I have been obedient in this matter for two years at least, I do not experience any sense of devotion?

Spiritual Director: Now, I see your problem. You say you have not experienced any sense of devotion. Are you seeking the will of God in all you do or are you in search of consolation and spiritual sweetness? If you wish to walk the path of holiness from now on seek only the will of God, who certainly wishes to make you a saint but may not wish to fill you with consolation in this life. If you do not find consolation, rest contented with the fact that you have within you the Consoler himself. You complain of two years of spiritual aridity. St. Jane Frances de Chantal suffered for forty years. St. Mary Magdalen de' Pazzi bore pain and temptations for five full years and at the end of that period she herself asked the Lord never to allow her to experience sensible consolations in this life. St. Philip Neri was so full of the love of God that he prayed: "Jesus, I have never really loved you as much as I would wish to love you." And again he said: "I do not know you, Lord. That is why I seek you. I wish to love you Lord, and I do not know how. I go in search of you and cannot find you." This is the language of the saints. Then why are you upset that you suffer lack of devotion and cannot find the Lord even when you seek him?

Soul: But these were all saints. I do not know whether God has forgiven me the offenses I have committed against him on account of my lack of genuine sorrow.

Spiritual Director: So, you are really happy that you committed those past sins.

Soul: Certainly not. I detest them more than anything else.

Spiritual Director: And then why do you fear that the Lord has not forgiven you? According to the Doctors of the Church whoever detests past sins is absolutely certain of God's forgiveness. As St. Teresa says, whoever is determined to suffer even death itself rather than offend God is certain of being sorry for all past sins. Are you determined to suffer whatever comes rather than lose God's grace?

Soul: Yes, by the grace of God, I am determined to allow myself to be torn to pieces rather than deliberately commit a venial sin.

Spiritual Director: Very good. And why then should God reject you? You fear that God has rejected you. Oh, if only you could realize the love which, at this very moment, God has for you, you would faint from the intensity of the consolation you would experience. Don't you know that Jesus Christ is the Good Shepherd who has come on earth to give his life to save his sheep, even if they have deliberately strayed away? And how could he abandon one of his flock who is ready to die rather than cause him the slightest offense?

Soul: But how do I know that I have not consented to some grave sin and that the Lord has not abandoned me?

Spiritual Director: You are not correct in what you say. Mortal sin is such a detestable thing that there is no way it could be on your soul without your being aware of it. Sinners who are at enmity with God can have no doubt but that they have lost the grace of God. All the masters of the spiritual life are in agreement that when scrupulous souls are in doubt as to whether they have lost the grace of God or not, it is certain that they have not. No one can lose the grace of God without being aware of it. And so every time you begin to doubt whether you have lost the grace of God or not, be certain that you have not.

Soul: Well then, why is it that I do not feel any sense of confidence?

Spiritual Director: Listen to me. True confidence does not consist in feeling it but in willing it. Do you wish to have trust in God? If you want to have trust in God then you already have it.

Soul: But the love of God. How can I know that I possess it?

Spiritual Director: The same rule holds good for the love of God as for confidence in God. Love for God is in your will. Do you want to love God? If you really want to love him, then you already do. And now you would like to experience the consolation of that confidence and that love. But God in his wisdom and for your greater merit does not wish to allow you to experience that consolation. So then, be satisfied with having confidence and love without experiencing consolation.

And I say the very same thing to you about your faith. It is sufficient that you want to believe all that the church teaches without experiencing the consolation of your belief. The time will certainly come when all the clouds will be driven away and you will then enjoy the light all the more. In the meantime rest contented to walk in obscurity and abandon yourself into the hands of God's Providence and mercy.

Take courage then from the words of scripture. The Lord says: "Return to me, says the Lord of hosts, and I will return to you" (Zec 1:3). If we want the Lord, let us then turn away from creatures. Let us turn with love toward him and he will turn with love toward us. He says to us all, "Come to me, all who you who labor and are burdened and I will give you rest" (Mt 11:28). And in another place he says "Come now let us set things right, says the Lord. Though your sins be like scarlet they may become white as snow; though they be crimson red, they may become white as wool" (Is 1:18). So, in point of fact, the Lord says to the sinner who repents, come to me and if I do not receive you, you can reprimand me and accuse me of being untruthful. But no. No matter how sinful your conscience may be, I, with my grace, shall make it as white as snow. He seeks out sinners full of compassion for them, lest they should lose their souls: "Turn, turn from your evil ways! Why should you die, O house of Israel?" (Ez 33:11). In a word, the Lord says why do you wish to lose your souls when I am ready to save you if you come to me. And if the Lord addresses himself in this way to sinners, how is it possible that he would reject a soul who wishes to love him?

And now, tell me in all sincerity, do you harbor any human attachment to any person or thing on this earth, are you ambitious to appear before others, to see yourself preferred to them? Recall the warning of St. John of the Cross that even the slightest attachment, the slenderest thread, can prevent us from flying to God and belonging totally to him.

Soul: No. By God's grace there is nothing on this earth for which I would commit a deliberate offense against God. All the same, I know I am full of defects. For example, I feel very much being thought little of and at times I show resentment on account of it.

Spiritual Director: And when you are resentful, what do you do?

Soul: I humble myself before the Lord and ask him to forgive me. I then determine not to fall into this defect again trusting in Jesus Christ who will strengthen me. And despite all this I am fearful and uneasy and it seems to me that it is impossible for me to attain to holiness of life. And it appears to me to be my pride that makes me even think of it.

Spiritual Director: Very well. Keep on acting just like that. But do not allow yourself to be disturbed. Even if you fall a hundred times a day continue to behave as you are, be sorry for your fault,

207

determine not to commit that fault again with God's grace. Put your trust in Jesus Christ and be at peace. Be convinced that it is certainly not pride to wish to attain holiness of life even after committing a fault. It would more likely be pride if you thought little of yourself after your fault and allowed yourself to be upset, as if our resolutions could guarantee that we would never commit another fault. Just be humble and trust in the Lord.

That is all. I have listened carefully to you and I understand all the fears that you have expressed about not knowing whether you will be saved or whether you are in God's grace or not. What you have told me is sufficient. From now on please do not tell me any more of your doubts nor recount what you suffer on account of them. I know your conscience and now I wish to give you some thoughts which I hope will give you peace when you are suffering as you have been. I say "peace," but not the peace that removes all shadow of anxiety. This peace God keeps for us in heaven. While we are here on our earthly pilgrimage his will is that we should always have some slight anxiety so that we should not neglect to ask him for his help and to put our trust in his divine mercy. If it were otherwise we would frequently neglect to have recourse to Our Lord and this is the reason he permits us to be troubled by these and similar fears in order to make sure that we do have recourse to him.

Peace for Scrupulous Souls

Introduction

Editor's Note: Alphonsus suffered greatly from scruples for most of his life. They were particularly troublesome in the early years of his clerical and priestly ministry. They had their source in his sensitive and anxious temperament, which he inherited from his mother and which was aggravated by family tensions and his father's opposition to his vocation.

There then followed his initiation in the rigorous moral theology teaching and practice of François Genet (1640–1703) whose manual *Morale de Grenoble* was the text studied in the Naples seminary. Alphonsus suffered considerably as he gradually moved away from the system of the Rigorists to his own compassionate and more benign practice. Furthermore, his growth in prayer, which led him through its various stages to the grace of contemplation, entailed the purification of his conscience, which can be one of the salutary effects of scruples.

Alphonsus found peace only in total and absolute obedience to his confessor. The result was that, in his priestly ministry as a director of souls, he was able to empathize with those who suffered from this conscience condition. He deals with scruples and their treatment in many of his writings from the *Moral Theology* to the *True Spouse*. The work translated here appeared for the first time as a separate publication in Naples in 1751. From that year onward it appeared in nearly all the collections of his spiritual writings.

* * *

The suffering that affects scrupulous souls comes, not from the fact that they have a scruple about what they are doing, but from the fear that what they are doing might be sinful and that they are, in fact, committing sin. But they should realize that whoever obeys a competent and holy director does not, in fact, act in doubt but acts with the greatest certainty that one can have here on earth, namely, the certainty which comes from the divine word of Jesus Christ who declares that whoever listens to

the instructions of his ministers listens to himself. "Whoever listens to you listens to me" (Lk 10:16). That is why St. Bernard
declares: "Whenever a confessor, speaking in the name of God,
prescribes something which is clearly not displeasing to God, he
is to be obeyed as if his instructions came from the mouth of
God himself."[1]

There is no doubt but that in the matter of direction of conscience, the confessor is one's legitimate superior. On this point
there is unanimity among the masters of the spiritual life. Father
Pinamonti in his *Spiritual Director* declares:

> Scrupulous souls should be told that their greatest security
> consists in accepting the decisions of their spiritual direc-
> tors in all those matters which are not clearly sinful. It is evi-
> dent from the lives of the saints that there was no more
> secure way for them than the way of obedience to their spir-
> itual directors. The saints had more confidence in the voice
> of their confessors than they had even in the direct voice of
> God. Scrupulous souls, on the other hand, rely more on
> their own fallible judgment than on the words of the gospels
> which assure us: "Whoever listens to you, listens to me."[2]

Blessed Henry Suso is of the opinion that God does not
demand of us an account of what we have done in obedience to
our spiritual director. St. Philip Neri is of the same opinion. Let
those who wish to make progress in the ways of God choose for
themselves a competent spiritual director whom they should
obey as they would God himself. In this way they will not have to
render an account to God of their actions. Moreover, he urges
souls to trust in the advice of their spiritual directors since God
will not allow them to err. There is no surer way of restraining
the devil than to obey one's director in spiritual matters just as
there is nothing more dangerous than to direct oneself. Speaking, as it were, in the name of God, St. John of the Cross warns,
"If you refuse to obey your confessor, you refuse to obey me since
I have said 'who despises you despises me.'" Furthermore, he
asserts that it is pride and lack of faith which makes one refuse to
accept the advice of one's confessor. It is essential therefore to

have this solid conviction that in obeying the directions of one's confessor, one will never commit sin. In a word, to quote St. Bernard, "The great remedy for scruples is blind obedience to one's confessor." John Gerson relates that on one occasion St. Bernard commanded one of his monks, who suffered from scruples, to go immediately to celebrate Mass, relying only on this command of St. Bernard. The monk obeyed and was cured of his scruples as a result of his obedience.[3]

Some, however, may well respond, quoting Gerson again, would to God that I had a St. Bernard for my director! Mine is only an ordinary confessor. The answer is simple. Whoever speaks like this is making a serious mistake. You did not entrust yourself spiritually to your director because he is a learned person, but because he is your guide. Therefore you should obey him not because of what he is but as if he were God. St. Teresa is very much to the point when she says: Choose your spiritual director with a determination not to make any further excuses. Simply trust in the words of the Lord, "Whoever listens to you, listens to me." The Lord values this submission to such an extent that despite all the battles we have to fight, despite the fact that again and again we feel that the advice of our director is not correct, we still follow his directions, no matter what we have to suffer. As a result, the Lord will assist us in every way since we have totally accepted his divine will.

St. Francis de Sales recommends spiritual direction as the surest way of advancing in the way of God. "This is the one piece of advice above all others; no matter how long you search or where you search, you will never find a more secure way of ascertaining the will of God than the way of humble submission to one's spiritual director. This is the way recommended and practiced by all the saints." Father Alvarez goes so far as to say that even if the spiritual director should err, his penitent is certain of not erring for the simple reason that the penitent is obeying the one given to him by God as his guide and director. Father Nieremberg is of the same opinion. "Obey your confessor and you will not sin even if what is in question is sinful since you are acting with the intention of obeying the person who stands in the place of God for you. Your obligation is to obey what that person directs." Fathers Rogacci and Lessio state that the spiritual director is the interpreter of the will of God for us. If what the director commands is doubtful or even if it is indeed wrong, the fact that one has obeyed excuses from sin. In a word, then, one should obey one's confessor, and scrupulous souls must renounce themselves in favor of their spiritual directors.[4]

St. Francis de Sales has three very consoling maxims for scrupulous souls: (1) An obedient soul has never been lost. (2) One should be quite at peace simply to know from one's spiritual director that all is well without seeking for further reasons. (3) The most perfect way is to walk blindly under divine Providence amid the darkness and perplexities of this life. And so all the great moral theologians, among them such names as St. Antonino of Florence, Navarro, Silvestro, and so forth, state that the surest norm for walking in the ways of God is obedience to one's confessor. Fathers Tirillo and La Croix assert that this is the teaching of all the Fathers of the church and all the great masters of the spiritual life.[5]

Scrupulous souls should realize, secondly, that not only is the path of obedience the secure way for them but that they are obliged to obey their spiritual directors and at the same time to disregard their scruples and to act quite freely in all their doubts. "Scruples are to be completely disregarded, and one is to do the very opposite to what they suggest, provided one is following the advice of a prudent, competent and devout spiritual director." Father Wigandt states that "the person who acts contrary to scruples does not commit sin. One is at times bound to do so and, especially, when following the advice of one's confessor." This is the common opinion of all those theologians who belong to the more rigid school of thought. I repeat that this is the common view of theologians. And the simple reason is that if scrupulous souls do not overcome their scruples they are in danger of not fulfilling their other religious obligations or at least they render themselves unable to make progress in their spiritual lives. They could even lose their mental balance, ruin their health, fall into despair, or develop a totally relaxed conscience. And that is why

St. Antonino, in agreement with Gerson, issues this warning to scrupulous souls who out of unfounded fears do not follow the path of obedience in their efforts to overcome their scruples: "Be careful lest in your desire to possess total certainty you do not fall into a more dangerous situation still."

Father Wigandt lays it down that scrupulous souls should quite simply obey the instructions of their director of conscience provided what he commands is not clearly sinful. The teaching that one is bound in all doubtful occasions to obey one's spiritual director, provided there is no obvious and clear sin, is the common and certain teaching of moral theologians. This is St. Bernard's teaching in the quotation given above. St. Ignatius declares that one must obey in everything that is not evidently sinful. Blessed Umberto, who was Master General of the Dominicans, says the same thing: "Unless what is commanded is clearly wrong it should be obeyed as if it were the command of God himself." And Denis the Carthusian: "If you are doubtful whether a command is contrary to the law of God you should follow the command of your director because even if it is against the law of God, the one who obeys does not sin." And St. Bonaventure agrees with this.[6]

Gerson puts the whole matter succinctly. He says that one must take a very determined stand against scruples. Philip Neri suggested that the best remedy for scruples is to treat them with contempt. In his life it is recorded that as well as advising the accepted remedy of total submission in everything to the judgment of one's confessor, he also advised his penitents to treat scruples with disdain and contempt. His practice with scrupulous persons was to forbid them to confess frequently. And when they did confess to him and mentioned their scruples he ordered them to go to Holy Communion without listening further to their scruples.

So to conclude. Scrupulous souls should follow the way of obedience. They should totally disregard their scruples and act with full freedom in the matters about which they have scruples. And it is not necessary that in every single act they should have to recall that this is a scruple, or that they have received a command to obey their spiritual director. It is sufficient that they act as a result of what they have previously determined. As a result of their past experiences they are acting by virtue of a conscience previously formed even though they do not advert specifically to the directions at the moment. And by way of confirmation, La Croix, Tambur with Vasquez and others,[7] point out that even if the scrupulous souls cannot at once lay aside their fear of sinning or recall explicitly the advice of their confessors (which is almost impossible for scrupulous souls in the midst of their fears and perplexities) they still do not sin even though they act with a definite fear of committing sin. The reason is that having previously been advised about similar scruples and having received instructions to treat them with contempt, they can take it for granted that these instructions still apply even though they may not at once advert to them. Moreover, any fear that scrupulous souls may have should be treated with contempt since such fears are not authentic norms of conscience.

Here is how Gerson deals with the matter. A formed conscience exists when, after discussion and reflection, one's reason decides that a certain course of action should be followed or avoided. To act against this judgment is sinful. A scruple of conscience arises when one's reason hesitates in the midst of doubts, unable to decide what course of action to follow and at the same time not wishing to omit what would be pleasing to God's will. If I might paraphrase Gerson's explanation: He says in substance that one sins in acting with a practical doubt, when the *doubt precedes* the proper formation of one's conscience. One's conscience is formed when having examined all the circumstances one comes to the conclusion that such and such a course of action must be followed and that something else must not be followed. One would then commit sin by acting against the dictates of such a formed conscience. But when one's mind is in doubt and vacillates between one point of view and another and at the same time one does not wish to offend God in what one does, this, according to Gerson, is not a rational doubt but a vain fear which should be rejected and treated with contempt as far as is possible.

So when scrupulous persons have an habitual intention of never offending God it is quite certain that even if they act with a doubtful conscience, they do not sin. And the reason for this is that what they think is a doubtful conscience is nothing more than a fear which has no foundation. On the other hand, it is certain that to commit a mortal sin there must be full knowledge in one's mind and perfect consent of one's will in wishing an action which gravely offends God. There is not the slightest doubt about the truth of this teaching. It is held by all the theologians of the *Salmanticenses* and even by Rigorists such as Giordanini, Habert, and even by the most Rigorist of all, Genet.[8] He says that if there is imperfect deliberation it is only a venial and not a mortal sin. St. Thomas and all the others agree. St. Thomas expresses it as follows: "What could be a mortal sin is simply venial if the act is imperfect, that is, if the act is not fully deliberate but unpremeditated."

Scrupulous souls should therefore accept the sufferings which their scrupulosity causes in a spirit of resignation; they should not forget in the midst of their trials that God permits these for their benefit, that they might grow in humility, that they might be more careful in avoiding certainly gravely dangerous occasions of sin, that they might more frequently recommend themselves to the Lord, and that they might have greater trust in the divine goodness. They should have frequent recourse in prayer to the Mother of God, who is called Mother of Mercy and Comforter of the Afflicted. Certainly they should fear offending God but seeing that they are determined to die a thousand deaths rather than lose the grace of God, they should fear much more disobedience to the directions of their confessor. They should be convinced that by obeying blindly their spiritual director they will never be abandoned by the Lord, who wishes all to be saved and will never allow a truly obedient soul to be lost.

"Has anyone hoped in the Lord and been disappointed?" (Sir 2:10). "Cast all your worries upon him because he cares for you" (1 Pt 5:7).

"The LORD is my light and my salvation; whom do I fear?" (Ps 27:1). "In peace I shall both lie down and sleep,/for you alone, LORD, make me secure" (Ps 4:9).

"You are my help and deliverer;/my God, do not delay!" (Ps 40:18).

DEVOTIONAL WRITINGS

Novena to the Sacred Heart

Introduction

Editor's Note: Margaret Mary Alacoque was born in 1647 and entered the Visitation convent at Paray-le-Monial in 1671. Two years later she experienced her revelations concerning devotion to the Sacred Heart of Jesus. Despite considerable opposition from a variety of sources, the devotion took root and a number of devotional manuals appeared in French. Prominent among them was the work of the French Jesuit Jean Croiset (1656–1738), whose *De la dévotion au Coeur de Jésus* was published in Lyons in 1691 and was immediately translated into Italian. The devotion had a strong appeal to Alphonsus. He was familiar with the life of Margaret Mary written by Monsignor Languet, bishop of Sens, and also with the writings both in Latin and French of another French Jesuit, Father Gallifet (1663–1749), the spiritual director of Claude de la Colombière, S.J., who dedicated his life to the propagation of devotion to the Sacred Heart. However, the main influence in convincing Alphonsus of the theological orthodoxy of this devotion was probably the writings and preaching of St. John Eudes (1601–1680).

Alphonsus's familiarity with the devotion and its theological basis is evident from one of his earliest publications, *Visits to the Blessed Sacrament* (1745/1748). In the Introduction and in Visit 24 he quotes the words of Margaret Mary and apparently makes explicit reference to the work of Father Croiset. In 1758 Alphonsus preached a triduum in the Claretian convent in Nola on devotion to the Sacred Heart and this he subsequently expanded into a full nine-day novena, which was published in Naples some months later. Besides the nine meditations and appropriate prayers to the Sacred Heart and Our Lady, Alphonsus prefaced the work with a theological *mis-au-point,* clarifying the true nature of the object of this devotion. This short treatise went a long way toward removing the obstacles to full acceptance of the devotion into the church's liturgy. A few years later, in

1765, Pope Clement XIII approved the establishment of the liturgical feast of the Sacred Heart of Jesus.

The publication of this novena filled the Jansenists throughout Italy and France with intense rage. The work was denounced in all the Jansenist publications and especially in the Jansenist bible, the *Annali Ecclesiastici* of Florence, which castigated Alphonsus for his support for this "outlandish, incoherent, pharisaical, false, superstitious and nestorian devotion to the heart of flesh of Jesus Christ which had its origins in the hallucinations of the visionary Alacoque." One of the first acts of Alphonsus as bishop of Sant'Agata of the Goths was to establish the feast of the Sacred Heart in his diocese in 1765, the very same year the feast received liturgical approval.[1]

*   *   *

Devotion to Jesus Christ in which we concentrate on the love our Redeemer has shown, and continues to show us, is the devotion which surpasses all others. A spiritual writer has recently lamented the fact that there are many who practice a variety of other devotions but neglect this. Many preachers and confessors, too, are eloquent about many subjects but speak very little about love for Jesus Christ, when, in point of fact, love for Jesus Christ should be the principal, not to say, the only devotion of a Christian. Consequently, the principal object and effort, both of preachers and confessors, should be to awaken and increase in their audience and penitents this love for Jesus Christ. Negligence in this matter is the fundamental reason why souls make such little progress in virtue, why they continually fall into the same defects and are frequently guilty of serious faults. Since they are not admonished and encouraged to grow in love for Jesus Christ they are deprived of that golden thread which binds their souls to God.

It was for the purpose of making himself loved that the Eternal Word came into this world: "I have come to set the earth on fire, and how I wish it were already blazing!" (Lk 12:49). And it was for this very same purpose that the Eternal Father sent his Son into the world, namely, to reveal to us his Father's love and in this way elicit our love in return. The Father declares that he loves us since we love Jesus Christ: "For the Father himself loves you, because you have loved me" (Jn 16:27). Moreover, he gives us his graces when we ask them in the name of his Son: "Amen, amen, I say to you, whatever you ask the Father in my name he will give you" (Jn 16:23). Finally, he admits us to his eternal happiness as we conform ourselves to the example of the life of Jesus Christ: "For those he foreknew he also predestined to be conformed to the image of his Son" (Rom 8:29). But we shall never achieve this likeness to Jesus Christ, indeed, we will never even wish to possess it, if we do not reflect on the love which Jesus Christ has shown us.

We read in the life of the Venerable Margaret Mary Alacoque, a religious of the Visitation, that Our Lord revealed to her his wish that a feast in honor of his Sacred Heart should be established, and devotion to it propagated in the church in our time. The purpose of this feast would be to enable souls to reverence his Sacred Heart and to make reparation for the insults which he receives especially when the Most Blessed Sacrament is exposed for veneration on the altar.

In the life of this religious, written by Monsignor Languet, the bishop of Sens, we read that while she was praying before the Most Blessed Sacrament, Our Lord appeared to her and showed her his heart surrounded by thorns, with a cross above it and in the midst of flames. "Behold this Heart," he said to her, "which has so loved all men and women, even to the extent of sacrificing itself as proof of love for them. And, in return, my Heart receives nothing but ingratitude and irreverence from the great majority of people. And what displeases me most is that many of these are persons whose lives are consecrated to me."[2]

And then he commissioned her to strive to secure that on the first Friday after the octave of the feast of Corpus Christi a special feast should be established in honor of his Sacred Heart. This feast would have three ends. (1) That the faithful would be able to express their gratitude for the great gift of the Most Blessed Sacrament. (2) That souls would have an opportunity of making reparation by their prayers and devotion for the numerous offenses and irreverence which the Sacred Heart has received, and continues to receive, in this sacrament from sinners. (3) That souls would be able to make up to Our Lord for the lack of respect which is shown to him in churches where the Blessed Sacrament receives little reverence. And Our Lord promised that he would dispense the riches of his Sacred Heart on those who showed him honor on his feast and also on those who visited him in the Blessed Sacrament. In a word, this devotion to the heart of Jesus Christ is above all a manifestation of love toward our Loving Savior.

As regards the *object* of this devotion. The *spiritual* object is the love which the heart of Jesus Christ has for all men and women since it is commonly said that the heart is the source of love: "My son, give me your heart" (Prv 23:26); "My heart and flesh cry out/for the living God" (Ps 84:3); "God is the rock of my heart, my portion forever" (Ps 73:26); "Because the love of God has been poured out into our hearts through the holy Spirit that has been given to us" (Rom 5:5). The *material* or sensible object of this devotion is the Sacred Heart of Jesus, not in itself, but as united with his sacred humanity, and consequently, with the divine Person of the Word of God.

This devotion has spread rapidly in a very short space of time. It has been introduced into many contemplative monasteries; over four hundred confraternities consecrated to the Sacred Heart of Jesus have been established in France, Savoy, Flanders, Germany, and Italy and also in missionary countries. These confraternities have been enriched by the Holy See with many indulgences and with authority to erect sanctuaries and churches bearing the title of the Sacred Heart. All this appears from the apostolic letter of Pope Clement X dated 1674, which is printed in the work of Father Eudes, as Father Galliffet of the Society of Jesus tells us in his work *The Excellence of Devotion to the Heart of Jesus*, p. 266.[3]

Many people hope that one day the church will grant its approval for a special Office and Mass in honor of the Sacred Heart of Jesus. This request was first made by Father Galliffet in 1726. He explained that the Sacred Heart of Jesus merits this special reverence since it is the *co-principle*, that is, the source and the seat of all the sentiments, and especially of love, of the Redeemer for us. And at the same time, it is the center of all the interior sorrows that he has suffered during his life. But, as far as my information goes, Father Galliffet did not pursue his intention further since what he relied upon to be the unassailable basis of his request proved to be, in fact, doubtful. The objection was made, and quite rightly, that it was not at all certain whether all the sentiments of the soul could be said to have their source in the heart and not in the head. Many modern philosophers, amongst them Ludovico Muratori in his moral philosophy (Chap. II, p. 14), favored the second opinion, namely, the head. The church, with its usual caution in such matters, has made no pronouncement on this question, with the result that Father Galliffet's request, based as it was on a doubtful supposition, could not be granted. So it was not considered opportune to grant the request for a special Office and Mass in respect of the heart of Jesus since further requests could well be made in the course of time for similar favors in honor of, say, the ribs, the tongue, the eyes, and other members of the human body of Jesus Christ. This is all clearly stated in the well-known work of the late Pope Benedict XIV, *De Servorum Dei beatificatione et Beatorum canonizatione,* Lib. 4, pars. 2, cap 30. No. 17 (Bologna 1738).[4]

However, let it be stated at once that our hope of seeing a special Office and Mass being granted in honor of the Sacred Heart does not rely on the aforementioned opinion of ancient philosophers. Rather does it rely on the *common opinion* of philosophers both ancient and modern, that even if the heart is not the seat of the affections and the principal of life, it is still, in the words of the learned Muratori, *one of the principal sources and organs of all human life.* Physicians commonly assert nowadays that the heart, to which is attached the arteries and the veins, is the source and principal of the circulation of the blood. Other parts of the body, consequently, are energized from the heart. So, since the heart is one of the primary sources of human life, it is beyond doubt that the heart has one of the most important parts to play in the whole range of human emotions. Experience teaches us that the internal movements of sorrow and love make a far greater impression on the heart than on any other part of the human body. This is particularly true of the emotion of love. Leaving aside all the other saints let us recall that in the life of St. Philip Neri it is recorded that the ecstasy of his fervor toward God was so intense that the heat of his heart could be felt exteriorily on his breast; his heart beat so strongly that it could be felt by those who placed their heads on his chest. It was claimed that his rib-cage expanded, so great was the agitation of his heart. St. Teresa writes in her *Life* (Book I, Chap. 4) that the Lord sent an angel to wound her heart with the result that she felt herself burning with divine love and fainted away. These experiences make us realize that the Lord allows the effects of his love to be felt in the hearts of his saints. And the church has granted to the Discalced Carmelites a special Mass to honor the Wounded Heart of St. Teresa.[5]

The church has also felt it appropriate to permit veneration of the Instruments of Our Lord's Passion, such as the lance, the nails, and the crown of thorns, and a special Mass has been authorized for these occasions. Benedict XIV in the work I have already mentioned quotes the words of Pope Innocent VI: "We think it fitting that a special feast should be celebrated in honor of the Instruments of Our Lord's Passion especially in those placed where it is said that these Instruments are preserved. Our intention in granting these special Offices is to encourage the devotion of the faithful."[6]

If, then, the church has considered it fitting to venerate with special devotion the lance, nails, and thorns which caused the body of Jesus Christ such suffering in his Passion, can we not hope, all the more, that the church will grant similar favors in honor of the Sacred Heart of Jesus Christ which played such an important part in his love and in the terrible sufferings he endured as he saw the torments being prepared for him and, at the same time, the ingratitude which men and women would show him in return? How was it that Our Lord sweated blood in the Garden of Olives if not because his heart was constricted, with the result that his blood was forced out through the pores of his body? And that constriction of the heart was caused by nothing else than the fear, sorrow, and revulsion which he experienced, as the evangelists describe: "He took with him Peter, James, and John, and began to be troubled and distressed. Then he said to them, 'My soul is sorrowful even to death'" (Mk 14:33–34; cf. also Mt 26:37–38).

However, leaving aside this matter for the moment, let us now facilitate the devotion of those souls who, enamored of the Sacred Heart, wish to meditate on his love and honor him in the Most Blessed Sacrament of the Altar during this novena.

First Meditation:
The Heart of Jesus, Deserving of Our Love

Whoever is in every way lovable necessarily attracts the love of others. Oh! if we could only fathom how lovable are the characteristics of the heart of Jesus we should all be under the happy constraint of loving him. And, what heart, among all hearts, is more deserving of love than the heart of Jesus? A heart unsullied, holy in every way, full of love for God and for us, with no other wish than the glory of God and our good. This is the heart in which God himself finds all his delight. In this heart every perfection, every virtue, is to be found: an ardent love for God his Father united with the greatest possible humility and reverence; total dismay at the thought of our sins which are laid upon him, with, at the same time, the supreme confidence of a most loving son; complete revulsion at the sight of our offenses united with the greatest sympathy for our misery; intense suffering united with a perfect acceptance of the divine will. In a word, everything that is most worthy of our love is to be found in the heart of Jesus.

We are led to love others on account of their beauty, their innocence, their graciousness, their fidelity. But supposing there was a person in whom all these beautiful traits were to be found united. Would that person not attract everyone's love? And supposing we heard that somewhere away from us there was a prince, gracious, humble, courteous, devout, full of charity, gracious to everybody, who repays with good those who do him evil, would we not feel ourselves drawn to love him even if we did not know him or he us? How then does it come about that Jesus Christ who possesses all these virtues to the highest degree and who loves us so tenderly is so little loved by the great majority of people? How is it that he is not the sole object of all our love? O God, how is it that Jesus who is so worthy of our love and who has given us so many proofs of his love has the misfortune, if I may so express it, to be the only one not to be loved by us, as if he were unworthy of our love! This thought brought tears to the eyes of saints like Rose of Lima, Catherine of Genoa, Teresa of Avila, Mary Magdalene de' Pazzi. As they meditated on such ingratitude they exclaimed: "Love is not loved!"

Affections and Prayers[7]

O amiable Redeemer, who, more worthy of love than you, could the Eternal Father have commanded us to love? You are the very beauty of heaven, the very love of your Father; in your heart are found all the virtues. O amiable heart of Jesus, you have merited the love of all our hearts; how deprived and unhappy must be the heart that does not love you! I have been that unfortunate person when I did not love you. But I do not wish to continue in this way. I love you now and wish to love you always.

Holy Virgin Mary, my mother and my hope, assist me; pray to Jesus that by his grace I may become what he wishes me to be.

Second Meditation:
The Loving Heart of Jesus

Oh, that we could realize the love that burns in the heart of Jesus for us! He has loved us to such a degree that if the love of all men and women, the love of all the angels and of all the saints were united together they would not be equal to one thousandth part of the love of the heart of Jesus. He has loved us immensely more than we can love ourselves. He has loved us almost to excess. What greater excess could there be than that a God should die for his creatures? He has loved us to the very end: "He loved his own in the world and he loved them to the end" (Jn 13:1). There has never been a moment from all eternity in which our God has not

226

thought of us and loved each one of us: "With age-old love I have loved you;/so I have kept my mercy toward you" (Jer 31:3). For love of us he became man and chose a life of suffering, ending with death on the Cross. He has loved us more than his own honor, his own comfort, more even than his own life since he sacrificed all these to show us the extent of his love for us. Is not this, in fact, an *excess* of love which must fill with amazement the very angels of heaven for all eternity?[8] It is this very same love which has prompted him to remain with us in the Most Blessed Sacrament, as on a throne of love. He remains there motionless under the appearance of a little bread in the Ciborium, without any external signs of his divine majesty, and with apparently no other purpose than to demonstrate his love for us all.

Love makes us wish to be in the presence of the one we love. It is this love which makes Jesus Christ remain with us in the Blessed Sacrament. His thirty-three years on this earth were insufficient for him to demonstrate his love for us and so his desire to be with us led him to perform the greatest of all his miracles, namely, the institution of the Holy Eucharist. Since the work of our redemption had been completed and we had been reconciled with God our Father for what purpose did Jesus wish to remain with us in this sacrament? He remains with us since he is reluctant to leave us, saying that it is with us he finds all his delight. This love for us has led him to become the food of our souls, to unite himself with us so that our hearts and his would become one and the same: "Whoever eats my flesh and drinks my blood remains in me and I in him" (Jn 6:56). What an outpouring of God's love is this! If anything could shake my faith in the mystery of the Eucharist, declared a servant of God, it is not how the bread could become the flesh of Jesus or how he could be contained in such a small space or be in so many places at the same time. One answer suffices for all these problems—God can do all things. But there is one thing I cannot comprehend and that is how God could love us to such an extent as to become bread for us. This love is a truth of faith totally beyond my comprehension. O love of Jesus, make yourself known to us and loved in return![9]

Affections and Prayers

"You shall love the Lord, your God, with all your heart, with all your soul, and with all your mind" (Mt 22:37). Yes, my God, you wish to be loved by me and I wish to love you. I wish to love you above all others since you have loved me to such an extent. O heart of Jesus, burning with love for me, inflame my heart with love for you. Mary, Mother of Divine Love, you who desired to see your Son Jesus loved, unite me with your Son. And obtain for me the grace never to be separated from him.

Third Meditation:
The Heart of Jesus Longing to Be Loved by Us

Jesus has no need of us; whether we love him or not, he is equally happy, rich, and powerful. And yet, as St. Thomas writes, since Jesus Christ loves us he so desires our love in return almost as if we were his God and all his happiness depended on us.[10] It was this thought that made Job exclaim: "What is man, that you make much of him,/or pay him any heed?" (Jb 7:17). How can it be that a God desires, indeed seeks so eagerly the love of a mere creature? The fact that God would have permitted us to love him would have been in itself a great condescension on his part. If a servant were to say to his king, "Sir, I love you," it would be regarded as affrontery. But what could one say if the king were to say to his servant, "It is my wish that you should love me?" The rulers of this world do not abase themselves to this extent, but Jesus, who is the Lord of Heaven, has gone so far as to demand our love: "You shall love the Lord, your God, with all your heart" (Mt 22:37). He urges us to give him our hearts. And if he ever sees himself rejected by a soul, he refuses to depart but remains at the door of that person's heart and knocks: "Behold, I stand at the door and knock" (Rv 3:20) and he requests admission, addressing the soul in loving words: "Open to me, my sister, my beloved" (Sg 5:2). In a word he finds his greatest joy in being loved by us and finds his consolation when a soul repeats to him, "I love you." This is the result of the great love which he bears toward us since one who loves, of necessity, desires to be loved in return. One heart seeks another, love calls for love.

What is the purpose of God's love, writes St. Bernard, except that he wishes to be loved in return. These are the very words of God himself when he says: "And now, Israel, what does the LORD, your God, ask of you but to fear the LORD...to love and serve the LORD, your God, with all your heart and all your soul" (Dt 10:12). He is that good shepherd who, when he finds the lost sheep, calls his neighbors to him: "Rejoice with me because I have found my lost sheep" (Lk 15:6). He is the kind father who not only pardons his lost son when he returns but lovingly embraces him. He tells us that whoever does not love is destined to die: "Whoever does not love remains in death" (1 Jn 3:14) and on the other hand that those who love are loved by God and God remains with them: "God is love, and whoever remains in love remains in God and God in him" (1 Jn 4:16). Will so many requests, such insistence, so many promises and even threats, not move us to love our God who desires so much to be loved by us?

Affections and Prayers

Lord, I now realize that on account of my sins I deserve to be deprived of your grace and as a result condemned not to be able to love you any more. But I understand that you persist in asking me to love you and I feel a great desire within me to do so. This is a grace from you. Give me then the strength to love you and grant that from now onward I shall be able to say with all my heart and in all sincerity, My God, I love you. You desire my love, I desire your love. Jesus, do not remember the offenses I have committed against you in the past. Let us now be united in love. I shall never abandon you and you will never abandon me. You will forever love me and I shall always love you. My dear Savior, I trust in your merits. Make me love you, make a sinner who has offended you, love you.

Immaculate Virgin Mary, come to my assistance. Pray to Jesus for me.

Fourth Meditation:
The Sorrowful Heart of Jesus

It is impossible for us to consider how much the Sacred Heart of Jesus suffered for us while on earth and not be moved to sympathy. He himself has made it clear that his heart was so deeply afflicted by sorrow that it would have been sufficient in itself to cause his death were it not that he was miraculously preserved by the power of his divinity: "My soul is sorrowful even to death" (Mk 14:34). The greatest suffering the heart of Jesus experienced was not from the vision of the torments and the insults that his executioners were preparing for him but from the ingratitude which would be shown to the immense love of his heart. He saw clearly all the sins we would commit despite all his sufferings and his bitter and ignominious death. He foresaw in a special way all the insults which his Sacred Heart would have to endure in the Most Blessed Sacrament which he would leave us as a testimony to his love. My God, what outrages has not Jesus Christ had to endure from us in this sacrament of his Love for us! It has been trodden under foot, thrown away, used in blasphemous ceremonies. And yet the vision of all these outrages did not deter him from bequeathing to us this pledge of his love. He hated sin but his love for us overcame this hatred; he was prepared to permit so many acts of sacrilege rather than deprive us of this divine food for our souls. Is all this not sufficient to make us love this Sacred Heart? Has Jesus Christ not done enough to deserve our love? Will we, in our ingratitude, leave Jesus abandoned on our altars as so many others do? Or shall we not rather join those devout souls who know how to honor him and who are consumed with love for him just as the candles that burn around the Monstrance are consumed by the flames? The heart of Jesus is burning with love for us and in his presence shall we not burn with love for him?

Affections and Prayers

O adorable heart of Jesus, behold prostrate before you one who has caused your loving heart such bitterness! My God, how could I have caused such sorrow to one who has loved me so greatly and who spared no effort to entice me to love him? But permit me to say, my Savior, that now as a result of your grace I feel the deepest remorse for the offenses I have caused you and I could die from shame. Grant me, dear Lord, a hatred for my sins similar to what you experienced in your lifetime.

Jesus, grant me from now onward such a hatred for sin that I would detest the slightest fault against you since they displease you who, far from deserving the very least offense, merits all my love. Mary Most Holy, obtain for me the grace always to pray to you and say: Mary, my Mother, help me to love Jesus Christ.

Fifth Meditation:
The Compassionate Heart of Jesus

Where could we find a more compassionate and loving heart than the heart of Jesus who has shown such compassion for our miseries? This love made him come down from heaven to earth, made him declare that he is that Good Shepherd ready to lay down his life for his sheep. In order to obtain for us the pardon of our sins, he did not pardon himself but willed to sacrifice himself on the Cross to satisfy, with his sufferings, what we deserved for our sins. This mercy and compassion made him say even to us: "Why should you die, O house of Israel? For I have no pleasure in the death of anyone who dies" (Ez 18:31–32). My poor children, he seems to say, why do you wish to destroy yourselves by fleeing from me? Do you not realize that by fleeing from me you are in danger of eternal death? I have no desire to see you lost; do not delay, turn to me when you will and find your life once more. His compassion leads him to declare that he is that loving father who, even though he sees himself despised by his son, does not reject him when he returns penitent but rather embraces him tenderly and does not remember all the insults he has received. "None of the crimes he committed shall be remembered against him" (Ez 18:22). This is not what we are wont to do. Even though we forgive, we very often harbor the memory of the offenses received and we are inclined to vindicate ourselves. And even if we omit to vindicate ourselves on account of the fear of God, we experience very great repugnance in conversing and dealing with those who have insulted us.

Jesus, you pardon penitent sinners and you even give yourself to them completely in Holy Communion; in the next life you give yourself to them in Eternal Glory and you do not harbor the slightest repugnance in embracing, for all eternity, the soul who has offended you. Where could we find a more loving and compassionate heart than yours, O Savior of the world?

Affections and Prayers

Compassionate heart of Jesus, have mercy on me. Even before I offended you, my Redeemer, I did not deserve the great graces you have given me. You created me, gave me so many inspirations and all totally undeserved on my part. But having offended you, not only did I not deserve your favors, I certainly deserved to be abandoned by you for all eternity. But you, in your great mercy, have waited for me and preserved my life even when I was at enmity with you. Your mercy allowed me to see my misery and you called me to conversion; you gave me sorrow for my sins and a desire to love you. Now, I hope that, with your grace, I am in your friendship once again.

And I ask you, my mother Mary, not to permit me ever again to cut myself off from my merciful Savior.

Sixth Meditation:
The Generous Heart of Jesus

People of generous disposition are anxious to help all those who are in need, especially those who are most in want and afflicted. Where could one find a person more generous than Jesus Christ? He who is infinitely good has a supreme desire to share his riches with us: "With me are riches and honor.../granting wealth to those who love me" (Prv 8:18–21). It was in order to make us rich that he became poor, as the Apostle said: "For your sake he became poor although he was rich, so that by his poverty you might become rich" (2 Cor 8:9). And it was for this purpose also that he has wished to remain with us in the Most Blessed Sacrament where (according to the vision of Father Balthasar Alvarez) he has his hands full of graces for us when we visit him. And it is for this very same reason that he gives himself totally to us in Holy Communion to convince us, as it were, that there is nothing he will deny us since he has, in fact, given us his very self: "He who did not spare his own Son but handed him over for us all, how will he not also give us everything else along with him?" (Rom 8:32).[11]

So we find in the heart of Jesus every good, every grace that we need: "I give thanks to my God always on your account for the grace of God bestowed on you in Christ Jesus, that in him you were enriched in every way...so that you are not lacking in any spiritual gift as you wait for the revelation of our Lord Jesus Christ" (1 Cor 1:4–7). Let us realize that it is to the heart of Jesus that we owe all the graces of our redemption, of our calling, of the inspirations we receive, of our forgiveness, of the help to overcome all temptations, of the courage we need to bear our sufferings. Yes, without his grace we could do nothing of good: "Because without me you can do nothing" (Jn 15:5). And, if in the past you have not received further graces, do not blame me, for the fault is yours since you neglected to ask me for them: "Until now you have not asked anything in my name; ask and you will receive" (Jn 16:24). Oh, how rich and generous to us is the heart of Jesus when we appeal to him: "The same Lord is Lord of all, enriching all who call upon him" (Rom 10:12). What great mercies do those souls receive who have recourse to Jesus Christ! David sang: "Lord, you are kind and forgiving,/most loving to all who call on you" (Ps 86:5). Let us then go to this heart and with confidence ask for what we need and we shall obtain it.

Affections and Prayers

Jesus, you did not hesitate to pour out your blood and give your life for my sake and shall I, in return, be reluctant to give you my poor heart? No, my Redeemer, I offer you all that I have and all that I am; I offer you my will; accept it and do with it what you please. I have nothing and can do nothing of myself but I have my heart which you have given me and which no one can take from me. I can be robbed of my possessions, of my blood, of my very life, but not of my heart. With this heart I can love you and with this heart I wish to do so.[12]

Teach me then, my God, to forget myself totally. Teach me what I have to do in order to attain that perfect love for you which your grace has inspired me to seek for. I feel within myself a great desire to please you in everything and I look for your grace to be strengthened to do so.

Immaculate Mother, how blessed you were to have your heart always and ever conformed to the Heart of Jesus. Obtain for me the grace that, for the future, I shall never wish or desire anything except what Jesus wishes.

Seventh Meditation:
The Grateful Heart of Jesus

The heart of Jesus is so full of gratitude that not even the slightest good deed done out of love for him, not even the slightest word spoken in honor of his glory, not even the slightest fleeting thought in his favor, goes without its reward. He is so grateful that he rewards everything done for him a hundredfold: "Everyone... will receive a hundred times more and will inherit eternal life" (Mt 19:29). Even those who are renowned for their gratitude repay the favor they have received only once; they pay their debt, as the saying is, and that is the end of the matter. Jesus Christ does not act in this way with us. Every good deed done to please him is not only recompensed a hundred times in this life but is rewarded over and over again in every moment for all eternity. Who then could be so indifferent as not to do everything possible to please this Sacred Heart which is so full of gratitude? But, my God, what do we do to give pleasure to this Sacred Heart? Rather should I say how can we be so ungrateful to our Savior? If he had shed but one drop of his blood or even one tear for our salvation we would have been under an infinite degree of obligation to him since this tear or this one drop of blood would have been of infinite value in the sight of God to obtain for us every grace. Instead, Jesus has expended every moment of his life for us, has given us his merits, his sufferings, all the contumely he suffered in his Passion, all his blood and his very life. So we are not only under one obligation to him but we are infinitely in his debt. And then when we think how grateful we are to animals: When they show us the slightest sign of affection we are compelled to love them in return. How is it then that we can be so utterly ungrateful to God? It would seem that we consider all the good things he has done for us as so many injuries since instead of being grateful and showing our love for him, we repay him with offenses and insults. Help us, O Lord, to recognize our ingratitude for the love you have shown us.

Affections and Prayers

Jesus, behold at your feet one who has been so ungrateful. I have shown gratitude to others but only to you have I shown ingratitude, to you who have died for me and who could do nothing more to place me under the obligation of loving you. My only consolation is that I am dealing with a heart of such infinite goodness and mercy who is ready to forget all the injuries and offenses of a sinner who repents and wishes to love. Dear Jesus, in the past I have offended you and despised you but now I love you above all things, more than myself. Tell me what you wish from me and I am ready to do it with the help of your grace.

Mary, my Mother, do not allow me to show any further ingratitude to your son. Pray to Jesus for me.

Eighth Meditation:
The Despised Heart of Jesus

There is no more bitter suffering for a heart which has loved than to see its love despised. And the greater the love the greater the ingratitude. If every person on this earth were to renounce their possessions, and were to go to live in a desert, were to eat only wild herbs, sleep on the bare ground, practice the most severe penances, and, finally, give their lives for Jesus Christ, what recompense would all this be for the sufferings, the blood, the life which the Son of God has sacrificed out of love for us? If we, then, were to sacrifice ourselves every moment of our lives until death, we would not repay in the least degree the love which Jesus Christ has shown to us in giving us the Most Blessed Sacrament. For a God to hide himself under the appearance of bread and to make himself the food of creatures! And, O God, what is the recompense and the thanks which we have shown to Jesus Christ? Ill-treatment, disrespect for his laws and his teaching, injuries and insults such as we would not inflict on our worst enemy, or even our slave or the vilest creature on earth. How can we reflect on all this ill treatment which Jesus Christ has received and continues to receive every day and not feel regret? And should we not seek through our love to recompense the great love of this Sacred Heart in the Most Blessed Sacrament? There he burns with love for us and is anxious to share with us all that he possesses and to give us himself, and to receive us into his heart as often as we visit him: "I will not reject anyone who comes to me" (Jn 6:37). We have grown too familiar with the words *creation, incarnation, redemption, Jesus born in a stable, Jesus dead on a cross.* Oh, God! if we had heard that another creature had done this for us how could we not have been moved to love? It is only our God, if I may so express it, who has had the misfortune to be treated by us in this manner. There is nothing more that he could do to make himself loved by us, nothing more to achieve his purpose. Instead of seeing himself loved he has been despised and disregarded. And it all flows from our forgetfulness of God's love for us.

Affections and Prayers

O heart of Jesus, abyss of love and mercy, how is it that at the very sight of the goodness you have shown me and of my ingratitude, I have not died from sorrow and remorse? You, my Savior, have given me my being, and then you have given me your blood and your life; you have suffered ignominy, even to death, out of love for me. And not content with this you have devised another means of sacrificing yourself every day for me by your presence in the Blessed Sacrament. You have not refused to subject yourself to every form of insult—which you foresaw would take place—in this sacrament of your love. My God, how can I reflect on this ingratitude without dying of shame? Put an end, O Savior, to my ingratitude by rooting my heart from now onward in your love and make me wholly yours. Remember the blood and tears you shed for me and forgive me. Grant that all these sufferings for me have not been in vain.

Mary, your heart was always on fire with divine love. Ask your Son, who never denies you what you request, to grant me the grace of a similar love for him.

Ninth Meditation:
The Faithful Heart of Jesus

The heart of Jesus Christ responds faithfully to all whom he calls to his divine love: "The one who calls you is faithful, and he will also accomplish it" (1 Thes 5:24). This divine fidelity gives us confidence to hope for everything from him even though we are worthy of nothing. Even if we have driven the Lord from our heart, once we open the door to him, he enters at once just as he has promised to do: "If anyone hears my voice and opens the door, [then] I will enter his house and dine with him, and he with me" (Rv 3:20). If we wish to receive God's grace, let us ask for it in the name of Jesus Christ and we shall obtain it: "I chose you and appointed you to go and bear fruit that will remain, so that whatever you ask the Father in my name he may give you" (Jn 15:16). If we are tempted let us trust in his merits and he will not permit the forces of evil to tempt us beyond our strength: "God is faithful and will not let you be tried beyond your strength" (1 Cor 10:13).

It is much more satisfactory to deal with God than with human beings. When we have dealings with our fellow men and women, they very frequently do not live up to their promises, either because their promises were deceitful or because, having promised, they changed their intentions. But as the Holy Spirit asserts, "God is not man that he should speak falsely,/nor human, that he should change his mind" (Nm 23:19). God simply cannot be unfaithful to his promises since being truth itself he cannot deceive nor can he alter his intentions, since all that he wishes is just and right. He has promised to receive everyone who comes to him, to assist those who ask his help, to love those who love him. And will he not do as he says? "Is he one to speak and not act,/to decree and not fulfill?" (Nm 23:19). Oh, that we were as faithful with God as he is faithful with us! How often in the past have we not promised to belong to him, to love and serve him. And then we have betrayed him, and, abandoning his service, have become the slave of the powers of evil. Let us pray to God that he will give us strength to be faithful in the future. How happy we would be if we were faithful to God in the very few things he demands of us. He, for his part, will always be faithful in rewarding us out of all proportion to what we have done. He will allow us to experience what he promised to his faithful servants in the gospel: "Well done, my good and faithful servant. Since you were faithful in small matters, I will give you great responsibilities. Come, share your master's joy!" (Mt 25:21).

Affections and Prayers

My Redeemer, would that I were as faithful to you as you have been to me! As often as I have opened my heart to you, you have entered to pardon me and to accept me back into your grace. Whenever I have called on you, you have come to my assistance. You have been faithful to me at all times but I have been so unfaithful to you. I promised to serve you but then too many times have I turned my back on you. I promised you my love and then have refused it on so many occasions. It almost seems, my God, that despite the fact that you created me and redeemed me I considered you less worthy of my love than creatures and my own unworthy desires for which I have abandoned you.

Mary, my Mother, help me to be faithful to your Son.

The Blessed Virgin Mary

Introduction

Editor's Note: The name of Alphonsus has become almost synonymous with excesses in Marian piety in the history of Roman Catholic spirituality.[1] Protestant controversialists of the nineteenth century almost invariably pointed to *The Glories of Mary* as the classic example of the exaggerated emphasis Roman theology gave to Mary. Even John Henry Newman, who read and admired St. Alphonsus, felt it necessary to disassociate himself from aspects of Alphonsus's Marian piety that seemed to him expressive of an overly effusive Neapolitan temperament.[2]

A fair estimation of the place of Mary in the spirituality of St. Alphonsus must keep two factors in mind. First, of the over one hundred works written by Alphonsus, only one, *The Glories of Mary,* is devoted entirely to the Blessed Virgin Mary. Merely on a statistical basis the attention paid by Alphonsus to Our Lady is minor compared to his writings devoted to various aspects of the person of Jesus the Redeemer. Second, all of Alphonsus's writings must be viewed through the optic of the central choice in his life and ministry—to preach the good news of plentiful redemption to the most abandoned, especially the poor, who have the least recourse to the church's ordinary ministry. Preaching on the Blessed Virgin Mary was a powerful pastoral instrument for that population. Alphonsus himself remarked that the sinner who remained untouched by sermons on hell would be moved by a sermon on the Mother of God. Alphonsus's apostolic genius consisted in his ability to use the popular piety of the poor of eighteenth-century Naples as a way of integrating them more fully into the church's life and of teaching them a more integral spirituality.

The Blessed Virgin Mary figured prominently in the religious formation of Alphonsus. Eighteenth-century Naples was full of churches dedicated to Mary under a variety of titles. Images of Mary were displayed in public on almost every corner. From his youth, Alphonsus was immersed in an atmosphere of

239

Marian piety. The figure of "la Madonna" exercised a powerful influence on Alphonsus's religious imagination as it did on that of his contemporaries. Alphonsus was formed in all the practices of Marian devotion typical of the age. He remained faithful to recitation of the rosary throughout his life and as an old man became agitated at the thought that he might have forgotten to say the rosary on a given day. On receiving his law degree in 1713, Alphonsus, as custom required, wrote out in his own hand and swore an oath to uphold and defend the doctrine of the Immaculate Conception of the Blessed Virgin Mary.[3] This act was more than a pious convention for Alphonsus; it was the setting of a direction that was to mark his life and ministry ever after. He was later to write in his introduction to *The Glories of Mary,* "All the benefits I have ever received, my conversion, my vocation to leave the world and so many other graces I have received from God, I recognize them all as coming through you, O Mary. You know well that, in order to see you loved by everyone as much as you deserve and to give you thanks for all the many benefits you have obtained for me, I have always sought, everywhere, whether in public or private, to spread your sweet and saving devotion."[4]

The conversion of life precipitated by the loss of a crucial law case in 1723 was manifested symbolically when Alphonsus, on August 29, 1723, entered the church of Our Lady of Mercy, Ransom of Captives, and placed his cavalier's sword at the foot of the image of Jesus and Mary.[5] Alphonsus was always extremely reticent about his own spiritual experiences. All the more notable therefore is his remark of 1786, recorded by his confessor, Father di Costanzo. Alphonsus recalls with great emotion the early days of the Redemptorist Congregation in Scala when he used to retire to a cave to pray and where, he said, the Blessed Virgin advised him on the future of the Congregation and told him "many wonderful things."[6] One of the few decorations Alphonsus permitted himself was a picture of Our Lady of Good Counsel kept on his desk and under whose gaze the majority of his works were written. In his old age Alphonsus moved his companions to tears to watch the crippled old man struggle to fall to his knees to pray the angelus. As the angelus rang on August 1, 1787, Alphonsus died, holding an image of Mary.

Alphonsus gave a strong tradition of Marian devotion to the Redemptorist Congregation. Under the title of the Immaculate Conception, Mary was the official patroness of the Institute and the early Redemptorists bound themselves by vow to defend the doctrine of the Immaculate Conception. Saturdays and the vigils of the principal feasts of Mary were observed as days of penance in Mary's honor. What later became the Redemptorist habit began as the typical cassock of a Neapolitan secular priest with the significant addition of a fifteen-decade rosary worn from the cincture. On missions Redemptorists were never to omit the sermon on the Blessed Virgin Mary, which was to focus on "the confidence we should have in the protection of this divine Mother."[7] An appealing image of Mary was always placed near the pulpit and the mission sermon was always preceded by the recitation of the rosary and instruction on its mysteries. In their own churches the Redemptorists were always to preach on Saturdays in honor of Mary and the formation of Marian confraternities was an important element in Redemptorist pastoral activity.

Alphonsus also applied his considerable musical and artistic skill to propagating devotion to Mary. He himself painted a number of pictures of Mary and commissioned his friends to paint several others. Invariably Alphonsus depicts Mary not as the distant sovereign of heaven surrounded by adoring cherubs but rather as a peasant woman in humble dress. One of the images of Mary that Alphonsus owned and venerated was by an unknown artist, entitled "La Divina Pastora"—the Divine Shepherdess. Mary is shown with the child Jesus on her lap. Both of them are in peasant dress including straw hats. A shepherd's hut is seen in the background and the child Jesus leans from his mother's lap to play with the sheep.[8] The painting is an eloquent representation of Alphonsus's Marian theology. Jesus and Mary are not distant supernatural figures but ever close to the poor, in their midst, and involved in the struggles of their lives. Alphonsus also composed a number of popular songs in honor of Mary, setting religious lyrics to familiar peasant tunes. The refrain of one of them sums up both the essence of Alphonsus's theology of Mary and his genius at translating it into terms accessible to the lowest segment of his society: "Evviva Maria, Evviva Maria, Evviva Maria e chi la creo!"—"Long live Mary ('evviva' in Italian has the sense of the English 'hurrah') and the One who created her!"

Some of Alphonsus's earliest literary efforts were devoted to the Blessed Virgin Mary. Among the earliest, probably written in the 1730s, was *Prayers to the Divine Mother for Each Day of the Week* (one of which is included below). His *Visits to the Blessed Sacrament,* originally written as sample meditations for Redemptorist novices and later expanded to include one for each day of the month, was published in 1748. Each daily visit also included a brief visit to Mary and one of his most famous prayers to Mary, the "Most Holy." (One of the visits to Mary and the text of the "Most Holy" are given below.)

Only the *Visits to the Blessed Sacrament* (1748) and the first edition of the *Moral Theology* (1748) antedate *The Glories of Mary* (1750) among Alphonsus's major works. The full title of the work is *The Glories of Mary, a work useful for reading and preaching. Divided into two parts: In the first are treated the many and bountiful graces that the Mother of God dispenses to those devoted to her as demonstrated in the various parts of the Salve Regina. In the second part are treated the principal feasts of Mary, her sorrows, in general and in particular. Also included are her heroic virtues and the accustomed devotions in her honor; finally there are added some selected stories by way of examples.* As Alphonsus indicates, the first part of this work is structured as a commentary on the ancient Marian hymn *Salve Regina* or "Hail, Holy Queen," sung or recited by custom in the Latin Church after night prayer of the Liturgy of the Hours during a large part of the year.

Alphonsus is making a theological point in the selection of the *Salve Regina* as a basis for his work. Devotion to Mary was looked on with some suspicion by clergy and theologians who had been influenced by the philosophers of the Enlightenment, even more so by those who were Jansenists or had Jansenist leanings. Of particular concern to Jansenist theologians was the *Salve Regina,* since it referred to Mary as *spes nostra*–our hope.

Since the Jansenist doctrine of grace proffered hope of salvation, even in Jesus, to very few, it was insufferable to the Jansenists that Mary should be seen in any way as a motive for hope of salvation. Some breviaries printed under Jansenist influence went so far as to omit the *Salve Regina* altogether. In choosing to base a mariology on the *Salve Regina*, Alphonsus is making a clear theological option against the Jansenist pessimism about salvation, their elitist attitude toward popular piety, and their individualism. Alphonsus opts instead in favor of an optimism about the power of grace more characteristic of Jesuit theology, an option in favor of the religion of the ordinary people, and in favor of the communitarian theology in which all creation is a mediation of the presence of God rather than in competition with it.[9] In his response to the criticisms of certain passages in *The Glories of Mary* made by the great theologian Ludovico Muratori, Alphonsus makes reference to his reliance on the *sensus fidelium:* "I add another argument, which has great weight with me: the greater part of the faithful have always had recourse to the intercession of the divine mother for all the graces which they desire....I shall always rejoice that I have believed and taught it to others, if for no other reason, at least because it inflames my devotion towards Mary; whereas the opposite opinion cools it, which is certainly not a slight evil."[10] Alphonsus's mariology seeks to be not only in continuity with the tradition of the church but also to be pastoral—capable of moving hearts with love for the goodness of God meditated through the figure of Mary. The frontispiece of *The Glories of Mary* is an engraving designed by Alphonsus of Mary in peasant dress, with the caption *Spes nostra,* our hope. In art Alphonsus summarizes what he attempts to teach by theological reflection—that the love of God continues to draw near to the church and the world through the Blessed Virgin Mary. She is a sign and instrument of plentiful redemption.

The theological nucleus of *The Glories of Mary* is found in Alphonsus's frequent assertion that in the Blessed Virgin Mary God's power meets God's compassion; that Mary not only feels great tenderness toward us but that it is God's will that she also enjoy the power to help us. This is a particularly liberating message for the poor since in their experience those who love them can do little for them and those who have the power to help them are not interested in them. Just as Alphonsus typically depicts God as in search of humanity, ever moving toward us in our misery and need, so also his image of Mary is an intensely apostolic one. In *The Glories of Mary*, Our Lady is presented not merely as a past historical figure but as a present and active force in the world. Alphonsus compares Mary to the Old Testament figure of Ruth, who was permitted by Boaz to gather the ears of corn after the reapers (Ru 2:3).[11] So also does Mary follow after apostolic workers in the church to save the souls who fail to be touched by the ordinary ministry of the church.

Alphonsus presents Mary as the instrument used by God as a first opening of grace into the person of the sinner. This is both a theological conviction and a psychological intuition. Alphonsus recognizes the unique entry of God into human history that attended on Mary's act of consent in the annunciation. His pastoral experience taught him that, given the experience and world view of the eighteenth-century Neapolitan peasant, Mary touches hearts like no other element of the gospel message. Alphonsus also associates Mary with perseverance in God's grace until the end. A poor person who can be convinced to wear a medal of Our Lady on a dirty cord around his neck can, with the help of a careful pastoral program, be brought, step by step, to great holiness. In his "Notice to the Reader" that begins *The Glories of Mary*, Alphonsus sees Mary as the midwife of God's grace in souls.[12] The entire progress of the Christian life is touched by the gracious and powerful interest of the Mother of God.

Alphonsus's conviction of the present activity of Mary in the church is seen in the use in which he makes of the *esempi* in *The Glories of Mary*. Alphonsus concluded each section of his commentary on the *Salve Regina* with an "example," a story that illustrates in narrative form the truth on which he has just commented. He adds at the end of the book a further collection of more than eighty Examples that can be used in Marian preaching. Much of the material in Alphonsus's writing on Mary that is troubling to contemporary sensibilities is found in the *Examples*, for example, stories of damned souls who, through Mary's inter-cession, were returned to life in order to go to confession. One such story tells of the severed head of a thief in Normandy that shrieked for a confessor and was heard. Alphonsus himself admits that some of these stories might strain credulity but he warns of the cynical spirit, foreign to Catholic piety, that would reject anything out of hand that would redound to the glory of Mary. The parables of Jesus in the gospels, despite some implau-sible elements of their own, served to introduce their listeners to an experience of the reign of God that was erupting into the ordinary stuff of human life—into kitchens, fields, and pastures, into wedding feasts and fishing expeditions. Alphonsus's use of *esempi* served a similar purpose. They often relate examples of the intervention of God, through Mary, into the lives of the poor and helpless. The *esempi* offer an entry into the reign of God—a world in which God subverts the structures of the status quo to bring justice and freedom to the oppressed.[13]

As a work of theology, *The Glories of Mary* breaks no new ground nor would Alphonsus, with his constant reference to sources in Christian tradition, want it to. Due to its immense pop-ularity, with numerous editions in many languages, *The Glories of Mary* was a formative influence on the Marian piety of genera-tions of Catholics. Alphonsus's work was influential in forming a theological and popular consensus on two questions of mariol-ogy, the Immaculate Conception and Mary's role in the media-tion of grace. Well in advance of the solemn definition of the Immaculate Conception as a dogma of the faith by Pope Pius IX in 1854, Alphonsus argued in favor of the Immaculate Concep-tion based on the tradition of the church evidenced in the belief of the faithful and on the church's liturgy. Alphonsus also argued in favor of Mary as the universal mediatrix of God's grace, "a mediation of grace by way of prayer."[14] The church has never solemnly defined whether or how Mary is involved in the media-tion of God's grace, although there was considerable enthusiasm among some bishops for such a definition at the Second Vatican Council.[15] The council merely acknowledged that the church invokes Mary under the title "mediatrix" in such a way as neither to add to nor to detract from the unique role of Jesus in the mediation of grace (cf. *Lumen Gentium,* ch. VIII, n. 62).

The following selections from the writing of Alphonsus Liguori on the Blessed Virgin Mary include a selection from *Orazioni alla Divina Madre per ciascun giorno della settimana (Prayers to the Divine Mother for Each Day of the Week)* from 1734, among the first writings of Alphonsus on Mary; from *Visite al SS. Sacramento (Visits to the Blessed Sacrament,* 1745), one of the "Visits to the Blessed Virgin" and the prayer that followed it; from *The Glories of Mary* "The Notice to the Reader" and "The Introduction," and some sections of the work that deal with the mediation of grace by Mary and with her Immaculate Conception.

In style and tone, Alphonsus's writings on Mary have perhaps survived the test of time least well among his ascetical works. Perhaps they can be best defended in the words of Alphonsus's countryman Giuseppe de Luca, expert on the spirituality of eighteenth-century Italy:

> How they carried on about *[The Glories of Mary]!* They accused it of exaggeration and could not understand that the excesses they saw in it stemmed from the poverty of their own love and from their own coldness. Not one of the saint's statements can be criticized if we examine them from a strictly theological point of view, and consequently any excess cannot be doctrinal. Then it must be the tone, they say; for it is the tone that shapes the music. True enough: The tone of the book is full of fire and unbearable heat, but this heat is no more and no less than love. And since when must love be judged by those who do not love?[16]

*　　*　　*

Selected Writings

Prayers to the Divine Mother for Each Day of the Week

PRAYER FOR SATURDAY[17]

O most holy Mother, how many are your gifts to me and how ungrateful have I been! An ungrateful person is unworthy of further gifts but I will never lose confidence in your mercy. O my great Advocate, have pity on me. You are the dispenser of all the graces that God grants to us unhappy creatures. It is for this reason that he has made you so powerful, so rich, and so generous, so that you might help us. I am resolved to save my soul. Therefore I place my eternal salvation into your hands and I offer myself to you. I wish to count myself among your most devoted servants. Do not drive me away. You go in search of the miserable in order to relieve them. Do not then abandon a miserable sinner who comes searching for you. Speak in my favor: Your Son does whatever you ask of him. Take me under your protection and it will be enough for me. If I have your protection I will fear nothing; neither from my sins because I hope you will obtain forgiveness of them from God; nor from the devils because you are more powerful than all hell together; nor even from Jesus, my judge, because one prayer from you will appease him. Protect me, therefore, my Mother, and obtain for me the pardon of my sins, a love for Jesus, holy perseverance, a good death, and heaven at last. It is true that I am undeserving of these favors, but if you ask the Lord for them for me, I will obtain them. Pray then to Jesus for me. O Mary, my Queen, I trust in you. On this hope I rely. In this hope I live and with it I hope to die. Amen.

Visits to the Blessed Sacrament

NINTH VISIT TO MARY[18]

Mary is like her Son Jesus in everything. Since she is the Mother of Mercy, she is filled with joy whenever she is able to help and console those in misery. So great is the desire of this Mother to obtain graces for everyone that Bernardino de Bustis says, "She is more interested in doing good for you and in giving you graces than you are to receive them."

Most Holy Immaculate and my Mother Mary, to you who are the Mother of my Lord, the Queen of the world, the Advocate, the Hope, the Refuge of Sinners, I direct myself today, I who am the most miserable of all. I offer you my most humble homage, O great Queen, and I thank you for all the graces you have obtained for me until now, particularly for having kept me from hell which I have so often deserved. I love you, O most lovable Lady, and because of my love for you I promise to serve you always and to do all that I can to make others love you too. I place all hope in you. To you I entrust my salvation. Accept me as your servant and welcome me under your mantle, O Mother of Mercy. And since you are so powerful with God, save me from all temptations, or rather obtain for me the strength to vanquish them until death. Of you I ask a perfect love for Jesus Christ. Through you I hope to die a good death. O my Mother, by the love which you bear to God, I beg you to help me at all times but especially at the last moments of my life. Do not leave me, I pray you, until you see me safe in heaven; blessing you and singing your mercies for all eternity. Amen. So I hope, So may it be.

The Glories of Mary[19]

Author's Note[20]

If perhaps some of the statements in this book might seem outlandish to some, I declare that I have made them and understood them in the same sense in which the Holy Catholic Church and sound theology understand them. For example, by calling Mary "mediatrix" I intend to refer to her as a mediatrix of grace in contrast to Jesus, who is the prime and unique mediator of justification. By calling Mary "all-powerful" (as have St. John Damascene, St. Peter Damian, St. Bonaventure, Cosmo Gerosolimitano, and others), I mean this in the sense that as Mother of God she can obtain from God by her prayers whatever she asks in favor of those devoted to her; neither this nor any other divine attribute can properly be applied to a creature, and Mary is but a creature. By calling Mary "our Hope" I intend by this (as is taught by St. Bernard) that all graces come to us by her hands.

The Notice to the Reader[21]

In order that my little work might not provoke a reaction from the overly critical, I thought it well to clarify certain statements found in it which may seem outlandish or perhaps obscure. I have noticed some, and should others attract your attention, kind reader, I request that you understand them according to the sense of true and sound theology and of the Holy Roman Catholic Church of which I am a most obedient son.

In the Introduction, referring to chapter five of this book, I have said that God wishes that all graces should come to us through the hands of Mary. This truth is a source of great consolation to those who are tenderly devoted to Mary Most Holy and for the poor sinners who wish to be converted. This should not appear as foreign to sound theology; the very Father of theology, St. Augustine (*Liber de Sancta Virginitate*, ch. 6.), gives voice to the general consensus that Mary has cooperated by her love in the spiritual birth of all the members of the church. A celebrated author, whom no one accuses to be given to exaggerations or to the fantasies of the falsely devout (Monsignor Nicole, *Instruzioni teologiche e morali sopra l'orazione domenicale, salutazione angelica, ecc.*), says that "since it was precisely on Calvary that Jesus Christ formed his church it is clear that the holy Virgin cooperated in a singular and excellent manner in the accomplishment of this work." While it can be said that she gave birth to the head of the church without pain it cannot be said that she gave birth to the body of this head without great pain. It was on Calvary that Mary began to be in a special way the Mother of the whole church. In short: the most holy God, to glorify the mother of the Redeemer, has decided and arranged that Mary, because of her great love, should pray for all those for whom her divine Son has paid and offered the superabundant price of his precious blood in which alone is our life, our salvation, and our resurrection.

On the foundation of this doctrine and those in accord with it, I have based my propositions—propositions which the saints in their tender conversations and fervent discourse with Mary have not hesitated to make. Thus the celebrated Father Vincenzo Contenson, citing an ancient Father, has written, "In Christ was the fullness of grace as in a head; Mary was the neck through which it flowed." This opinion is clearly taught by the Angelic Doctor Thomas Aquinas, who says,

There are three ways in which Mary is full of grace....The third is so that through her grace might be transfused to all. In any saint there is grace sufficient for the salvation of many; in Christ and Mary there is enough for the salvation of the whole world. In every danger you can obtain salvation from this glorious Virgin. Thus the Song of Songs says, "Your neck is like David's tower girt with battlements; a thousand bucklers hang upon it..." (Sg 4:4); therefore in Mary is the remedy for every danger. In every work of virtue you may have her as a helper for she says of herself, "In me is all hope of life and virtue" (Sir 24).

The Introduction[22]

My dear reader and brother in Mary, the devotion which has inspired me to write and you to read this book makes us both happy children of such a good mother. You may hear some say that I might have saved myself the effort since there are already many learned and renowned books available on this subject. If you hear this I ask you to respond in the words of the Abbot Francone, who says the praise of Mary is an inexhaustible fountain: The fuller it gets, the wider it is; the fuller it is, the more it expands. Thus this holy Virgin is so great that the more she is praised still more remains to praise....

I have seen countless works, large and small, which treat of the glories of Mary but they are often too rare or too voluminous or do not accomplish the purpose I have in mind. Therefore I have tried to collect as many books on Mary as I could get my hands on and in this book I have tried to select the choicest and most moving passages of the Fathers and theologians. I have done this for the convenience of the devout so that they might with little effort or expense set themselves afire by reading of the love of Mary and also to provide material for sermons for priests who wish to motivate others to devotion to this divine Mother.

Worldly lovers often speak in praise of those they love in order that the object of their affections might be esteemed and acclaimed by others. Paltry indeed is the love of those who consider themselves lovers of Mary but hardly speak or think of her and do little to make her loved by others. The true lovers of this most lovable Lady do not act in that fashion; they long to see her praised everywhere, to see her loved by the entire world. Therefore they never miss a chance whether in public or in private to set afire the hearts of others with the same blessed flame with which they themselves burn toward their Beloved Queen.

So that everyone might realize how important it is for one's own benefit and that of others to promote devotion to Mary, it is important to hear theologians on this topic. St. Bonaventure says that those who seek to extol the glories of Mary are assured of heaven. This opinion is confirmed by Richard of St. Lawrence, who says that to honor the queen of angels is to win life eternal. He adds that this Lady is most grateful to those who honor her in this world and will surely be honored by her in the next. And who is not aware of the promise made by Mary herself in the book of Ecclesiastes, "They that explain me shall have everlasting life" (Eccl 24:31). This text is applied to Mary in the liturgy of the feast of the Immaculate Conception. St. Bonaventure, who did so much to make Mary's glories known, says, "Rejoice, my soul, and be glad in her because many good things are held in store for those who praise her." He says further that all of scripture speaks in praise of Mary; let us then always praise her with hearts and tongues, so that we might be led by her into the company of the blessed...

St. Anselm says that devotion to Mary is of great profit to all. As her most holy womb was the means of salvation for sinners, so unless Mary be preached sinners will not be converted and saved....It is well known that in this way St. Bernardino of Siena made Italy holy; in this way St. Dominic converted so many provinces; St. Louis Bertrand never omitted in his sermons to promote devotion to Mary; so many others have done the same.

The celebrated missionary Paul Segneri the younger preached a sermon on Mary in all of his missions and said that it was his favorite sermon. In our own missions [i.e., of the Redemptorists] we have an inviolable rule never to omit the sermon on the Madonna. We can attest in all truth that scarcely any sermon is more profitable or produces more compunction in the hearts of the people than the sermon on the mercy of Mary. I say "the mercy of Mary" because, as St. Bernard says, we praise her humility, we admire her virginity, but as poor sinners it is especially hearing of her mercy that delights and pleases us. We embrace mercy with more love, we remember it with more ease, we invoke it more often.

For this reason I will leave to other authors to detail the other praises of Mary. I prefer in this book to speak mostly of her tender mercy and powerful intercession. I have collected as far as I am able, with the work of many years, everything that the Fathers and distinguished authors have said on the mercy and power of Mary. These are described in a marvelous way in the great prayer the "Hail, Holy Queen," which is approved by the church and whose recitation is required of the clergy and religious for a great portion of the year. In the first place I will devote a number of discourses to the various parts of this beautiful prayer. Then I will provide, for the pleasure of those devoted to Mary, a series of discourses on the principal feasts and virtues of this divine Mother; finally, in a third part, I will include the practices of devotion most used by those dedicated to Mary and approved by the church.

Devoted reader, if this work pleases you as I hope it will, I beg you to recommend me to the Blessed Virgin Mary, that she might give me a greater confidence in her protection. This grace which I seek for myself, I promise I will seek for you as well, whoever you may be, if you do me this charity. Oh, blessed are they who cling with confidence and love to these two great anchors of our salvation, Jesus and Mary. Surely such people can never be lost.

Dear reader, let us both speak from the heart the words of the devout Alphonsus Rodriguez, "Jesus and Mary, my sweet loves, for you may I suffer, for you may I die, may I be in all things yours, in nothing mine." Let us love Jesus and Mary and we will become saints. What finer fortune could we hope for or desire? Farewell until we see one another in paradise at the feet of this most sweet mother and this most loving son, there to praise them, to thank them, to love them, together, face to face, for all eternity. Amen.

Chapter V, I[23]
Mary, Our Mediatrix
The Necessity of the Intercession of Mary for Our Salvation

It is an article of faith that it is not only permissible but useful and holy to invoke and to pray to the saints, and more especially to the Queen of the saints, Mary most holy, in order that they might obtain divine grace for us. This has been defined by councils against the heretics who condemned it as an insult to Jesus Christ, who is our unique mediator. But if Jeremiah after his death could pray for Jerusalem (2 Mc 15:14); if the elders in the Book of Revelation (5:8) presented the prayers of the saints to God; if St. Peter promised his disciples that he would remember them after his death (2 Pt 1:15); if holy Stephen prayed for his persecutors (Acts 7:59); if St. Paul prayed for his companions (Acts 26:24); if then the saints can pray for us, then why can we not pray to the saints to ask them to pray for us? St. Paul recommends himself to the prayers of his disciples: "Brothers, pray for us" (1 Thes 5:25). St. James tells us to pray for each other (Jas 5:16). Therefore we also can do the same.

Who would deny that Jesus Christ is our only mediator of justice, and that by his merits he has obtained reconciliation with God for us? On the other hand it is lacking in piety to assert that God is not pleased to grant graces through the intercession of the saints, and especially through his mother, Mary, whom he wants to see loved and honored by us. Who does not know that any honor paid to a mother redounds also to her son? "The glory of children is their parentage" (Prv 17:6). Thus says St. Bernard: "Let us not think that we might obscure the glory of the son by praise of the mother; the more the mother is honored, the more the son is honored as well. There can be no doubt that whatever is said in praise of the mother is in equal measure praise of the son." St. Ildephonsus also says that all the honor that is paid to the queen mother is doubtless bestowed on the king too. All the authority that Mary might have to be mediatrix of our salvation was granted to her through the merits of her son. Mary is indeed a mediatrix not of justice but of grace and intercession as St.

Bonaventure calls her "Mary, the most faithful mediatrix of our salvation." And St. Lawrence Justinian asks, "How can she be other than full of grace, who has been made the ladder of paradise, the gate of heaven, the most true mediatrix between God and humanity?"

St. Anselm rightly observes that we pray to Mary for grace not because we distrust the mercy of God but rather because of our own sense of unworthiness; we recommend ourselves to Mary that her dignity might supply for our lowliness.

Therefore only those without faith can deny that recourse to the intercession of Mary is holy and useful. But what we intend to demonstrate here is that the intercession of Mary is necessary for our salvation: not absolutely necessary but morally necessary, to speak precisely. We maintain further that this necessity stems precisely from the will of God that all graces should pass through the hands of Mary, according to the opinion of St. Bernard, which today is the common opinion of theologians and doctors, as is asserted by the author of *The Reign of Mary*. This opinion is followed by Vega, Mendoza, Pacciuchelli, Segneri, Poire, Crasset and by innumerable other learned authors....

This proposition (that all the good we receive from the Lord comes through Mary) is not very attractive to a certain modern author.[24] In other respects he speaks with great learning of true and false devotion. But when he speaks of the devotion due to the Mother of God he is rather stingy and reluctant to concede to her the glory given without scruple by St. Germanus, St. Anselm, St. John Damascene, St. Bonaventure, St. Antoninus, St. Bernardino, the Venerable Abbot of Celles, and so many other learned people. They have no difficulty in affirming that the intercession of Mary is not only useful, but necessary. The aforementioned author says that the proposition that God grants no grace except through Mary is but a hyperbole and an exaggeration that fell from the fervent lips of some saints. Saner discourse would require us to understand these words to mean that through Mary we received Jesus Christ, by whose merits we obtain all graces. To believe that God grants us no grace except through Mary's intercession would be in error since St. Paul states, "There is also one mediator between God and/the human race,/Christ Jesus" (1 Tm 2:5).

With all due respect, the same author points out in his own book that it is one thing to speak of a mediation of justice by merit and another to speak of mediation of grace by way of prayer. It is one thing to say that God cannot grant grace except through Mary; it is another thing to maintain that God does not will to do so. We maintain fully that God is the source of every good and the absolute master of all grace, and that Mary is but a creature who has received all she has gratuitously from God. But who can deny that it is reasonable and fitting to assert that God would wish to exalt this great creature? She loved him more than all other creatures during her life. He chose her to be the mother of his Son, the Redeemer of us all. Would he not will that all graces which he wishes to grant to the redeemed should pass through her hands? We readily admit that Jesus Christ is the only mediator of justice, according to the distinction we have already made, and that by his merits he obtains for us all grace and salvation. But we say that Mary is the mediatrix of grace. Everything she has she receives through Jesus. When she prays, she prays in the name of Jesus. Yet all the graces we seek come to us through her intercession.

There is nothing contrary to the sacred dogmas in all this. It is in accord with the sentiments of the church, which, in the approved prayers, teaches us to have continual recourse to the Mother of God and to invoke her as the health of the sick, the refuge of sinners, the help of Christians, our life, our hope. The same holy church in the divine office assigned for the feast of Mary applies to her the words of the book of Sirach, "In me is all hope of life and virtue...all grace and truth" (Sir 24:25, Vulgate ed.). In Mary is the hope of every grace. In Mary we find life and salvation: "Who finds me finds life" (Prv 8:35)....Surely such expressions as these are sufficient to prove that we need the intercession of Mary.

Moreover, we are supported in this opinion by so many Fathers and theologians that it is surely unjust to say, as does the aforementioned author, that they spoke "hyperbolically" and that "excessive exaggerations" fell from their lips. To exaggerate and to speak in hyperbole is to exceed the limits of truth. Surely we cannot say this of the saints who were animated by the spirit of God, which is the spirit of truth.

If I may be permitted to make a small digression, in order to give my own opinion. When a theological opinion tends in some way to give honor to the Blessed Virgin Mary, when it has some good foundation and is not repugnant to the faith nor to the decrees of the church, nor to the truth—then to refuse to hold such an opinion because the reverse may be true shows little devotion to the Mother of God. I do not wish to number myself among those of such little devotion nor would I hope to number my readers among them. I prefer to be counted among those who will believe everything that can be believed of the greatness of Mary without error. The Abbot Rupert numbered among the acts of homage that are pleasing to Mary to firmly believe what redounds to her glory. If nothing else were available to quell our fears of going to excess in praise of Mary, the word of St. Augustine should suffice. He declares that whatever we might say in praise of Mary is small in comparison with what she deserves, because of her dignity as Mother of God. We speak with the church in the text of the Mass of the Blessed Virgin Mary: "How blessed are you, O Virgin Mary, and most worthy of all praise...."

Conclusion of the Discourse on the Feast of the Immaculate Conception[25]

I wish finally to conclude this discourse, on which I have spent more time than all the others, because our least Congregation has for its principal patroness the Blessed Virgin Mary, precisely under this title of her Immaculate Conception. I wish to conclude by giving as briefly as possible the reasons which make me certain, and which, in my opinion ought to convince everyone of the truth of this pious belief, and one which contributes so much to the glory of the divine Mother, that is, that she was preserved from original sin.

There are even many Doctors who maintain that Mary was also exempt from contracting even the debt of sin; for example, Cardinal Galitino, Cardinal Cusanus, De Ponte, Salazar, Catharinus, Novarino, Viva, De Lugo, Egidio, Richelio, and others. This opinion is quite probable. Even if it is probable that the will of all people were included in the will of Adam, as being the head of all (as is held as probable by Gonet, Habert, and others, basing themselves on the text of Paul, "Therefore, just as through one person...all sinned," in Romans 5:12), it is also probable that Mary did not contract the debt of sin. Since God so distinguished Mary by grace from common humanity, it ought piously to be believed that the will of Adam did not include that of Mary.

This opinion is only probable, but I subscribe to it as being more glorious for my Lady. But I consider as certain the opinion that Mary did not contract the sin of Adam. I hold it as certain and even as proximately definable as *de fide*, as do also Cardinal Everard, Duval, Raynauld, Lossada, Viva, and many others. I leave out of consideration those revelations which confirm this opinion, especially those of St. Bridget, which were approved by Cardinal Torrecremata and by four Popes and which are found in various parts of the sixth book of her *Revelations*. I cannot fail to consider the opinions of the holy Fathers on this subject and thus to demonstrate how unanimous they are in conceding this privilege to the divine Mother. [Alphonsus here cites texts of fifteen Doctors and Fathers of the church in support of the Immaculate Conception of the Blessed Virgin Mary.] And many other Doctors speak in the same way.

But, finally, there are two arguments that are conclusive proof of this pious belief. The first is the universal consensus of the faithful on this question. Father Egidius of the Presentation assures us that all the religious orders follow this opinion. A modern author tells us that even in the order of St. Dominic while there are 92 against this opinion there are nevertheless 136 in favor.[26] But what should persuade us above all that our pious belief is in accord with the general sentiment of Catholics is that it is attested to in the celebrated bull of Pope Alexander VII, *Sollicitudo omnium ecclesiarum*, of 1661. The bull states, "This devotion and homage toward the Mother of God has so spread and increased that when the universities adopted this opinion it had already been embraced by nearly all Catholics." In fact, this opinion is defended in the universities of the Sorbonne, Alcala, Salamanca, Coimbra, Cologne, Metz, Naples, and many others. To receive a doctorate in these universities the candidates must swear an oath to defend the Immaculate Conception of Mary. The learned Petavius bases his belief in the Immaculate Conception on the argument of the general consensus of the faithful. This argument, writes the most learned bishop Giulio Torni, cannot fail to convince us. What else makes us certain of the truth of the sanctification of Mary in the womb and of her Assumption, body and soul, into heaven, than the general consensus of the faithful? Why then should not the same general consensus of the faithful make us certain of her Immaculate Conception?

The second reason to believe that Mary was free from original sin is stronger than the first: that the universal church commands the celebration of the feast of the Immaculate Conception. The church celebrates the first moment in which the soul of Mary was created and infused into her body. Alexander VII in the bull mentioned above states that the church in its liturgy gives the same veneration to Mary as do those who hold the pious opinion that she was conceived without original sin. I maintain as certain that the church cannot celebrate anything which is not holy, according to the teaching of Pope St. Leo and of the bishop St. Eusebius: "In the apostolic see the Catholic religion was always preserved spotless." All the theologians, including Augustine, Bernard, and Thomas, agree on this point. In fact, Thomas uses this very argument to prove that Mary was sanctified before her birth, that is, from the fact that the church has a liturgical celebration of her birth. Thus he states, "The church celebrates the birth of the Blessed Virgin. The church celebrates feasts only of saints. Therefore, the Blessed Virgin was sanctified in her mother's womb." But if it is certain, as the Angelic Doctor states, that Mary was sanctified in the womb because the church celebrates her birth, why is it not equally certain that Mary was preserved free from original sin from the first moments of her conception knowing, as we do, that the church celebrates this fact by a feast?

As further confirmation of this great privilege of Mary, we may note the innumerable graces and miracles that the Lord is pleased to work daily throughout the Kingdom of Naples by means of pictures of the Immaculate Conception of Mary. I could refer to many which passed through the hands of a Father of our own Congregation; I will tell the story of only two that were truly admirable.

Examples

A woman came to one of the houses our little Congregation has in this kingdom to tell one of our priests that her husband had not been to confession in many years. The unhappy woman was at her wits' end to think what more she could do to convince him. If she so much as mentioned confession, he would beat her. The priest instructed the woman to give him a picture of Mary Immaculate. When evening came the woman once again begged her husband to go to confession. As usual he pretended to be deaf and so she gave him the picture. He had barely received the picture when he said, "Well, I'm ready. When are you going to take me to confession?" The woman, seeing such an instantaneous change, began to weep for joy. In the morning he came to our church. When the Redemptorist asked him how long it had been since his last confession, he answered, "Twenty-eight years." "How is it," asked the priest, "that you felt moved this morning to come to confession?" "Father," he said, "I was stubborn. Last night my wife gave me a picture of the Madonna and immediately I felt my heart change. Throughout the night every moment seemed a thousand years to me, so anxious was I for the day to arrive so that I could go to confession." He then went to confession with great compunction, changed his life, and continued to go frequently to confession to the same Father.

In another place in the diocese of Salerno, while we were giving a mission, there was a man who had a great enmity for someone who had offended him. One of our Fathers spoke to him to encourage him to be reconciled but he answered, "Father, have you ever seen me at the sermons? No, and for this very reason I do not go. I already know that I am damned. Nothing will satisfy me but to have my revenge." The priest went to great lengths to convert him but, seeing that his words were useless, he said, "Take this picture of the Madonna." At first the man answered, "A lot of good a holy card is going to do me!" No sooner had he taken it, then as if he had been willing to be reconciled all along, he asked the priest, "Father, what else do I need to do to be reconciled? I am willing to do it." The time for reconciliation was set for the next day. But when the morning came he had changed his mind again and wanted nothing to do with it. The priest offered him another holy card, but he refused it. Finally, with great resistance, he took it. What do you imagine happened? Immediately on taking the card he said, "Let's hurry. Where is the *mastrodatt* [i.e., "maestro d'atti," a Neapolitan dialect word that means a notary public. The man was willing to resolve his dispute by a public act]. At once everything was resolved and the man afterward went to confession.

Prayer

Ah, my Immaculate Lady, I rejoice with you to see you enriched with such great purity. I give thanks, and I resolve to give thanks always, to your Creator and mine, for having preserved you from every stain of sin. I hold this great and singular privilege of yours to be certain and in defense of it I am ready to swear an oath, or even, if necessary, to lay down my life.

I wish that the whole world knew you and confessed you to be that beautiful Dawn, always illumined by the light of God; that Chosen Ark of salvation, free from the shipwreck of sin that afflicts us all; that perfect and immaculate Dove that your Divine Spouse declared you to be; that Garden Enclosed in which God delights; that Sealed Fountain whose waters were never disturbed by the enemy; that white Lily, born among the thorns of the children of Adam who are conceived in sin and as enemies of God, yet conceived pure, spotless, and in everything a friend of your Creator.

Permit me to praise you as you are praised by God: "You are all-beautiful, my beloved,/and there is no blemish in you" (Sg 4:7). O most pure Dove, all pure, all lovely, ever a friend of God. "Ah, you are beautiful, my beloved,/ah, you are beautiful!" (Sg 4:1). Ah, most sweet, most lovable, immaculate Mary, you who are so beautiful in the eyes of your God, do not disdain to cast your compassionate eyes on the foul wounds of my soul. Look at me, take pity on me and heal me. O beautiful magnet of hearts, draw my unhappy heart to you. You who from the first moment of your life appeared beautiful and pure before God, have pity on me, who was not only born in sin but also have again stained my soul with sin after Baptism. God has chosen you as his daughter, his mother, and his spouse, has preserved you from every stain, and in his love preferred you to every other creature—what grace could God possibly deny you? Immaculate Virgin, you have to save me. I address you in the word of St. Philip Neri: "Grant that I might always remember you; and may you, for your part, never forget me. It seems like a thousand years before I can see your beauty in paradise, to praise and love you, 'mamma mia,' my Queen, my beloved, my most beautiful, most sweet, most pure, Immaculate Mary. Amen."

PRAYER

Introduction

Editor's Note: No aspect of the spiritual life is more central to the spirituality of St. Alphonsus Liguori than prayer. Alphonsus himself states about his preaching: "No matter what my sermon may seem to be about, the real topic is always prayer." All the apostolic efforts of Alphonsus were in some way oriented toward teaching prayer and toward forming Christians into communities of prayer. Much of his writing was to provide material for prayer or for instruction in prayer. The very way in which Alphonsus structured his ascetical works indicates his preoccupation with prayer. Each chapter of his ascetical works is concluded by a section of *affetti e preghiere*–affections and prayers. They form an insight into the heart of Alphonsus at prayer. He could not write for a very long time without breaking into prayer himself. He would have expected as much of the reader. To read a work of Alphonsus without being drawn to prayer is not to have read it at all.

Alphonsus himself received an impressive formation in the doctrine and practice of prayer from an early age.[1] It is a telling detail that all his life Alphonsus used a hand-written book of simple prayers, acts of love and trust, given to him as a boy by his mother. As a young man, he made an annual retreat with Don Giuseppe, his father; they alternated years between the Vincentians and the Jesuits. Thus Alphonsus is among the countless figures whose spirituality was formed by contact with the Spiritual Exercises of St. Ignatius. As a member of the Sodality of San Giuseppe for Young Noblemen, directed by the Oratorians, Alphonsus was exposed to the joyful and optimistic spirituality of St. Philip Neri. Alphonsus's religious formation was rich and solid. He was nourished by the finest elements of Christian tradition, which he would later weave into a synthesis all his own.

Notable in his life of prayer was his devotion to the Eucharist. His contemporaries remarked on his frequent assistance at the Forty Hours devotion held almost continually in one or another of

Naples's many churches. Alphonsus himself attributed his conversion and vocation to prayer before the Blessed Sacrament.

As a founder, Alphonsus insisted on the primacy of personal and communal prayer for the Redemptorist Congregation. The daily rhythm of prayer that Alphonsus handed on to the Congregation was simple and rooted in the perennial tradition of the church. The celebration of the Eucharist was the center of the day. Alphonsus mandated recitation of the Liturgy of the Hours in common for communities that were sufficiently large. This was unusual for an apostolic Congregation since the Jesuits had established a model apostolic religious life without choral recitation of the Office.[2] Alphonsus himself did not mandate the recitation of the Office during the intense activity of the mission season. In 1774 Alphonsus published his *Translation of the Psalms and Canticles That Are Contained in the Divine Office,* a translation and commentary on the Psalter to foster devout recitation of the Office for clergy and religious. For Alphonsus, mental prayer, especially meditation on the scriptures, was always to be preferred to the recitation of vocal prayers: "Nothing is better able to enkindle the love of God in a person than the Word of God itself contained in the Sacred Scriptures."[3] The schedule of community prayer for the Redemptorists centered around half-hour periods of mental prayer made in common morning and evening with another half-hour made privately in the afternoon outside of the mission preaching season. One of the goals of a mission was precisely to encourage the faithful to establish the practice of making mental prayer in common in the parish church or at home in the family circle. Alphonsus's companion, Gennaro Sarnelli (1702–1744), published a book in 1738 whose very title expresses the importance of meditation, *The World Sanctified by the Practice of Mental Prayer Made in Common.*[4]

One of Alphonsus's own favorite times of personal prayer was after the reception of the Eucharist and he required of the community a half-hour period of thanksgiving after communion (reduced to fifteen minutes during the mission time). Devotion to the Eucharist was fostered further by a daily visit to the Blessed Sacrament that was always to include "an act of spiritual communion" as a reminder that the Eucharist is first and foremost food for the pilgrim journey and that visits to the Blessed Sacrament should serve to whet our hunger for the sacramental Lord. The characteristic Alphonsian devotion to the Blessed Virgin Mary was expressed by daily recitation of the rosary and a brief "visit to the Blessed Virgin Mary" made in conjunction with the visit to the Blessed Sacrament. The Redemptorists were not a monastic congregation, and Alphonsus clearly made adaptations in the requirements of community prayer for the sake of ministry. Nevertheless the prayer regimen he considered normative for his community is substantial and Alphonsus always intended the Redemptorist community to be an example and a center of prayer for the surrounding neighborhood.[5] Alphonsus specified that the early Redemptorist houses should have a public church with a vigorous program of prayer and that the houses should be large enough to accommodate retreatants who would share in the life of prayer of the community.

Prayer, for Alphonsus Liguori, is the fundamental and defining act of the human person. A refrain that runs throughout his work makes this point: "Whoever prays is saved; whoever does not pray is lost." Prayer, more than words, is the fundamental option of the person—to rejoice in creatureliness, in grateful openness of the self to the Creator, or to die in suffocating self-enclosure. Alphonsus sees the root of human sin in the failure to pray; Adam and Eve brought sin into the world because, in time of temptation, they did not pray.[6] Consequently the theology of prayer of Alphonsus puts great emphasis on the absolute necessity of prayer of petition for salvation. In an age when Jansenism made salvation seem to be a prize reserved for spiritual Olympians, Alphonsus made salvation available literally for the asking.[7]

Alphonsus's writing on prayer must be situated in the context of the theological controversies *De Auxilliis* about the relationship between divine grace and human freedom that raged from the time of the Reformation well into the eighteenth century.[8] A large portion of Alphonsus's most extended theological investigation of prayer, *Del Gran Mezzo della Preghiera* (1759),[9] is devoted to a refutation of the Jansenist theology that denied the universality and sufficiency of God's grace. While Alphonsus did not resolve the *De Auxilliis* in any theoretical way, he offered a practical solution in his writings on the prayer of petition.[10] God gives to all the grace to pray as an expression of a universal salvific will. Alphonsus is confident that faithfulness to this initial grace through perseverance in prayer will place salvation within the reach of everyone.

Alphonsus emphasizes as well the practice of meditation or mental prayer. While mental prayer does not have the same absolute necessity for salvation that prayer of petition has, it is morally necessary for salvation. Prayer for Alphonsus is the natural response of the human heart when it has genuinely heard the gospel. "If we do not love so good a God," says Alphonsus, "it is because we do not really know him." For Alphonsus, God's very nature is an outpouring of love. God has gone out of himself to the point of folly in order to make himself lovable to us. To the "age of reason" Alphonsus preached *Iddio Pazzo*, the Crazy God. This self-outpouring of God erupts into history in Jesus Christ and is evident for Alphonsus in a special way in the Incarnation, the Passion, and the Eucharist. The Christian who prayerfully considers these mysteries will be led to respond in gratitude and love to God. Thus mental prayer, while it has a cognitive component, is not essentially an intellectual activity according to Alphonsus. The time of mental prayer should mainly be spent in the making of "affections," acts of the will oriented toward growing in love of God and conformity to the divine will.

Alphonsus was by temperament suspicious of extraordinary spiritual experiences and nothing will be found in his works to compare with the detailed analysis of the higher states of prayer found in the works of Teresa of Avila or John of the Cross.[11] Given the orientation of his ministry to the evangelization of the poor, the higher states of prayer would have been of little practical interest to Alphonsus. Furthermore, the Quietism controversy of the previous century had thrown an unfavorable light on the question of passive contemplation.[12]

Alphonsus does treat of the stages of prayer and contemplative and mystical prayer in his *Praxis Confessarii* (1757), a guide for confessors in the exercise of the various aspects of their ministry. Obviously Alphonsus thought it important that the average confessor have some familiarity with basic information on the higher states of prayer. His treatment is solid and traditional and heavily dependent on Teresa of Avila. A characteristic touch is Alphonsus's warning that one should not leave off making affections in prayer in the state of acquired contemplation. His preference is clearly in favor of active response to God until God clearly wills otherwise.

Alphonsus's insistent focus on prayer represents a kind of "democratization" of the spiritual life. For Alphonsus salvation and holiness did not depend on arduous spiritual exercises but on prayer, an act of religion that is accessible to everyone, especially to the poor and uneducated. One of the earliest ministries of Alphonsus was the direction of the *capelle serotine,* "evening chapels" or gatherings of laity in the back rooms of shops or in the corners of city squares for prayer, for religious instruction, and for mutual support in virtue.[13] Antonio Tannoia, Alphonsus's confrere and first biographer, tells of the kind of people that frequented the evening chapels: cowherds and carpenters, those who sold eggs, capers, and chestnuts in the streets; all of them enamored of Jesus Christ. Alphonsus was not convinced of the possibility of holiness through prayer for the ordinary person merely out of theological conviction. He had witnessed in his own life and ministry the works of God's grace in the people who were at the margins of the ecclesial and social structures of his society.

In the last years of his life Alphonsus, crippled and racked with illnesses, was visited by the Neapolitan architect Giuseppe Mauro. Alphonsus asked him if his beloved *capelle serotine* were still functioning. Mauro replied that they were and were so successful that there were even saints among the coachmen of Naples. "There are saints among the coachmen in Naples. Glory be to God!" Alphonsus exclaimed.[14] Holiness, the fruit of prayer, flourishing among the least citizens of a harsh and loveless country—Alphonsus could not hope for a greater assurance that his life and ministry had been worthwhile.

PRAYER

The following selections from Alphonsus' work are included:

1. *A Way of Conversing Continually with God as with a Friend;*
2. Selections from *Prayer, the Great Means of Salvation;*
3. *The Practice of Mental Prayer,* and *Outline of a Simple Method of Making Mental Prayer*

A Way of Conversing Continually with God as with a Friend

Introduction by Brendan McConvery, C.SS.R.

Editor's Note: This short work was first published in Naples in 1753 as *A way of conversing continually with God as with a friend derived from a French work which has been favorably received by the devout, enlarged with other devout thoughts, affections and practices by Father Alphonsus Liguori.*[1] The "French work" alluded to in the title was *La Méthode pour Converser avec Dieu* by the French Jesuit Michel Boutauld (1608–1689), published in 1684 and translated into Italian in 1735.[2] Boutauld's work was to suffer an unusual fate. It was put on the "Index of Prohibited Books" in 1723, due, it has been suspected, to additions of a Jansenist tendency in posthumous editions, and the restriction was only formally lifted for the 1910 edition. This may explain Alphonsus's reticence in acknowledging the French author by name.

While Boutauld provided the title and general framework, Alphonsus drew on other sources, principally St. Jure's *De la Connaissance et de l'Amour du Fils de Dieu* and Lorenzo Scupoli's *Combattimento Spirituale.*[3] Despite its derivative nature, *A Way of Conversing* has remained one of Alphonsus's most popular short works. It was, with the *Visits to the Blessed Sacrament,* one of the first to be translated into German (Wurzburg and Bamberg, 1766). It is a serene and gentle work, at times almost lyrical in its appreciation of the goodness of creation that compels the person of faith to enter into communion with God. The essence of prayer, he assures the reader, is familiar and intimate conversation with a loving God. Although Alphonsus's principal metaphor for prayer is friendship, he recognizes its limits, for God is not only friend, but is also lover and mother and even these expressions of human love cannot fully capture the power of divine love (par. 1 and 2). The initiative in the dialogue of love does not lie with human beings, for God has spoken the first word in the mysteries of creation and redemption, and Alphonsus invites his readers to interpret the whole of the natural world as a set of signs recalling the mysteries of redemption (31–35).

The direct tone of the work suggests that it was intended for a wide general readership. There are no citations from the Fathers, but he weaves a rich tapestry of scriptural quotations, particularly from the psalms, the wisdom writings, and the New Testament. The *exempla* are for the most part taken from the lives either of familiar saints, or of those who enjoyed a reputation for sanctity in eighteenth-century Naples, such as Carlo Caraffa and Seraphina of Capri.[4] Alphonsus's experience with the lay movement of the *capelle serotine* (the "evening chapels" or groups of working men coming together for religious instruction and prayer) during the early years of his ministry had made him keenly aware of the hunger for a rich prayer life that existed among the ordinary people of his time. He offers them here encouragement and a simple rule of life (par. 28) that included daily meditation, spiritual reading, and familiar prayers such as the rosary and visits to the Blessed Sacrament.

For all its simplicity, a hard spine of theology runs through the work. Two obstacles had to be overcome in order to dispel the fear that a life of prayer of this kind was beyond the means of his readers. The first was the fear that the spiritual life could become an all-absorbing escape into a realm of spiritual fantasy. For Alphonsus, the reality of the Christian love affair with God rests on the recognition that God is love and allowing that to shape the rest of life. He insists: "You do not have to be so constantly applying your mind that you forget all your other duties and recreations. All that is required of you is that you simply carry on and continue to think of God the way someone who is in love would think of their beloved" (par. 7). The other argument was that faults committed through human weakness or a past history of serious sin were incompatible with a life of prayer. In Alphonsus's eyes, this was a more pernicious argument because it concealed a latent Jansenism and moral Rigorism that touched deeply on the complexity of the moral response. Rigorism fails to read the story of human striving for God and moral goodness accurately. It can discount human effort too easily, unless it is 100 percent successful, and in face of the reality of human failure it not infrequently proceeds to the implicit assumption that moral goodness is largely determined, either genetically or culturally. Determinism of this kind is not a long step from a theology of predestination. Alphonsus offers the reader in outline an intensely biblical view of God's purpose as universal salvation and notes: "I have placed all these texts before you so that when you are anxious at the thought that there is no salvation for you or that you are already predestined, you can find relief in knowing how much God desires to save you, if you are resolute in his service and in loving him as he has asked" (par. 18).

A modern reader will notice that Alphonsus touches only very lightly on the social world in which the call to holiness is to be lived. He does, however, mirror something of the social inequality of Naples with his unflattering references to the scramble for power and prestige into which so many people could be drawn, and it is easy to see where his sympathies lay.

This translation is based on the text of the Italian critical edition of the *Opere Ascetiche I: Practica di Amar Gesu Cristo e Opuscoli sull' Amore Divino* (Rome, 1933), 313–334, which it follows in the paragraph numbering. The only omission is paragraph 30, which is a list of indulgences then applicable to certain acts of devotion.

*   *   *

1. Holy Job was struck with wonder to consider that our God is so devoted to doing good for us that God's heart has no greater concern than to love us and to make itself loved by us. Speaking to God, Job exclaimed: "What is man, that you make much of him,/or pay him any heed?" (Jb 7:17). How mistaken it is to think that to relate to God with great confidence and familiarity would be a lack of respect for the infinite majesty. You ought, devout soul, to respect God in all humility and to lower yourself in the divine presence, especially when you remember the ingratitude and offenses of the past. But all this should not prevent you from relating to God with the most tender and confident love of which you are capable.

God indeed is infinite majesty but at the same time, infinite goodness and limitless love. You have in God the most sublime master imaginable but you also have in God the greatest lover for whom you could hope. God does not disdain your familiarity but rather rejoices that you would relate to God with the same confidence, freedom, and tenderness with which children relate to their mothers. Hear how you are invited to God's feet and the caresses you are promised: "As nurslings you shall be carried in her arms, and fondled in her lap; as a mother comforts her son, so I will comfort you" (Is 12b–13a). As a mother delights in placing a child on her lap so as to feed and caress him, so our good God delights to treat with the same tenderness those who love without reserve and have placed all their hopes in God's goodness.

2. Consider that you have neither friend nor brother, not father or mother, spouse or lover who loves you more than God does. Divine grace is that treasure by which we, lowly creatures and servants, become the dearest friends of the one who made us. "For to men she is an unfailing treasure;/those who gain this treasure win the friendship of God" (Wis 7:14). In order to increase our confidence, God emptied himself, became nothing (Phil 2:7), humble to such an extent as to become human in order to converse with us like a friend (Bar 3:38). God went so far as to become an infant, to become poor, and even went so far as to become a spectacle on the Cross. God went farther still in hiding under the appearances of bread and wine in order to be our companion forever and to be united with us with the greatest intimacy: "Whoever eats my flesh and drinks my blood remains in me and I in him" (Jn 6:56). In short, God loves you as much as if he had no other object of love except you alone. And so you should love none other than God. Of God you might say, indeed you ought to say: "My lover belongs to me and I to him" (Sg 2:16). My God is given to me completely and I give myself to him totally in return. God has chosen me as beloved and I chose God above all others as my only love. "My lover...stands out among thousands" (Sg 5:10).

3. Say to God often: O my Lord! Why do you love me so much? What good do you see in me? Have you forgotten how I have offended you? Instead of casting me into hell, you loaded me with favors. Since you have treated me with such love, who

better to love, from this day forward, than you, my good, my all? O most lovable God, if I have offended you in the past what disturbs me most is not the punishment I deserve but the displeasure I have given you, worthy of limitless love. What more could I possibly want, in this life or the next, but you? "Whom else have I in the heavens?" And when I am with you the earth delights me not: "God is the rock of my heart, my portion forever" (Ps 73:25, 26). You are and will forever be the only master of my heart, of my will. You are my only good, my paradise, my love, my all: the God of my heart, the God who is my destiny forever.

4. In order to strengthen your trust in God, recall the loving way in which God has dealt with you and the tenderness with which God has rescued you from a disordered life and the attachments of this world and drawn you to holy love. Now you have finally decided to love and please God as much as you can; how can you possibly dare to lack trust in God now? God's past mercies toward you are the surest guarantee of the love God bears you. The only thing that displeases God is a lack of trust in a heart that loves him and whom he loves. If you wish to give pleasure to his loving heart then trust with the greatest confidence and tenderness of which you are capable. "See, upon the palms of my hands I have written your name;/your walls are ever before me" (Is 49:16). Beloved one, says the Lord, why are you afraid or uncertain? I have engraved you on the palms of my hands so as never to forget to do you good. Do you perhaps fear your enemies? Your defense is ever before my eyes; how could I possibly forget it?

For this reason David rejoices and says: "For you, O Lord, bless the just...you surround [them] with the shield of your good will" (Ps 5:13). Who could possibly harm us if you surround and defend us with your goodness and bounty? Above all, revive your confidence with the thought of the gift that God has given us in Jesus Christ: "For God so loved the world that he gave his only Son" (Jn 3:16). How could God deny us anything, exclaims the apostle Paul, having given us his only Son? (Rom 8:32).

5. "And I found delight in the sons of men" (Prv 8:31). Heaven for God is the human heart. Does God love you? Then love in return. God's greatest pleasure is to be with you; you

should delight to be with God, to spend your whole life in the loving company of the God with whom you hope to spend an eternity of delight.

6. Accustom yourself to speak to God, one to one, in a familiar manner as to the dearest friend you have and who loves you best of all. It is a great mistake to treat God with uncertainty and to enter God's presence like a slave who, ashamed and full of fear, comes trembling with terror into the presence of a prince. It is even a greater mistake to think that conversation with God is nothing but boredom and tediousness. Nothing could be farther from the truth. "For association with her involves no bitterness/and living with her no grief,/but rather joy and gladness" (Wis 8:16). Ask people who love God with a true love and they will tell you that in the troubles of their lives they have found no greater or more genuine relief than in loving conversation with God.

7. This loving conversation does not demand that you constantly strain your mind at the expense of your other activities or even your recreation. It only requires that, without neglecting your other obligations, you act on occasion toward God in the same way that you act toward those whom you love or who love you.

8. Your God is ever at your side, indeed, within you. "'In him we live and move and have our being'" (Acts 17:28). You don't need to work through a doorman if you want to approach God. God delights in your intimacy. Discuss all your business with God, your plans, your troubles, your fears—anything at all that concerns you. And do so with confidence, with your heart open wide. God can scarcely speak to the person who does not speak to God. Those who are not accustomed to speaking to God will scarcely recognize God's voice when he does speak. And so the Lord remarks with regret: "As far as love is concerned, our sister is but a child; how can I succeed in speaking to her if she isn't capable of understanding me?" ([ed.] Sg 8:8). When we despise God's gift, God might seem to us to be a mighty and fearsome Lord. When we love God we find a most affectionate friend. That is why God desires to converse with us often—like a friend, without the slightest embarrassment.

9. It is true of course that we owe God the greatest reverence but when God makes his presence felt to you and makes known to

you his desire that you speak to him as one who loves you above all else, then express your feelings with full freedom and trust. "He who watches for her at dawn shall not be disappointed,/for he shall find her sitting by his gate" (Wis 6:14). God doesn't even wait for you to take the first step. When you desire his love he leaps ahead and presents himself to you bringing with him the graces and gifts you most need. God waits for just a word from you to show you how near he is, how ready he is to hear and comfort you. "The LORD has eyes for the just/and ears for their cry" (Ps 34:16).

10. God by his immensity can be found everywhere but there are two places that are his home in a special way: One is in heaven in the glory which he shares with the blessed; the other is on earth, in the humble who love him. "I dwell...with the crushed and dejected in spirit" (Is 57:15). This then is our God: Dwelling in the highest heaven he does not consider it beneath him to spend night and day among his faithful ones in their caves and huts. He shares with them there his divine consolations which surpass the greatest pleasures the world can offer. Only the person who has not experienced this can fail to long for it. "Learn to savor how good the LORD is" (Ps 34:9).

11. Friends in the world have times when they speak together and times when they are apart: but between God and you there need not pass a second of separation, if that is your wish. "When you lie down, you need not be afraid,/when you rest, your sleep will be sweet..../For the LORD will be your confidence" (Prv 3:24, 26). You may sleep and the Lord will place himself at your side and ever watch over you....While you sleep he is as close as your pillow and he remains always thinking of you so that, if you happen to awaken in the night, he might speak to you with his inspirations and to hear from you some expression of love, of self-offering, of thanksgiving. Even in the hours of the night he does not want your loving and sweet conversation to be broken. Sometimes God may even speak to you as you sleep and cause you to hear his voice so that, on awaking, you may put your good inspirations into action. "In dreams will I speak" (Nm 12:6).

12. God awaits you in the morning to hear from you some word of affection or of trust; to receive from you your first

thoughts, the promises of the actions which you will perform that day for his pleasure; and to hear of the sufferings that you will endure for the sake of his love and glory. God does not fail to be present to you from the moment you awaken; do not fail then, on your part, to give God a glance of love and rejoice to hear the joyful news that your God is not distant from you as he once may have been because of your sins. God loves you and wants nothing more than to be loved by you. From the first moment of the day he imposes on you the loving commandment: "You shall love the LORD, your God, with all your heart" (Dt 6:5).

13. Never forget the sweet presence of God, as do the majority of people. Talk to God as often as you can for he never tires of listening to you as do the great ones of this earth. If you truly love God, you will never lack for things to say to him. Tell him everything that happens to you; tell him about all your concerns just as you would to the dearest friend. Don't treat him as if he were a self-impressed prince who only deigns to speak to the great and about great things. It delights our God to come down to our level and he is thrilled to hear from us about all our concerns, no matter how small they may appear to us. He loves us so much and takes as good care of you as if you were his only care in the world. God is so devoted to your interests; it is as if Providence existed only to aid you; omnipotence only to help you; the divine mercy and goodness only to sympathize with you, to do you good, to win your confidence by the delicacy of his affection. Open your inner world to God with perfect freedom and pray that he guide you to do his holy will perfectly. Let your every desire and plan be directed only to the discovery of God's good pleasure and to give joy to the divine heart. "Commit your way to the LORD" (Ps 37:5); "ask him to make all your paths straight and to grant success to all your endeavors and plans" (Tb 4:19).

14. Never say: What is the point of revealing all my wants to God since God sees them already and knows them better than I? God knows them all, but God acts as if he doesn't know whatever needs you experience about which you do not speak or seek his help. Our Savior knew well that Lazarus was dead but acted as if

he didn't until he heard it from Mary Magdalene and then consoled her by returning her brother to life.

15. Whenever you are afflicted by some illness, temptation, persecution, or other problem, go at once to God so that his hand may reach out to help you. It is enough for you to present your trouble to him saying: "Look, Lord, upon my distress" (Lam 1:20). God will not fail to comfort you or at least to give you the strength to suffer the difficulty with patience. In that case, everything will turn out better for you than if he had released you from the difficulty. Tell God all about the thoughts of fear or depression that torment you and say: My God, in you is all my hope. I offer this trouble to you and I resign myself to your will; but please have pity on me. Either free me from this suffering or give me the strength to bear it. God will not fail to keep the promise made in the gospel to all those who suffer—to comfort and to strengthen all who come in search of help: "Come to me, all you who labor and are burdened, and I will give you rest" (Mt 11:28).

16. God is not put out that you would go to your friends and find support in your times of trouble but he wishes you to come to him above all. So then, after you have looked for relief in creatures and are unable to find it, turn to your Creator and say: Lord, human consolation is nothing but words. "Wearisome comforters are you all!/Is there no end to windy words?" (Jb 16:2-3). These offer me no comfort and I no longer wish to seek comfort there. You are all my hope, all my love. I wish only to be comforted by you. May my comfort in this situation be that I may do what pleases you. I am ready to suffer this grief for my whole life, even for eternity, if that is your good pleasure; but you, for your part, must help me.

17. Don't be afraid that you will offend God if sometimes you gently complain and say: "Why, LORD, do you stand at a distance/and pay no heed to these troubled times? (Ps 10:1). Lord, you know that I love you and desire nothing except your love. Have pity on me and do not abandon me. And when your desolation seems too hard and lasts too long, unite your voice with that of Jesus suffering the pains of death on the Cross and beg for mercy, saying: "My God, my God, why have you forsaken me?" (Mt 27:46).

This will serve to increase your humility as you recognize that one who has offended God by sin does not deserve consolation; but even more it will revive your confidence as you realize that God does or permits everything for our good: "We know that all things work for good" (Rom 8:28). The more confused and discouraged you feel, the greater should be your courage as you say: "The LORD is my light and my salvation;/whom do I fear?" (Ps 27:1). Lord, it is you who must save me; you who must give me light. In you I trust: "In you, LORD, I take refuge;/let me never be put to shame" (Ps 31:2). In this way you will find peace, knowing that no one who ever hoped in God was lost....Reflect that your God loves you even more than you love yourself; what then is there to fear? David consoled himself by saying: "Though I am afflicted and poor,/the Lord keeps me in mind" (Ps 40:18). Therefore say to God: I throw myself into your arms. I wish to think of nothing but to love you and please you. Here I am, ready to do whatever you wish. You not only desire my well-being, you are preoccupied with it. I leave my salvation in your hands. I rest in you and there will I ever rest because I have placed all my hopes in you: "In peace I shall both lie down and sleep,/alone, LORD, make me secure" (Ps 4:9).

18. "Think of the Lord in goodness" (Wis 1:1). With these words the author of the Book of Wisdom tells us we should have more hope in the divine mercy than fear of the divine justice because God is immeasurably more inclined to do good to us than to punish; as the Letter of James says: "Mercy triumphs over judgment" (Jas 2:13). Thus the apostle Peter tells us that in all our concerns, whether temporal or eternal, we ought to abandon everything over to the goodness of our God who takes the greatest care for our well-being: "Cast all your worries upon him because he cares for you" (1 Pt 5:7). How beautiful is the title that David gives to God—"God is a God who saves" (Ps 68:21). This means, as St. Robert Bellarmine explains, that the distinctive activity of God is not to condemn but to save all. God threatens with displeasure those who ignore him but to those who fear him he promises his mercy. As Mary sings in the Magnificat: "His mercy is from age to age/to those who fear him" (Lk 1:50). I have

placed before you, devout soul, all these passages of scripture so that when the thought afflicts you: "Am I saved or not? Am I predestined or not?" you may take courage from the promises God has made of this great desire to save you. You need only resolve to love and to serve him as he asks.

19. When you receive some happy news, don't act like some negligent people who run to God in times of difficulty but forget and ignore him when things are going well. You should be faithful to God as you would be to a friend who loves you and rejoices in your good fortune. Go to God and share your happiness with him, give him praise and thanks, recognizing everything as a gift from his hands. Rejoice in your fortune and know that it comes to you through God's good pleasure. Rejoice and be glad in God alone: "Yet will I rejoice in the LORD/and exult in my saving God" (Hb 3:18). [In citing Habbakuk, Alphonsus makes an allusion to the name of Jesus that means "God Saves."] Say to him: My Jesus, I bless and will ever bless you for the many graces you have given me especially since I have deserved not kindness from you but the punishment of my sins. Say to him in the words of the Beloved of the Song of Songs: "Both fresh and mellowed fruits, my lover,/I have kept in store for you" (Sg 7:14). O God, I give you thanks, and I hold in memory all your acts of kindness to me, both past and present, so that I may praise and thank you for them forever.

20. If you truly love God you should rejoice in God's happiness more than in your own. Whoever loves a friend rejoices in that person's well-being as if it were one's own. Console yourself therefore with the thought that your God is infinitely happy. Often say to God: My beloved Lord, your happiness gives me more joy than any good fortune of mine; yes, because I love you more than I love myself.

21. Another sign of confidence which is most pleasing to your most loving God is this: Whenever you have committed any fault do not let shame prevent you from going at once to God's feet to ask forgiveness. Know that God so greatly longs to forgive sinners that he grieves bitterly over their loss, when they flee from him and live as if dead to his grace. With love God cries out

281

and says: "Why should you die, O house of Israel...return and live!" (Ez 18:31–32). He promises to welcome those who have abandoned him, as soon as they return to his embrace. "See, I come to you, it is to you that I turn" (Ez 36:9). Oh, if sinners only knew the tender mercy with which the Lord waits to pardon them! "Yet the LORD is waiting to show you favor,/and he rises to pity you" (Is 30:18). If they only understood God's desire not to punish them but to see them change their lives that God might embrace them and press them to his heart! God declares: "As I live...I take no pleasure in the death of the wicked man, but rather in the wicked man's conversion, that he may live" (Ez 33:11). God says further: "Come now, let us set things right..../Though your sins be like scarlet,/they may become white as snow" (Is 1:18). It is as if God says: Sinners, repent of having offended me and come to me. If I don't forgive you then you can accuse me, upbraid me, and treat me as a fraud. But I will never fail of my promise. Come to me and know: Though your consciences are dyed deep as crimson by your sins, by my grace I will make them as white as snow.

22. In fact God has said that when sinners repent, their sins are as good as forgotten: "None of the crimes he committed shall be remembered against him" (Ez 18:22). Whenever you fall into a fault, immediately raise your eyes to God, make an act of love, and, confessing your fault, you may rest assured of pardon. Say to God: "Master, the one you love is ill" (Jn 11:3). The heart which you love is sick, is covered in sores. "LORD, have mercy on me;/heal me, I have sinned against you" (Ps 41:5). You, O God, go out in search of sinners; here is one at your feet who has come in search of you. The evil has been done, what should I do now? You do not want me to lose confidence in you. Even now, after my sin, you wish me only good and I love you as well. Yes, my God, I love you with all my heart and I regret the displeasure I have given you. I resolve never to do so again. Forgive me, you who are a God, "kind and forgiving, most loving to all who call on you" (Ps 86:5). Let me hear those words you said to Mary Magdalene: "Your sins are forgiven" (Lk 7:48). Give me the strength to be ever faithful to you in the future.

23. In occasions of sin, so that you might not lose courage, cast a glance to Jesus on the Cross and offer his merits to the Eternal Father. Thus you may be secure in your hope of pardon since in order to forgive you God did not spare his only son (Rom 8:32). Say to God with confidence: "Look upon the face of your anointed" (Ps 84:10). My God, look at the Son, dead for my sake. For the love you bear your Son, pardon me.

Pay great attention, devout soul, to the advice commonly given by all the masters of the spiritual life: go immediately to God after each act of unfaithfulness, even if it be a hundred times a day. After your fall, have recourse at once to God and then put your soul at peace. Otherwise you will be depressed and preoccupied with your fall and you will be reluctant to converse with God. Your confidence in God will diminish, your longing to love God will grow cold, and you will scarcely be able to advance along the way of the Lord. On the other hand, if we go to God immediately to ask pardon and promise improvement, our falls themselves will serve to help us advance in divine love. Between friends who love one another from the heart it often happens that when one has offended the other and then humbles himself to ask forgiveness, the bonds of friendship became stronger than ever. Do the same yourselves: Let your very faults be a means to bind you ever more closely in love to God.

24. Don't ever allow any doubt to arise about this from within yourself or from another. Always act toward God like faithful friends who consult with each other on everything. Never cease to confer in great confidence with God and to ask God to enlighten you about what will give him the greatest pleasure....Lord, tell me what you will that I may do it. Speak, Lord, your servant is listening.

25. In perfect freedom, recommend to God not only your own needs but those of others as well. How it pleases God that you would forget your own need and speak to him of the advancement of his glory, of the sufferings of others, especially those who groan in their afflictions, of the souls in purgatory who are his spouses and long to see him, and of the poor sinners who live deprived of grace. Pray especially for these sinners and

say to him: Lord, you who are so lovable, indeed worthy of an infinite love; how can you stand to see so many in the world who have received so many gifts from you and yet wish neither to know nor to love you and who even offend and despise you? O my God, supremely worthy of love, make yourself known, make yourself loved! "Hallowed be your name, your kingdom come" (Mt 6:9, 10). May your name be loved and adored by all; may your love reign in every heart. I will not leave you until you grant some grace to those unhappy souls for whom I pray.

26. It is said that those souls in purgatory who, while on earth, had but little longing for heaven suffer a special pain called the pain of languor. Not to long for that eternal kingdom which our Savior won for us at the price of his blood is truly to esteem it little. Do not forget then, devout soul, to long for heaven often, saying to your God that it feels like a thousand years must pass before you can see him and love him, face to face. Long to leave this exile, this place of sin and of danger of losing his grace, and desire to arrive in your true homeland, that country of love where you might love God with all your strength. Say often to God: Lord, as long as I live on this earth, I run the risk of leaving you and losing your love. When will I leave this life, where I am ever offending you, and come to love you with my whole self and unite myself to you without fearing to lose you ever again? St. Teresa would always sigh in this way and would rejoice when she heard the clock strike, thinking that another hour of life had passed and with it the danger of losing God. She so greatly desired to die so that she could see God that she was dying of the desire to die. Thus she composed the canticle of love: "I die because I do not die."

27. In short, if you wish to please the loving heart of your God, take care to speak to God whenever you are able, continually and with the greatest confidence possible. God is not reluctant to answer you and to speak to you in return. God will not make himself heard by you in a voice that reaches your ears but rather in a voice that only your heart knows well. Leave off conversation with creatures and speak one-to-one with your God: "I will lead her into the desert/and speak to her heart" (Hos 2:16). God will then

speak to you with such inspirations, such inner light, with such demonstrations of his bounty, with such sweet touches of the heart, with tokens of forgiveness, with such experiences of peace, with such hope of paradise, with such inner joy, with such sweetness of grace, with such loving and close embraces, with such a voice of love that is well understood by those whom God loves and who seek nothing for themselves save God alone.

28. To summarize what has already been said above, I do not wish to finish without suggesting to you a devout practice by which you may perform all your daily activities in a manner pleasing to God. When you awaken in the morning your first thought should be for God, offering in his honor all that you will do or suffer in the course of the day and asking for the help of his grace. Then make your other morning prayers, acts of thanksgiving, love, and petition, and resolve to live the day before you as if it were to be your last. Father St. Jure recommends making an agreement with the Lord every morning. Each time you make a certain sign, such as placing your hand on your heart or raising your eyes toward heaven or toward the crucifix, you desire by that sign to make an act of love, to see God loved by all, of offering of yourself, or other similar desires. After you have made these acts, place yourself in the wounded side of Jesus and under the mantle of Mary and pray the Eternal Father that for the love of Jesus and Mary he would protect you during the day. Take care before anything else to spend at least half an hour in mental prayer or meditation. Let your preferred meditation be on the sorrow and contempt that Jesus embraced in the Passion. This is the subject dearest to loving souls and the one which most enkindles divine love in them. There are three devotions which you must take very much to heart if you wish to make progress in the spiritual life: devotion to the Passion of Jesus Christ, to the Blessed Sacrament, and to Mary most holy. In your meditation make frequent acts of sorrow, of love of God, and of self-offering. The Venerable Father Charles Caraffa, founder of the Pious Workers, said that one fervent act of the love of God made during the morning prayer should be enough to maintain a person in fervor for the entire day.

29. Besides more specific acts of devotion (confession, communion, the divine office, etc.), whenever you are engaged in external occupations such as study, work, or in any activity that may be involved in your state in life, never forget when beginning any action to offer it to God, praying for his help to accomplish it without fault. Try to enter into the chamber of your heart and to unite yourself there with God, as St. Catherine of Siena used to do. Whatever you do, do it with God and for God.

On leaving your room or your house and on returning always say a Hail Mary to recommend yourself to the Mother of God. When you sit down to a meal, offer to God the pleasure or the disappointment you might feel in what you will eat or drink. At the end of the meal, say to God: Lord, how good you are to one who has offended you so much! During the day do not fail to spend some time in spiritual reading and to make a visit to the Blessed Sacrament and to the Blessed Virgin Mary. In the evening recite the rosary and make an examination of conscience and pray the Christian acts of faith, hope, and love; of contrition and purpose of amendment and of your desire to receive the sacraments during your life and at the hour of your death with the intention of gaining all the indulgences you can. In going to bed, reflect that you deserve to fall into the fires of hell, and compose yourself to sleep, embracing the crucifix and saying: "As soon as I lie down I fall peacefully asleep for you alone, O Lord, bring security to my dwelling" (Ps 4:9).

30. [This passage regarding indulgences is omitted since current church regulations on indulgences make it irrelevant.]

31. In order to keep yourself as much as possible in a state of recollection and union with God in this life, try to turn your every sight and sound into an opportunity of raising your mind to God or of glancing into eternity. For example, when you see running water, reflect that your life too runs on its course and that death draws near. When you see a lamp going out because of lack of oil, reflect that your life will one day too come to an end. When you see a cadaver or cemetery, consider that you too will be like that some day. When you see the great ones of this world rejoicing in their wealth or rank, take pity on their folly and say: God is

enough for me. "Some are strong in chariots; some in horses; but we are strong in the name of the Lord, our God" (Ps 20:8). Let them glory in such emptiness. I wish to glory only in God's grace and God's love. When you see elaborate funerals or the magnificent tombs of the great lords of the earth, say: If they are damned, what good did all this display do them? When you look at the sea, whether calm or tempestuous, reflect on the difference between a soul that enjoys God's grace and one that does not. When you see a withered tree, reflect that a person without God is good for nothing but to be cast into the fire. If you happen to see someone who has been accused of a great crime and who stands trembling with shame and fear before a judge or his parents or a bishop, consider the panic of the sinner before Christ the judge. When it thunders and you are afraid, reflect on how it must be for those unhappy ones who are damned when they hear continually in hell the thunder of the divine wrath. If you ever see someone who has been condemned to capital punishment and who cries, "Is there now no hope that my life might be spared?" consider the despair of the soul condemned to hell who says, "Is there now no hope that I may be spared from eternal ruin?"

32. Whenever you see the countryside or the seashore, flowers or fruits, and you are delighted by the sight or the fragrance of them, say: How many beautiful creatures God has created for me in this world so that I might love him! What greater delights must he have in store for me in paradise! St. Teresa used to say that when she saw a beautiful hillside or slope, their beauty seemed to reproach her for her ingratitude toward God. The Abbot De Rancé, founder of the Trappists, used to say that the beauty of creatures reminded him of his obligation to love God. St. Augustine said the same, exclaiming: "Heaven and earth and all they contain tell me to love you." There is a story of a holy man who, while walking through the fields, would strike with his walking stick all the flowers and plants he saw, saying: "Be quiet. Don't reproach me any more for my ingratitude to God. I have understood you. Be quiet!" Saint Mary Magdalene de' Pazzi, whenever she held in her hand a beautiful fruit or flower, would feel herself moved with divine love and would say to herself: "My

God has thought from all eternity to make this fruit, this flower for me, to give me a token of the love he bears me."

33. Whenever you see rivers or brooks, reflect that just as the water flows on to the sea without ever stopping so also you ought to be drawn ever toward God, your only good. Whenever you are in a coach drawn by a beast of burden, say: Look how these innocent animals exhaust themselves in my service; what trouble do I go to in order to serve and give pleasure to my God? When you see a little dog that is so faithful to its master for a scrap of bread, think how much more reason you have to be faithful to God who created you, who preserves you and provides for you and who heaps you with blessings. When you hear the birds sing, say to yourself: Listen to the praise these little creatures give to their Creator; and what are you doing? And then praise God yourself with acts of love. On the other hand, when you hear a rooster crow, remember that there was once a time when you, like Peter, denied your God; renew your repentance and your tears. Whenever you see a house or a place where you have sinned, turn to God saying: "The sins of my youth and my frailties remember not" (Ps 25:7).

34. When you see valleys, recall that their fertility is due to the water that cascades from the mountains; likewise, grace flows from the heavens on the humble and by-passes the proud. When you see a beautifully decorated church, consider the beauty of a soul in the state of grace which is the true temple of God. When you look at the sea, consider the immensity and the grandeur of God. When you see a fire or lighted candles on an altar, say: For how many years have I deserved to burn in the flames of hell? But since you, O Lord, have not sent me there, make my heart now burn with love for you as these logs or these candles burn. When you look at the night sky, thick with stars, say with St. Andrew Avellino: "O my feet, one day you will tread upon those stars!"

35. In order to recall often the mysteries of our Savior's love, when you see hay, a manger, or caves, remember the child Jesus in the manger of Bethlehem. When you see a saw, a hammer, a plane, or an ax, recall Jesus working as an ordinary boy in

the carpenter shop of Nazareth. If you see rope, thorns, nails, or pieces of wood, recall the sufferings and death of our Redeemer. St. Francis of Assisi, on seeing a lamb, would begin to weep and say: "My Lord was led to death like a lamb for me." Whenever you see altars, chalices, or patens, recall the greatness of the love of Jesus Christ in giving us the Blessed Sacrament of the Eucharist.

36. During the day, offer yourself often to God as did St. Teresa, saying: "Here I am, Lord; do with me whatever pleases you. Tell me what you wish me to do for you; I want to do it all." As often as you can, repeat acts of the love of God. St. Teresa said that "acts of love are the fuel which feeds the fire of holy love in the heart." Venerable Sister Seraphina of Capri, thinking how the mule owned by the monastery was not capable of loving God, sympathized with it, saying: "Poor beast, you can neither know nor love your God." The mule began to weep until tears streamed from its eyes. And so when you see an animal that is incapable of knowing and loving God you should be moved to make even greater acts of love, you who can love God. When you fall into some difficulty, immediately humble yourself, and by an even more fervent act of love seek to rise again. When any adversity befalls you, immediately offer your sufferings to God and seek to conform yourself to his holy will. Accustom yourself in every adversity to repeat the words: This is what God wills; I want it too. Acts of resignation to God's will are the acts of love dearest and most pleasing to the divine heart.

37. Whenever you have to decide on anything or give advice on a matter of importance, first recommend yourself to God and then act or give your opinion. Following the example of St. Rose of Lima, repeat as many times as you can in the course of the day the prayer: O God, come to my assistance; do not leave me in my own hands. Turn your attention often to the image of the Crucified or to that of Mary most holy which you have in your room. Never fail to invoke the names of Jesus and Mary frequently, especially in times of temptation. God, who is infinite goodness, desires nothing more than to share with us the fullness of his graces. The Venerable Father Alphonsus Alvarez one day saw our Savior with his hands full of graces and going about in

search of those with whom to share them. It is his will that we should ask them of him. "Ask and you will receive" (Jn 16:24); otherwise he will draw back his hand. But God opens his hand willingly to those who call upon him. For whoever has called upon God and found his prayer despised? David writes that the Lord acts, not merely with mercy, but with great mercy toward those who call upon him: "LORD, you are kind and forgiving, most loving to all who call on you" (Ps 86:5).

38. Oh, what goodness and liberality the Lord shows to those who seek him with love! "Good is the LORD to one who waits for him,/to the soul that seeks him" (Lam 3:25). If God allows himself to be found even by those who do not look for him—"I was found [by] those who were not seeking me" (Rom 10:20)—how much more willingly will he be found by those who do seek him; indeed who seek him in order to love and to serve him.

In conclusion: St. Teresa says that the just in this world conform themselves by love to what the blessed do in heaven. Since the saints in heaven occupy themselves only with God, and have no other thought or pleasure than in God's glory and love, so also must be the case with you. While you are in this world may God be your only happiness, the only object of your affections, the only end of all your actions and desires, until you arrive at that eternal kingdom where your love will be entirely perfected and completed, and your desires will be perfectly fulfilled and satisfied.

Prayer, the Great Means of Salvation [Selections]

The Great Means of Prayer in order to gain eternal life and all the graces we desire from God. A theological-ascetical work useful for every type of person. Divided into two parts. The First Part treats of the necessity, value, and conditions of Prayer. The Second Part demonstrates that the grace of prayer is given to everyone and treats of the ordinary way in which grace operates.

To Jesus Christ, the Word Incarnate
Beloved of the Eternal Father
Blessed by the Lord
Author of Life
King of Glory
Savior of the World
Long Awaited by the Nations
Desire of the Everlasting Hills
Heavenly Bread
Universal Judge
Mediator between God and Humanity
Master of Virtue
Fount of Graces
Good Shepherd
Lover of Souls

to you Alphonsus, the sinner, consecrates this work.

Part 1: Introduction Which Is Necessary to Be Read

I have published several spiritual works but I judge that none of them is as useful as this little work, in which I speak of prayer, the necessary and surest means of obtaining salvation and all the graces necessary to attain that goal. While I do not have the means to do so, if I were able I would have as many copies of this book printed as there are faithful in the world. I would give each one a copy so that everyone might know how necessary prayer is in order to be saved.

I say this because, on the one hand I see the absolute necessity of prayer taught by the sacred scriptures and all the Fathers of the Church; on the other hand, I see that so few Christians practice this great means of salvation. And what afflicts me all the more, I see that preachers and confessors speak but little of prayer to their listeners and penitents. I see that spiritual books, even the most popular, scarcely speak enough about prayer. There is nothing that preachers, confessors, and books should insist on with greater warmth and urgency than prayer. It is true that they teach many excellent means of remaining in God's grace, for example, the avoidance of occasions of sin, frequenting the sacraments, resisting temptations, hearing the Word of God, meditation on the eternal truths, and other means. I do not deny that these are useful. But, I say, what good are sermons, meditations, and all the other means given us by the masters of the spiritual life without prayer? Our Lord has declared that he does not give his grace to those who do not pray. "Ask and you will receive." Without prayer (I am speaking of the way in which Providence ordinarily operates) all our meditations, all our resolutions, all our promises, are useless. If we do not pray we will always be unfaithful to the lights we have received from God and to the promises we have made. This is so because in order to do the good, to overcome temptations, to practice virtue, in short to observe the divine commandment and counsels, it is not enough to be enlightened by God, or to reflect and make resolutions ourselves, but we need above all the actual assistance of God. The Lord gives this actual assistance (as we shall see) only to those who pray and who pray with perseverance. The light we have received, our reflections, and the good resolutions we have made—these benefit us, in times when we stand in danger of violating God's law, only if we pray. With prayer we obtain God's help which preserves us from sin. In such moments if we do not pray we will be lost.

I have wished, dear reader, to preface this work with these sentiments of mine so that you will give thanks to the Lord who, by means of this little book, gives you the grace to reflect more deeply on this great means of prayer. All those who are saved (I speak here of adults) are saved ordinarily by this means alone. And that is why I invite you to give thanks to God since he acts with exceptional mercy toward those to whom he gives the light and the grace to pray. I hope that you, my dear brother, after reading this little work, from this day forward you will never fail to have recourse to God in prayer, especially when you are tempted to offend him. If perhaps in the past your conscience has been afflicted by many sins you must understand that this is because you neglected to pray and to ask God for the help to resist the temptations that afflicted you. I beg you then to read and to reread this book with the greatest attention, not because it is mine but because it is a means the Lord has chosen to obtain your eternal salvation. It is a sign that the Lord wishes your salvation in a special way. After having read the book, as far as you are able, I beg you to encourage your neighbors and friends to read it too. Now let us begin in the name of the Lord.

The apostle Paul writes to Timothy: "First of all, then, I ask that supplications, prayers, petitions, and thanksgivings be offered for everyone" (1 Tm 2:1). St. Thomas Aquinas explains that prayer properly speaking is the raising of the mind to God. (*Summa Theologiae* 2a2ae, q.83, art.17). The act of asking which properly constitutes prayer when the request is directed toward a specific thing is called "petition"; when the object is unspecified is called "supplication" as, for example, when we say: "O God, come to my assistance." "Obsecration" is a pious demand when we indicated the ground by which we ask for a favor as, for example, when we say: "By your Cross and Passion, deliver us, Lord." Finally, "thanksgiving" is the offering of gratitude for benefits received, by which, St. Thomas teaches, we merit to receive great favors. Prayer in the strict sense, says St. Thomas, is having recourse to God but in a more general sense includes all the forms mentioned above. This more general sense is what we mean by prayer in this work.

In order to become more fond of prayer, this great means of our salvation, we need to consider first how necessary it is for us and how effective it is in obtaining all the graces we need from God, if only we knew how to pray as we ought. Thus in the First Part we will speak of the necessity and value of prayer and next of the conditions necessary to make it efficacious with God. In the Second Part we will show that the grace of prayer is given to everyone; there we will treat of the way in which grace ordinarily works.

Chapter I: The Necessity of Prayer

Prayer is not necessary for salvation; this is an error from the time of the Pelagian controversy. Pelagius, the impious author of that heresy, held that the human person would lose salvation only for lack of knowledge of the necessary truths. With great perception, St. Augustine said: "Pelagius discussed everything, except how to pray." Pelagius treated everything except prayer, which is the only means to acquire the science of the saints, as St. Augustine held and taught. As the letter of James states: "But if any of you lacks wisdom, he should ask God who gives to all generously and ungrudgingly, and he will be given it" (Jas 1:5).

All too clear are the scriptures in maintaining how necessary it is for us to pray if we would be saved. [It is necessary to] "pray always without becoming weary" (Lk 18:1); "Ask and it will be given to you" (Mt 7:7).

The majority of theologians hold that these words "necessary," "pray," "ask," impose a precept. Wycliff held that these words referred not to prayer but to the necessity of good works (since for him prayer is nothing but a kind of good work); this error has been expressly condemned by the church. Thus the learned Doctor Leonardo Lessius wrote that one cannot deny that prayer (for adults) is necessary for salvation without compromising a truth of the faith. The scriptures hold that prayer is the only means to obtain the help necessary for salvation....

The reason for this is clear. Without the aid of grace we can do nothing good; "without me you can do nothing" (Jn 15:5). Regarding this passage Augustine remarks that Jesus did not say that "without me you can bring nothing to completion," but "without me you can do nothing." Thus, without grace, we cannot even begin a good work. St. Paul goes further in saying that of ourselves we cannot even desire to do good. "Not that of ourselves we are qualified to take credit for anything as coming from us; rather, our qualification comes from God" (2 Cor 3:5). If we cannot even think of a good thing, much less can we desire it. Many other biblical texts teach the same: "There are different workings but the same God who produces all of them in everything" (1 Cor 12:6); "I will put my spirit within you and make you live by my statutes, careful to observe my decrees" (Ez 36:27). As Pope St. Leo the Great wrote: "No one does any good thing unless enabled by God to do so." Thus the Council of Trent condemned the proposition that anyone, without the previous inspiration and assistance of the Holy Spirit, can believe, hope, love, or repent so as to obtain the grace of justification.

The author of the *Opus Imperfectum* says regarding animals, that God has given swiftness to some, to others wings, all in order to preserve their lives. God has so designed the human person that God alone would be the defense of human life. And so the human person was made helpless to procure salvation so that it would be received only by the help of divine grace.

In the ordinary Providence of God, this grace is not given except to those who pray, according to the famous expression of Gennadius: "We believe that no one comes to salvation except at God's call; no one is called to salvation, except by God's aid; no one is promised God's aid, except through prayer." We can do nothing without the help of grace and God ordinarily gives this grace only to those who ask. Who could fail to arrive at the conclusion that prayer is absolutely necessary for salvation? It is true that the first graces come to us without any cooperation on our part, such as the call to faith or to penance; St. Augustine teaches that God grants these graces even to those who do not pray. Nevertheless, this saint holds for certain that other graces, especially the grace of perseverance, are not given except in response to prayer....Thus it is the common teaching of theologians, following St. Basil, St. John Chrysostom, Clement of Alexandria, and others including Augustine, that prayer is necessary (for adults) not only with the obligation of precept but also because it is a necessary means of salvation. In the ordinary Providence of God, it is impossible that a Christian be saved unless that person ask God for the graces necessary for salvation. St. Thomas teaches the same....According to the Angelic Doctor, in order to be saved we must fight and conquer. "An athlete cannot receive the winner's crown except by competing" (2 Tm 2:5). Without the aid of divine grace we cannot resist the assaults of so many and such powerful enemies. This divine help is obtained only by prayer; thus without prayer no one can be saved.

Prayer is the only ordinary means for receiving God's gifts. St. Thomas proves this in another place when he says that all the graces that God has willed from all eternity to give to us will be given by no other means except prayer.

Prayer is not necessary so that God will know our needs but that so we will know our need of God. We must have recourse to God to receive the necessary aids toward our salvation and thus recognize the Author of our every good....God has willed that whoever wants bread must sow the grain; whoever wants wine must tend the vines. In the same way, whoever wants the graces necessary for salvation must pray for them. "Ask and it will be given to you" (Mt 7:7).

We are but poor beggars. We have nothing but what God gives us as alms. "I am afflicted and poor" (Ps 40:18). St. Augustine says that the Lord deeply desires to bestow graces upon us but does so only to those who ask..."and it will be given to you." Thus St. Teresa concluded that whoever fails to ask will not receive. Chrysostom says that prayer is as necessary for our salvation as moisture is necessary to prevent a plant from drying up and dying. Elsewhere he says that just as the soul is the life of the body so prayer is the life of the soul and the soul without prayer emits a foul odor. He speaks of a foul odor because whoever fails to have recourse to God soon begins to rot through sin. Prayer must also be called the food of the soul. As the body cannot survive without nourishment neither can the soul survive without the nourishment of prayer, as Augustine says. All these images are used by the holy Fathers to teach us the absolute necessity of prayer for anyone who wishes to be saved....

Chapter II: The Value of Prayer

St. Bernardino of Siena says that prayer is a faithful ambassador, well known to the King of heaven, accustomed to entering his private chambers and to plead with importunity that the tender heart of the King will grant every help to us in our unhappiness as we lament our state, full of conflicts and struggles, in this vale of tears....The prophet Isaiah also assures us that when the Lord hears our prayers, he is moved at once with compassion toward us, and does not leave us long in our crying but answers us immediately and gives us what we need. "No more will you weep;/He will be gracious to you when you cry out,/as soon as he hears he will answer you" (Is 30:19). In another place the Lord, speaking in the words of the prophet Jeremiah, complains about us, saying: "Have I been a desert to Israel,/a land of darkness?/Why do my people say, 'We have moved on,/we will come to you no more?'" (Jer 2:31). Why do you say you will come to me no more? Has my mercy become a barren land to you, unable to produce the fruits of grace; or perhaps it is an inferior plot of land that produces harvest too long delayed? God wishes to assure us that he never fails to hear us, indeed to hear us instantly, when we pray. God reproaches those who fail to pray because they are unsure they will receive a hearing.

It would be an immense favor if God were to admit us to his presence to present our petitions once a month. The kings of this earth give an audience but a few times a year. God gives a continual audience. Chrysostom writes that God is always ready to hear our prayers and that no one ever prayed and was not received....Elsewhere he says that when we pray, even before we have finished pouring out our needs, God has already responded. God himself has promised this: "Before they call, I will answer" (Is 65:24). The Lord, says the psalmist, is near to all who pray, to console them, to hear them, to save them: "You, LORD, are near to all who call upon you,/to all who call upon you in truth" (Ps 145:18). "In truth" means those who call upon God as they ought. "You satisfy the desire of those who fear you;/you hear their cry and save them" (Ps 145:19). Moses gloried in this truth and so said: "For what great nation is there that has gods so close to it as the LORD, our God, is to us whenever we call upon him?" (Dt 4:7). The gods of the Gentiles were deaf to those who called to them since they were mere human inventions and capable of nothing. But our God, who can do all things, is far from deaf to our cries, but is ever near to the one who prays and is anxious to grant whatever is asked. Lord, the psalmists say, this is how I have come to know that you, my God, are all goodness, all mercy—whenever I had recourse to you, immediately you came to my aid.

We are poor, lacking in everything. But if we pray we are poor no longer. If we are poor, God is rich. God is all liberality to anyone who calls for help: the "Lord...enriching all who call" (Rom 10:12). We are dealing with a Lord of infinite power and infinite wealth. Let us not waste our time asking for some insignificant trifle but ask for something great. As St. Augustine says: "You are asking the Almighty; ask mightily!" If a person were to go to the king and ask him for small change, for a penny, the king would feel insulted. We honor the mercy and liberality of God when, miserable as we are and unworthy of any kindness, we nonetheless ask for great graces. We trust in the goodness of God and that God will be faithful to the promise to grant to those who pray whatever graces they may ask. St. Mary Magdalene de' Pazzi used to say that God feels so honored and so consoled when we seek graces that God is in a sense grateful to us. When we open ourselves to receive God's gifts we do God a favor since we allow God to act in accord with the divine nature which is none other than to do good to us. Let us be persuaded that when we ask of God we receive far more than we request. "But if any of you lacks wisdom, he should ask God who gives to all generously and ungrudgingly, and he will be given it" (Jas 1:5). James points out that God is not like us, stingy with our goods. The richest among us, even the kind and generous, when they give alms usually give less than they are asked. Their wealth, great though it is, is also finite. The more they give the less they have for themselves. But when God is asked, he gives of his good "generously," with an open hand, always giving more than is asked, because God's wealth is infinite. The more God gives, still more remains to be given. "LORD, you are kind and forgiving, most loving to all who call on you" (Ps 86:5). The psalmist says, Lord, you are too courteous to those who call upon you; your mercies are abundant, far more than what is asked.

Thus all our attention should be placed in praying with confidence. Prayer will open to us all the treasures of heaven.... Prayer is a treasure; whoever prays more, receives the most. St. Bonaventure said that every time we pray we receive something that is of greater value than the entire world....Some devout souls spend a great deal of time in reading and meditation but give little attention to prayer. Doubtless spiritual reading and meditation on the eternal truths are very useful things. St. Augustine points out that prayer is even more useful. In reading and in meditation we become aware of our obligations but in prayer we obtain the grace to fulfill them....What good does it do us to know our obligations and then not fulfill them? It just makes us the more guilty in the eyes of God. We can read and meditate all we want but we will never fulfill our duties unless we pray for that grace from God.

St. Isidore remarks that the devil goes to the greatest length to distract us with thoughts of worldly care precisely when he sees that we are praying and seeking grace of God....Why? Because the enemy sees that at no other time do we gain so many treasures of heavenly goods as when we pray. The main fruit of mental prayer is to ask God for the graces we need for perseverance and for eternal salvation. This is the main reason why mental prayer is morally necessary for the person who wants to persevere in the grace of God: The person who does not remember to ask for graces during the time of mental prayer is unlikely to do so at another time either. Without meditation we do not ask for grace; we may even forget that we need to ask. On the other hand, if we meditate every day we will easily see the needs of our soul, the dangers to which we are exposed, and the necessity we have of prayer. And thus we will pray and we will obtain the graces we need for the salvation of our souls. Speaking from experience, Father Segneri said that when he began to meditate he was more concerned with exciting affections than with praying. But then he became aware of the necessity and the immense usefulness of prayer, even after he devoted himself, in his long periods of mental prayer, to making petitions.

Devout King Hezekiah prayed: "Like a swallow I utter shrill cries" (Is 38:14). Baby swallows do nothing but cry, seeking help and nourishment from their mothers. If we wish to preserve the life of grace we should do the same. We should cry out continuously to God for the help to avoid the death of sin and to grow in holy love. Father Rodriguez relates that the Desert Fathers, who were the first masters of the spiritual life, held a meeting to discuss which exercise was the most useful and necessary for eternal salvation. They decided that it was to repeat over and over the short prayer of David: "O God, come to my assistance." This, writes Cassian, is what anyone who wishes to be saved must do—say constantly: "My God, help me! My God, help me!" We ought to do this as the first thing on arising in the morning; we should continue to do it in all our needs and in all our activities, whether spiritual or material. We ought to do this especially when we find ourselves bothered by some temptation or passion. St. Bonaventure says that often we can obtain a grace more surely by a short prayer than we can by any other good. St. Ambrose adds that even while we pray we have already gained what was sought. The very act of prayer is the same as receiving. Chrysostom writes that there is nothing more powerful than a person who prays because such a person partakes in the very power of God. To arrive at perfection, says St. Bernard, we need meditation and prayer. By meditation we see what we lack; by prayer we receive what we need.

In conclusion, to save oneself without prayer is most difficult, even impossible (in the ordinary workings of Providence as we have already seen). With prayer, salvation is secure and even easy. To obtain salvation it is not necessary to give up our life working among the unbelievers; it is not necessary to move to the desert and survive on herbs. What does it cost us to say: My God, help me. Lord, help me. Have mercy on me! Could anything be easier? This little thing is sufficient to save us if we are faithful to it. St. Lawrence Justinian reminds us especially to pray whenever we begin an action....Cassian attests that the central advice of the Desert Fathers was to have recourse to God by short but frequent prayers. St. Bernard says that no one should make light of the value of prayer because God esteems it highly and gives to us either what we ask or something even better for us....Let's be clear that if we don't pray we have no one to blame but ourselves because the grace of prayer is given to everyone. The power to pray is always right in our hands. As the psalmist says: "At dawn may the LORD bestow faithful love/that I may sing praise through the night,/praise to the God of my life." (Ps 42:9). In my Second Part [not included here], I will treat of this point at length to make it quite clear that God gives to all the grace of prayer. Thus we can obtain all the help we need, and even more than we need, to observe the divine law and to persevere until death. For the moment, I will only say that if we are not saved it is nobody's fault but ours. It is for no other reason than that we failed to pray.

The Practice of Mental Prayer

Introduction

Editor's Note: This outline dealing with mental prayer appeared as an appendix to Alphonsus's *Praxis Confessarii* published in Italian in 1755 and in a Latin translation in 1757. Its purpose was to encourage and assist confessors and preachers to instruct the faithful in the practice of daily reflective prayer. This was the logical outcome of the importance Alphonsus attached to prayer and of his constant efforts during his missionary career to instruct the faithful in a simple method of prayer. Despite considerable opposition from local clergy, Alphonsus insisted on introducing the practice of mental prayer in common for the ordinary faithful in the course of his missions. He composed an outline of his thinking on the importance of mental prayer as early as 1742, which he apparently had printed and distributed during his missionary campaigns. Various reworkings of this original manuscript were published either separately or in collections of devotional works in the following years. He also published a short instruction to assist children in making mental prayer in church before morning Mass.

By 1755 Alphonsus's original draft had assumed its final shape, which he then incorporated as instructions for confessors and preachers in his abbreviations of his *Moral Theology* and which is given here. A few years later, in 1760, a considerably extended version appeared in Volume 2 of *La Vera Sposa di Gesu Cristo.*

*   *   *

Before we speak of the method and practice of mental prayer it will be of help to say something about its importance. It is important for two reason. The first reason, to which St. Augustine refers, is that it is impossible for those who walk with eyes closed to see clearly the way which leads to salvation and the means of acquiring it. The eternal truths are of supernatural origin and cannot be perceived by human eyes; only by the eyes of the mind, that is, by reflection and consideration, can we come to appreciate them. So those who do not devote some time to mental prayer do not reflect and consequently they do not realize what is conducive to their eternal salvation and they do not see the way that leads to it. This is precisely what St. Bernard wrote to Pope Eugene: "I fear for you, Eugene, lest in the midst of so many affairs you may come to neglect prayer and reflection. Your heart, as a result, will grow hard and you will not be disturbed on that account as you should be, because you will not be aware of it" (Book I, *De Consideratione*).[1]

In order to attend to one's eternal salvation it is necessary to possess a docile and sensitive heart, one ready to recognize divine inspirations and to follow them. This is what Solomon asked of the Lord: "Give your servant, therefore, an understanding heart to judge your people and to distinguish right from wrong" (1 Kgs 3:9). St. John declares that souls who belong to God listen to his divine inspirations and put them into practice: "'They shall all be taught by God.' Everyone who listens to my Father and learns from him comes to me" (Jn 6:45). Our hearts, by their very nature, are stubborn and inclined to follow the desires of the flesh and are opposed to the law of the spirit. However, they are softened by the inflow of God's grace which comes to them through prayer. In prayer, souls are moved to reflect on the divine goodness and the love which God bears toward them. As a result they are inflamed with love, their hearts are opened, and they become responsive to God's call. Just as happened to David who exclaimed: "In my thoughts a fire blazed up,/and I broke into speech: LORD, let me know my end, the number of my days,/that I may learn how frail I am" (Ps 39:4–5). Without prayer, the heart will remain stubborn, resistant to grace, and disobedient, and will reap its due reward on the last day: "A stubborn man will fare badly in the end,/and he who loves danger will perish in it" (Sir 3:25). If it persists in its stubbornness the heart will suffer the misfortune of not knowing itself for what it is: The heart that does not reflect, says St. Bernard, is not afraid of itself because it does not know itself. It is not aware of its defects or of the obstacles which it will encounter on the way of salvation. And realize that the Pope whom St. Bernard warned about omitting prayer (if it is true that he sometimes did so) did not neglect his prayer on account of some worldly affairs but on account of matters which were of importance for the glory of God and of the church. Priests should realize that they have all the greater need of the assistance of divine grace when they are overwhelmed with demands on their time for important matters. Consequently, they need to devote themselves all the more to prayer in order to obtain the strength that they need to carry out their duties. And this holds good not only for those who might be inclined to neglect prayer in order to attend to secular affairs but also for those who omit prayer in order to assist others spiritually, as for example, by hearing their confessions, preaching, or writing.

The example of St. Teresa of Avila is to the point in the letter that she wrote to the bishop of Osma, who was a model of zeal for his flock but who was not assiduous in prayer; at times he neglected it. The saint, when she became aware of this defect in the bishop by a special light from above or perhaps by way of a special revelation, let nothing deter her from writing to him to get him to amend his ways. And this despite the fact that he was her confessor. She even wrote to him in Latin: "When I gave thanks to God for all the graces with which he has adorned you, humility, charity, zeal, I asked him at the same time to give you an increase of every virtue. He allowed me to see that you were lacking in nothing except the one grace which is the most necessary of all and without which the whole edifice will crumble and collapse. You are lacking in prayer and in perseverance in prayer with the result that the main support of your union with God and the presence of the Holy Spirit is weakened. From this result aridity and a sense of futility." And she then concluded: "Although we are unable to detect imperfections in ourselves, nevertheless when God opens our eyes, as he is wont to do in prayer, we come to realize the existence of our many imperfections."[2] This is what the Holy Spirit declared, namely, that the world is full of sinners and hell is filled with them: "Desolate, all the land,/because no one takes it to heart" (Jer 12:11).

Another basic principle and one that is more relevant to the question of the necessity of mental prayer is that souls who do not meditate invariably neglect prayer with consequent danger to their eternal salvation. Even though at times many virtues can be found in those who do not give themselves to prayer, they are mainly of a passing nature and are lacking in constancy. Perseverance in virtue is only obtained by asking God for it and asking him with perseverance. Those who do not ask with perseverance will not persevere. For this reason St. Paul urged his disciples to pray without ceasing: "Pray without ceasing" (1 Thes 5:17). And our Lord himself said that we should never cease to pray: "Then he told them a parable about the necessity for them to pray always without becoming weary" (Lk 18:1). So meditation is morally necessary for souls if they wish to remain in the grace of God. I say *morally necessary* because, even though, absolutely speaking, one could remain in God's grace without meditating, at the same time it is morally impossible, in other words, extremely difficult, to avoid falling into serious sin if one does not meditate.

The reason for this is, quite simply, as I have already suggested, that souls who do not devote time to prayer and are distracted by other cares do not realize their spiritual needs, make light of the spiritual dangers they face, neglect the steps they should take to avoid the dangers, and, finally, fail to realize how necessary it is for them to pray. They then abandon prayer completely and so expose themselves to moral danger.

The famous Bishop Palafox in his annotations to the letter of St. Teresa which I have already quoted—he calls her the most spiritual of all the saints—writes as follows:

> We prelates should learn that it is not sufficient for us to be zealous or charitable without the accompanying grace of prayer. Virtues which are not supported by prayer will fail and we shall be in moral danger. The reason is obvious. How long can charity remain in us if God does not give us the grace of perseverance? And how will God give us this grace if we neglect to ask him for it? And how can we ask him for it if we do not pray? How can this miracle take place (namely to obtain perseverance without prayer) if we remove the aqueduct which brings all the heavenly graces into our souls, in a word, prayer? If we cease to pray we cease

to be in communication with God to secure our perseverance in virtue. There is no other way, no other means of
obtaining graces from God.

On the other hand, the Lord himself assures us that those
who meditate on the great eternal truths—death, judgment, the
two eternities that face us, one of happiness, the other of unhappiness—will be able to keep themselves free from sin: "In whatever you do, remember your last days, and you will never sin" (Sir
7:36). David declared that his reflection on eternity encouraged
him in the exercise of virtue and helped him to purify himself of
his defects: "I consider the days of old;/the years long past I
remember./In the night I meditate in my heart;/I ponder and
my spirit broods" (Ps 77:6, 7). A certain author writes that if one
were to ask the souls of those who are lost the reason for their
being in hell, the greater part of them would reply that they
found themselves there because they did not reflect on its existence. Whoever reflects on the eternal truths during the spiritual exercises, considers them fully and with faith, will certainly
be converted to the Lord. St. Vincent de Paul said that it would
be unheard of if a sinner who attended a mission and followed
the spiritual exercises with attention were not converted to the
Lord. And the preacher who preaches the spiritual exercises is a
mere creature while in mental prayer it is God himself who
speaks to our souls: "I will lead her into the desert/and speak to
her heart" (Hos 2:16). God speaks more wisely to us than any
preacher. All the saints become saints through meditation. Experience teaches us that those who are faithful in prayer will not
easily fall into serious sin. And if, perhaps, they do so occasionally, they will immediately pull themselves together and return to
God, as a result of their persistence in prayer.

Mental prayer in sin cannot exist together. A servant of God
has declared that many people recite the rosary, the office of the
Mother of God; they fast and still remain in sin. But it is not possible for those who are assiduous in prayer to remain in enmity
with God. They will either abandon prayer or give up sin, one or
the other. And if they persevere in prayer, not merely will they

turn away from sin but they will be freed from inordinate love of creatures and will give their love to God: "In my thoughts a fire blazed up" (Ps 39:4).

Prayer is a furnace in which souls are enkindled with the love of God. It is impossible for us to reflect sincerely on the divine goodness, on the reasons why God should be loved, on the love with which he loved and still loves us, and not be inflamed with love for him. David, the royal prophet, as he thought of God and meditated on his great love for creatures, declared that he felt himself on fire, as it were, with a desire to love God; his spirit fainted as he received the overwhelming consolations with which the Lord inundated him at that moment: "When I think of God, I groan;/as I ponder, my spirit grows faint" (Ps 77:4).

Let us move on to the practice of mental prayer. The church is the most appropriate place in which to give oneself to prayer. If one is unable to get to a church or to remain for some time in it, one can pray by raising one's mind to God no matter where one is: at home, in the country, walking, working. Whoever seeks God can find him everywhere and at all times.

As regards time, the morning is the most suitable. Our daily affairs go better when preceded by prayer. We should pray twice in the day, in the morning and the evening, but if we cannot find a suitable time in the evening we should at least pray in the morning. Father Charles Caraffa, the founder of the Congregation of Pious Workers, declared that one fervent act of love in prayer in the morning is sufficient to preserve our souls in fervor right throughout the day. Regarding the amount of time to be given to prayer, that is a matter to be decided by the prudent judgment of one's pastor or confessor. But it is quite certain that a half an hour a day is not sufficient if one aspires to a high degree of perfection. Half an hour is adequate for those who are beginning and it is important for them to be encouraged not to omit their prayer when they experience aridity.

We now come to how we should instruct others to pray. There are three parts in prayer: preparation, meditation or reflection, and conclusion. Preparation consists of three acts of faith, namely, acts of the presence of God, humility, and petition for light. Here are examples: (1) "My God, I believe you are present with me here and I adore you from the depths of my nothingness." (2) "My Lord, I have deserved eternal punishment for my sins, but I repent of my sinfulness. Out of your great mercy spare me, O Lord." (3) "Eternal Father, for the love of Jesus and Mary enlighten my mind in this prayer that I may profit by it." After this say a Hail Mary to Our Lady that she may obtain this grace for you and a Glory be to the Father in honor of St. Joseph, your angel guardians, and your patrons. These acts should be made with deep attention but quite briefly. Then one should pass directly to reflection or meditation.

As regards meditation, it is useful for those who are able to do so to use some suitable book, dwelling on those sections which the soul finds most moving. Francis de Sales said that in this we should imitate the bees, since they remain on one flower as long as they are able to extract some honey; when this is exhausted they move on to another bloom. Those who find reading difficult should turn their thoughts to the Last Things, the goodness of God, and, above all, to the life and Passion of Jesus Christ. Reflection on the Passion, according to St. Francis de Sales, should be the usual subject of their meditations. What a beautiful book the Passion of Our Lord is for devout souls! In it we perceive better than in any other writing the awful wickedness of sin and the great love God has for us. Brother Bernard of Corlione, who was unable to read, enquired of an image of the Most Holy Redeemer on one occasion if it would be pleasing to him if he should learn to read. The image replied: "Why do you wish to read? What need have you of books? I am your book and that should be sufficient for you."

It is important to understand that the perfection of mental prayer does not consist in reflection but in acts of affection, petition, and resolution. These are the three great fruits of meditation, as I have already pointed out. Accordingly, when we have meditated on some eternal truth, and when God has enlightened our souls, we should then speak to God by making acts of faith, thanksgiving, adoration, humility, and, above all, acts of love and sorrow for sin, which is itself an act of love. Love is that golden link which binds the soul to God—charity is the bond of perfection. Every act of love is a grace which confirms us in the friendship of God: "For to men she is an unfailing treasure;/those who gain this treasure gain the friendship of God" (Wis 7:14). "Those who love me I also love" (Prv 8:17). "And whoever loves me will be loved by my Father, and I will love him and reveal myself to him" (Jn 14:21). "Love covers a multitude of sins." (1 Pt 4:8). (See also what I have written in my *Moral Theology,* Bk 6, n. 442.)[3]

The saintly Sister Maria Crucifixa had a vision of a very great fire in which bundles of straw were immediately consumed. She was given to understand by this that our souls are cleansed of their faults and sins by every genuine act of love.[4] St. Thomas teaches that every act of love acquires for us a further degree of glory for all eternity; every act of love of God merits eternal life. Here are some examples of acts of love: "My God I love you above all else. I love you with my whole heart." Or we can submit ourselves wholly to God's will by saying: "My God, let me know what you wish of me since I am ready for whatever you ask." Or again, we can offer ourselves without reservation to God, saying: "Here I am, O Lord. Do with me and whatever I have, as you please." These acts of offering oneself to God are the acts of love which are most pleasing to the heart of God. St. Teresa offered herself to God more than fifty times a day. The most perfect act of love, however, is to rejoice and take one's delight in the thought of the infinite happiness of God himself.

When souls become aware that they have achieved union with God by the grace of supernatural or infused recollection, they should make no further effort to elicit any other acts than those to which the Lord gently draws them. They should turn their loving attention to the union which God is granting them since otherwise they might place obstacles to God's action. An important point has been made by St. Francis de Sales when he states that if the Holy Spirit inspires us with certain affections even before we begin to meditate or reflect, then we should freely omit the initial period of reflection and give ourselves over immediately to making affections. The purpose of the initial period of reflection or consideration is to move us to make acts of affection; when this has been achieved in some other way there is no need for reflection.

It is very much to be recommended that in our prayer we should continue to ask the Lord with humility and confidence for his inspirations, the forgiveness of our sins, perseverance, the grace of a happy death, entrance to heaven, and, above all else, the grace of his holy love. St. Francis de Sales exhorts us to ask the Lord most earnestly for the grace of divine love, since once this has been obtained all other graces will follow. And the greatest grace will be if the soul should suffer spiritual desolation and can do nothing more than repeat over and over again the prayer of David: "O God, come to my aid. O Lord make haste to help me. Assist me and be near to me." Father Paul Segneri said that he learnt from experience that there is no more profitable exercise for a soul than to make frequent acts of petition in the course of meditation. It is important to make our petitions in the name of Jesus Christ and through his merits, since he has promised: "Amen, amen, I say to you, whatever you ask the Father in my name he will give you" (Jn 16:23).

It is also important that in our prayer (at least toward the conclusion) we should make resolutions and not only in general terms, such, for example, as to avoid all deliberate faults even of a minor nature or to offer oneself to God. We should resolve in particular to pay more attention to avoid some specific fault into which we frequently fall, or to practice some specific virtue more assiduously, like bearing with the defects of some companion with greater patience, to be more obedient to such and such a superior or a certain rule of life, or to be more diligent in denying oneself in such and such a matter. We should not leave prayer without having made at least one particular resolution.

Our prayer should conclude with three acts: (1) thanks to God for the inspirations granted us during our prayer; (2) acts of determination to attend to whatever resolutions we have made; (3) acts of petition to the Eternal Father, through the intercession of Jesus and Mary, for the grace of remaining faithful. We should then conclude our prayer by reciting a *Pater* and *Ave,* recommending to God the souls in purgatory, the ministers of the church, sinners, and our own friends, relations, and benefactors. The Our Father and the Hail Mary are the most useful of all prayers as Jesus Christ and the church teach us.

When our prayer is over we should follow the advice of St. Francis de Sales and enjoy the sweet smell of the flowers we have gathered, that is, we should recall to ourselves, as the day progresses, one or another thought which most moved us in the course of our prayer.

We should be attentive to put into practice, when the occasions arise, whatever resolutions we made in the course of our prayer, for example, the resolution to tolerate with great gentleness the person who gets on our nerves, to deny ourselves in looking, hearing, or speaking. Especially should we endeavor to preserve a spirit of recollection in silence, since if we allow ourselves to become totally engrossed in idle conversations and occupations, the spirit of devotion which we had achieved in prayer will be dissipated.

Spiritual directors should recommend to their penitents never to omit their prayer and still less to shorten the time if they are going through a period of aridity. They should not be upset even if they have to suffer a prolonged period of spiritual desolation. We approach the Lord in prayer with the intention of honoring him. If he deigns to speak with us and to grant us his favors we should be immensely grateful. But if not, we should be content to remain peacefully in the divine presence, adoring God and laying our needs before him. Even if God does not speak to us we can be certain that our presence and our fidelity are pleasing to him and we can rest assured that he will hear our prayers.

An Outline of a Simple Method of Making Mental Prayer[5]

1. The preparation consists of three acts: of faith, to adore God present here; of humility, to humble ourselves before God and to ask forgiveness; a request for enlightenment, to seek light from God, for the love of Jesus and Mary, in order to spend this period of prayer well. After having said a Hail Mary to Our Lady, we pass to the meditation proper.

2. Several observations need to be made regarding the meditation. First of all, it is good to read something on the subject of meditation, especially something that lends itself to reflection and leads us to recollection. However, when the soul feels itself moved by some devout sentiment, then reading should be left aside and you should occupy yourself with reaping the fruits of meditation.

Meditation has three fruits: affections, prayers, and resolutions. Regarding affections: The soul should occupy the will, but with sweetness and without violence, in making affections toward Jesus and Mary, either of confidence, humility, sorrow, of love, or resignations, of self-offering, and so forth. Prayer enkindles the affections; they inflame the soul and unite it to God: These are the most important fruits of prayer.

Regarding prayers [of petition]: The soul ought to seek from Jesus and Mary the grace which it needs, not only in general, but also in particular, for example, over some vice, the love of God, holy perseverance, and so forth. This way of prayer is most useful, even essential, especially in times when the affections are dry. In such a case there is nothing better than to humble ourselves, to resign ourselves, and to seek the mercy of the Infinite Goodness. Otherwise we run the risk of leaving off prayer because of boredom or of making it with little profit.

Regarding resolutions: Before finishing the prayer, the person ought to make or renew some particular resolution, to overcome some habitual fault or to practice some necessary virtue.

3. The conclusion is made with three brief acts:
(a) to thank Jesus and Mary for the graces received.
(b) to offer to God, by the hands of Jesus and Mary, the acts and resolutions that have been made; and
(c) to ask the Lord, for the love of Jesus and Mary, to give the strength to put the resolutions into action.

For fuller information on the method of prayer, refer to *The Spiritual Guide* by da Ponte, or *The World Sanctified* by Sarnelli.

MORAL THEOLOGY

Introduction

Editor's Note: The temper of the times shaped the *Moral Theology* of Alphonsus. In civil and ecclesiastical life there was a mentality of strict social control through innumerable laws. Moral problems were seen within the context of these laws: Were they obligatory, or were they not? Moral theology sought to answer these questions.

What is characteristic about Alphonsus is the spirit of his approach to this task. He was anxious to establish a solid basis for peace of conscience within the plethora of conflicting opinions about law, and to do so in a way that would help a person on the way to salvation. His method is largely shaped by his missionary experience among the Neapolitans: In the light of this experience he read the standard authors and interpreted them.

Alphonsus is a theologian of his time and place. His interest for us is his astute observation of human nature, his balanced reading of the standard theological opinions, and his ability to encourage people prudently to solve their moral problems for the sake of their eternal salvation. Morality for him was never a simple matter of the lazy application of universal rules to particular acts. His moral theology is one of practical reasoning in which the value of the correct intention is decisive. It is the practical application of the rules of charity to the situations in which people found themselves and the colorful Neapolitans were capable of finding themselves in some tricky corners. His concern, however, is never limited to the production of a neat and self-enclosed moral solution. Gaining salvation is the reason behind the solutions proposed.

Alphonsus presumed that moral problems would be dealt with in confession—the sacrament of reconciliation. He differs from most authors of his time by ensuring that this sacrament is celebrated with care, charity, and courtesy: a look at the readings included here—"The Confessor as Father," "A Careful Judgment," and "The Importance of Studying Moral Theology"—will

315

confirm this. Alphonsus is a master of the solution of the practical problems that can arise in confession; the readings "Returning Stolen Goods" and "The Scrupulous Person" show his skill as a practitioner of the art of moral theology: know the people you are dealing with, understand what is possible and not possible, and lead them with a touch of kindness to a better way of life.

It would be deceptive and thoroughly unfair to limit the moral contribution of Alphonsus to the level of the confessional and the solution of practical problems. He thinks deeply about the important issues and phrases them with a subtlety that is easily missed: "What is Conscience?" and "The Importance and Limit of the Law" show a theologian for whom precision of language and balance of judgment are important. But even here it should be noted that Alphonsus is writing to help ordinary people rather than to impress other theologians. "The Importance of the Right Intention" and "The Practice of Charity" confirm this purpose in his writings.

Alphonsus wrote under pressure. The pressure was not just that of the complicated moral problems to be solved. The temper of the times, as noted, was replete with a love of law, and within the church there was a virulent debate about which system of applying the law was the correct one. Alphonsus was under pressure to explain that the system he was following was both solid and in keeping with Catholic doctrine. Although the terminology may be foreign to us, and the debate itself obscure, no presentation of Alphonsus as a moral theologian would be complete without at least a glimpse of the agonies he went through on this point. He was a prolific letter writer and it is in two of these letters, "Study and Reflection" and "Explaining the Moral System to a Friend," that we get a sense of the personal care he attached to being correctly understood.

Alphonsus's journey as a moral theologian had led him from the strict theory he studied in the seminary, through the experience of mission work among ordinary people, to a less strict theory in later years. He finally came to the realization that kindness and a compassionate understanding of the vagaries of human nature could contribute to what he most desired—the salvation of souls.

The Confessor as Father[1]

The confessor, to be a kind father, should be full of charity. This charity should be shown, in the first place, in the way everyone is welcomed: It does not matter whether they are poor, rough-mannered, or sinners.

Some priests wish only to hear the confessions of the devout or of people with social standing, because they will not be confronted with the need to send them away. If some poor sinner comes, they reluctantly hear their confession and then send the person away in an abrupt manner. As a result it happens that a troubled person, who has made a great effort to go to confession, develops a hatred for the sacrament and is frightened to go again because of the rude reception and dismissal. Having no confidence about finding someone to help and give absolution, they give themselves over to an evil life and to despair.

Good confessors act differently. When a person of this type comes, there is an open-hearted welcome. There is a victorious sense of joy because of the prize that has been won, seeing the good fortune of having snatched a soul from the hands of the evil one. These good confessors know precisely that this sacrament was instituted more for sinners than for pious people. Indeed, the smaller sins do not need sacramental absolution to be forgiven; they can be wiped out in many different ways. They know what Jesus meant when he said: "I did not come to call the righteous but sinners" (Mk 2:17).

That is why confessors, clothed with compassion as the apostle Paul urges, should act in this way: The deeper they find that a person has sunk into the mire of sin, the greater the love they will show in order to draw the soul back to God. These or similar words should be used: "Come on now, be happy"; "Make a good confession"; "Say everything with a sense of freedom, don't be embarrassed about anything"; "It doesn't matter if you haven't fully examined your conscience; it is enough to answer whatever questions I put to you"; "Say thanks to God who has

317

been waiting until now for you to come; now your life is to be changed"; "Be happy, God certainly forgives you if you have the proper intention. Indeed, God has been waiting just to be able to forgive you."

A Careful Judgment[2]

The final role of the confessor is that of judge. This involves the following. A judge is first bound to hear the facts, then examine the merits of the case, and, finally, pass sentence. In the same way, the confessor ought first to become aware of the penitent's state of conscience, then examine the penitent's disposition, and afterward impart or deny absolution.

As regards the first task, which is to know the sins of the penitent. Although the obligation of the examination of conscience is primarily with the penitent, nonetheless the following point should not be doubted, whatever may be the opinion of other theologians quoted by Lohner.[3] If the confessor sees that the penitent has not made a sufficiently careful examination of conscience, the confessor himself is bound to make a personal inquiry. This inquiry is, firstly, about the sins that the penitent would have been likely to commit, and, afterward, about their species and number.

There are some points to be noted about this. Those confessors who send away uneducated persons so that they may make a better examination of conscience act in a mistaken way. Father Segneri, S.J., calls this an intolerable error and quite correctly so.[4] The reason is that people of this type, no matter how hard they try, find it difficult to examine their consciences or to do it as well as the confessor would be able to do. Besides, there is the danger that they become terrified about the difficulty of an examination of conscience arising from the fact of their dismissal. They will stay away from confession and become hardened in sin. With such people, the confessor should personally inquire about their sins, asking them according to the list of the commandments. This is especially the case with penitents who are servants, coach-drivers, mule-drivers, soldiers, attendants, inn-keepers, or the like.

Such folk are in the habit of leading a life neglectful of their eternal salvation and are ignorant about spiritual matters. It is far from sermons and churches that they spend their time.

The mistake would be all the greater if the confessor sent away, because of a defective examination of conscience, an uneducated person who, out of shame, concealed some sin in the past. Even if this meant doubling back on the confessions of many years, it is worth doing because of the greater danger that the penitent would not return and would be lost.

It should be noted, all the same, that the confessor should not examine such people in minute detail. Questions should be asked only about sins that could easily have been committed, judging from the condition and capability of the penitent.

The Importance of Studying Moral Theology[5]

In order to fulfill the role of teacher correctly, it is necessary that the confessor have a good knowledge of the law. One who does not have knowledge cannot teach others. Attention ought to be given to what St. Gregory wrote concerning the task of leading people to eternal life being the art of arts: "The guidance of souls is the art of arts." St. Francis de Sales wrote that the role of the confessor is the most important and the most difficult of all. That is quite correct. It is the most important because it embodies the purpose of all the sciences, which is everlasting life. It is the most difficult, since, in the first place, the role of confessor demands a knowledge of almost all the sciences, all the other roles and arts. Secondly, the science of moral theology spans so many varied themes. And, in the third place, it is to a great extent made up of so many positive laws, each of which has to be assessed according to its correct interpretation. Besides, each of these laws is made extremely difficult because of the many circumstances of particular cases: On these depend the duty of changing the decisions to be taken.

There are some who pride themselves on being well read and on being theologians of high repute but who would not lower themselves to read the moral theologians: Casuists, they call them, with an insulting tone. They say that it is enough, for hearing confessions, to have the general principles of moral theology, since with these all the individual cases can be solved. Who denies that all the cases have to be solved with principles? But, here is the problem: how to apply to individual cases the principles that are appropriate to them. This cannot be done without a serious discussion of the arguments on one and the other side. This is precisely what the moral theologians have done. They have tried to clarify which principles should be used in the resolution of individual cases. What is more: There are today, as noted above, so many positive laws, official church declarations and decrees, that it is not possible to know about them if you do not read the casuists who have recorded them. The modern authors are certainly more useful than the older ones for doing this.

It is with good reason that the erudite author of the *Instruction for New Confessors*[6] says that many great theologians, for all the depth of their knowledge of the speculative sciences, are very ill-informed when it comes to morals. It was Gerson who wrote that moral theology is the most difficult area of all theology: There is no one so erudite or so well-informed that one will not always be coming across new things and new difficulties. The conclusion from this is that the confessor must never overlook the study of moral theology.

Returning Stolen Goods[7]

It is not possible to outline here everything that confessors ought to know about the subject of restitution: It is a vast and complex subject....Here I wish to note only a few of the things that occur and which are of a practical nature.

Firstly: When someone has committed a robbery along with others, there are distinctions to be made in order to judge whether or not this person is obliged to make restitution of the whole amount. If a person had been merely goaded on by companions, and the theft would have happened all the same without this person's involvement, that person is obliged to restore only what he individually took. But if they acted as a group in going to make the theft, each one encouraging the other, then each one is required to restore the full amount.

That is the theory. In practice, however, rough-mannered people, especially those who are not of an overscrupulous conscience, will not easily be persuaded that they are bound to give back what has been taken by others. And on the other hand, the owners themselves will be happy, for the same reason, if each one restores his own part. If people were obliged to restore the whole amount they might easily omit to give back, not just what others had taken, but even what they themselves had taken. For that reason, the confessor makes known to penitents that they are bound to restitution, without explaining the amount, letting each person make restitution as conscience dictates.

It should be noted that one is not bound to restore damage that has been done if it has not been of personal benefit, or if the person did not foresee the damage even in a vague way, unless the person has been forced by the sentence of a judge to make up the damage.

If the theft is uncertain, that is, if it is not clear who the person is who has been robbed, the penitent is obliged to make restitution by having Masses said, or by giving alms to the poor or to holy places. If the penitent is a poor person, the restitution can be applied in favor of himself or his family. But if the identity of the person robbed is clear, restitution should be made to this person.

If one has cheated a number of customers, but is not quite sure which ones, through small tricks (for example, when selling wine, olive oil, etc., by lessening the volume or the weight), I hold that restitution is bound to be made to the customers themselves, and not just to the poor of the locality as some authors allow. This can be done by either lowering the price or increasing the weight and measure.

Even if the obligation to restitution is certain, but the penitent remains in good faith and the confessor is sure that a warning would go unheeded, then the warning should be omitted. The reason is that what is a material sin should not be made into a formal sin, with the danger of the loss of one's soul.

The Scrupulous Person[8]

We will now deal with the scrupulous conscience though this subject deserves a longer treatment than is offered here. A conscience is scrupulous when, for a frivolous reason and without rational basis, there is a frequent fear of sin even though in reality there is no sin at all. A scruple is a defective understanding of something. These are the signs of a scrupulous conscience:

1. Obstinacy of judgment: The scrupulous person rejects the advice of the wise, consults various people but accepts the judgment of none of them. Indeed, the more the views heard, the more perplexed the scrupulous person becomes.

2. Frequent changes of judgment, for frivolous reasons: Because of this there is a fickleness of action and a confusion of mind, especially with regard to external actions, such as the celebration of Mass, the recitation of the Hours, or the administration or reception of the sacraments.

3. Having irrelevant ideas about the various circumstances that were, or could have been, present in some action.

4. A fear of sin in everything and obstinately holding out against advice, even against one's own judgment. As a result, the scrupulous person is never happy with the statement of a confessor but is always asking whether it is possible to be free from sin when acting in accordance with the advice given.

The remedies to be applied to scrupulous people of this kind are as follows. Once the confessor sees from the signs mentioned above that the person is scrupulous he is to prescribe: (1) that the virtue of humility be strongly cultivated, scruples often have their origin in the vice of pride; (2) that the reading of books which provoke scruples be avoided as well as the company of scrupulous persons; (3) that there should not be a long time given to the examination of conscience, especially about those things that are causing the greatest distress;

(4) that idleness be avoided, as it is because of this that the mind is often filled with worthless fears; (5) that trust in God be cultivated vehemently, so as to receive help in obeying the advice of the director.

This last is the most important of all. Indeed, it can be said that this is the only remedy for illness of this sort: to give oneself totally to the judgment of one's superior or confessor, as all the Fathers, theologians, and spiritual experts teach.

What Is Conscience?[29]

The first rule for acting in a good manner is the divine law, to which our conscience should then conform. But, since the goodness or evil of actions is apparent to us insofar as conscience grasps them, we say: The remote or material law of our actions is the divine law, the proximate and formal law is our conscience. This is what St. Thomas teaches when he says (*Summa Theologiae* IaIIae, q. 19, a.4) that human reason is the rule for acts of the human will so that it measures their goodness. This is more clearly expressed in another place (*Quodlib.*3, a.27): A human act is judged to be good or bad according to the good understood as it is pursued by the will, and not according to the material object of the act. So in this first tract we will deal with conscience and in a following one with law.

When we talk about conscience some distinctions are necessary. In the first place, conscience should be distinguished from *synderesis*. Synderesis is the knowledge of general principles, for instance: God is to be honored, evil to be avoided, do not do to others what you would not wish to be done to yourself, and so forth. Conscience, then, is the practical judgment which is formed by these principles in respect of current actions which we have to do or to avoid in the present moment, in accordance with the circumstances that are present. Hence conscience is defined: the dictate of reason by which we judge what is to be done, or avoided, in the here and now.

MORAL THEOLOGY

The Importance and Limit of the Law[10]

In the first place, I say that if an opinion which is on the side of law appears to be definitely more probable, we should absolutely follow it. We cannot follow an opposite opinion which is on the side of freedom. The reason is, because in matters of doubt, we are bound to seek and follow the truth in order to act in a lawful manner. Moreover, where it is impossible to discover the truth in a clear manner, we are at least bound to follow the opinion which comes nearest to the truth, and that is the more probable opinion....

In the second place, I say that if an opinion in favor of freedom is only probable, or of the same probability as the opinion in favor of the law, we cannot follow this opinion either, just because it is a probable opinion. In order to act lawfully, probability alone is not enough. Moral certainty about the goodness of an action is required, as St. Paul says: "Whatever is not done out of faith is a sin" (Rom 14:23). The phrase used is "out of faith," and that clearly means from a definite dictate of conscience such that a person, in conscience, is convinced that he has acted rightly. This is in accordance with the explanation of "out of faith" which is given by St. John Chrysostom, St. Ambrose, and others along with St. Thomas in *On Truth* q.17, a.5. Consequently, I hold that the saying which is common among the probabilists is false, namely: The person who acts according to probability acts prudently.

In the third place, I say that, given two opinions of equal probability, any less safe opinion cannot be followed. The real reason is, as we said, that probability alone (note the words: probability alone) definitely does not provide a sure basis for acting correctly. However, the opinion in favor of freedom, since it has a probability equal to the one in favor of the law, places a serious doubt whether there is indeed a law forbidding the action and, consequently, it cannot be said that the law is sufficiently promulgated. And because it is not promulgated in that case, it does not oblige. This is all the more so since an uncertain law cannot impose a certain obligation....

Indeed, a law, to be obligatory, not only has to be promulgated but has to be promulgated "as certain." We say therefore that no one is obliged to follow any law unless that law has been shown to be certain.

The Importance of the Right Intention[11]

Purity of intention consists in doing everything we turn our hands to with the sole intention of pleasing God. The good or bad intention with which we do something makes it good or bad before God. St. Mary Magdalene de' Pazzi said: "God rewards our actions in proportion to the purity of intention."

In the first place, we ought to seek God and not ourselves in everything we do. If we seek our own satisfaction we cannot expect any reward from God. This applies also to spiritual works. There are those who work hard and wear themselves out in preaching, hearing confessions, helping out, and doing other charitable works but they can lose everything because they seek themselves, not God, in doing all these things. The sign that we have worked for God in something is when we do not seek approval or thanks from others. We are not distressed when the work we undertake is not successful. We take as much pleasure in some good work that has been done by others as if it had been done by ourselves. Besides that, when we have done something good to give pleasure to God we do not have to struggle against vainglory if we are not praised. It is enough to say "to God be the honor and glory." And we never neglect to do good works for the edification of our neighbor out of a fear of vainglory. The Lord wishes that we do good in the presence of others so that they may benefit from it: "Just so, your light must shine before others, that they may see your good deeds and glorify your heavenly Father" (Mt 5:16). So when you do what is good, first of all, have the intention of pleasing God, and then that of giving good example to your neighbor.

In the second place, we also give glory to God when we perform physical actions like working, eating, sleeping, taking justified recreation. Let us do all this to give pleasure to God. Purity of intention can be called a heavenly alchemy by means of which iron becomes gold: That is to say, the slightest and most ordinary of actions become acts of divine love when done to give pleasure to God.

The Practice of Charity[12]

The person who loves God also loves the neighbor, and the person who does not love the neighbor does not love God either, as the divine precept says: "Whoever loves God must also love his brother" (1 Jn 4:21). We ought, then, to love our neighbor in an interior and exterior way.

And how ought we to love our neighbor? Here is the rule: "You shall love the Lord, your God, with all your heart,...and your neighbor as yourself" (Lk 10:27). We ought, then, to love God above everything and more than ourselves, and our neighbor as ourselves. Then, as we wish good for ourselves and are happy when we have it, and are, on the other hand, pained about our hurts, in the same way we ought to wish good for our neighbors and be happy when it comes. And we ought to be pained when misfortune happens to them. In the same way, we should not judge or imagine evil of our neighbors without a real basis. This is interior charity.

Next, exterior charity, which consists in the words and works we direct to our neighbor. As for words, we ought, in the first place, refrain from every shadow of rumor-mongering. The gossip is hated by God and everybody. On the other hand, the person who speaks well of all is loved by God and everybody. Such a person finds an excuse for the intention even if the fault cannot be excused. There is a second point. Let us be on our guard against telling someone the hurtful thing which another has spoken. In such sentiments one often finds hidden long-standing enmities and vendettas. Scripture says that the person who sows discord is hateful to God.

In the third place, we should be careful about hurting our neighbor with some unpleasant remark, even if it is only by way of joke. Would you like to be made fun of in the way you make fun of your neighbor? A fourth point. Avoid quarrels. Sometimes disputes can be made out of nothing, and these go on to beget insults and grudges. We should also be careful about becoming persons of a contrary temperament as you find with some who just love to be in a position to contradict everything. When necessary give your opinion on some point or other and then calm down.

In the fifth place, let us use gentle words with everybody, including our inferiors. In this way we will save ourselves from cursing and saying hurtful things. When others lose their temper and say something abusive to us, let us answer with gentleness and the trouble will suddenly disappear. "A mild answer calms wrath,/but a harsh word stirs up anger" (Prv 15:1). When we are upset with our neighbor, let us be careful not to speak, because it is then that we can be carried away by passion.

Study and Reflection[13]

I recommend to confessors the study of moral theology. They should not blindly follow some opinion of theologians without first judging the intrinsic arguments. I speak, in particular, of those opinions which I no longer regard as probable in the second edition of my *Moral Theology*. What I say, and what the Probabilists say as well, is that every confessor is obliged to act as follows: The first thing to be assessed in every question is whether there is an intrinsic argument that is persuasive, since in this case the opposite opinion is made improbable. It is only when we are not convinced by reason that we can then use an argument of extrinsic probability. Be careful about this, because I fear that some members of the Congregation are seriously mistaken in this matter. Notice that in the second edition I generally admit as probable only those opinions that are expressly so called.

I am not demanding that my opinions have necessarily to be followed. But, please, before you reject my opinion read my book and think about what I have written with so much effort, discussion, and study, Confrères, I didn't go through all that effort for others or to get praised. If all I was going to get from it was a whiff of vainglory, I would certainly have done a lot less. God knows the cost to me in terms of fatigue and trouble. I wrote only for you, confrères, so that you would have a solid doctrine to follow or at least that you would act in a reflective way. I admit that there were a number of opinions in the past that I held to be sound but then I saw that they were improbable. So I ask you all, both the young and the confessors, to read my book since I wrote it for this purpose and then let you follow whatever opinion you form before God.

Explaining the Moral System to a Friend[14]

I think I have clearly proved, with the grace of God, the principle that a doubtful law is not obligatory. The reason is that the law is not obligatory if it is not promulgated, as St. Thomas and all the theologians say. When you have two probable opinions, it is not the law that is promulgated but only a doubt whether there is a law or not. So when there are equally probable opinions the law, because it is doubtful, is not obligatory.

Before I wrote my book, this point had not been made clear. But now everyone says that it has been made clear as daylight, as you can see from the letters that I had printed. What does it matter if some learned people, following the fashion of the day, say the opposite? They do not get the point that is at stake and speak in a loose way. Father Patuzzi has confirmed me in my view, seeing that he has made so many replies but has not replied to this precise point. Even his friends admit this.[15]

But you object, that the rule to be followed is, "In doubt, take the safer view, and so forth." This rule refers to cases where we are in doubt. But whoever works with the reflex principle explained above is not acting in doubt but with a moral certainty. So we are not dealing with the point that is at issue.

Let us come now to your feeling that one has to follow a rigid opinion which has one or two degrees of greater weight. This rule seems to me to be very confused and likely to cause scruples, since it is difficult to find the measuring scale which identifies these one or two degrees of greater weight. My rule seems very clear and certain to me. When the view in favor of the law is definitely more probable, I say that you cannot follow the less probable view. Thus, I am a true Probabiliorist, but certainly not a Tutiorist.[16] When I know that the rigid view is more probable, I say that it has to be followed—here I am against the system of the Jesuits. But when the rigid opinion is only equally probable or very doubtfully more probable, then it is safe to follow the more benign opinion. And why? Because when a view is equally probable or there is a doubt about it being a little bit more probable, the law is doubtful in the real sense of the word. So then the principle that a doubtful law does not oblige comes into play, since what has been sufficiently promulgated is the doubt about the law, but not the law itself....

I hope that I have made myself sufficiently clear.

Advice for Priests Who Minister to
Those Condemned to Death

Introduction

Editor's Note: In 1725 while still engaged in his studies for the priesthood, Alphonsus became a member of the *Confraternitá dei Bianchi*. The *Compagnia di Santa Maria succerre Miseris,* or simply the *Bianchi della Giustizia,* was an association of priests and laymen whose function was to attend to the spiritual needs of criminals in the Naples prisons and specifically to assist spiritually at the execution of criminals and to bury them. The *Bianchi* wore a white habit with a capuche and white cincture, hence their name. Dressed in their habits, the members of the confraternity accompanied the condemned persons on their last journey to the gallows erected in the Piazza del Mercato. Executions took place in public before a large crowd, which witnessed the gruesome routine culminating in the spectacle of the *tirapiedi,* who clung to the prisoner's feet and swung with him into space to ensure that the spinal cord was effectively severed.

Entry into the sodality or confraternity was not automatic; a candidate had to be strongly recommended and capable of performing satisfactorily the important priestly duties attached to membership. Alphonsus's application, supported by two Oratorian Fathers and the Jesuit provincial, was favorably received and he became a member in April 1725. The registers of the confraternity show that Alphonsus assisted at several executions after his ordination to the priesthood. When an execution was to take place, the Courts of Justice would inform the confraternity. The members were then summoned to assemble in their own oratory to begin a program of prayers for the condemned person. Certain members were then assigned to immediate participation in that particular execution. They visited the condemned man in his cell and accompanied him in procession through the streets to the Piazza del Mercato. They remained with him to the last moments of life and the final anointing.

As a result of the experience gained in this priestly ministry,

Alphonsus later included in his moral theology writings instructions for priests who would have to assist at executions. They are to be found in Italian in the *Pratica del Confessore* (1755) and in Latin in the *Praxis Confessarii* (1757) and the *Homo Apostolicus* (1759). Years later, in 1775 and 1777, he published a final version of these instructions in Italian, in both Naples and Venice, *Avvertimenti a' Sacerdoti che assistono a' Condannati a Morte*. There are thus four versions of this pastoral work, differing in minor details. For example, the Latin version in the *Homo Apostolicus* has suggestions for prayers to be said when the priest accompanies the condemned person from the prison to the gallows, when the criminal is blindfolded, when he begins to ascend the steps to the gallows platform, and finally just before the sentence is carried out. The translation here is of the 1777 Venice edition in Italian.

*   *   *

To assist spiritually those who are dying is a work of great charity. But it is a far greater charity still to assist those who are condemned to be executed for their crimes. They merit our greatest sympathy on account of the sad plight in which they find themselves. They are facing death; in a few days they are destined to leave this world. St. Paul's words come to our minds: "Blessed be...the Father of compassion and God of all encouragement, who encourages us in our every affliction, so that we may be able to encourage those who are in any affliction with the encouragement with which we ourselves are encouraged by God" (2 Cor 1:3–4). The Apostle urges us to console those who "are in any affliction." Who are in greater affliction from every point of view and who are more deserving of our compassion than the unfortunate criminals who are condemned to die within a short while for their misdeeds? They find themselves confined in a prison cell guarded by the agents of justice, abandoned by their relations and friends. (1) They are sorely troubled by the thought of hell which they have merited on account of all their misdeeds; (2) they dread the thought of dying at the executioner's hands while they are yet at an age in which they could have hoped for many more years of life; (3) they are dejected at the prospect of

331

being subjected to a shameful death in public; (4) they are heart-broken at the thought of leaving their parents, relations, wives, and children without someone to protect and provide for them.

The priest whose duty it is to assist these unfortunate persons must do everything possible to bring them consolation in their terrible sufferings.

At the very outset he should be extremely careful not to speak to those who are condemned to death about the rigors of divine justice or about any other similar subject which inspires terror. He should rather emphasize the divine mercy and God's will that all should be saved. So, from the very first moment that he comes in contact with the condemned persons, he should address them in a joyful and friendly manner, calling them by their Christian names. He should say to them: "God wishes to save you. He is calling you to leave this world which is full of sorrows, to bring you to another world where he wants to make you happy for all eternity. Now is the time for a genuine of confession of your sins. All you have to do is to repent of the offenses you have committed against God. He is waiting for you with open arms to embrace you and to make you happy for all eternity in paradise."

After these and similar words of encouragement, endeavor to console the unfortunate persons condemned to death and specifically in regard to the four areas of anxiety which I have outlined above. As regards the first source of their anxiety, namely, the fear of damnation for the evil they have done, endeavor to reassure them by pointing out that God does not wish the death of the sinner but that he be converted and live for all eternity. "Why should you die, O house of Israel? For I have no pleasure in the death of anyone who dies, says the Lord God. Return and live!" (Ez 18:31, 32). And in another place he says that when sinners repent of what they have done wrong, he forgets all their sins: "But if the wicked man turns away from all the sins he committed, he shall surely live, he shall not die" (Ez 18:21).

Of course, when one is speaking with those who are unlettered, one is not to quote any of these texts in Latin. Even in the case of an educated person who has been condemned to death, only the briefest quotation in Latin can be tolerated. To increase their confidence place before the condemned persons the image of Jesus Crucified. And then you should say to them, "How could we possibly doubt for a moment that our sins will be forgiven when we realize that Jesus Christ died in order to forgive sinners their sins? 'I did not come to call the righteous but sinners'" (Mk 2:17). And in another place, Jesus Christ declared that he will not reject anyone who comes to him repentant: "I will not reject anyone who comes to me" (Jn 6:37). And, furthermore, he adds in Matthew's gospel (18:12) that he continues to go in search of the lost sheep and when he finds it he places it triumphantly on his shoulders.[1]

And then we have Mary, the Mother of God, who also goes in search of sinners to bring them to God. She revealed to St. Brigid of Sweden that when sinners have recourse to her, she disregards their sins and considers only the intention with which they come to her. When they come with a determination to change their lives she endeavors to heal all the wounds their sins have caused them and she obtains for them the grace to make their peace with God.

Supposing, then, that the condemned persons object that they are going to their death with very little confidence since they have done little or no penance for their sins, you should reply as follows: "My child, realize that to accept your death as a penance for your sins is the greatest penance you could perform and the one most acceptable to God. Accept your death then as coming to you from the hands of God and, for this authentic act of resignation, God will pardon you all your sins and remit all the punishment they have merited" (cf. 1 Pt 2:20–26).

As regards the bitterness of having to die before one's time, endeavor to point out to them that they should thank God that they did not die when they were in their sins and in great danger of losing their souls. Now they are dying, strengthened with all the sacraments of the church and with such great hope of eternal salvation. Perhaps if the Lord had permitted them to live longer they would only, with great difficulty, have succeeded in saving their souls.

As regards the fact that they are going to die a shameful death, endeavor to console them with the thought that they are going to die just as Jesus Christ did, who was the Son of God and Lord of the universe. He died in shame on a cross which was the most ignominious of all deaths for those condemned to be executed. Encourage them to unite their deaths with the death of Jesus Christ and so make of their deaths an offering to God. It is recounted that on one occasion a man condemned to death confided to his priest that he was totally innocent of the crime with which he was charged. The confessor then suggested to the condemned man that he would do everything in his power to make known his innocence. "No, Father," replied the condemned man, "for many years I have asked the Lord to allow me to die in shame just as he wished to die on the Cross. And now that he has granted me this favor would you wish to deprive me of it? I wish to die in this shame since this was the way my Lord Jesus Christ died."

Finally, as regards the anguish of leaving their families and relatives abandoned console them by pointing out that since they are certainly going to save their souls they will be able to assist their families and relatives from heaven much more efficaciously than they could have done on earth. And moreover, God, who loves them more than the condemned persons do, will certainly come to their assistance.

The greatest sorrow that a priest who assists those who are going to be executed can experience is when he comes across those who are so hardened that they do not wish to repent and are not willing to pardon their enemies who, they say, were the cause of their being condemned to death. In such cases the priest should do his best to point out to them that if they do not forgive, and if they die with hate in their hearts, they will certainly lose their souls. Our Lord has said: "Forgive and you shall be forgiven." And so whoever forgives is forgiven.

Say then: Be sure that if you forgive, you yourself will be forgiven. Your salvation is assured since God has promised to forgive those who forgive their enemies. However, if you do not wish to pardon others, then all you will receive in return is justice and you will certainly lose your soul. You now realize that in the past God pardoned you so many sins which you have committed against him and will you now refuse to forgive your enemy as the

Lord demands? Do you mean to say to me that it makes no difference to you whether you go to hell or not? If you speak like that it is clear that you have no idea of the reality of hell. One hour in hell is worse than all the accumulated sufferings this earth can produce over thousands of years. Do not allow the devil to deceive you in this way in order to drag you into this place of torments. Know also that if you lose your soul on account of the hatred which you harbor in your heart, the bitterest suffering you will endure in hell will be the realization that, if you had overcome this hatred, you would have saved your soul. Once in hell there is no further hope for your eternal salvation. So to overcome this temptation, pardon your enemies for the love of Jesus Christ who died for you and is ready to embrace you once you pardon others out of love for him.

If those who are condemned insist that they are unwilling to pardon the judges who have unjustly condemned them, endeavor to convince them that the judges are obliged to mete out justice and to pronounce sentence according to the evidence given in the trial. So it is not fair to hate them.[2]

It is especially difficult to bring to a right frame of mind those condemned persons who, as a result of all their crimes, have arrived at the stage of hating God. However, we must, at least, make the effort. Those who are condemned to death declare that God hates them, that they are the objects of his hatred, that he created them only for the purpose of sending them to eternal damnation. All the misfortunes that happened to them were decreed for this end. The priest should reply to them in this way: No, God does not hate you; he only hates your sins. Remove your sins and God cannot hate you any further. And even at this very moment when you say you hate God, he, for his part, still loves you and is ready to embrace you and bring you to paradise. All you have to do is to ask his pardon and to love him. It is certainly not true that God created you for hell; he has created you for paradise. You are the one who has set yourself on the road to perdition as a result of the sins you have committed. And, despite all this, God is ready to pardon you if only you are sorry for having offended him. How can you say that

God hates you when in fact he died for you on the Cross out of the love which he has for you? Love him then, do not hate him any more since he has not deserved this ingratitude from you.

If the condemned persons still remain obstinate, be sure to encourage them to have recourse to the Virgin Mary, and get them to pray to her in these words: "Mary, Mother of God, you see that I am on the verge of losing my soul. You can help me, come to my assistance."[3]

All these thoughts and exhortations are very good and effective but when you find a condemned person totally obstinate, then there is more need for an increase of prayer than for more words. The priest himself should recommend these souls to Jesus Christ, to the Mother of God, and to different communities of religious. Endeavor to celebrate Mass for their conversion since it is unlikely that they will be moved to repentance without considerable prayer.

LETTERS

Introduction

Editor's Note: The eighteenth century was the great era of letter writing in Europe; it became an art form in itself. Alphonsus was an indefatigable correspondent in Latin and Italian on a variety of subjects from moral theology to business matters concerning the publication of his books. He addressed his correspondence to popes, bishops, clergy, kings, theologians, religious men and women, married men and women as well as to candidates for the priesthood and religious life. Nearly three thousand of his letters have been preserved. A considerable section of his letters deals with matters of spiritual direction and of affairs connected with the government and development of the Congregation of the Most Holy Redeemer of which he remained Superior General even during his years as bishop of the diocese of St. Agatha of the Goths. Apart from the specific purpose of his letters, they shed a revealing light on many aspects of life, civil, social, political, and ecclesiastical, of his time.

A short selection of his letters on various subjects is given in the following pages.

*   *   *

Letter 1. To Sister Maria Celeste Crostarosa

Live Jesus, Joseph, Mary, Teresa

March 1733

Celeste, my dear Sister in Jesus Christ and Mary.[1]

I asked you not to reply to my letter but since you have wished to do me that honor I ask you to read this letter and then to do whatever the Lord inspires you. However, please read it with a serene spirit, and not with the intention of finding counter-arguments to what you have just read. If you read with the intention of rebutting what I have written you will certainly find many opportunities for doing so but you will miss the opportunity of getting to the truth. Heretics in their search for arguments against the church have been able to quote the scriptures for their purpose. Please then read this letter and pray about it for three days but serenely and with a spirit of indifference. Do no write to me or make notes of what you wish to say in reply. After that you may act as you wish.

And since you wish confidentiality from me, so do I request similar confidentiality from you. This letter and everything that it contains is not to be communicated to others, not to Don Silvestro (Tosquez) nor to anyone else whomsoever. You think that I know everything. Well, if you wish in earnest just to please God by seeking the truth and accepting it rather than wishing to be justified and approved in the eyes of others, please, Sister, allow me the liberty of speaking clearly and placing before you what I consider to be the truth. I have no other motive in doing so than the glory of God and the good of your soul which, for me, is of paramount importance. At the outset, let us separate the question of your soul from the whole matter of the new Institute.

First as regards your soul. Why, tell me, Celeste, did you leave Monsignor Falcoia? He is a holy person, enlightened, as you yourself have told me several times. You know for certain that he was given to you by God and has guided you very well for many years. You should prostrate yourself before God in a spirit of thanksgiving for this. So what fault have you now found in him? Has he allowed you to fall into some error? Or have you left him because you are upset that he has humiliated you and been severe with you? But, Sister, do you not realize that this treatment was absolutely necessary in order to bring your proud spirit under control and to divorce you from your attachment to your own judgment? He was not alone in discerning this defect in you since Don Bartolomeo and others had already become conscious of it.[2] St. Philip Neri declared that this was the most dangerous of all defects for one's spiritual life. St. John Chrysostom declared that even a saint who relies on his own judgment is in greater danger from this than from those who direct him. Another saintly authority declared that those who rely on themselves have no need of devils to tempt them.

340

So then, who has approved your decision to abandon Falcoia? You say it was an inspiration from the Lord, that you are at peace in your decision, and that the results confirm the decision. And who has assured you that these inspirations, this peace, the results themselves are for your good? Can you not recall the case of the penitent who for eight years imagined she had received an inspiration from heaven, which was confirmed by a feeling of serenity, and the good effects it had on her? Even her confessor, judging by the results, was led to believe that the inspiration was from God. And then Father Colellis, as is clear from his life, revealed that it was all a delusion.[3] Since in a matter such as this even the most diligent of spiritual masters can make mistakes, how is it that you are able to convince yourself that all is well? Maybe it was Don Silvestro Tosquez who has reassured you? But if you find Falcoia unacceptable because he has humiliated you, a thousand times more should you suspect the verdict of Don Silvestro who considers you greater than even St. Teresa of Avila. He has been singing your praises everywhere from here to Vienna. He approves everything you do or say to the extent that he is totally dependent on you, which is something, as you are certainly aware, spiritual directors should avoid at all costs, if they wish to guide souls correctly and to preserve their humility.[4]

My dear Celeste, do you realize to what extent Don Silvestro has led you to lose your humility and helped you to become attached to your own judgment? You have now arrived at the stage of declaring to all in the monastery that there is no obligation of obeying the injunction of the Mother Superior even imposed *sub gravi*. What Doctor of the Church, my dear Celeste, has come up with such nonsense: that it is not a mortal sin for those with a vow of obedience to disobey deliberately a command of the Mother Superior imposed in a serious matter? A serious matter is one which entails a serious evil or can lead to a serious evil. And it is to be taken for granted that the Mother Superior has considered this when she has announced her precept. It is the very height of pride for a woman who has not studied theology to contradict, in this matter, those whom the church has declared to be experts.

My dear Celeste, where has the old Celeste gone? How has this collapse come about? I could almost die when I think about it. Who has deluded you to such an extent as this? Where has all your old obedience to superiors gone? Where is all your beautiful humility and the desire you professed to be despised and thought little of? Having totally departed from your spirit of obedience, you are now going about looking for public approval and the esteem of others under specious pretexts of seeking the glory of God. God does not need you to defend his glory. No, indeed. When he perceives that you are genuinely humble, and the more he sees you accepting humiliation, the more will he come to your defense and the defense of your undertaking. You know what I am talking about.

I want you to know that in the matter of correct teaching, Don Silvestro, who is the source of your attractive new doctrine of obedience, is as out of line as he could be. I myself have heard from his own mouth that on fast days of the church it is not permitted to eat before twenty-one hours and that in the evening one is not permitted to have the usual *collation*.[5] He was thereby arrogantly condemning all those religious and holy people who followed a different practice. And I will not mention other erroneous opinions which he expressed in moral theology. He even had the audacity to declare—and maybe you yourself have heard him say this—that all those who allowed themselves to be directed spiritually by Falcoia were damned! There is not the slightest doubt but that your vision to leave Falcoia is a delusion. If you consulted a thousand unbiased theologians they would unanimously confirm this. The fact that Falcoia, who was still your spiritual Father at the time, told you it was all a delusion should have been sufficient to convince you. Tell me this, Celeste: Was it possible that it was all an illusion or not? I think you should at least have some reasonable doubts in the matter since a saint such as Teresa of Avila in the account which she gives of her visions on page 227 writes: that even if she could have sworn on oath that God had spoken to her, she would not have been convinced of it until a third party had confirmed it for her.[6] And she goes on to say in the same place that she never once put into practice what she learnt in prayer without revealing everything first to her confessor. And if, occasionally, they directed her to do the very opposite of what the Lord had revealed to her, she immediately obeyed. A good example of this is the foundation of Malagone (Chapter 10). It was initially revealed to her that she should refuse any source of revenue for the foundation. Her confessor, on the other hand, insisted that there should be a regular source of income. She obeyed and the Lord approved her act of obedience.

Now, taking into account the reasonable doubt you should have had about the authenticity of your vision, if you wished to proceed without fear of being mistaken, whose judgment should you have sought if not that of your spiritual Father if you did not wish to go outside the norms of obedience which Jesus Christ has bequeathed to his church when it is a question of discerning his will? You communicated your vision to your spiritual Father, he told you it was a delusion, and you immediately do the very opposite! Tell me, would St. Teresa have acted as you did? It is quite wrong to behave in this way to your spiritual Father who was once so highly esteemed by you. Could you imagine that so holy a man would have advised you to do something contrary to the will of God and thus go against his own conscience? One should obey one's spiritual Father on every occasion that it is not certain he is acting under the influence of some prejudice or other. Falcoia is prejudiced but Don Silvestro is not prejudiced? Celeste, do what is pleasing to God and give up Don Silvestro. I realize full well that this will entail a great effort on your part but the greater the difficulty you will experience in overcoming yourself, so much greater will be your advance in the way of perfection. Tell me, if God wants you to leave him what is going to be your response? "But God does not want it," you reply, O my dear Celeste in Jesus Christ, can it be that you do not see clearly that you are being deceived and what is worse, that you are being deceived because you wish it yourself? Since you have been advised by so many of the real truth I cannot imagine what excuse you will have to offer to Jesus Christ on the day of judgment. Perhaps you will reply: "Well, that is my affair." Very well, let us leave this point and pass on to the question of the new Institute.

As regards the matter of the new Institute it is obvious that the rules drawn up by you are in need of a thousand further determinations. And do you not recall telling me on the very first occasion that I visited the monastery that Falcoia was quite correct in separating the divine from the human since the rules contained many matters of purely personal opinion? You told me the very same thing about the Men's Congregation when I came here to Scala to make the foundation. It was precisely for this that I consulted you and we were both of the same opinion. Besides the many clarifications that the rules are in need of, they also require many other sections and particular constitutions to deal with the question of schools, the missions, the houses for study, the various religious exercises to be performed, the apostolic works that are permitted or forbidden, the different academies that should be held, the community meetings, and many other things. Just for the questions of missions and schools alone we would need two complementary volumes besides the rules so that everything will be quite definite both for the present and the future and in order to secure uniformity throughout.

Now, who is going to draw up all these explanations and constitutions? Both D. Vincenzo and myself have little experience of community; for myself I can say that I am totally ignorant in the matter. D. Silvestro Tosquez is even less equipped than either of us. Don Giovanni Battista di Donato cannot see beyond his own old Rule. As you know, he is adamant in his opposition to the recitation of Office in choir, which is one of our basic principles.[7] In a word, all he wants is to impose his own rules on us. So if we abandon Falcoia and decide among ourselves to make these rules, Don Silvestro would certainly assume the position of director and, at the same time, infallible interpreter of the revelations you have received and even of those to come in the future. He has made every effort up to the present to cast himself in the role of leader but never of disciple. God help the one who goes against him in this whole matter. All he wants, as I know only too well from experience, is to come out on top. You are aware that he had no sooner visited the convent, as a layman, than he presumed to undertake the spiritual direction of some unfortunate sisters who have now withdrawn themselves from his direction and feel as if they have emerged from a dark tunnel. This alone, Celeste, should make you reconsider your position. I repeat, that he was hardly in the door than he insisted that whoever wished to write to Falcoia should first get his permission. What would he not have done to the rest of us if we had left Falcoia? And it has now occurred to me, Celeste, that this is precisely what you have in mind, namely to get us all to leave Falcoia and to depend blindly on the oracle of Don Silvestro, like yourself. If such were the will of God, I would do it. But, for the moment I feel no such inspiration. Now, let us come back to consider our position.

The only way forward for us to get things in order is for all of us to place ourselves under the guidance of one person. Having made known our opinions to him we should then follow blindly whatever he determines. This person should be well experienced, have lived in community, be skilled in the giving of missions and other spiritual exercises, and equipped with the learning necessary for an apostolic worker. At the same time he would need to be a spiritual person with the gift of discernment. It would be up to him to resolve the various problems and to make decisions in all doubtful matters without divisions on our part. This would be the best way to preserve amongst us the gifts of charity and union which are so necessary for the launching of this bark, as you say, and as I have said so often until I am exhausted. What Rule of a religious order or congregation was not made in this way, depending totally on one sole director? The only doubt I ever had about this was as regards the Teresian Reform, especially about the doubts which arose concerning the Rule of St. Albert which had been adopted by St. Teresa. And then I discovered that, despite the fact that all those first companions were holy people and well versed in community life, the reform was on the point of self-destruction for the simple lack of one sole director. There was such a diversity of observance being introduced that St. Teresa herself feared for the success of the Reform. When Father Gratian visited the Reformed houses and found such diversity of practice in the different monasteries, he took it upon himself to draw up the constitutions, as is reported in the Chronicles, and it is these which were adopted from then on.

So in order to establish solidly a set of rules and the Institute itself it is essential to leave everything to someone who is capable of doing this. The first reason is because we are not capable of doing it, then because this is the easiest and simplest way of doing things and because this is how all rules have been drawn up. Only in this way can unity be preserved among us. Otherwise, on one hand there will never be perfect harmony amongst us since each one will be advocating and adducing reasons for what he thinks should be established and on the other hand, the task of finalizing a set of rules will drag on *ad infinitum* and end up in interminable squabbles.

It was precisely to avoid this that you wrote to me suggesting that one side should give in to the other. My dear Celeste, this is impossible. That one side should give in to the other is a possibility when it is a question of honors, of one's personal convenience, or of matters of little importance. But when it is a question of establishing something for the glory of God, without the binding force of obedience and of agreement to accept the decision of one person, no one will give in, in matters which are considered to be for the greater glory of God. And our own experience has borne out the truth of this wisdom since even in matters of trifling importance we have not been able to agree among ourselves up to the present. So in every one of our disagreements, yes, in each and every one, we have had to have recourse to one person to settle matters. Anyone who has a brain in his head and is capable of reasoning knows this is the truth; even your own Don Vincenzo has finally admitted it to me.

You say to me: "Well, you yourself should obey your present superior."[8] I have respect for the Father Superior and I am aware of my obligation to obey those rules already confirmed. But I have never had any intention of obeying the rules which Don Giovanni Battista lays down. I shall obey in all this matter only those rules determined by Monsignor Falcoia, my spiritual director, and also director of this whole enterprise. I want you to know, sister, once and for all, that I have come to this Institute not to be the head of it or director or to take the first place in anything, as you point out to me. Nor was it to please anybody, as you are well able to recall, since, when Falcoia begged me to solicit Monsignor Guerriero for the approval of your rules, I made it clear to Falcoia that he should excuse me since what he requested was against obedience to my director of conscience at that time. I have come this far solely out of obedience to God. And I hope never to abandon this work no matter what appeals are made to me by others. I am thinking particularly of the efforts being made to make me return to Naples. I want you to know that in all this I have not been following your revelations as I made clear from the very outset. I have followed only the ordinary secure way of holy obedience to my spiritual fathers. To them has been promised by Jesus Christ certainty in discerning the will of God, in a way that has not been accorded to all the revelations in the world, as all masters of spirituality are agreed. St. Teresa in the tenth chapter of her *Foundations,* basing her opinion on the words of our Lord *Who hears you hears me,* says that while here on earth we must place ourselves blindly in the hands of just one judge, be it either one's superior or confessor. The Lord so values this submission that even if what we are commanded to do seems incorrect, simply by obeying our superiors, whether with or without difficulty, we finally arrive at doing the will of God perfectly.[9]

As regards myself, as you are aware, I have placed myself completely under obedience to Falcoia and I hope to live and die under obedience. If you wish to follow a different way, well then goodbye to you, wherever you will end up. I, if I am faithful to obedience will sanctify myself. As regards yourself, I do not know how you hope to achieve holiness if you abandon your spiritual guide. And I declare to you that I am not going to leave Falcoia even if everyone else were to leave themselves in my hands, if such an outcome were possible. And I cannot make up my mind whether it would not be better to abandon one's vocation rather than withdraw oneself from obedience, presuming that it was possible to have a genuine vocation against obedience. In a word, to put an end to all this speculation, I would rather leave the Institute and remain obedient than abandon obedience and remain in the Institute. St. Philip Neri valued much more a person who leads an ordinary life under obedience than one who does extraordinary things without obedience. I want you to know that when I begin to have doubts about the authenticity of all your revelations, from the very beginning the one thing that gives me courage and makes me determined to continue is the realization that I have not followed your revelations but rather the path of obedience to my spiritual Father. (By the way, it is certain that all the inspirations and revelations which confirm you in your present obstinacy are delusions, as Falcoia has stated to you and everybody else knows it as well.) So, to sum up, even if all your revelations were delusions, I am able to go ahead without hesitation since I follow the way of obedience and so cannot be deceived as regards my true vocation.

Let us now come back to the question of ourselves. Since we must choose among ourselves one who will resolve the various doubts, difficulties, and problems that arise at the moment, Don Vincenzo declares that we must choose someone other than Falcoia. But why should we have to choose someone else, I say, and not Falcoia, except that we are going to act from prejudice? We have clear and certain indications from God that Falcoia has been chosen to establish this work. It was sufficient for all of us in the beginning to know that Falcoia was your director to realize that it was to him that God gave the initial burden of this work. It was his duty and no one else's to confirm and explain the inspirations you received, just as the confessor of St. Teresa, whose duty it was to direct the saint in the matter of her revelations concerning the Reform, had also to direct the whole matter of the Reform itself.

As well as all this, we have confirmation from Sister Maria Columba who from the very outset wrote to me (and I have now reread her letter) as follows: "It is my belief that Our Lord wishes you to be head of the new Institute but *in dependence on your revered Thomas Falcoia,* since our Lord has chosen him as the principal leader to take charge of this great undertaking.[10] Columba wrote to me that this was the message she received time and time again from Our Lord. Maybe, of course, Columba has been deluded? And I say, Celeste, maybe *you* have been deluded? While I am prepared to admit that both of you are holy persons, I am also aware that Our Lord is accustomed to permit even souls very dear to him to be deceived as we know from the example of Sister Maria Serafina of Capri and others. Why then should I consider Columba to be deluded and not you, since she follows the path of obedience and you do not? To add to this, I recall that you yourself wrote to me several times that in this whole affair we should depend in everything on Falcoia. In one letter which I can send you if you wish and which the Lord's Providence made me preserve safely, you wrote the following words: "Be at peace and leave everything to the judgment of our good Father whom God has placed over this undertaking so that we should all be guided by him." And the rest of your letter confirmed this attitude. But now you will tell me you have received contrary inspirations. And who has approved these blessed contrary inspirations? Why should I now have to accept what you tell me and not what you informed me before? Finally, Celeste, we know that as regards this new Institute Falcoia did not rely solely on your revelations but sought counsel from the discernment of others as well as from the inspirations which he himself received before he ever came to know you. For a number of years he made efforts both in Naples and in Rome to establish just such an Institute basing the idea on the gospels, which is worth more than all your and his own inspirations together.

Supposing we did not have any of these supernatural inspirations and that we had to submit ourselves to one person for the simple reason that we realized this was the shortest and securest way to preserve harmony among ourselves and to establish this undertaking, why should we not then choose Falcoia? And we would have chosen him were it not that Don Silvestro came on the scene. No one other name was mentioned amongst us; we consulted no one else amongst us except Falcoia—a man of years, with experience, enlightened, learned, versed in community, the giving of missions, and with practical experience of worldly affairs. It would be difficult to find another in whom all these qualities are united, qualities which are necessary for the establishment of this undertaking and which are to be found in this holy old man. Or maybe you have received another revelation from God that we should depend on some specific person other than Falcoia?

My God, Celeste, what a dangerous hallucination this is of yours! This is what happens when a soul who has received special inspirations from heaven falls into hallucinations due to a specific character defect. It is my belief that it will take a miracle from heaven to bring you back to the authentic light of God's inspirations. We are now completely disunited as you can see and you are the cause of it. Celeste, I am now speaking to you seriously as if from God. Realize that, at this moment, you, as a result of your obstinacy, are engaged in ruining this whole Undertaking which is not yours but the Lord's. It is true that neither you nor all the rest of us together can succeed in destroying the Undertaking if it is something that God wills to establish. I now feel that God will assist us all the more even if you remain in your obstinacy because if we omit all reference to special revelations we shall have more hope of approval from Rome. In the meantime, what will be the outcome of all this for your soul before the judgment seat of Christ if you wish to carry the responsibility of having brought this Undertaking to the verge of ruin? As regards myself, if I am excluded from the Institute as you continue to say I will be, I admit that this is what I deserve and I shall be at peace provided I am not excluded from the path of obedience. However, realize that it is not up to you nor to Don Silvestro to drive me out. That belongs to God who has no need either of you or of Don Silvestro. I believe that I have been called to this Institute because obedience tells me so.

As regards yourself, I believe that you are on the edge of a great precipice and my heart goes out to you if you do not reconsider your position. You have withdrawn from obedience to Falcoia whom you are obliged to obey, at least as the general director of the convent. In a word, one could say that you have withdrawn yourself from obedience to your legitimate superior. Consequently you must have lost your interior tranquillity. Take care that you do not also lose your soul since you have already entered on that path. I have requested different people to make novenas on your behalf. But I find that you are obdurate and I fear that God may be about to abandon you.

Sister, I have spoken to you in this manner solely for the glory of God and for the good of your soul. Don't be indignant with me and do not trouble yourself to reply to me. I am fully aware that that head of yours would be well able to reply and go on the offensive. But I doubt if these answers would be of much worth before the tribunal of Jesus Christ. Indeed, the very fact of searching for reasons to reply might only lead you to further obstinacy in your attitude rather than to helping you along the path to holiness.

My dear Celeste, listen to me. Humble yourself. If you humble yourself the Lord will certainly enlighten you. Obey your superiors and you will be certain not to go astray. Falcoia is a holy man, he is understanding and do not think that he is not well disposed toward you. If you are humble before him believe me that he will be kinder to you than he was before. At least, resign yourself to the will of God in total indifference and in this frame of mind give yourself over to prayer. Otherwise prayer will be of little benefit to you. Every reason you adduce will come from passion; all your inspirations and lights will be illusions and your own imaginings. If you do not wish to listen to me or to Falcoia, take advice from other impartial persons. Seek counsel, do not walk blindly on the way of perdition, and take advice, not with the purpose of proving yourself to be right but with the intention of knowing and accepting whatever is placed before you as the truth.

Everything that I have written to you, Celeste, I have written because I love you in Jesus Christ. If you dislike me as a result you are doing me an injustice. May Jesus and Mary grant that we may both do only the Will of God.

My letter is finished but I feel I must add these few words. Celeste, pardon me if I conclude by speaking even more clearly to you. Do you not realize the attachment you have for Don Silvestro and the attachment he has for you? "Oh, but this attachment is from God because I wish only God." I am convinced that there has been no sin in it. But is it not true to say that in all this there is much that is earthy? In Don Silvestro you are not seeking only God, you are seeking for something that is not God. Realize that at the moment you are an earthenware vessel. By following Don Silvestro you are placing yourself voluntarily in great danger of losing God. "But I place my trust in God." No. I tell you, Celeste, you are not trusting in God since God does not assist those who place themselves voluntarily in danger; rather does he abandon them. In a word, this is certain. If you follow Falcoia you will certainly achieve holiness. If you follow Don Silvestro you will certainly not achieve holiness. God alone knows if you will even achieve salvation.

Live Jesus and Mary.
Alfonso de' Liguori. A Poor Sinner.

Letter 2. A Letter to a Priest of the Diocese of Naples

1746

Reasons why the habit of cursing the dead does not constitute the formal sin of blasphemy.[1]

1. I am not dealing with the question of cursing the saints or the souls in purgatory. Certainly to curse them would always be a grave sin. The words of the curse if they are taken literally are a curse or a malediction uttered either against those already damned (who are the real dead since they are dead to the real life) or against the bones of the dead. I cannot see how saying *mannaggia i morti* (that is, damn the dead) and understanding it as I explained above can possibly be a mortal sin.

2. Words that are ambiguous in meaning—and this is even the most rigid opinion—provided that the intention of those who utter them is not to blaspheme or to offend God in a serious matter, should be understood according to the general estimation of the people. They will be blasphemous if the ordinary people consider them so. I have asked those who confessed this matter what they intended by the use of thee words and if they had in mind holy people or the saints or the souls in purgatory. They replied in horror: "May God preserve me! I only had in mind the dead." This, therefore, is their honest belief. They all made a distinction between the souls of the saints and the dead.

3. Blasphemous expressions are such either because they are commonly considered to be so by the people or because those who use them intend them to be so. Ask those who "blaspheme the dead" if they intended to curse saintly souls either in heaven or in purgatory and they would without hesitation reply no. Where then can the blasphemy be if this is what is understood by those who utter these words and by those who hear them?

4. Those who confess these matters are clear in their accusation of what they have done, and they make a distinction between cursing the saints, cursing the souls in purgatory, and cursing the dead. Therefore this last means something quite different from the first two. And as a result of my observations to them, some who have been guilty of cursing the souls in purgatory are horrified when they come to accuse themselves.

5. The contrary opinion does not make any distinction between the words of the following Neapolitan expressions: damned be Saint N., damned be the souls in purgatory, and damned be your dead! Everybody knows that this is completely untrue. Both those who are inveterate in this habit of cursing the dead and those who are accustomed to listen to it realize that there is a distinction to be made between simply cursing the dead and cursing the saints and the souls in purgatory.

6. Very many who accuse themselves of cursing the dead will add that they had the intention of cursing the souls in purgatory and you yourself will be aware of this from your own experience.

7. If one follows the opposite opinion to mine, sins are immediately multiplied. The ordinary person on hearing that it is a mortal sin to curse the dead, then comes to the conclusion, as I have found out, that it is a mortal sin to curse their animals, curse the rain, the winds, and so forth.

8. It is our duty as confessors to prevent people falling into sin. By following my opinion very many sins are prevented. Since this practice of cursing is so widespread, how many sins are multiplied by declaring that it is a serious sin! So why should we not hold and accept the opinion that is so obviously in accordance with reason?

Alphonsus de Liguori

LETTERS

Letter 3. Concerning the Election of the Next Pope[1]

Live Jesus, Mary, and Joseph

Arienzo, 24 October 1774

Your Excellency
My dear friend and Lord,

As regards my opinions concerning the present state of the church with relation to the election of the new Pope, what opinion of any weight could a miserable, ignorant, and unspiritual person like myself possibly give? There is need for prayer and much prayer. All the human science and prudence that there is cannot extricate the church from the present state of relaxation and confusion in which every section finds itself; the all-powerful arm of God is necessary.

As regards the bishops, very few of them possess genuine zeal for souls. Almost all religious communities—and one could omit the "almost"—are relaxed. As a result of the present state of general confusion, observance has collapsed and obedience is a thing of the past. The state of the secular clergy is still worse: so, in a word, there is need for a general reform of all clerics and ecclesiastics if there is to be any improvement in the present great corruption of morals among the laity.

So we have to pray to Jesus Christ that he would give us as head of the church one possessed of more spirit and zeal for the glory of God than of learning and human prudence. He should be free of all party attachments and devoid of human respect. If, by chance, for our great misfortune, we should get a Pope that does not have the glory of God as his sole purpose, the Lord will not help him greatly and things from their present condition will go from bad to worse. However, prayer, which can provide a remedy for so many present ills, will move the Lord to put his hand to the problem and remedy the situation.

For this reason I have not only instructed all the communities of my humble Congregation to pray to God with greater fervor than ever for the election of the new Pontiff but I have also instructed all the priests of my diocese, both secular and religious, to recite the prayer *pro electione Pontificis* in all Masses. I also hope that the Lord will inspire the Sacred College of Cardinals to instruct Papal Nuncios throughout the whole Christian world to see to it that this prayer is recited by every priest at Mass. This is the first advice that a miserable old man like myself can give.

I shall not omit to pray several times each day for the election of the Pope but what use will my frigid prayers be? Nevertheless, I trust in the merits of Jesus Christ and Our Lady that, before my death, which is now quite near on account of my years and the infirmities which afflict me, the Lord will grant me the consolation of seeing the church restored.[2]

I assure you, my friend, that I desire, like yourself, to see remedies for so many and such unfortunate situations. In all this matter a thousand ideas circulate in my head which I feel like telling everybody about. But, mindful of my own unworthiness, I have not the effrontery to publicize them lest I should appear to wish to reform the whole world. So I share these ideas with you not from any arrogance but for my own peace of mind.

Since there are many vacancies in the College of Cardinals, I would hope, in the first place, that the new Pope would select as cardinals from among the candidates proposed to him only the most learned and zealous for the good of the church. He should convey to the princes of the various countries in the very first letter announcing his election that when they wish to nominate candidates to be promoted as cardinals they should propose only those of proven piety and learning. Otherwise, he could not in conscience promote them.

I should also like to see the new Pope being determined to refuse further benefices to those in the church who are already well provided for in this respect with sufficient income for their appropriate maintenance. In this matter I should like to see him standing firm against all efforts to the contrary.

I also wish that he would control the extravagance of all prelates. For this purpose he should determine precisely for everybody (otherwise there will be no remedy in this matter) the exact number of their retainers in accordance with what is appropriate for the different groups of prelates: so many butlers and no more; so many servants and no more; so many horses and no more. That will ensure that the enemies of the church will have no further reasons for their criticism.

The new Pope should be vigilant to confer benefices only on those who have loyally served the church and not just on anybody indiscriminately. He should use particular diligence in his choice of bishops since it is on them that the service of God and the salvation of souls mainly depends. He should pay great attention to informing himself beforehand about their moral conduct and their learning, both of which are necessary for the good government of their dioceses. And as regards those bishops already in their dioceses, he should inform himself secretly from their metropolitans and others about their conduct, to ascertain if they are paying little attention to the good of their flock.

I wish, furthermore, that he would let it be known to all and sundry that bishops who are careless in their duties, who transgress in the matter of residence or in the luxury of their retinue or in excessive expenditure on furnishings, life-style, and similar matters, will be suspended or replaced by the appointment of vicars apostolic in order to remedy the situation. It is important to make an example from time to time. Examples of this sort will make other bishops take notice and moderate their extravagance accordingly.

I hope that the next Pope will be very slow in granting privileges which weaken good discipline in the religious life. Such, for example, would be permission for enclosed sisters to leave the enclosure out of mere curiosity just to see the things of the world, readily to dispense religious from their vows and allow them to return to secular life—a practice from which many scandals result. Above all else I should hope that the Pope would be able to recall all religious to their primitive observances, at least in the most important matters.

That is all for now; I do not wish to bore you further. We can do nothing more than pray to the Lord that he will give us a Shepherd full of his spirit, one who will be able to deal with the matters I have mentioned here briefly and all for the glory of Jesus Christ.

Accept my deep respects as I declare myself your Excellency's devoted and humble servant,

Alfonso Maria, bishop of St. Agatha of the Goths.

Letter 4. To His Brother, Don Hercules de Liguori in Naples[1]

Live Jesus, Mary, and Joseph

Nocera, 21 March 1762

My dear Brother,

I have been so stunned by the command of the Holy Father the Pope[2] to accept my appointment as bishop under obedience, that I don't know where I am at the thought that I have to leave the Congregation after thirty years.

For the rest I am very grateful to you for agreeing to loan me money for the expenses involved. If you had not agreed I had determined, as a last resort, to write to the Pope informing him that I had not the wherewithal to pay for the Bulls and the other expenses involved. Who knows but that this inability might have been the means of allowing me to escape the episcopacy? I wrote to Cardinal Spinelli to enlist his assistance in securing my release but he has done quite the opposite.[3] What can one do? I sacrifice myself to the will of God.

Please realize that I shall require a considerable sum of money. I am awaiting word from Rome as to the precise amount. I reckon that for all the expenses that will have to be met both in Rome and Naples I shall require about 4,000 ducats; certainly, at least, 3,500. Yes, I understand that the loan will have to be repaid with all the interest you yourself will have to pay.[4] But do understand that I shall not be able to repay it all in one lump sum. If the revenue of the bishopric comes to around 5,000 ducats per year, I presume I shall be able to repay 1,500 ducats per year together with the interest. There will also be charges on the bishopric and there shall be much expenditure in the beginning.

Please get everything arranged as soon as you can since I wish to leave for Rome as early as possible. I shall have to bring the money with me to Rome to pay for the Bulls and other expenses and I wish to have everything concluded before the Pope goes off for his holidays in May.

As regards a house (in Naples) I do not wish to incur further expenses. I think it will be sufficient for me to have one or two rooms on the bottom floor of your apartments so that I can receive whoever wishes to visit me when I come to Naples. The rooms on the upper floor can remain for the members of the Congregation when they visit Naples. The other areas are not suitable for me to receive those who come to visit me.

Now, as regards a carriage, yes, certainly, I shall have to buy one. First, I must to find out if the late bishop has left one that could be used; I should be able to get it cheaply. In the meantime, do not buy the carriage of the Marquis Valva for the moment until I find out the position in the diocese. If the late bishop's carriage is not suitable I shall take the marquis's.

We can discuss these matters when I come to Naples this week or next. But I do not need to buy a carriage and mules immediately. I can use the Forcella carriage for the visits I have to make while there. One more thing at the moment. I have to go to Caserta to visit the Regents and for that I shall have to remain overnight at Caserta. I should like to remain that night in the convent of the Carmelites. Would you please request the Prior or send the concierge to ask him to do me the favor of allowing me to stay overnight in the monastery?[5]

I know you are delighted but all I can do is shed tears. How could I have been expected to accept a bishopric in my old age? But blessed be the will of God who wishes to make a martyr out of me in these my last years of life. I can't sleep, I have lost my appetite, and I am almost stupid when I realize that the Pope never issues such obediences but has nevertheless done it to me.

Regards to Donna Rachele.[6]

I greet you.

Your affectionate brother

Alfonso, bishop elect of Sant' Agatha.

P.S. Today, Sunday, I don't feel so well. I contracted a fever this morning and this evening, as I write, it has not yet left me.

Letter 5. To the Redemptorist Novices in the Noviceship at Deliceto

Live Jesus, Mary, Joseph, and Teresa

Nocera, 28 January 1762

My very dear Brothers,

God knows how greatly I envy you. If only I had had the good fortune to withdraw myself from the world in my youth and to enter God's house in the company of so many good young men who encourage each other to love God more and more, far from the sinful world where so many are on the road to perdition!

I envy you, I say, and I urge you to thank God always for the grace he has granted you to leave the world out of love for him. These graces are not given to everybody. How many of your young companions are still in your native places, distracted and full of preoccupations, in the midst of a thousand spiritual dangers and perhaps in some cases, far from God. Young people who remain in the world very easily fall prey to the power of the evil one. Be careful yourselves because the devil will do everything in his power to make you abandon your vocation; if he succeeds in this he will have gained everything.

Let everyone of you realize that each of you will have to face his own trials and temptations in the midst of darkness. There is no other remedy in this situation than to have recourse of the Lord in prayer, without dallying to argue with the temptation and to say to him: "Lord, I have given myself to you and I do not wish to abandon you. Even if everyone else leaves you I shall never leave you." And be certain to have recourse to Our Lady who is called the Mother of Perseverance. It is not possible that one who has recourse to her and perseveres in prayer to her could lose his vocation.

Be convinced that whoever does in the Congregation will not only be saved but will be saved as a saint and will enjoy a high place in heaven. Bind yourselves more and more to Jesus Christ. Love is that golden link which binds souls to God and binds them so securely that they can never be separated from him. I urge you to continually make acts of the love of God in your prayers, in your communions, at your visits to the Blessed Sacrament, in your spiritual reading, in your rooms, the refectory, in the woods—in a word—everywhere and at all times. Whoever loves Jesus Christ from his heart has no fear of losing him; he is happy to suffer every pain, every humiliation, and every privation for love of him. On the other hand, whoever does not follow this way is in danger of losing his vocation. And this, my dear Brothers, is the greatest disaster that could befall one. I pray to God that he would allow you to die rather than to suffer the misfortune of losing your vocation which would then bring down upon you all other possible misfortunes.

If you lose your vocation and return to the world having turned your back on the Lord, you will not have the heart to give yourselves to prayer because in prayer your will come face to face with your infidelity. And so having abandoned prayer, which is all too easy to do, and finding yourself once more in the world surrounded by so many evil companions, occasions of sin, and deprived of the special assistance of God (who is accustomed to deal in this way with those who are unfaithful to his call), what will be the outcome of it all for you both in this world and in the next? Even if you succeed in saving your souls, which will be difficult, you will at least have lost that crown which the Lord has prepared for you if you had remained faithful. And for the rest of your lives you will always be uneasy, full of regrets and remorse for having abandoned God out of some caprice or other.

And so I repeat, ask the Lord in your prayers that he would allow you to die rather than to suffer this misfortune. I bless you all now in the name of the Most Holy Trinity and especially in the name of Jesus Christ who has gained for you through his death the great and inestimable grace of vocation. I bless you also in the name of the virgin Mary so that she will obtain for you the grace of perseverance. Love her greatly and pray to her for help in your efforts to sanctify yourselves. Courage, then, in your struggle for holiness. Love Jesus Christ who has shed his blood and given his life for each of you.

As you struggle on the road to holiness pray to the Lord for me, an old man, now very near to death with nothing achieved for God. Do you at least remain faithful to love him for me. I hope before I die to see you all and to congratulate you all when you have pronounced your vows. I pray for you every day, indeed, many times. Do you do the same favor for me. I embrace you all now in the heart of Jesus Christ and I bless you again. Live Jesus, Mary, Joseph, and Teresa.

A final word. If anyone of you experiences a temptation against your vocation (I am talking of a real temptation and not of some passing whim) write to me at once and come to no decision without having my reply. When you have that you can make your decision as seems best.

Etc. Alfonso de Liguori.

Letter 6. To the Daughter of the Prince of Ardore[1]

Live Jesus, Mary, and Joseph

Arienzo, 31 October 1766

My dear Daughter,

Before replying to your very esteemed letter I must tell you what happened to me in a case similar to yours. I ask you to regard this as confidential, though you may speak to your confessor about it.

Seven years ago when I was preaching the spiritual exercises in Naples in the convent of St. Marcellino, one of the nuns, Sister Brianna Caraffa, came to consult me about her vocation to transfer to the Hermitage of Sister Ursola.[2] I investigated the life and conduct of the nun in question and other matters as appropriate, and finally encouraged her to follow her vocation. She then secured the permission of her confessor which she had not previously obtained. She wrote to the Pope for permission and the Holy Father entrusted the matter to the Cardinal Archbishop of Naples. The final decision concerning her transfer rested with him. But when the nuns of St. Marcellino heard of the matter, they did everything in their power and continue to do so, to prevent her carrying out her purpose.

Now, let me come to your case. Having considered all the circumstances which you have placed before me I believe that your vocation to transfer to the Hermitage is genuine. You have been attracted to a life of solitude for a long while. Your first inclination, as you outlined to me, was to join the Carmelite Sisters of St. Teresa who also profess a life of solitude. I am convinced that you do not have, in any way, a grudge against or an aversion to your present monastery. If you thought of leaving your present convent only to escape difficulties where you are you might well find a much heavier cross in the Hermitage which it would be beyond your strength to bear. I sincerely hope that your one intention in seeking a transfer is to find the Lord and to live a life totally free of worldly associations. I agree that it was the Lord who freed you from the burden of looking after that pupil.[3] And, accordingly, I urge you not to accept, on any pretext whatsoever, other pupils since they are a considerable distraction to anybody who wishes to serve the Lord wholeheartedly.

So from all these considerations and from the other matters that you mention in your letter I have no doubt but that you have a genuine vocation for the Hermitage. But I see a mountain of difficulties confronting you.

Your parents will raise a storm but that will be nothing compared with the storm the nuns in your present convent will raise. The next difficulty will be to settle financial matters with the monastery of S. Liguoro. The nuns will object to losing your dowry and will also make a claim on your annual income. And Roman decrees make it clear this would not be unjust. Donna Brianna wrote from St. Marcellino to inform me that she left fifty ducats of her annual income as well as her dowry to her sister, also a nun in the convent. She set aside fifty ducats for the Hermitage and St. Marcellino is to pay a further sixty ducats annually to the Hermitage. It is my understanding that this arrangement was made by the Roman authorities.

Now let us come to what I advise in your case. In the first place make sure, Sister, that you have the consent of your director of conscience. Without this you are not to take the slightest step. Then you should write to the Pope to obtain his authorization for your transfer and to arrange financial matters with your convent. Finally you will also have to have the consent of the Archbishop; without this you can do nothing.

God can do all things and when he wills something he will achieve it. My advice to you is to begin to live now as if you were in the Hermitage, silence, keep to your room, the choir. Carry out your present duties in the convent faithfully but devote the rest of your time to prayer and spiritual reading. Talk with visitors in the parlor as little as possible.[4]

We do not yet know precisely what God is asking of you. However, begin to take the necessary steps to secure your transfer (of course, with the permission of your director). It might well be possible that the Lord wishes to make you a hermit in your present monastery, cutting yourself off from your relations and from the parlors. This is the decision come to in the convent of Donna Alvina, in the case of the penitent of Father Torres of Sanfelice. It is quite possible that your parents and the nuns of St. Liguoro would agree to this course of action while they would not agree to your transfer to the Hermitage.

I recommend secrecy in this whole matter. Mention it to no one with the exception of your director of conscience and Father Pisanell, the Jesuit. If the nuns find out what you have in mind they will do everything to block your negotiations with Rome, the Cardinal Archbishop, and your parents.

Next, I recommend to you to do everything with serenity. If you do not succeed in what you have in mind or if some step which you take fails do not get upset since uneasiness never comes from God. You desire to become a hermit solely to please God. So if the Lord shows you definitely that it is his pleasure that you should remain in your present monastery you should say in all peace and serenity: *Lord I want only your pleasure and not my own.* In the meantime, let us await the outcome of what happens in the case of Sister Brianna Caraffa, the nun in S. Marcellino. From that we can gauge what is likely to happen in your case. For my part, useless that I am, I shall pray for you at Mass that the

Lord will make you entirely his own. For your part please do not omit to recommend me to Jesus Christ in your prayers and especially when you visit the Blessed Sacrament.
With all my respects,
I remain your humble and grateful servant,

Alfonso Maria, bishop of Sant' Agatha.

Letter 7. To the Fathers and Brothers of the Congregation of the Most Holy Redeemer

August 8, 1754

I beg all of you, my brothers in Jesus Christ, before you hear this letter read, to say the *Veni, Creator Spiritus,* and to ask of God the light to understand well and to put into practice what I write to you all in general and to each one of you in particular, in the name of Jesus Christ.

It is not yet twenty-two years since the commencement of the Congregation and it is only five years since it was approved by the Holy Church.[1] So, at this moment, it should not only have maintained its first fervor but should have increased it. Many, it is true, are behaving well but others, instead of advancing, show a want of spirit. What will become of these, I do not know, for God has called us into the Congregation (especially now at its beginning) to become saints and to save ourselves as saints. As for him who would simply save his soul in the Congregation, but not become a saint, I do not know if he will be saved at all. Poor Congregation if this want of spirit spreads! What will it be fifty years hence? One should have to weep and say, poor Jesus Christ! If he is not loved by a member of the Congregation who has received from him so many graces and such special lights, by whom will he be loved?

My God, of what use are so many communions? And why have we come to the Congregation and for what purpose do we remain in it, if we are not endeavoring to become saints? Is it to deceive the people who consider us all saints and to make them laugh at us on the Day of Judgment when they will know our

364

imperfections? We have now many good novices, but they and others who come after will, through our example, be worse than we are. In a short time the Congregation will become thoroughly relaxed, because imperfections will give place to scandals, and, if this happens, better far, my Brothers, that we pray the Lord to suppress the Congregation at once.

I am already old and in bad health and am drawing nigh already to the day of account.[2] I desire to be of as much service to you as I can and God knows how much I love each of you, more than my brothers and my mother. But it is not the will of God that I should endanger my eternal salvation through love (but an inordinate love) of any of you. We are all miserable creatures and we all commit faults but I am not pained by passing faults but by those which are permanent and by certain weaknesses which do harm to the whole community. If any one would, with his eyes open, condone such faults as these and defend them or, at least, excuse them as tolerable, I, for my part, declare that I cannot, and ought not, tolerate them. Such would be, for example, faults either against obedience or against poverty, against humility or fraternal charity. I hope, by the grace of God, to maintain this resolution until I die and to act upon it faithfully, since I have promised God never to allow myself to be overcome by human respect, which would lead me to see the brethren fail in important matters which are prejudicial to others, without correcting them.

You are already aware that perhaps my weakest point is to be too indulgent. But I hope that God will give me firmness not to bear with the imperfect who will not correct themselves and who even defend their imperfections. I beseech you who are young and who remain to govern the Congregation, never to tolerate a member of the community who should be so imperfect as not to humble himself after a fault but should even defend it. I protest that on the Day of Judgment I will accuse before the tribunal of Jesus Christ the superior who, in order to avoid causing pain to a member of the community, shuts his eyes to faults that do harm to the community and is the cause of the Congregation becoming relaxed. With regard, however, to the past, if there be any who have been guilty of some fault I do not intend now to reproach them with it; I speak only for the future.

But to come at once to certain special points, I beg each one to pay attention to the following remarks.

First, then, I beg each of you to value his vocation. It is the greatest blessing, next to creation and redemption, which God could bestow on you. Thank Almighty God for it every day and be afraid of losing it. Do not be deceived by the enemy of souls, who will say that you could do good even out of the Congregation, at home, and would enjoy greater peace out of it. And what good? *Nemo propheta acceptus in patria sua.* Everyone knows this and experience proves it. A priest will save more souls in one year in the Congregation than in his whole life out of it. And to speak of personal advantage, a member of the Congregation will gain more by practicing obedience for one year than he would gain in ten by living according to his own fancy out of the Congregation.[3]

And besides, we have to do the good that God wills of us and not that which we will ourselves. Now, God wills of one who is called to the Congregation that good and those labors which are imposed upon him by the Rule and by his superiors. Peace indeed! What kind of peace? *Quis restitit ei et pacem habebit?* We see it, my Brothers, in those who have abandoned the Congregation. What kind of peace will God give to those faithless ones who, out of some caprice and for want of mortification, lose their vocation and turn their backs upon the will of God? And especially when they come to die how shall they find peace when they remember that they are dying out of the Congregation? I will not say more on this point because everyone already well understands it. But the misfortune is that in the moment of temptation we are blind and the loss of vocation is not considered an evil.

I draw your attention in a special way to the following point. Let no one think to frighten us by saying that he wishes to leave. Thanks be to God the Congregation has, at the present moment, many good members and every day fervent and talented young men come to join us. This is because the good name of the Congregation has spread throughout the entire kingdom and even out of it. It is believed that there is great fervor and perfection in the

Congregation (would to God that only half were true!) and so the good subjects will remain with us to give missions and retreats.

And even were we obliged to give fewer missions, it will always be better to keep up the spirit of regular observance with a few subjects than to see the Congregation become relaxed. Those few who live conscientiously will please God more than a thousand who lead imperfect lives. So then, to sum up this point, unhappy he who loses his vocation! And by the way, I renew for each one the formal obedience which I have already given—not to leave the Congregation without first having obtained my express permission, together with the dispensation from the vows and oath of perseverance, unless this has been already obtained from the Sovereign Pontiff.[4]

Secondly, I beg each one to obey and to make no resistance to the commands of the local superior. If a member of the Congregation has some difficulty, he is allowed to make it known. But I beg him to make up his mind to obey even before he makes his representation, should it not be entertained. So resolved, let him go and explain his difficulty whatever it may be. If he does not act in this way he will remain disquieted; should his difficulty not be admitted and he remain disquieted, the devil will gain much with him.

Father de la Colombière made a vow always to go against his own will. Should anyone not have the courage to do as much (and I do not demand this) at least he ought to be careful on all occasions to mortify his self-will which is the ruin of souls. Speaking of obediences which are difficult (for there is no great merit in those which are easy), St. Catherine of Bologna says that we should perform them without murmuring *exteriorly,* for example, by complaining of the food, clothing, or the manner of acting of superiors. This latter is a great fault. And we should obey without *interior* murmuring, for this also disturbs the soul.

I beg in a special manner of each one not to wish to change his house without evident necessity. Should the necessity be evident, I, nevertheless, beg him, before he makes his request, to resign himself entirely to the judgment of his superior should the latter take a different view of his case. For my part, I declare that

I will not grant this to anyone without clear necessity, for to act otherwise might become the source of much disquiet for the members of the Congregation.

Thirdly, I beg of you all not to complain one to another of what the local superiors do. To do so may be the cause of great temptation both to yourselves and to the others.

Fourthly, I beg each of you to ask Jesus Christ for his holy love, otherwise all the good resolutions will be of little profit. And in order to obtain this holy love let us strive to have a great love for the Passion of Jesus Christ, by praying and making a little meditation on it during the day and, when it is possible, by making the Way of the Cross. Jesus Christ is surely much pleased when we think of the sorrows and the scorn which he endured for us. It seems to me impossible for one who thinks often of his sorrows and of his passion not to become full of love for Jesus Christ. I pray both present and future superiors often to insist at the Chapters on the love of Jesus Christ and of his Passion. There is nothing on which we insist in the missions more than on this love for the Passion of Jesus Christ. What a shame, then, for one of us to be found at the day of judgment to have loved Jesus Christ less than some poor woman!

I beg each one to love his cell and not to become dissipated by wandering about here and there during the day. Let us husband our time in order to spend it in prayer, in visits to the Most Holy Sacrament which we have in our midst for this very purpose, and also in study because this too is absolutely necessary for us.[5]

Lastly I recommend to superiors, both present and future, the observance of the rules. Regular observance is in their hands. The Rector Major is far away; if the local Rector does not attend to it, the Rector Major cannot remedy what is amiss.[6] Therefore it is necessary for superiors not merely to preach this observance but to be the first to practice it. That which is seen makes far more impression than that which is heard.

At the same time I recommend to superiors charity toward the members of the community, in supporting them in their temptations and in endeavoring to assist them in their necessities as far as possible and by inquiring expressly in their account of conscience if they are in need of anything.

I recommend above all the account of conscience each month—if possible on the first Monday of the month and when it cannot be made or finished on the first Monday, then on the second.

I especially recommend attention and charity to the sick, in visiting them and providing them as far as possible with the necessary remedies and in asking them if they are in want of anything. If this or that request is not compatible with poverty, the superior should be understanding with them as much as possible.

I also advise superiors to correct in private, because public corrections do little good except in cases where the fault was public. Then the correction does good to the others. But even here it is better first to correct the member of the community in private and only afterward publicly.

So much for superiors. As for the members of the Congregation I beg them never again to say that the Congregation is not as strict as it was and that the primitive observance is relaxed. Even if, on account of the increased number of subjects, more faults are committed each one should endeavor to correct himself and to live in observance of the Rule. Let him understand that the inobservant, who will not correct themselves, will not be tolerated in the Congregation. Hence when anyone commits a fault let him at once humble himself interiorly if the fault was interior and exteriorly, by accusing himself of it, if the fault was exterior. On falling into any fault let him at once make a purpose of amendment.

If anyone has some grievance against one of his brethren or against his superior, let him be careful to take no step in the heat of passion. Let him first get calm, recommending himself to God and then, if he thinks it necessary, let him act or let him go and speak or write to the superior. For the love of Jesus Christ I beg you to pay attention to this point. Oh! if this were observed, how many faults would be avoided. In the heat of passion many things appear very different from what they really are. On this account I beg superiors also not to correct while they are under the influence of anger, but to wait until the mind becomes calm, otherwise their corrections will avail but little.

I recommend as strongly as I can detachment from relations who are certainly, as Jesus Christ says, the greatest enemies of our perfection.[7]

Let every one be on his guard not even to mention the word *honor (stima propria)* in the Congregation.[8] The greatest honor that a member of the Congregation should desire is to love obedience and to be despised and to be thought little of. To be despised as Jesus Christ was despised was the desire of the saints. He who does not make up his mind to become a saint cannot persevere in the Congregation. Jesus Christ himself who loves this Congregation exceedingly will drive him out. It is not the will of God that the first stones of this, his own building, should be so weak as to be not only unable to encourage and to give good example to those who shall come after us, but even to give little edification to those who are in it at present. Let each one well understand this.

I recommend also the love of poverty and beg all to take notice that faults against the two virtues of poverty and obedience are not and cannot be tolerated in the Congregation. If the practice of these two virtues fail, the spirit of the Congregation is wholly destroyed and at an end.

I again assure you that what I have now written, just as it came into my mind, is not against any one in particular but, in general, for all and rather for the future than for the past. I moreover beg all of you after hearing this letter not to suppose that I have any ill-feeling toward any one who has committed some faults in the past. I declare that as Jesus Christ has forgotten the faults of those who have humbled themselves for them, so, also, do I forget them. Let each one understand that when any one has the misfortune to fall into a fault, if he will only heartily humble himself for it, he may be sure that I will heartily forgive him. By his humiliation he will make himself more dear to me than before. I say this in order that no one may lose courage if by chance he should ever fall into some fault. On the other hand let all guard against committing faults, even the smallest, with open eyes. The devil is wont to make use of such faults as these to lead us into more serious ones and then to tempt us to lose our vocation. By this snare the devil has been able to drive more than one out of the Congregation.

Lastly, be assured, my Brothers, that I love each of you, after God, as my only love on this earth, and I offer for you, from this moment, my blood and my life. You who are young may do much for the glory of God, but, as for me, who am old and ill and useless, what more service can I render? Therefore, I beg each of you, if you are at a distance, to write to me whenever you need to and to banish the idea, which the devil has been making use of to disquiet me and others, that you will annoy me by speaking or writing to me. Be sure the more one shows me this confidence the more he binds me to himself. Remember that where there is question of consoling one of my brethren and children I leave everything. I consider it of greater importance to help one of my children than to do any other good work. God demands this of me in my office more than anything else.

To conclude then, my Brothers. Let us—in what remains of our lives, long or short (within a short time three of our young men, Muscarelli, Blasucci, and Zabbati, and Father Paul who in health was younger than all, have died)—let us, I say, become saints.[9] Let us love Jesus Christ very much for he deserves to be loved and especially by us whom he has loved more than others. Let us love a God who died for the love of us. Let us enliven our faith and remember that we have but a few days to live on this earth and that eternity is awaiting us. We preach these truths to others and, indeed, they are truths of faith. So then we have no longer to live for ourselves or for the world but for God alone, for eternity alone, and in order to become saints. Therefore, let us continually offer ourselves to Jesus Christ that he may do with us as he pleases. Let us continually beg of the Most Blessed Virgin to obtain for us the great treasure of the love of Jesus Christ. And when the devil tempts us against our vocation—and this is his great business with each one of us—let us recommend ourselves to the Mother of Perseverance and we shall certainly not lose our vocation.

I bless and embrace you all in the Heart of Jesus Christ, that having loved him exceedingly on this earth we may all, one day, be united in loving him in our heavenly home. Let us not lose the beautiful crown which I see prepared for every one who lives in observance and dies in the Congregation.

Live Jesus, Mary, Joseph, St. Francis Xavier, and St. Teresa!

NOTES

General Introduction

1. Francois Bourdeau, *Le Livre des "Visites au Saint Sacrement"* in *Alphonse de Liguori, Pasteur et Docteur.* Theologie Historique, No. 77 (Paris: Beauchesne, 1987).

2. Ciencia Tomista, 1925, 14.31; 1926, 53, 321–97; J. F. Hidalgo, *Doctrina Alfonsiana acerca de la accion de la Gracia Actual, Efficaz y Suficiente* (Marietti, 1954).

3. Bernard Häring, Foreword, *The Practice of the Love of Jesus Christ* (Private Edition).

4. A chronological list of Alphonsus's publications can be found in the Reference Matter section.

5. Giuseppe Cacciatore, *La Letteratura degli "Exempla,"* in S. Alfonso M. de Liguori, *Opere Ascetiche,* Introduzione Generale (Rome, 1960); Giuseppe Orlandi, *L'Uso degli "Exempla" in S. Alfonso M. de Liguori. Spicilegium Historicum C.SS.R.,* XXXIX (Rome, 1991).

6. S. Alfonso de Liguori, *Selva di materie predicabili ed istruttive,* etc. (Naples, 1780), II.181. Cf. Also S. Alfonso, *Lettera ad un religioso amico ove si tratta del modo di predicare all'apostolica etc. Opere Ascetiche,* III.299 (Turin: Marietti, 1847).

7. S. Alfonso, *Selva,* etc., ut supra, I.3.

Divine Love and the Means of Acquiring It

1. Alphonsus here uses the thought of hell as a proof of God's wish to be loved by his creatures. This inversion of the usual use of the thought of hell is a common "conceit" found in the writings of the seventeenth- and eighteenth-century mystics.

2. Alphonsus quotes St. Thomas Aquinas to this effect: *quasi sine te beatus esse non posset,* without, however, giving the precise reference.

3. Alphonsus does not give a precise reference for the quotation from St. Gregory of Nyssa, (c.330–390) but he is doubtless referring to Gregory's *In Canticum Canticorum,* Hom. 4. The arrow theme to describe God's grace and its effect on souls was widely used in Alphonsus's time. Many spiritual works had a frontispiece showing arrows emanating from God the Father or the Trinity or the Holy Spirit, and piercing human hearts as they knelt in prayer, especially before the Blessed Sacrament.

The mystical writings of St. Catherine of Genoa (1447–1510) were much in vogue in the eighteenth century.

4. Alphonsus often cites or paraphrases passages from Bernard of Clairvaux's *Sermones Super Cantica Canticorum.* He concludes here with a long list of similar short prayers, only a few of which are included. The Italian quatrain deserves to be quoted in full:

Gesu mio, diletto mio,
Io non voglio altro che te:
Tutta a te me do, mio dio,
Fanne pur che vuoi di me.

5. Vincenzo Giiberti (Gilberti) (1562–1656), Superior General of the Theatines, wrote extensively on the psalms. He was one of the most widely read spiritual writers of the seventeenth and eighteenth centuries. He was in the same mold as Alphonsus, two centuries later, in that his devotional works were intended for the general faithful.

6. Pope St. Gregory the Great (590–604) wrote the *Moralia in Job,* a storehouse of dogma, morals, asceticism, and mysticism. It is more acceptable in contemporary spiritual writings to speak positively of our love for others, especially parents and relations, as being ultimately directed toward God. Alphonsus, rather negatively, warns of any love that might separate us from the love of God. This approach, quite common at the time, is to be seen against the background of the discussions in contemporary writings about "pure love"—that is, love without any admixture of selfish interest.

7. This work, entitled *Riflessioni ed Affetti sopra la Passione di Gesu Cristo esposta semplicemente secondo la discrivono i sagri Vangelisti,* was published for the first time in 1761 as an appendix to the second volume of *The True Spouse of Jesus Christ.* Cf. B.G.E.R Vol. I No. 48.

8. Alphonsus gives a general reference to St. Thomas's work on the Blessed Eucharist. Cf. *Summa Contra Gentiles,* Lib. IV.61. The *Stimulus Amoris* attributed to St. Bonaventure is now considered to be the work of Frater Jacobus Mediolanensis, O.Min.

9. St. Bernard, *Sermones ad Fratres.*

10. This is another example of the language of the mystics.

11. The Latin text of the Vulgate, *Domine, quid me vis facere,* can be translated "Lord what would you have me to do," which suits Alphonsus's argument. The N.A.B. translation of Acts 9.6 does not convey the sense Alphonsus intended. John of Avila (1499–1569) was beatified by Pope Leo XIII. Preacher, writer, spiritual director, he was one of the reformers of the sixteenth century. His *Audi Filia* was a much

quoted work on Christian perfection. He is frequently referred to as Venerable Master of Avila.

12. In this section Alphonsus understands by "mental prayer" reflection on the Word of God and on the great eternal verities. In section 20 he insists on the necessity of "prayer," that is, on the necessity of the prayer of petition. One of the key elements in Alphonsus's spirituality and teaching was the necessity of asking God with confidence for all the graces we need for our eternal salvation.

13. Alphonsus uses the phrase *orazione mentale* in paragraph 19 with the meaning "reflection" or "meditation" in the strict sense. In paragraph 20 he uses *preghiera* in the sense of "prayer of petition." He is quite logical then when he writes here that the lives of saints were lives both of *orazione e preghiere.*

14. This last paragraph is typical of the spontaneous nature of Alphonsus's devotional writings. He had already treated in paragraph 13 of the Passion of Jesus Christ as a motive for loving God. Another aspect of this thought then occurred to him at the end of what he had written and he added this paragraph as an afterthought.

Conformity to the Will of God

1. Alphonsus gives a reference to Chap. 4 of "The Divine Names" and refers to the author as St. Denis. Centuries of controversy are connected with the works of the "pseudo-Denis." At the time of Alphonsus these works were widely accepted and referred to in Naples by even the most learned and critically minded authors, such as Giulio Torni, the author of commentaries on the works of Estius and the Sentences of Peter Lombard. Alphonsus frequently quotes from "The Divine Names." S. Alfonso M. de Liguori, *Opere Ascetiche,* Introduzione Generale (Rome, 1960).

2. Henry Suso, (1295–1366), Dominican preacher and mystic, pupil of the great Meister Eckhart and companion of Tauler. Suso's *Little Book of Eternal Wisdom* was the most popular book of simple mysticism until it was displaced by *The Imitation of Christ.*

3. Blessed Stefana Quinzana (1457–1530). An account of her life was published in 1658.

4. The division of this work into various sections is the work of different editors over the years. Alphonsus apparently wrote the work as one simple devotional treatise without chapter divisions.

5. Blessed John of Avila (1500–1569). His treatise *Audi Filia,* which Alphonsus quotes here, is regarded as a masterpiece of sixteenth-century spiritual literature.

6. Accounts of these less than well known martyrs are to be found in H. Rosweyde, S.J., *Acta Sanctorum.*

7. Caesarius (c. 1180–1240), a Cistercian monk of Heisterbach. An ascetical and historical writer whose *Dialogus Miraculorum* is a classic of the *exempla* tradition, which Alphonsus used extensively in his devotional writings.

8. Alphonsus V of Aragon (1438–1481), known as the Troubadour of Our Lady.

9. Salvian, a priest of Marseilles in the fifth century who addressed letters to the Christian world as if coming from Paul's disciple, Timothy.

10. John Tauler (c. 1300–1361), the great German Dominican preacher and mystic. Like Suso, he was a pupil of Eckhart.

11. Laurentius Surius (van der Schuur) narrates this anecdote in his life of St. Vedastus in his *De probatis Sanctorum historiis.*

Motives for Confidence in the Divine Mercy

1. "Iurans etiam, vivo dicens, cupit sibi credi." Tertullian, *On Penitence,* Chap. 4, Ancient Christian Writers, Vol. 28 (Newman Press, N.Y., 1959), pp. 20–21.

2. Denis Petau (Petavius), S.J., *De Theologia Dogmatica* (4 vols., 1644–1650). In 1644 Petau published *De la pénitence publique,* etc., against Arnauld's *De la fréquente Communion.* His advocacy of frequent and even daily communion made Petau most acceptable to Alphonsus, who quotes him frequently.

3. Alphonsus translated literally the Latin of the Vulgate, *Domine quid me vis facere?* which I have retained. The translation of the N.A.B. is not quite as appropriate: "Now get up and go into the city and you will be told what you must do" (Acts 9:6).

4. In Alphonsus's day the Liturgical Prayer of the Church was the preserve of the clergy and religious.

5. Right up to the end of the nineteenth century one's spiritual director regulated the frequency of one's reception of Holy Communion. The penitent was encouraged to request permission as often as

possible. Freedom to receive Holy Communion daily came officially with the reforms of Pope Pius X.

6. Three and a half paragraphs that detail the physical sufferings of St. Liduvina have been omitted here.

7. Alphonsus appends a long prayer to Jesus Christ Crucified at the end of this treatise.

The Practice of the Love of Jesus Christ

1. "Having now given you this book on the confidence we should have in Mary, I hope before very long to offer you another on the love of Jesus her son which I hope will be equally pleasing to you" (*Opere Ascetiche*, Vol. 6, p. 19, note 1.) This sentence was omitted from subsequent editions.

2. It has been published by Noel Londoño: "S. Alfonso de Liguori: Prontuario de textos. Un manuscrito ineditio. Introduction y notas," *Spicilegium Historicum C.Ss.R.* XLI/2 (1993): 277–349. The notebook contains sermon outlines and points for the examination of candidates for orders, but the largest section of it is an outline and collection of biblical and patristic texts for what is clearly the projected book on Jesus Christ.

3. The correspondence with Remondini enables us to follow the fortunes of the composition; see Letters 193, 194, 196, 198, 200, 205, 209, in *Letters. Vol. 4: Special Correspondence* (Part II) in *Complete Works of St. Alphonsus,* ed. Eugene Grimm (New York, 1886).

4. Letter to Remondini, no. 198, supra.

5. In 1933, De Meulemeester listed 255 editions in French alone as well as others in languages as diverse as Arabic, Armenian, and Chinese; cf. *Bibliographie Générale* I. 138ff.

6. A careful study of the *Visits to the Blessed Sacrament* (1745), one of his earliest published works, for example, has shown his indebtedness to St. Jure for the examples contained in a considerable number of the "visits." Cf. François Bourdeau, "Essais sur la composition par étapes du 'Livre des Visites au S. Sacrament' à la lumière des sources" in *Spicilegium Historicum C.Ss.R.* XXXV/2: 233–309. Henri Bremond has described St. Jure's work as a masterpiece of French religious literature, but remarks that it is of thoroughly Ignatian stamp, unlike some of his later works, which belong more properly to the French School (*Histoire*

Littéraire du Séntiment Réligieux en France, Vol. III, Chap. 5, "Jésuites Bérulliens").

7. St. Jure devotes the first part (Livre 1) of his work to the motives of love, the second to the exercises of love, and the third to the effects of divine love.

8. D. Capone, *Suor Celeste Crostarosa e S. Alfonso de Liguori: Incontri–Spiritualitá: Per la Storia della Spiritualitá nel Settecento* (Materdomini, 1991), pp. 153–60.

9. Bernard Häring, *Free and Faithful in Christ: Vol. 1: General Moral Theology* (Slough, 1978), p. 57.

10. Ibid., "Una morale per i redenti": in *Morale e Redenzione,* ed. L. Alvarez Verdes and S. Majorano (Rome: Edacalf, 1983), p. 19.

11. Ibid., *Free and Faithful, Vol. 1,* pp. 57ff.

12. Brian Johnstone, "St. Alphonsus and the Theology of Conversion," *Readings in Redemptorist Spirituality* 2 (Rome, 1988), pp. 72–85.

13. One of the few studies is Rita Librandi's "S.Alfonso: Grammatico e Rettore" in *S. Alfonso M. de Liguori e la Società Civile del Suo Tempo* (2 vols.), ed. P. Giannantonio (Florence, 1990), Vol. 1, pp. 494–504.

14. *Opere Ascetiche Vol. 1: Practica di Amar Gèsu Cristo e Opuscoli Sull'Amore Divino* (Rome, 1933), pp. 1–243.

15. This is a summary, rather than a direct quotation, of the thought of the Bishop of Geneva. See particularly *Introduction to the Devout Life, 1,* Chap. 1.

16. Alphonsus's teaching on gratitude as the foundation of love and source of moral action finds an echo in the thought of the contemporary Redemptorist moral theologian Bernard Häring in his *Free and Faithful in Christ: Vol. 1: General Moral Theology,* pp. 202–05.

17. Alphonsus, following the Vulgate, translates *nimiam caritatem* in its sense of "excessive love" and we have attempted to preserve this nuance here. The idea of the extravagant quality of divine love returns at several other places in his writings, e.g., he reads the Latin word *excessum* in the Lucan transfiguration account as "excess" rather than the "departure" demanded by a literal translation of the Greek.

18. Lawrence Justinian (1381–1456), Patriarch of Venice and theologian. The foolishness of divine love is one of the favorite themes of Alphonsus.

19. John of Avila (1499–1569) was a leading figure in the reform of the Spanish Church through his educational apostolate and the work

of parish missions. He had contact with many of the leading figures of the time, being a correspondent of Teresa of Avila and Ignatius Loyola among others. The *Tratado del Amor de Dios* from which this lengthy quotation is taken has been described as one of the pearls of Castilian literature. He was beatified in 1894 and canonized in 1970.

20. Thomas Aquinas, *De Duobus Praeceptis Caritatis et Decem Legis Praeceptis* 1, "De delectione Dei."

21. Johannes Tauler (c.1300–1361), Dominican preacher and writer.

22. Bernardine de Bustis (d. 1500), Italian Franciscan.

23. Giovanni Tiepolo (Tiepoli) (1557–1631), Patriarch of Venice 1619 and an eclectic popularizer.

24. Session 13, Chap. 2: "The reasons for the institution of this most holy sacrament." Cf. *The Decrees of the Ecumenical Councils* ed. Norman Tanner (Georgetown, 1990), Vol. 2, p. 694.

25. *Office of Corpus Christi,* Magnificat antiphon at second vespers.

26. Baptisa (Camilla) Varani (1458–1524), Italian Poor Clare and mystic. From her spiritual writings on the passion and interior sufferings of Jesus ("I Dolori Mentali di Gèsu nella sua Passione") she is regarded as an early precursor of devotion to the Sacred Heart of Jesus. Cf. "Baptiste Varani" in *Dictionnaire de Spiritualité* 1, col. 1240–42.

27. "Louis da Ponte" is Alphonsus's Italianized spelling for Luis de La Puente (1554–1624), Spanish Jesuit and spiritual writer, who was a disciple and biographer of Alvarez. Cf. note 31 below.

28. There were two Italian Jesuits of the seventeenth to eighteenth century called Paolo Segneri, Paolo Segneri (senior, 1624–1694) and his nephew (1673–1713) (cf. *Dic Spir* 14, cols. 519–24). The latter was a figure of particular significance in the evolution of the popular mission in the period immediately prior to Alphonsus. On Segneri as a popular missioner, see G. Orlandi, "L.A. Muratori e le missione di P. Segneri Jn.," *Spic. Hist. C.Ss.R.* 20/1 (1972): 151–294.

29. Alphonsus may here be reflecting somewhat ruefully on his relationship with his father, Don Joseph, whose "long years in the galleys had left their mark upon his character, making him harsh in manner, a martinet at home, and altogether unaccustomed to the experience of having his decisions questioned, as Alphonsus was to learn to his cost" (Jones, *Alphonsus Liguori: The Saint of Bourbon Naples,* 10).

30. Pier Matteo Cardinal Petrucci (1636–1701) was an Oratorian and noted spiritual writer.

31. Balthasar Alvarez (1533–1580), Spanish Jesuit and spiritual

writer. He was for six years confessor of Teresa of Avila, who devoted a few lines to him in her autobiography: "I had a confessor who mortified me very much and was sometimes an affliction and a great trial to me because he disturbed me exceedingly, but he was the one who also profited me the most, as far as I can tell" (*Life,* Chap. 26). Alvarez taught a form of mystical prayer of the simple presence of God, which brought him into conflict with his Jesuit superiors for a time, who forbade him to teach any other method of contemplation than the one contained in the spiritual exercises.

32. The gloss was originally a short marginal or interlinear explanation added to the biblical text in the Middle Ages. Eventually, the glosses grew in length and acquired an important exegetical role in the medieval theological schools. St. Thomas discusses the meaning of this verse of Romans, quoting this gloss with approval (cf. *Super Epistolam ad Romanos* Lectio VI, n.698). Alphonsus would have known the glosses through their use, particularly in apolgetic commentary on scripture, by the post-Tridentine biblical commentators. See "Glosses, Biblical" in *Catholic Encyclopedia.* (On the influence of the gloss, see Beryl Smalley, *The Bible in the Middle Ages,* 3rd ed. [Oxford, 1984]).

33. It is not possible to convey adequately in English the nuance of the Italian in Alphonsus's distinction between the third method, *orazione mentale,* and the fifth, *la preghiera. Orazione mentale* is not simply intellectual meditation on the truths of faith; it is the entire dialogue of love that is born of it and that is "prayerful" in the widest sense. *La preghiera,* on the other hand, is strictly speaking what we might call "prayer of petition." As will be seen, Alphonsus does not consider this a lower form of the activity of prayer, suitable only for those who cannot either give themselves to the heart-warming prayer of affection or to contemplation. The prayer of petition is essential for everyone and has been laid upon Christians by the words of Jesus, "ask and you shall receive."

34. Catherine of Bologna (1413–1463), Italian Poor Clare who was known as a mystic, artist, and writer.

35. Anthony Torres (1637–1713) was a member of the Congregation of the Pii Operarii and an assiduous missioner in Naples. It was through Torres that Thomas Falcoia, the collaborator and *direttore* of the nascent Redemptorist Congregation, was drawn to the Pii Operarii, and later chose Torres as his spiritual director. Torres was denounced to the Inquisition on suspicion of promoting Quietest ideas, and was suspended for a time from the exercise of his priestly ministry; see

Oreste Gregorio, *Mons Tommaso Falcoia (1663–1747)* (Rome, 1955), pp. 13ff.

36. Juan Palafox y Mendoza (1600–1659), a Spanish spiritual writer and defender of the Indians.

37. As Alphonsus has noted, much of this section has already been set forth in Chapter 2 and is omitted here. He marshals strong arguments here in favor of frequent communion. The evolution of the Latin liturgy from medieval times onward had limited reception of communion by the laity to a few times a year. By Alphonsus's time, even this minimum had been undermined further by the residues of Jansenism. The conditions he lays down, including daily meditation and the permission of the confessor, may appear excessively severe today, but would have been regarded in his time as pastorally bold.

38. This is one of the most quoted lines of Alphonsus. For Alphonsus's understanding of the economy of grace, see the Introduction and the section on the writings on prayer in this volume.

39. Thomas Aquinas, *Summa Theologiae*, 3a, q.39 a.5c.

40. Alphonsus is wrong in ascribing this curious story to St. Augustine. It may, however, come from the *Apologeticus adversus gentes pro christianis* of Tertullian.

41. Responsary in the Rite of Consecration of Virgins of the Roman Pontifical.

42. *Summa Theologiae*, 2a, 2ae, q.10, a.5. Alphonsus's view on this matter was the bitter fruit not merely of the family opposition he encountered, but also of several incidents among the early applicants to his Congregation.

43. Louis Habert, *Theologia Dogmatica et Moralis:* "De Sacramento Ordinis," par. 3, Chap. 1.2. Habert (1635–1718), was a French theologian, some of whose opinions attracted the opposition of Archbishop Fénélon, who wrote a propos of his theory of grace: "If this system is not heretical, then the condemnation of Jansenius is unjust and Jansenism is only a phantom and an imaginary heresy which the Jesuits used to persecute faithful disciples of St. Augustine and to tyranize consciences in favor of the position of Molinos" (*Dictionnaire de Theologie Catholique,* Vol. 6, cols. 2013–15).

44. Probably Fray Luis de Grenada (1504–1586), Spanish Dominican spiritual writer and theologian.

45. Alphonsus is here describing his practice in this matter as can be seen from his letters. One of his benefactors had recommended a person for ordination, but was refused courteously but firmly: "The

extreme kindness with which you have seconded my episcopal ministry has long since made me your debtor; but you will pardon me if I say that I cannot this time comply with your request to confer orders upon your friend. Some persons use every means to reach holy orders which they would receive to the injury of their souls, and this I cannot permit." *General Correspondence* 3, 284.

Direction of Souls Who Wish to Lead a Deeply Spiritual Life

1. St. Francis de Sales actually wrote that "one *ounce* of prayer in the midst of desolation is more pleasing to God than a hundred *pounds* in the midst of sensible consolations."

2. Terminology in the area of the various states of prayer is always a difficulty. The saints/mystics found it difficult to describe precisely degrees of prayer that differ from each other only by insignificant shades. And frequently they use different words to describe the same state. Alphonsus mainly follows Teresa of Avila. The prayer of recollection is also called the prayer of simplicity or of simple regard. Teresa of Avila occasionally regards "recollection" and "prayer of quiet" as synonymous.

3. P. Segneri, S.J. (1624–1694), *Concordia tra la fatica e la quiete nell'orazione.* (Florence, 1680). As A. Poulain, S.J., *The Graces of Interior Prayer* (London, 1912), p. 61, explains, Alphonsus is not here speaking of affective prayer, which he includes in meditation. Between meditation and "infused contemplation" he places "acquired contemplation," which he also calls "active recollection" and then, one of his special states, which he names "contemplative repose," the loving attention to God.

4. Teresa of Avila, *The Book of Her Life,* Chap. 14. In his quotations from the saints, Alphonsus was inclined to give the meaning of the saints' words rather than to quote them literally. This is particularly true with regard to quotations in spiritual matters from saints such as Teresa of Avila, John of the Cross, and Francis de Sales.

5. *The Way of Perfection,* Chap. 31.

6. A reference to Pseudo-Dionysius, *De Mystica Theologia,* Chap. 1.

7. The references to the statements of Teresa of Avila in this section concerning the grace of union with God are to be found throughout her works and Alphonsus gives references in general to *The Way of*

Perfection, Chap. 17; *The Interior Castle*, 5, 6; *The Book of Her Life*, Chap. 18; *Meditations on the Song of Songs*, Chap. 3.

8. Poulain, *The Graces of Interior Prayer*, p. 266, No. 55, suggests that this incident refers to Alphonsus himself.

9. This is a traditional metaphor. Alphonsus avoids the exaggerated descriptions of the grace of union to be found in some mystics.

10. This traditional distinction of three kinds of visions goes back to St. Augustine, *De genesi ad litteram*, Bk. 12.

11. John of the Cross, *The Ascent of Mount Carmel*, Bk. 2.Chap. 23.

12. The references to Teresa of Avila are from *The Interior Castle*, 6.9.

13. John of the Cross. *The Ascent of Mount Carmel*, 2.32.4. Alphonsus joins the majority of saints, Ignatius of Loyola, Philip Neri, John of the Cross, Teresa of Avila, in laying down severe restrictions for spiritual directors in dealing with revelations. He had firsthand experience in the matter as a result of his dealings with Venerable Maria Celeste Crostarosa.

14. Teresa of Avila, *The Book of Her Life*, Chap. 15; *The Interior Castle*, 6, Chap. 9.

15. Number 3 Concerning Mortification. Alphonsus gives no references to his sources for this whole section.

16. Pope Innocent XI (1676–1689), Decree *Cum ad Aures* 1679. Alphonsus felt considerably restrained by this decree of the Congregation of the Council. He went as far as he could in his liberal interpretation of it. His own instincts were leading him to advocate daily reception of the Eucharist—a practice that had to wait a further 150 years for official church approval. See Alfonso M. de Liguori, *Opere Ascetiche* (Rome, 1933), Vol. I, p. 416.

17. Pope Benedict XIV (1740–1758), *De Synodo diocesana*, 7.12.9. Alphonsus altered his opinion on this point. In the *Homo Apostolicus* (1759), the Latin translation of *Istruzione e pratica per li confessori*, often referred to as the *Pratica Grande*, he supported the opposite opinion.

18. Alphonsus's references to the *Roman Catechism* are from the section "De Eucharistiae Sacramento."

19. Francis de Sales, *Introduction to the Devout Life*, II.20. St. Thomas, *In IV Sent.*, dist. 12, qu. 3, art. I, solutio 2. Most of the references to St. Thomas are from this section of the work.

20. Pope Alexander VIII (1689–1691) condemned these Jansenist positions in 1690. They were not the errors of Michael Baius, who was condemned by Pius V in 1567.

21. A French proverb from the area of the Alps.

22. Sayings also attributed to St. Augustine.

23. The *Salmanticenses* were a group of Carmelite theologians teaching at Salamanca who compiled a massive commentary on Thomas Aquinas's *Summa* between 1600 and 1725.

24. *De Profectu Religiosorum,* 77. The attribution of this work to St. Bonaventure is, at best, very doubtful.

Peace for Scrupulous Souls

1. St. Bernard, *De Praecepto et Dispensatione.*

2. Giampietro Pinamonti, S.J. (1632–1703), *Il Direttore.*

3. St. Alphonsus quotes Henri Suso from Pietro Brencola (1673–1749), *Strada della Perfezione* (Naples, 1731). John Gerson (1363–1429) was a theologian, ascetic, mystic, moralist, man of affairs, and pastoral theologian. Alphonsus here cites from his *De Preparatione ad Missam.* St. Philip Neri is one of the saints most frequently quoted by Alphonsus. He would have had available to him G. Crispino, *La Scuola di S. Filippo Neri* (Naples, 1675).

4. Giacamo Alvarez di Paz, a Spanish ascetic whose writings greatly influenced Alphonsus, especially his *De Perfectione Vitae Spiritualis.* His works were published in Lyons, 1608–1617; Giovanni Eusebio Nieremberg, S.J. (1590–1658), *Opere Spirituali* (Venice, 1715); Benedetto Rogacci (1646–1719), *L'Uno Necessario* (Rome, 1697–1707); Leonardo Lessio, S.J. (1554–1623), *De Statu Vitae Eligendo* (Paris, 1637).

5. St. Francis de Sales (1567–1622). Alphonsus read Francis de Sales in the Italian translation of the saint's works by Giuseppe Fozzi, S.J., and Daniello de Nobili, published in Venice 1732–1735. Many of the references are paraphrases of what Francis de Sales actually wrote. St. Antonino of Florence, O.P. (1389–1459), was a moral theologian of considerable influence. Due to printers' errors he appears occasionally in Alphonsus's writings as "St. Anthony" and at least once as "St. Augustine." Martinus ab Azpilcueta (1493–1587), commonly referred to as *Doctor Navarrus,* was professor at Salamanca and Coimbra. Silvestro de Prierio, O.P. (d. 1523), author of *Summa Sylvestrina* (1515), was often quoted by Alphonsus. Tirillo is James Tirinus, S.J. (1580–1636). Claude La Croix, S.J. (1592–1714), whose *Theologia Moralis* was published Milan in 1724.

6. Martin Wigandt, O.P., *Tribunal confessariorum* (Venice, 1754).

Blessed Umberto or Humbertis de Romanis (d. 1277) was Master General of the Dominicans. His *Speculum Religiosorum* was published in Colgone (1616).

7. Thomas Tamburini, S.J., a Sicilian whose *Theologia Moralis* was published in Venice (1726). Gabriel Vasquez (1549–1604), famous Spanish theologian.

8. G. Giordanini, C.M. *Istruzione per i novelli confessori* (Bassano, 1780, Louis Habert (1635–1718), and François Genet (1640–1703) were all well-known theologians of the Rigorist school whom Alphonsus here quotes as supporting his own more liberal opinion.

Novena to the Sacred Heart

1. See Alfonso M. de Liguori, *Opere Ascetiche*, Vol. 4 (Rome, 1939), pp. 499–524; Francois Bourdeau, *Le Livre des "Visites au Saint Sacrement,"* pp. 321–65, in *Alphonse de Liguori. Pasteur et Docteur.* Theologie Historique No. 77, (Paris: Beauchesne, 1987). F. M. Jones, *Alphonsus de Liguori, The Saint of Bourbon Naples,* 1696–1787, p. 294.

2. See Languet, *Vie de Marguerite-Marie Alacoque,* livre 4.n.LVII.

3. Father Gallifet's work was published first in Latin in Rome in 1726 and then in French in a translation by the author himself.

4. Benedict XIV's work was published under his name before he was elected Pope, Prosperus Lambertinus.

5. Mass in honor of the Wounded Heart of St. Teresa, or the feast of her Transverberation, is celebrated by the Carmelite Sisters on August 26. Bernini's statue of the Ecstasy of St. Teresa or her Transverberation is preserved in the Chiesa di S. Maria della Vittoria in Rome.

6. Pope Innocent VI (1352–1362), a pope of the Avignon papacy.

7. Alphonsus was insistent, as we know from his method of mental prayer, that all prayer, except perhaps the highest form of contemplative union with God, should issue in affections and petitions. These consisted, in the main, of acts of love, sorrow for sin, acceptance of God's will, and offering of oneself to the Lord. I have shortened, somewhat, the affections and prayers that are appended here to each of the nine meditations in preparation for the feast of the Sacred Heart.

8. The translation of the Latin word *excessus* referring to Our Lord's death to mean *eccesso* and *excess* in the Italian and English sense is a liberty of translation that Alphonsus frequently allowed himself in his devotional writings.

9. This sentiment is taken virtually word for word from a sermon of Father Claude de la Colombière, S.J. See Alfonso M. de Liguori, *Opere Ascetiche*, Vol. IV, p. 510.

10. S. Thomas Aquinas, *Opusculum* 63, cap. 7, Secundum principale.

11. See Alfonso M. de Liguori, *Opere Ascetiche*, Vol. IV, p. 517.

12. There are clear echoes of the prayer of St. Ignatius Loyola here. Alphonsus was a diligent student of Ignatius's life and writings.

The Blessed Virgin Mary

1. See Hilda C. Graef, *Mary: A History of Doctrine and Devotion*, Vol. 2, *From the Reformation to the Present Day* (New York: Sheed and Ward, 1964), pp. 74–77.

2. John H. Newman, *Apologia Pro Vita Sua*, Chap. 4, pt. II.

3. Frederick M. Jones, C.SS.R., *Alphonsus de Liguori, The Saint of Bourbon Naples*. Dublin, 1992, p. 20; T. Rey-Mermet, C.SS.R., *Le Saint du Siècle des Lumières*. Paris, 1987, p. 92.

4. *Le Glorie di Maria*, pp. 15–16.

5. Jones, *Alphonsus de Liguori*, p. 86; Rey-Mermet, *Le Saint*, p. 122.

6. Rey-Mermet, *Le Saint*, p. 229.

7. Alphonsus de Liguori, *The Complete Works of St. Alphonsus de Liguori*, ed. Eugene Grimm, C.SS.R., Vol. 15, *Preaching* (New York: Benziger Brothers, 1890), p. 229.

8. Domenico Capone, C.SS.R., *Il Volto di Sant'Alfonso nei Ritratti e nell'Iconografia* (Rome: Padri Redentoristi, 1954), pp. 116–17.

9. For a treatment of Jesuit optimism about the availability of grace, see John O'Malley, *The First Jesuits* (Cambridge: Harvard University Press, 1993), pp. 80–84.

10. Liguori, ed. Grimm, C.SS.R., vol. 8, *The Glories of Mary*, p. 694.

11. Ibid., p. 192.

12. Ibid., pp. 25–27.

13. For a treatment of the power of story to present an alternative vision of reality, see John J. Navone, *Towards a Theology of Story* (Slough: St. Paul Publications, 1977).

14. Liguori, ed. Grimm, C.SS.R., *The Glories of Mary*, p. 153.

15. Richard P. McBrien, *Catholicism* (Minneapolis, Minn.: Winston Press, 1981), pp. 882–84.

16. Giuseppe de Luca, *Sant'Alfonso, il mio maestro di vita cristiana* (Rome: Edizioni di Storia e Letterature, 1983), pp. 126–27.

17. Liguori, *Opere Ascetiche*, Vol. 7, *Le Glorie di Maria, Parte Seconda* (Rome: Redentoristi, 1937), pp. 482–83.

18. Citation of critical edition of *Visits*.

19. The following texts are all translations from the Italian of the critical edition of *Le Glorie di Maria*, pts. 1 and 2.

20. *Le Glorie di Maria*, Vol. 6, p. 12.

21. Ibid., pp. 12–14.

22. Ibid., pp. 15–20.

23. Ibid., pp. 157–63.

24. Alphonsus refers here to one of the most notable theologians of the eighteenth century, Ludovico Muratori (1672–1750). For information on Muratori and the mariology of Alphonsus see Jones, *Alphonsus de Liguori*, pp. 267–74, and Rey-Mermet, *Le Saint*, pp. 448–52.

25. *Le Glorie di Maria*, Vol. 7, pp. 32–42.

26. This fact is significant for Alphonsus since Dominicans would be expected to follow the opinion of St. Thomas Aquinas. Thomas taught the sanctification of Mary in her mother's womb but not the Immaculate Conception, which he found hard to reconcile with the universal necessity of redemption through the death and resurrection of Jesus. Cf. McBrien, *Catholicism*, p. 876.

Prayer

1. Jones, *Alphonsus de Liguori*, pp. 12–14; Rey-Mermet, *Le Saint*, pp. 37–55.

2. O'Malley, *The First Jesuits*, pp. 159–64.

3. Alphonsus de Liguori, *The Complete Works of St. Alphonsus de Liguori*, ed. Eugene Grimm, C.SS.R., Vol. 5, *The Passion and Death of Jesus Christ* (New York: Benzinger Brothers, 1890), p. 15.

4. Gennaro Maria Sarnelli, *Il mondo santificato, dove si trata della meditazione e della preghiera. Opera istruttiva ed illuminativa, utilissima ai secolari, ecclesiastici e religiosi per facilitare a ciascuno stato di anime, l'esercizio della vita devota e per introdurre nelle chiese, communita e famiglie l'uso dell'orazione in commune* (Naples, 1738).

5. For information on the life of prayer of the Redemptorist Congregation see Francesco Chiovaro, C.SS.R., ed., *Storia della Congregazione*

del Santissimo Redentore, Vol. 1, *Le Origini,* 1732-1793 (Rome, 1993), pp. 431-517.

6. S. Alfonso M. de Liguori, *Opere Ascetiche,* ed. Giuseppe Cacciatore, C.SS.R., Vol. 2, *Del Gran Mezzo della Preghiera e Opuscoli Affini* (Rome, 1962), p. 16.

7. Giuseppe Cacciatore, S. *Alfonso de Liguori e il Giansenismo* (Florence, 1944).

8. For a popular discussion of the history of the question, see McBrien, *Catholicism,* pp. 158-61.

9. For information on the background and composition of his work, see S. Alfonso M. de Liguori, *Opere Ascetiche: Introduzione Generale* (Rome, 1960), pp. 220-24.

10. For a treatment of the relationship of Alphonsus's theology of grace and his writing on the prayer of petition, see B. Häring, C.SS.R., "Sant' Alfonso: una morale per i redenti," in *S. Alfonso de Liguori e la sua opere,* ed. Ermelindo Masone and Alfonso Amarante (Naples: Valsele Tipografica, 1987), pp. 129-42; Theodule Rey-Mermet, *La Morale selon St. Alphonsus de Liguori* (Paris: Les Editions du Cerf, 1987), pp. 88-89.

11. For a treatment of Alphonsus's own mystical experiences, see Antonio Muccino, "La vita mistica de S. Alfonso Maria de Liguori," in *S. Alfonso de Liguori e la sua opere,* ed. Masone and Amarante, pp. 194-203.

12. There are two brief works by Alphonsus on Quietism. See *"Due Scritti inediti intorno al quietismo"* in *Spicilegium Historicum Congregationis Ssmi Redemptoris* (1965), pp. 85-97.

13. For information on the evening chapels, see Jones *Alphonsus de Liguori,* pp. 62-65, and Rey-Mermet, *Le Saint,* pp. 173-83.

14. The story is related by Rey-Mermet, *Le Saint,* p. 678.

A Way of Conversing Continually with God as with a Friend

1. The Italian title reads "Modo di conversare continuamente ed alla familiare con Dio. Ricavato da un' operetta francese ricevuta con molto gradimento da' divoti; con altri santi pensieri, affetti e practiche aggiunte dal P[adre]. Alfonso de Liguori."

2. S.v. Boutauld, Michel, in *Dictionnaire de Spiritualité,* tome 1, col. 1917.

3. According to G. Cacciatore, paragraphs 5-27 draw their

inspiration from Boutauld, 28–29 from St. Jure, and the remainder depends on Scupoli; see Le Fonti e I Modi di Documentazione" in *Opere Ascetiche: Introduzione Generale* (1960), pp. 236–37. Cacciatore regards Boutauld as a second-rate writer whose cheap (*gretta e meschina*) mysticism has been humanized by Alphonsus's adaptation.

4. Carlo Caraffa (1561–1633) founded the Congregation of the Pii Operarii in Naples in 1602 for the apostolates of catechizing and mission-giving. In his early years, ill health ended his attempt to join the Jesuits. After some years in the army, he was ordained priest in 1600. Due to the success of their missions and their influence in clerical circles, the Pii Operarii were a significant spiritual force in Naples in Alphonsus's time. Seraphina of Capri (1621–1699) founded at the age of forty a conservatory following the Teresian Carmelite Rule. Although bound to the Order by no juridic bonds, Seraphina's reform was to be influential in the convent life of Naples during her lifetime and for some time afterward. The Carmelite community of Marigliano, for instance, to which Maria Celeste Crostarosa originally belonged, was influenced by Seraphina's reform. Despite her lack of formal education, she composed several mystical treatises, which attracted the attention of the Holy Office during the Neapolitan Quietist controversy. The dominant characteristic of Seraphina's spirituality was its stress on the love of God.

The Practice of Mental Prayer and An Outline of a Simple Method of Making Mental Prayer

1. Bernard of Clairvaux, *Five Books on Consideration. Advice to a Pope* (Cistercian Publication, Kalamazoo, Mich., 1976), Book I, Chap. 2, no. 3. Chapters 7 and 8 deal with the necessity of reflection or meditation as an essential element of prayer. This explains why this work is frequently quoted by Alphonsus.

2. The Bishop of Osma was Alonso Valazquez, who died as Archbishop of Santiago in 1587. He was for some time Teresa's confessor and advisor. However, the letter in question is not from Teresa of Avila, although the sentiments may well be hers. Cf. Alfonso de Liguori, *La Vera Sposa di Gesu Cristo*, Vol. 2, Chap. XV.2, p. 85 (*Opere Ascetiche*, Vol. 15, Rome, 1935).

3. Alphonsus never ceased to insist that those who practiced mental prayer should not delay too long on reflecting or thinking about

what they had read. He persistently warned his penitents not to over *concettualizzare*. After some moments of reflection they were to make acts of love, sorrow, petition, etc., which went under the general heading of "affections."

4. Sister Maria Crucifixa was a Benedictine nun who died in 1699. Alphonsus was familiar with Girolamo Turano, *Vita della Ven. Suor Maria Crocifissa della Concezione, O.S.B.*

5. S. Alfonso M. de Liguori, *Opere Ascetiche*, ed. Giuseppe Cacciatore, C.SS.R. (Rome, 1962), *Ristretto Del Modo Di Fare L'Orazione Mentale*, pp. 223–24.

Moral Theology

1. *Pratica del Confessore per ben esercitare il suo Ministero*. Naples, De Simone, 1755, par. 3. From the text edited by G. Pistoni, Modena, 1948.

2. *Praxis Confessarii*. Remondini, Venice, 1757. Caput 1, Nos. 19 & 20. Text used is found in *Opera Moralia*, ed. L. Gaudé, Rome, 1905–1912, Vol. 4.

3. T. Lohner, *Instructio practica de Confessionibus* (Venice, 1736), Bk. 1, 3, 2, Quaer. 1. This work was later placed on the Index of Forbidden Books.

4. P. Segneri, S.J., *Il Confessore Istruito*, 2, XI. p. 239 (*Opere*. Turin, 1833).

5. *Pratica del Confessor per ben Esercitare il suo Ministero*. Naples, De Simone, 1775, par. 17. Text edited by G. Pistone, Modena, 1948.

6. P. F. Giordanini, *Istruzione per i Novelli Confessori* (Venice, Remondini, 1757), p. 26.

7. *Praxis Confessarii*, Remondini, Venice, 1757. Caput 2, No. 44. The edition used is found in the *Opera Moralia*, ed. L. Gaudé, C.SS.R., Rome, 1905–1912, Vol. 4.

8. *Theologia Moralis*, Lib. Primus, Tractatus Primus. Caput 1, Nos. 11 & 12. Edited by L. Gaudé, Rome, 1905–1912.

9. *Homo Apostolicus*, 1759, Tractatus 1, No.1. *Opere di San Alfonso*, Mariette, Torino, 1887, Vol. 7.

10. *Theologia Moralis*, Liber Primus, Tractatus Primus. Caput 3, Nos. 54, 55, 56, 58. Edited by L. Gaudé, Rome, 1905–1912.

11. Text from *Regolamento di Vita di un Cristiano*, 1754. *Opere Ascetiche*, Rome, 1968, Vol. 10, pp. 275–322.

12. *Regolamento di Vita di un Cristiano*, 1754. In *Opere Ascetiche*, Vol. 10, pp. 275–322. Rome, 1968.

13. *Lettere di San Alfonso. Corrispondenza Generale*, Vol. 1. Rome, 1887–90. No. 176, pp. 260–62. August 1754.

14. Letter to Father Pietro Paolo Blasucci, November 1768. *Lettere di San Alfonso. Corrispondenza Speciale*, Vol. 3, No. 217, pp. 342ff. Rome, 1887–1899.

15. Giovanni Vicente Patuzzi, O.P. (1700–1769), a native of Verona. An eminent theologian and apologist, styled the "Italian Pascal," who strongly opposed Probabilism. Despite his ill health and declining powers, he was persuaded to oppose Alphonsus's doctrine of Equiprobabilism under the pseudonym Adelfo Dositeo, with less than convincing arguments.

16. Tutiorism was the teaching that the safer position must always be followed, even when its opposite is equally probable or more probable.

Advice for Priests Who Minister to Those Condemned to Death

1. Since this text was intended for priests in the exercise of their confessional ministry, Alphonsus quoted scripture in Latin. He was leaving nothing to the good sense of his clerical readers when he warned them not to quote scripture in Latin to their penitents.

2. Alphonsus's plea for judges came from his own experience in the Naples Law Courts.

3. Alphonsus regarded prayer to Our Lady as an important apostolic instrument in securing the conversion of sinners. He insisted on a special sermon to the Mother of God in every parish mission.

Letters

Letter 1

1. Sister Maria Celeste Crostarosa was a Sister in the Visitation Convent of Scala above Amalfi. She experienced visions or supernatural communications concerning new religious congregations of sisters and missionary priests that were later to be approved in the church as the Redemptoristine Sisters and the Congregation of the Most Holy

Redeemer. Her spiritual director for many years had been Thomas Falcoia, later bishop of Castellamare di Stabia on the bay of Naples. Falcoia's direction severely tested Celeste's obedience and spirit of faith. A pseudo-pious layman, Don Silvestro Tosquez, insinuated himself into convent affairs and the formation of the two religious groups. Crostarosa, apparently under his influence, rejected Falcoia as her spiritual director. Alphonsus, who was never her spiritual director but who had investigated the alleged supernatural events in the convent at the request of the local bishop, had placed himself under obedience to Falcoia.

2. Don Bartolomeo Carace had been Celeste's director of conscience while she was a Carmelite sister.

3. The reference is to some alleged local revelations that were well known in the Scala convent at the time.

4. Don Silvestro Tosquez was in the Hapsburg service and was a frequent visitor to Vienna.

5. Twenty-one hours: sometime in the early afternoon, depending on the season of the year. A *collation* was the light repast allowed on strict fast days of the church.

6. This is apparently a reference to Teresa's *Life.*

7. Don Vincenzo Mannarini and Giovanni Battista di Donato were two of the original companions of Alphonsus in the founding of the Redemptorists, referred to in his letter as "the Institute" and "the Undertaking."

8. Di Donato was nominally Alphonsus's superior in the group at Scala.

9. Since this is a letter and not a formal tract, Alphonsus does not give any specific reference to the sources of his quotations from Teresa of Avila.

10. Sister Maria Columba was another sister of the Scala convent who claimed to be favored by spiritual revelations.

Letter 2

1. Alphonsus found as a result of his missionary preaching throughout the rural areas of the Kingdom of Naples that the habit of cursing the dead relations of one's neighbors or enemies was widespread. According to the rigorous interpretation of moral theologians at the time, this practice was regarded as formal blasphemy of God, always a serious sin. Alphonsus gradually came to the conclusion that

this was an incorrect interpretation of the habit. Greatly daring, he formulated his theological opinion on the matter and forwarded it to bishops, university theologians, and priests to find out their reaction. This is one of those letters to a priest of Naples.

Letter 3

1. Pope Clement XIV (Ganganelli) died in September 1774 with, according to certain accounts, some mysterious spiritual assistance from Alphonsus. During his pontificate he had failed to nominate cardinals, with the result that the College of Cardinals was seriously depleted at his death, a fact referred to in this letter of Alphonsus. The conclave to elect his successor dragged on for over four months until in February of the following year (1775) Cardinal Angelo Giovanni Braschi was elected and assumed the papacy under the title of Pius VI. Alphonsus would have been familiar with him since he had been Papal Nuncio in Naples. In the year of his election he accepted the resignation of Alphonsus as bishop of St. Agatha of the Goths and allowed him to return to his monastery in Pagani. Unfortunately, Pius VI carried out few of the recommendations proposed in this letter by Alphonsus.

2. Alphonsus announced that his death was near from as early as 1754 when he was not quite sixty years of age. Despite the fact that he suffered from ill health and many infirmities all his life he did not die until 1787, thirteen years after declaring once again in this letter that his death was imminent.

Letter 4

1. Hercules was the youngest male member of the Liguori family and the only one who did not become a priest. He did not get on too well with his father and was rather unfortunate in his two marriages. Alphonsus showed him considerable understanding while at the same time calling him to order on several occasions.

2. The Pope in question was Clement XIII (1758–1769).

3. Cardinal Spinelli was the Cardinal Archbishop of Naples for many years and was well known to Alphonsus. He had been transferred to a curial position in Rome when Alphonsus enlisted his support in his efforts to avoid accepting the episcopacy.

4. Hercules would have had to borrow at interest the money he loaned Alphonsus.

5. Alphonsus regularly stayed with the Carmelite Fathers in Caserta on the occasion of his visits to the Court. Here he asks Hercules to send the concierge of the family apartments to make the necessary arrangements.

6. Donna Rachele, Hercules's wife, died in October 1762, a few months after Alphonsus's appointment as bishop.

Letter 6

1. This young lady was a nun in the convent of St. Liguoro in Naples. She consulted Alphonsus about her vocation to the strictly enclosed Hermit Sisters of the Immaculate Conception.

2. The Venerable Ursola Benincasa (1547–1618) founded the contemplative hermitage for sisters, which was placed under the guidance of the Theatines.

3. Girls "entered" or were placed in enclosed convents in Naples as "educande" from the age of ten or eleven. They were entrusted to the tutelage of one of the professed sisters.

4. The parlor where the nuns conversed with their visitors was referred to as the "Grate" or "Grill." Excessive visits and prolonged conversations at the Grate were a serious abuse in convents at the time and were severely castigated by Alphonsus in his writings for nuns.

Letter 7

1. Founded 1732. Approved by Pope Benedict XIV 1749.

2. Alphonsus was fifty-eight at the time of writing this letter. He was to live for another thirty-three years, "prophesying" his approaching death in nearly every letter he wrote for the next thirty years!

3. A very high proportion of the clergy in Bourbon Naples lived at home and did not engage in any pastoral ministry. It is against this background that this statement of Alphonsus must be read. For a full description of the pastoral activity—or the lack of it—of the clergy at the time of Alphonsus, see Jones, *Alphonsus de Liguori*, p. 305.

4. For the canonical background to understanding this whole matter, see ibid., pp. 322–33.

5. The following paragraph of this circular letter deals with the

necessity of the study of moral theology. It has been included under *Study and Reflection* in the *Moral Theology* extracts.

6. At this stage in the development of the Congregation of the Most Holy Redeemer, the local superior was styled the Rector and the superior general was called the Rector Major.

7. This quotation from Alphonsus, which has so often been quoted out of context, must be understood and interpreted against the background of the social conditions prevailing in Naples at the time. *Prete in familia, si; religioso, no,* was the accepted adage. Cf. Jones, *Alphonsus de Liguori,* p. 312.

8. The natural pride and vanity of the Neopolitan nobleman went under the name of *stima propria.* A member of the Neapolitan nobility would defend his dignity in every way possible. Any slight to his social standing, real or imaginary, such, for example, as to be kept waiting in an ante-chamber for an appointment, was a serious insult to be immediately vindicated. Cf. Jones, *Alphonsus de Liguori,* p. 305.

9. The three "young men" mentioned here were students who died of tuberculosis, which was widespread at the time. Father Paul Cafaro was one of the pillars of the Congregation and a great ascetic. He was for many years Alphonsus's director of conscience.

REFERENCE MATTER

Chronological List of Alphonsus's Writings

1728	*The Eternal Truths*
1732	*Hymns and Verses*
1734	*Prayers to Our Lady for Each Day of the Week*
1743	*Novena in Honor of St. Teresa*
	Short Way of Perfection
	Precis of Christian Doctrine
1745	*Visits to the Blessed Sacrament*
	Reflections Useful for Bishops
1746	*Letter Concerning the Moral Implications of Cursing the Dead*
1748	*Annotations to the Medulla Theologiae Moralis* of H. Busenbaum, S.J.
	(In the course of the nine editions published during the saint's lifetime the title page changed to *Moral Theology*, Rev. Alphonsus de Liguori, Bishop of St. Agatha of the Goths, etc.)
1748	*Reply to Calumnies Concerning Letter Dealing with the Moral Implications of Cursing the Dead*
1749	*In Favor of the Moderate Use of the Probable Opinion*
1750	*The Glories of Mary*
	Considerations on Religious Vocation
1751	*Clock of the Passion*
	Concerning the Refusal of Absolution to a Cleric 'habituato in vitio turpi'
	Rest for Scrupulous Souls
1752	*Lives of Father Sarnelli and Brother Vito Curzio*
1754	*On Conversing Continually and Familiarly with God*
	Rules for Correct Living
1755	*Pratica del Confessore. Praxis Confessarii*
	On the Moderate Use of the Probable Opinion
	Conformity with the Will of God
1756	*Advice to Newly Approved Confessors*
	Against the Errors of Materialists and Deists
	Reply to an Anonymous Writer
1757	*Rules for Seminaries*
	A Short Treatise on the Necessity of Prayer
	Examination of Candidates for Ordination

Concerning the Cursing of the Dead
Advice to Priests for Assisting the Dying
Instruction and Practical Advice for a Confessor (Compendium, Pratica Grande, Homo Apostolicus)

1758 *Preparation for Death*
Discourses for Times of Calamity
Novena for Christmas
Novena for the Sacred Heart
Meditations in Honor of St. Joseph
Reply to a Letter Concerning Cursing the Dead
Preparation for Mass and Thanksgiving

1759 *Concerning the Prohibition of Books*
Prayer the Great Means of Salvation

1760 *The Selva (Dignities of the Duties of the Priest)*
The Exercises of the Mission
The Mass and Office Hurriedly Recited

1760/1 *The True Spouse of Jesus Christ*

1761 *Meditations for Private Eight Days Retreat*
Considerations on the Passion of Jesus Christ
The Way of the Cross
Letter on the Manner of Preaching with Apostolic Simplicity
Life and Death of Sister Teresa de Liguori
A Short Compendium of Christian Doctrine

1762 *Reply to Dom Cipriano Aristasio*
The Moderate Use of the Probable Opinion
The Truth of the Faith as Evidenced by the Motives of Credibility
Method of Making Mental Prayer with Children during Mass

1764 *The Direct Confessor (For Confessors Appointed to Rural Areas)*
Reply Concerning the Frequentation of Holy Communion against Don Cipriano Aristasio
Examination of Candidates for Confession Faculties
Questions to be Asked of Priests Who Wish to Engage in the Ministry of the Confessional
Apologia in Favor of the Use of Equally Probable Opinion
Defense of Dissertation in Favor of the Use of the Probable Opinion against Adelfo Dositeo
Rules for the Monastery of Our Lady Queen of Heaven at Airola

1765 *On the Moderate Use of the Probable Opinion*
Some Points Concerning the Matter of Frequent Communion
An Uncertain Law Cannot Induce a Certain Obligation

CHRONOLOGICAL LIST OF ALPHONSUS'S WRITINGS

1766	*The Way of Salvation*
	Life of Father Paul Cafaro
1767	*The Truth of the Faith*
	Refutation of the Book De l'Esprit
	Refutation of a work On Preaching
1768	*Practice of the Love of Jesus Christ*
	Arguments against Febronius
	Instructions on the Ten Commandments for the Faithful
	Five Points on which Preachers Should Instruct the Faithful
1769	*Exposition and Defense of the Points of Faith Discussed and Defined at the Council of Trent*
	On the Grace of Justification
	On the Acceptance Due to the Definitions of a Council
	Ceremonies of the Mass
	Honoraria for Masses
	Apologia for His Moral Theology *Attacked as Lax*
1770	*An Opinion Which Is Not Convincing in Favor of an Obligation, Does Not Impose an Obligation*
1771	*Sermons for all the Sundays of the Year*
	Letter to a Bishop on the Benefits of Missions
	Letter on the Benefit of Spiritual Exercises Made in Silence
1772	*Triumph of the Church (History and Refutation of Various Heresies)*
	Sermons for the Feast of St. Joseph
	Sermons for the Clothing of a Religious
1773	*Considerations on the Passion of Jesus Christ*
	Considerations on Some Spiritual Matters
	On the Truth of Divine Revelation
	Is the Use of a Probable Opinion Lawful?
	Miraculous Discovery of the Blessed Sacrament in a Parish in Naples
	Meditations on the Passion of Jesus Christ for Each Day of the Week
1774	*Explanation of the Psalms and Canticles*
	Explanation of the Author's Moral System
1775	*Advice to Priests Appointed to Assist Those Condemned to Death*
	Victory of the Martyrs
	The Sacrifice of Jesus Christ
	Exhortation to Religious

403

Select Bibliography (with Abbreviations)

1. Editions of Alphonsus de Liguori's Writings

Alphonsus M. de Liguori:

Opere Ascetiche (Editio Critica). 10 vols. Rome, 1933–1968.

Opere Complete. Edited by G. Marietti. Turin, 1845–1887.

Theologia Moralis. Edited by L. Gaudé, C.SS.R. I–IV. Rome, 1905.

Lettere di S. Alfonso Maria de Liguori. Vols. I–III. Rome, 1887–1890.

The Complete Works of St. Alphonsus de Liguori. Edited by E. Grimm, C.SS.R. 22 vols. New York, Benzinger, 1886–1897.

2. Bibliographies

Concessionis Tituli Doctoris...in honorem S. Alphonsi M. De Ligorio. Rome, 1870 (Sacra Rituum Congregatio). Contains Official List of Alphonsus de Liguori's Publications.

M. de Meulemeester, C.SS.R. *Bibliographie Générale des Écrivains Rédemptoristes.* 3 vols. Louvain, 1933 (B.G.E.R.).

Spicilegium Historicum C.SS.R. Rome, 1953. Sources for the History of St. Alphonsus and the Redemptorists in critically edited texts. Published by the Institutum Historicum C.SS.R., Rome, 1953–.

Studia et Subsidia de Vita et Operibus S. Alfonsi de Ligorio, Rome, 1990. Bibliotheca Historica C.SS.R. Vol. XIII.

3. Biographies

A. Berthe, C.SS.R. *St. Alphonse de Liguori,* Paris, 1990.

K. Dilgskron, C.SS.R. *Leben des Hl. Bischofs und Kirchenlehrers A.M.de Liguori.* Regensburg, 1887.

Frederick M. Jones, C.SS.R. *Alphonsus de Liguori, The Saint of Bourbon Naples.* Dublin, 1992.

T. Rey-Mermet, C.SS.R. *Le Saint du Siècle des Lumières.* Paris, 1987.

A. M. Tannoia. *Della Vita et Istituto del Ven. Servo di Dio, Alfonso Maria Liguori.* 3 vols. Naples, 1792–1802 (Ristampa Anastatica, 1982. Materdomini. Av.).

R. Telleria, C.SS.R. *San Alphonso Maria de Ligorio.* 2 vols. Madrid, 1950/1951.

4. Selected Studies and Monographs

G. Cacciatore, C.SS.R. *La Spiritualità di S. Alfonso de Liguori. (Le Scuole Cattoliche di Spiritualità.* Vita e Pensiero, Milano, 1949).

R. De Maio, *Società e Vita Religiosa à Napoli nell'Età Moderna, 1656-1799.* Naples, 1971.

C. Hoegerl, C.SS.R. *Founding Texts of Redemptorists. Early Rules and Allied Documents.*

———. *Heart to Heart: An Alphonsian Anthology* (Private Circulation, Rome, 1981).

Jorge R. Colon Leon, C.SS.R. *La Oracion de Petition en la Doctrina de San Alfonso M.De Ligorio.* (Pont. Universitas Gregoriana, Rome, 1986).

G. Lievin, C.SS.R. *La Route vers Dieu. Jalons d'une Spiritualité Alphonsienne.* St. Paul. Fribourg-Paris, 1963.

———. Alphonse de Liguori, Biographie, Préparation, Analyse des Oeuvres, Doctrine. *Dictionnaire de Spiritualité, Ascetique, et Mystique,* T.I., 357–389.

E. Marcelli, C.SS.R., and S. Raponi, C.SS.R. *Un Umanista del 700 Italiano. Alfonso Maria de Liguori.* Rome: Bettinelli.

E. Masone, C.SS.R., and A. Amarante, C.SS.R. *S. Alfonso de Liguori e la Sua Opera.* Naples, 1987.

J. W. Oppitz, C.SS.R. *Alphonsian History and Spirituality.* (Private Circulation).

Giannantonio Pompeo, a cura de. *Alfonso M. De Liguori e la Societa Civile del suo Tempo.* Florence, 1990.

B. Ullanov, ed. *The Way of St. Alphonsus de Liguori.* London, Burns Oates, 1961.

G. Velocci, C.SS.R. *Sant'Alfonso de Liguori. Un Maestro di vita Cristiana.* Edizione San Paolo. Milan, 1990.

M. Vidal, C.SS.R. *La Morale di Sant'Alfonso. Dal Rigorismo alla Benignità.* Editiones Academiae Alphonsianae. Rome, 1992.

Index

References in **boldface** are to material in Introduction.

INDEX

Scripture Index

Other Volumes in This Series

Other Volumes in This Series

Other Volumes in This Series

THE CLASSICS OF **WESTERN SPIRITUA**
A LIBRARY OF THE GREAT SPIRITUAL MA

"The texts are first-rate, and the introductions are informative and reliable. The books will be a welcome...addition to the bookshelf of every literate religious person."
The Christian Century

In one series, the original writings of the universally acknowledged teachers of the Catholic, Protestant, Eastern Orthodox, Jewish and Islamic traditions have been critically selected, translated and introduced by internationally recognized scholars and spiritual leaders.

ALPHONSUS DE LIGUORI—SELECTED WRITINGS
edited by Frederick M. Jones, C.SS.R.
with the collaboration of Brendan McConvery, C.SS.R.,
  Raphael Gallagher, C.SS.R., Terrence J. Moran, C.SS.R., and
  Martin McKeever, C.SS.R.
consultants Sean O'Riordan, C.SS.R., and Carl Hoegerl, C.SS.R.
preface by Sean O'Riordan, C.SS.R.

"I cannot refrain from expressing my displeasure that there are so few preachers and confessors who speak about prayer. Even when they do, they do so inadequately. Conscious as I am of the necessity of prayer in our own lives, I would wish that authors of spiritual books, as well as preachers and confessors in their spiritual direction of souls, would insist on nothing more than on prayer. Let their advice be 'pray, pray, pray and never cease to pray.'"
From *A Short Treatise on the Necessity of Prayer* (Chap. I, Sec. I), 1757

Beyond the tercentenary of the birth of Alphonsus de Liguori in September 1696, we focus our attention on the extensive corpus of his writings, which led to his being declared a doctor of the church in March 1871, in the immediate aftermath of the First Vatican Council. In an age of great philosophical and theological activity—the so-called Age of Enlightenment—he produced over one hundred and ten publications dealing with moral theology, dogmatic theology and apologetics, spirituality and devotional subjects.

His achievement was immense. Single-handedly, he steered moral theological teaching and practice away from the paths of excessive rigorism through his thirty-two moral theological publications. His dogmatic writings—some fifteen in all—vindicated the position of the papacy against anti-Roman attitudes prevalent at the time in the Catholic Church. Other dogmatic works helped to clarify the doctrinal basis of devotion to the Sacred Heart and paved the way for the definition of Our Lady's Immaculate Conception.

His devotional writings, which form the major section of this volume—over sixty in all—determined, to a very large extent, the practices of Catholic piety right up to the Second Vatican Council.

These selections from Alphonsus de Liguori's variety of writings illustrate at once his theological acumen and his practical good sense.

WITH THE COLLABORATION OF
BRENDAN McCONVERY, C.SS.R., RAPHAEL GALLAGHER, C.SS.R.,
TERRENCE J. MORAN, C.SS.R., AND MARTIN McKEEVER, C.SS.R.
CONSULTANTS
SEAN O'RIORDAN, C.SS.R., AND CARL HOEGERL, C.SS.R.
PREFACE BY
SEAN O'RIORDAN, C.SS.R.

ISBN 0-8091-3771-2

52495>

9 780809 137718

PAULIST PRESS
NEW YORK • MAHWAH
$24.95